The First Crusade

THE MIDDLE AGES SERIES

Ruth Mazo Karras, General Editor
Edward Peters, Founding Editor

A complete list of books in the series
is available from the publisher.

The First Crusade

The Chronicle of Fulcher of Chartres and Other Source Materials

SECOND EDITION

Edited by Edward Peters

PENN

University of Pennsylvania Press

Philadelphia

First edition published 1971 by University of Pennsylvania Press
Copyright © 1971 University of Pennsylvania Press
Second edition copyright © 1998 University of Pennsylvania Press

Printed in the United States of America on acid-free paper

10 9 8 7 6 5 4 3 2

Published by
University of Pennsylvania Press
Philadelphia, Pennsylvania 19104-4011

Library of Congress Cataloging-in-Publication Data
The First Crusade : the chronicle of Fulcher of Chartres and other
source materials / edited by Edward Peters. — 2nd ed.
    p.   cm. — (Middle Ages series)
  Includes bibliographical references.
  ISBN 0-8122-1656-3 (paper : alk. paper)
  1. Crusades—First, 1096–1099—Sources. I. Peters, Edward, 1936–
II. Series.
D161.1.F57 1998
940.1′8—dc21   98-12687
                                                CIP

Contents

Preface   ·   xi

Abbreviations   xiii

Introduction   1

I. Pope Urban II at the Council of Clermont, November 27,
1095   25

1. The Speech of Urban: The *Gesta* Version   25
2. The Speech of Urban: The Version of Robert of Rheims   26
3. The Speech of Urban: The Version of Baldric of Dol   29
4. The Speech of Urban: The Version of Guibert of Nogent   33
5. The Privilege of Urban to the Pilgrims   37
6. The Truce of God Proclaimed in the Diocese of Cologne   38
7. The Truce of God Proclaimed at the Council of Clermont   41
8. Urban's Letter to the Faithful in Flanders   42
9. Urban in Anjou, Lent, 1096: The Chronicle of Fulk
le Réchin   42
10. Urban's Letter to His Supporters in Bologna   44
11. Urban's Letter to the Monks of Vallombrosa   44
12. Urban's Letter to the Counts of Besalú, Empurias,
Rousillon, and Cerdaña and Their Followers   45

II. The Chronicle of Fulcher of Chartres, Book I (1095–1100)   47

Translated, with notes, by Martha E. McGinty

III. Peter the Hermit and the "Crusade of the People"
(March–October, 1096)   102

1. Peter the Hermit: The Version of Guibert of Nogent   103
2. Peter the Hermit: The Version of Albert of Aachen   103

3. Peter the Hermit: The Version of William of Tyre   107
4. The Slaughter of the Jews: The Version of Albert of Aachen   109
5. The Slaughter of the Jews: The Version of Ekkehard
    of Aura   112
6. *Gezerot Tatnu* 4856: The Version of the Anonymous
    of Mainz   112
7. *Gezerot Tatnu* 4856: The Version of Solomon ben Simson   125
8. Folcmar and Gottschalk in Hungary: The Version of Albert
    of Aachen   139
9. Folcmar and Gottschalk in Hungary: The Version of
    Ekkehard of Aura   140
10. The Crusaders in Hungary: The Version of Solomon
    ben Simson   140
11. The End of the "Crusade of the People": The Version of
    Anna Comnena   143
12. The End of the "Crusade of the People": The *Gesta*
    Version   144
13. The End of the "Crusade of the People": The Version of
    Albert of Aachen   146
14. The Byzantines Save Peter the Hermit: The Version of
    Anna Comnena   150

IV. The Journey to Constantinople (August, 1096–May, 1097)   152

1. The *Gesta* Version   152
2. The Deserters: The Version of Albert of Aachen   153
3. Bohemund: The *Gesta* Version   153
4. Raymond of Toulouse and Ademar of Le Puy: The Version
    of Raymond d'Aguilers   156

V. The Crusaders at Constantinople (October, 1096–May,
1097)   159

1. Hugh of Vermandois: The Version of Anna Comnena   159
2. Godfrey of Bouillon: The *Gesta* Version   161
3. Godfrey of Bouillon: The Version of Albert of Aachen   162
4. Godfrey of Bouillon: The Version of Anna Comnena   168
5. The Byzantines: The Version of Peter Tudebode   171
6. Bohemund: The *Gesta* Version   173

7. Bohemund: The Version of Anna Comnena 174
8. Raymond of Toulouse and Ademar of Le Puy: The Version
   of Raymond d'Aguilers 177
9. Raymond of Toulouse: The *Gesta* Version 178
10. Raymond of Toulouse: The Version of Anna Comnena 179

VI. The Siege and Capture of Nicaea (May–June, 1097) 180

1. The *Gesta* Version 180
2. The Version of Raymond d'Aguilers 182
3. The Version of Anna Comnena 184
4. The Letter of Emperor Alexius I to the Abbot of Monte
   Cassino 185

VII. The Siege and Capture of Antioch, Kerbogha's Attack,
and the Discovery of the Holy Lance (October, 1097–July, 1098) 187

1. Nicaea to Antioch: The Version of Peter Tudebode 188
2. The *Gesta* Version 189
3. The Version of Raymond d'Aguilers 191
4. The Suffering of the Crusaders: The *Gesta* Version 193
5. The Suffering of the Crusaders: The Version of Raymond
   d'Aguilers 196
6. The Suffering of the Crusaders: The Version of Peter
   Tudebode 199
7. The Fall of Antioch: The *Gesta* Version 202
8. The Fall of Antioch: The Version of Raymond d'Aguilers 205
9. Kerbogha's Attack: The *Gesta* Version 206
10. Kerbogha's Attack: The Version of Raymond d'Aguilers 211
11. The Discovery of the Holy Lance: The *Gesta* Version 213
12. The Discovery of the Holy Lance: The Version of
    Raymond d'Aguilers 215
13. The Defeat of Kerbogha: The *Gesta* Version 221
14. The Defeat of Kerbogha: The Version of Raymond
    d'Aguilers 224
15. The Firanj Seize Antioch: The Version of Ibn al-Athir 228
16. The Firanj Seize Antioch: The Version of Ibn al-Qalanisi 231
17. Kerbogha's Attack: The Version of Ibn al-Athir 233
18. Kerbogha's Attack: The Version of Ibn al-Qalanisi 235

19. The Firanj Take Ma'arrat an-Nu'mān: The Version of
    Ibn al-Athir   235
20. The Firanj Take Ma'arrat an-Nu'mān: The Version of
    Ibn al-Qalanisi   236

VIII. The Siege and Capture of Jerusalem (June–July, 1099)   238

1. The March to Jerusalem: The *Gesta* Version   238
2. The March to Jerusalem: The Version of Raymond
   d'Aguilers   239
3. The Fall of Jerusalem: The Version of Peter Tudebode   245
4. The Fall of Jerusalem: The Version of Raymond d'Aguilers   249
5. The Fall of Jerusalem: The *Gesta* Version   255
6. The Frankish Triumph: The Version of Raymond
   d'Aguilers   256
7. "The Vision of Peace": The *Gesta* Version   261
8. "The Vision of Peace": The Version of Raymond
   d'Aguilers   261
9. "May God Restore It Forever": The Geniza Letters   263
10. The Firanj Conquer Jerusalem: The Version of Ibn al-Athir   272
11. The Firanj Conquer Jerusalem: The Version of Ibn
    al-Qalanisi   274
12. Ascalon and Its Aftermath: The Version of Ibn al-Qalanisi   275
13. Ascalon and Its Aftermath: The Version of Peter Tudebode   277
14. The Latins in the Levant: From the Chronicle of Fulcher
    of Chartres, Book III   281

IX. Letters of the Crusaders   283

1. The Patriarch of Jerusalem to the Church in the West
   (Antioch, January 1098)   283
2. Anselm of Ribemont to Manasses II, Archbishop of
   Rheims (Antioch, February 10, 1098)   284
3. Stephen, Count of Blois and Chartres, to His Wife, Adele
   (Antioch, March 29, 1098)   287
4. Anselm of Ribemont to Manasses II, Archbishop of
   Rheims (Antioch, July 1098)   289
5. The People of Lucca on Crusade to All Faithful Christians
   (Antioch, October 1098)   291

6. Godfrey of Bouillon, Raymond of St. Gilles, and Daimbert
      to Pope Paschal II (Laodicea, September 1099)   292
7. Manasses II, Archbishop of Rheims, to Lambert, Bishop
      of Arras (1099)   296
8. Pope Paschal II to the Clergy in Gaul (1099)   297

X. Three Problematic Texts   298

1. The "Encyclical" of "Sergius IV"   298
      Translated by Thomas G. Waldman
2. *La Chanson d'Antioche*   302
3. *Nomen a solemnibus*   307

Bibliographical Essay   309

Preface

Both the nine-hundredth anniversary of the First Crusade (1095–1099) and the appearance of a considerable number of texts, translations, and works of scholarship on the history of the First Crusade since the publication of this book in 1971 are more than adequate justification for a second edition. The new edition retains most of the original texts that have made it a useful book for teachers, students, and general readers. It also includes a number of additional texts in translation that historians have come to use routinely in understanding and explaining a series of related events and experiences that had far wider consequences even than the remarkable journey to and conquest of Jerusalem. The new material consists chiefly of sources written in Hebrew and Arabic, although it also includes some new works originally in Latin and one in Old French. Section VI of the first edition, on the evolution of crusading privileges, has been omitted from this edition. In its place I have included three problematic texts that illuminate the complex ways in which ideas related to war against infidels were represented in three different literary genres. The introduction has been extensively revised and expanded, indicating the most important and accessible items of recent scholarship, especially in English but occasionally in other languages. Crusade history has long been an international subject, and not all of the most important work is available in English. The bibliographical essay at the end of the book has also been expanded and revised.

I am grateful to readers of the first edition who have used and commented on it and to several learned societies that have invited me to participate in conferences sponsored by them, particularly the Association for Jewish Studies, for an invitation to comment on a group of papers on the massacres of 1096 presented at the 1995 annual meeting in Boston, and to the Medieval Academy of America, for an invitation to organize and preside at a session on "Clermont and Its Consequences" at its 1996 annual meeting in Kansas City. I am also grateful to the scholars at those meetings and elsewhere who have given help and advice in the preparation of the new edition, particularly Robert Somerville, Thomas G. Waldman, Robert Chazan, Ivan Marcus, David Berger, Richard Landes, James A. Brundage, Bruce Brasington, James M. Powell, Mona Hammad, and James Muldoon.

This book is dedicated to the memory of Donald E. Queller (1925–1995).

Edward Peters

Abbreviations

Autour de la Première Croisade	*Autour de la Première Croisade: Actes du Colloque de la Society for the Study of the Crusades and the Latin East (Clermont-Ferrand, 22–25 juin 1995)*, ed. Michel Balard (Paris, 1996)
Crusade and Settlement	*Crusade and Settlement: Papers Read at the First Conference of the Society for the Study of the Crusades and the Latin East*, ed. Peter W. Edbury (Cardiff, 1985)
Crusaders and Muslims	*Crusaders and Muslims in Twelfth-Century Syria*, ed. Maya Schatzmiller (Leiden-New York-Cologne, 1993)
The First Crusade	*The First Crusade: Origins and Impact*, ed. Jonathan Phillips (Manchester-New York, 1997)
Gabrieli	Francesco Gabrieli, ed., *Arab Historians of the Crusades, Selected and Translated from the Arabic Sources*, trans. E. J. Costello (Berkeley and Los Angeles, 1969)
Gibb	H. A. R. Gibb, trans., *The Damascus Chronicle of the Crusades, Extracted and Translated from the Chronicle of Ibn al-Qalanisi* (London, 1932)
Hagenmeyer	Heinrich Hagenmeyer, *Die Kreuzzugsbriefe aus den Jahren 1088–1100* (Innsbruck, 1901)
Hill and Hill	John H. Hill and Laurita L. Hill, *Historia de Hierosolymitano Itinere by Peter Tudebode* (Philadelphia, 1974)
The Holy War	*The Holy War*, ed. Thomas Patrick Murphy (Columbus, Oh., 1976)

The Horns of Hattin	*The Horns of Hattin,* ed. B. Z. Kedar (Jerusalem-London, 1992)
Krey	A. C. Krey, *The First Crusade: The Accounts of Eye-Witnesses and Participants* (Princeton, 1921)
MGH	*Monumenta Germaniae Historica*
SS	*Scriptores*
Munro, *Letters*	Dana C. Munro, *Letters of the Crusaders* (University of Pennsylvania, Translations and Reprints from the Original Sources of European History, Vol. I, no. 4, Philadelphia, 1896)
Munro, *Urban*	Dana C. Munro, *Urban and the Crusaders* (University of Pennsylvania, Translations and Reprints from the Original Sources of European History, Vol. I, no. 2, Philadelphia, 1895)
Outremer	*Outremer: Studies in the History of the Crusading Kingdom of Jerusalem Presented to Joshua Prawer,* ed. B. Z. Kedar, H. E. Mayer, and R. C. Smail (Jerusalem, 1982)
The Oxford Illustrated History	*The Oxford Illustrated History of the Crusades,* ed. Jonathan Riley-Smith (Oxford-New York, 1995)
RHC	*Receuil des historiens des croisades*
Occ.	*Historiens occidentaux*
Victory in the East	John France, *Victory in the East: A Military History of the First Crusade* (Cambridge, 1994)

Introduction

Clermont and Its Consequences

From the pontificate of Leo IX (1049–1054) through that of Urban II (1088–1099), a series of vigorous and determined popes assumed the direction of the movement for ecclesiastical reform that had spread from small monastic and episcopal centers in Italy, Burgundy, the Rhineland, and Lorraine. The new papal influence in the reform movement contributed to the growth of the recognition of papal authority throughout western Europe and began to redirect reform toward the whole of the universal Church and Latin Christian society.[1] At the heart of the reform movement lay the two principles of the freedom of the church (both churchmen and ecclesiastical office and property) from the domination of laymen and the spiritual purification of the clergy, the latter emphasized by a renewed insistence on clerical celibacy.[2] Although the movement had been opposed by strong lay, episcopal, clerical, and monastic resistance and had profoundly divided traditional allies, such as pope and emperor, the cause of reform was pursued diligently by popes who were diplomats and popes who were visionaries and their supporters, cleri-

1. The best recent general histories are those by Uta-Renate Blumenthal, *The Investiture Controversy: Church and Monarchy from the Ninth to the Twelfth Century* (Philadelphia, 1988); Colin Morris, *The Papal Monarchy: The Western Church from 1050 to 1250* (Oxford, 1989); Gerd Tellenbach, *The Church in Western Europe from the Tenth to the Early Twelfth Century*, trans. Timothy Reuter (Cambridge, 1993). See also H. E. J. Cowdrey, *The Age of Abbot Desiderius: Montecassino, the Papacy, and the Normans in the Eleventh and Early Twelfth Centuries* (Oxford, 1983), and Giles Constable, *The Reformation of the Twelfth Century* (Cambridge, 1997), as well as works cited in the bibliographical essay at the end of this book.

2. On the purity of the clergy, see Michael Frassetto, ed., *Medieval Purity and Piety: Essays on Medieval Clerical Celibacy and Religious Reform* (New York, 1998); and Amy G. Remensnyder, "Pollution, Purity, and Peace: An Aspect of Social Reform Between the Late Tenth Century and 1076," in *The Peace of God: Social Violence and Religious Response in France Around the Year 1000*, ed. Thomas Head and Richard Landes (Ithaca, N.Y.-London, 1992), 280–307. On the idea of pollution in the context of the Holy Land, see James A. Brundage, "Prostitution, Miscegenation and Sexual Purity in the First Crusade," in *Crusade and Settlement*, 57–65; and Penny J. Cole, " 'O God, the heathen have come into your inheritance' (Ps. 78.1): The Theme of Religious Pollution in Crusade Documents, 1095–1188," in *Crusaders and Muslims*, 84–111.

cal and lay. Although one important aspect of reform consisted in freeing the church from extensive lay control, the rich monastic/aristocratic culture of eleventh-century Christendom supported reform more often than not, and popes and other reformers frequently called on the services of laymen to aid in the great cause.[3] The result of the new universality of the ecclesiastical reform movement was the transformation of Christendom. Its most striking single enterprise was the First Crusade.

The reform movement and the crusade that it indirectly produced were not, however, exclusively the concern of the most powerful rulers and thinkers of eleventh-century western Europe. One of the most striking features of the reform was the variety of levels of society to which its arguments appealed and whose members acted upon them. The call for an armed pilgrimage to aid Christians in the East and liberate Jerusalem made by Pope Urban II (1088–1099) at the Council of Clermont on November 27, 1095, was answered by individuals from all social backgrounds, and their history must be traced in a wide variety of experiences and perceptions, from Urban's sermon to the capture of Jerusalem on July 15, 1099, the establishment of the Latin Kingdom of Jerusalem in 1100, the supporting expedition that set out from Europe in 1101, and the memories of these events recorded in many different kinds of sources.

The popes, knights, and others who traveled and fought were not the only ones involved in the consequences of Clermont. The Jews of the Rhine valley and elsewhere—Speyer, Worms, Metz, Trier, Regensburg, and Prague —experienced the first European pogroms at the hands of crusaders and local residents in the *Gezerot Tatnu* of 4856/1096.[4] Hungarians and Byzantines suddenly encountered vast armies in their lands whose purposes were either unknown or misunderstood, whose conduct was, more often than not, violent and abrupt, and whose need for food and other supplies greatly strained local economies. The capture of Jerusalem, its port city of Jaffa, and a number of other territories in Palestine and Syria for the first time established European colonies in the eastern Mediterranean. This created a new factor in the diplomatic and commercial policies of the East Roman Empire and its capital at Constantinople as well as an alien and threatening political and religious presence in the Muslim world. European traders, particularly those in the cities of the Italian peninsula, acquired new and protected access to the

3. The most recent version of this point is the study by John Howe, "The Nobility's Reform of the Medieval Church," *American Historical Review* 93 (1988), 317–339. See also Howe, *Church Reform and Social Change in Eleventh-Century Italy: Dominic of Sora and His Patrons* (Philadelphia, 1997), and Marcus Bull, "Origins," in *The Oxford Illustrated History*, 13–33.
4. On the massacres of the Jews in Europe, see below, "The Others," p. 13, and Section III of this volume.

commercial wealth of the East.[5] The need for settlers and reinforcements after 1099, the opportunities for pilgrims and other travelers to venture into a now Christian Holy Land, and the growth of successful resistance on the part of Muslim states created a continuing interest and concern in western Europe for the newly conquered lands in the East and resulted in a formalizing of both crusader status and the crusade movement itself at least until the end of the sixteenth century.

But the worlds of Jewish Europeans, Central Europeans, the East Roman Empire, and Muslim Syria and Palestine were not the only societies affected by the consequences of Clermont. In Europe itself the news of the Crusade spread swiftly, and memories of it lasted long. To many people in the twelfth century and later, it appeared to be a bridge between the heroic era of Charlemagne and their own world.[6] The Crusade's triumphs were characterized and mischaracterized in chronicles and poems. Perhaps its deepest legacy was the sense that God had intervened unmistakably and decisively in human history once again in favor of a sinful but chosen people. Its immediate achievements proved impossible to sustain, but its memory could be—and was. The First Crusade and its consequences touched the lives and thoughts of more people at more levels of society in more ways than any earlier event in European history.

5. The most recent summaries of the consequences for trade are the essays by David Abulafia, "The Role of Trade in Muslim-Christian Contact During the Middle Ages," in *The Arab Influence in Medieval Europe*, ed. Dionisius A. Agius and Richard Hitchcock (Reading, 1994), 1–24, and "Trade and Crusade, 1050–1250," in *Cross-Cultural Convergences in the Crusader Period: Essays Presented to Aryeh Grabois on His Sixty-Fifth Birthday*, ed. Michael Goodich, Sophia Menache, and Sylvia Schein (New York-Bern, 1995), 1–20. See also David Abulafia, *Commerce and Conquest in the Mediterranean, 1100–1250* (Aldershot and Brookfield, 1993); E. Ashtor, "Il regno dei crociati e il commercio di Levante," in *I Comuni Italiani nel Regno Crociato di Gerusalemme*, ed. Gabriella Airaldi and Benjamin Z. Kedar (Genoa, 1986), 1–49; *The Cambridge Economic History of Europe*, vol. 2, *Trade and Industry in the Middle Ages*, 2d ed. ed. M. M. Postan and Edward Miller (Cambridge, 1987), chs. 5 and 6; Robert S. Lopez, *The Commercial Revolution of the Middle Ages, 950–1350* (Englewood Cliffs, N.J., 1971); E. Ashtor, *A Social and Economic History of the Near East in the Middle Ages* (London, 1976). In general, see M.-L. Favreau-Lilie, *Die Italiener im Heiligen Land vom ersten Kreuzzug bis zum Tode Heinrichs von Champagne (1098–1197)* (Amsterdam, 1989).

6. On the late eleventh-century and later twelfth-century identification of Charlemagne (ruled 768–814) with Jerusalem and with relics associated with the majesty of Christ, see the discussion in Amy G. Remensnyder, *Remembering Kings Past: Monastic Foundation Legends in Medieval Southern France* (Ithaca, N.Y.-London, 1995), 150–64, and E. A. R. Brown and Michael Cothren, "The Twelfth-Century Crusading Window of the Abbey of St. Denis," *Journal of the Warburg and Courtauld Institutes* 49 (1986), 1–40.

The World of the Crusaders:
Islam, East Rome, and the Popes

The Muslim world into which Urban launched the First Crusade had grown out of the Arabian Peninsula in the seventh century and by the late eleventh century ruled much of the ancient Mediterranean world and the Persian Empire, including Palestine and Syria, lands of considerable religious significance to the Greek and Latin Christians.[7] Under the Sunni Abbasid Caliphate at Baghdad, the Fatimid, or Shi'ite, Caliphate at first in Tunisia, and then from 973 in Cairo, and the Caliphate of Córdoba on the Iberian Peninsula, Muslim civilization entered a golden age of religious, economic, and artistic productivity. But the tenth and early eleventh centuries saw the weakening of the Caliphates at Baghdad and Cairo and the appearance of local energetic dynasties of rulers in Mosul and Aleppo and of the nomadic Seljuk Turkish people in the Near East in the eleventh century. The Turks gradually converted to Sunni Islam, and by 1055 a Seljuk ruler, Tughrul Beg, controlled Baghdad as sultan (*power*), nominally under the authority of the Caliph but in fact as the effective ruler of the Caliphate.[8] Tughrul Beg's nephew, Sultan Alp Arslan (1063–1072), inflicted a serious defeat on Byzantine forces at the battle of Manzikert in 1071, bringing much of Anatolia under Seljuk rule. Under Alp Arslan's son, Malik Shah (1072–1092), the Seljuk empire reached its greatest extent, but with the death of Malik Shah the actual power of the Caliphate was divided among separate princely houses. In Anatolia itself a separate Seljuk sultanate, that of Rūm (= East Rome, Anatolia), was established in the late eleventh century.

The Fatimid Caliphate in Cairo also declined after the death of the Caliph al-Hakim in 1021. Al-Hakim had ordered the destruction of the Church of the Holy Sepulcher in Jerusalem in 1009, although his successors permitted its rebuilding in the years following, completing the work with Byzantine funds in 1040. Under a series of weak caliphs, the office of *wazir*, or first minister, became the real seat of power in Cairo. Thus, on the eve of the First Cru-

---

7. An excellent brief history is that of Hugh Kennedy, *The Prophet and the Age of the Caliphates: The Islamic Near East from the Sixth to the Eleventh Century* (London-New York, 1986).

8. The best short account is the volume on the period of Islamic history following Kennedy's: P. M. Holt, *The Age of the Crusades: The Near East from the Eleventh Century to 1517* (London-New York, 1986). See also Robert Irwin, "Islam and the Crusades 1096–1699," in *The Oxford Illustrated History*, 217–259. Two important recent studies are those of S. Loutchitskaja, "*Barbarae nationes*: Les peuples musulmans dans les chroniques de la Première Croisade," *Autour de la Première Croisade*, 99–107, and Carole Hillenbrand, "The First Crusade: the Muslim Perspective," in *The First Crusade*, 130–141, and below, n. 37.

sade, the Muslim world of the Middle East was fragmented among several different and rival powers, complemented by a group of smaller, independent powers from Anatolia to Iberia. Syria and Palestine remained disputed territories among the greater Muslim powers. As Holt sums up the situation:

When the Crusaders approached Syria in the autumn of 1097, they had before them a politically fragmented land, where the rulers were for the most part men of narrow vision and little experience. Behind these petty princes and governors were the two major powers, the Great Seljuk Sultanate [at Baghdad] and Fatimid Egypt, both in decline, and the former at least little interested in the fate of Syria.[9]

The East Roman, or Byzantine, Empire was the other great power in the Middle East. Under the Macedonian dynasty and its last great representative, the Emperor Basil II (963–1025), both Bulgaria and Kiev came under East Roman influence and a strong defense was mounted in Anatolia and Syria against Muslim powers.[10] Diplomatic and cultural influence, economic prosperity, and strong, centralized government created a golden age of Byzantine civilization that was threatened by the weakening of the dynasty after the death of Basil II and his far less capable successors and a period of political anarchy that lasted from 1057 until 1081. Tense relations with western Europe were also exacerbated in 1054 by the breach between the ambitious Patriarch of Constantinople, Michael Kerularios, and the representative of Pope Leo IX, Cardinal Humbert of Silva Candida. Likewise, the growth of Norman power in south Italy, culminating in the defeat of the East Roman forces at Bari in 1071, the same disastrous year as Manzikert, worsened East-West relations. The Norman power also invaded western Greece later in the century and appeared to threaten Constantinople itself. Although the Empire was in no immediate danger, the appearance of two new and powerful forces on the western and eastern frontiers caused concern in both the West and Constantinople.

The reign of Alexius I Comnenus (1081–1118) achieved a remarkable restoration of Byzantine fortunes and power. Moreover, Alexius began to cultivate and to understand western Latin Christians both as potential military allies and as pilgrims with a great veneration for the Holy Land. Not all Byzantine-Latin relations had collapsed as a result of the breach of 1054, and

---

9. Holt, *The Age of the Crusades*, 15.

10. The best recent histories are those of Mark Whittow, *The Making of Orthodox Byzantium, 600–1025* (London, 1997), and Michael Angold, *The Byzantine Empire, 1025–1204: A Political History* (London-New York, 1984). On Byzantine civilization, see A. P. Kazhdan and Ann Wharton Epstein, *Change in Byzantine Culture in the Eleventh and Twelfth Centuries* (Berkeley-Los Angeles-London, 1985). See also Anthony Bryer and Michael Ursinus, eds., *Manzikert to Lepanto: The Byzantine World and the Turks, 1071–1571*, Byzantinische Forschungen 16 (Amsterdam, 1991).

both Alexius and his Western counterparts worked hard to restore them.[11] Having established good relations with Robert, Count of Flanders, who visited Constantinople on his return from a pilgrimage to Jerusalem in 1087, Alexius also approved of his mother's negotiations with Pope Victor III (1085–1088) concerning Byzantine facilities for Jerusalem pilgrims. Before his election as pope, Victor III had been Abbot Desiderius of Monte Cassino, and relations between the monastery of St. Benedict and Alexius I were extremely cordial.[12] By the election of Urban II in 1088, Byzantine-Western relations had improved considerably, and Alexius had come to regard the West as a source of both pilgrims and soldiers. He certainly did not regard it as a source for a crusade: no one yet knew what a crusade was. Crusade was the new business of the pope and the warrior order of western Europe.

One of the most striking consequences of the reform movement of the eleventh century was the increasing claims by and recognition of the pope not only as the bishop and high priest of Rome and guardian of the tombs of the apostles Peter and Paul, but also as the spiritual leader of Latin Christendom. The energetic pontificates of Leo IX, Nicholas II (1059–1061), Alexander II (1061–1073), and Gregory VII (1073–1085) each contributed to the new political role of the papacy, often in ways that influenced the idea of the legitimacy of violence on behalf of churchmen and Christian society as a whole.[13]

But the reform papacy of the eleventh century was not the first papacy to justify war. In the ninth century popes Leo IV (847–855) and John VIII (872–882) had stated that all who fell in combat with Muslim or Viking invaders would certainly be saved.[14] The army of Leo IX in 1053 was assembled and commanded by the pope, and in the decades following the papal truce

11. In general, see Cowdrey, *The Age of Abbot Desiderius*, and Jonathan Shepherd, "Aspects of Byzantine Attitudes and Policy Towards the West in the Tenth and Eleventh Centuries," in *Byzantium and the West c. 850–c. 1200*, ed. J. D. Howard-Johnston, *Byzantinische Forschungen* 13 (Amsterdam, 1988), 66–118, as well as other studies in the same collection, and Jonathan Shepherd, "Cross-Purposes: Alexius Comnenus and the First Crusade," *The First Crusade*, 107–129.

12. See Herbert Bloch, *Monte Cassino in the Middle Ages*, vol. 1 (Cambridge, Mass., 1986), 40–112; G. A. Loud, "Abbot Desiderius of Montecassino and the Gregorian Papacy," *Journal of Ecclesiastical History* 30 (1979), 305–26; and Cowdrey, *The Age of Abbot Desiderius*, passim.

13. Frederick H. Russell, *The Just War in the Middle Ages* (Cambridge, 1975), and Carl Erdmann, *The Origin of the Idea of Crusade*, trans. Marshall W. Baldwin and Walter Goffart (Princeton, N.J., 1977). See also the essays in *The Holy War*, and two essays by Jonathan Riley-Smith: "An Approach to Crusading Ethics," *Reading Medieval Studies* 6 (1980), 3–19, and "Crusading as an Act of Love," *History* n.s. 65 (1980), 177–192.

14. The question of the papacy and war has most recently been reexamined by John Gilchrist, "The Papacy and War Against 'the Saracens,' 795–1216," *International History Review* 10 (1988), 174–197, with extensive references to the scholarly literature and a substantial discussion of the influence of Carl Erdmann. Gilchrist's is the strongest argument that papal attitudes

with the Normans and the formal Norman subjection to the papacy in 1059, enemies of the reform popes often waged war against them and Rome both in the city and in the towns surrounding it. In 1063–64 Alexander II sent a papal banner and an indulgence for those who fell in battle against the Muslims to the army preparing for the siege of Barbastro in Spain.[15] In 1064 Alexander sent a papal banner to Erlembald, leader of the forces supporting ecclesiastical reform in Milan, and in 1066 he sent a similar banner to William of Normandy, who was setting out to conquer England, one dimension of which was the reform of the English church.[16]

In 1073–74 Gregory VII even proposed to lead an armed force to aid the emperor at Constantinople, a project that came to nothing but which indicates the extent to which the use of military force in matters considered crucial to the survival of the church and the pursuit of ecclesiastical reform had become ingrained in the minds of the reform popes of the later eleventh century.[17] And their conception of the world had greatly widened.

The Warriors

The military aristocracy of the eleventh century had achieved its precarious eminence in Western society by virtue of its prowess in war and its loyalty — and frequent strategic disloyalty — to the weakened kings and ambitious territorial lords who carved their principalities out of the old divisions of the Carolingian Empire and augmented them by purchase, marriage, cunning, and force. Kin groups claiming aristocratic status asserted their right to rule through their prowess in war and claimed public authority in their own terri-

---

toward war and policies that ruled its use did not substantially change at the mid-eleventh century. See also his earlier study, "The Erdmann Thesis and the Canon Law, 1083–1141," in *Crusade and Settlement*, 37–45, as well as H. E. J. Cowdrey, "Canon Law and the First Crusade," in *The Horns of Hattin*, 40–48, and the work of Michael McCormick, cited below, n. 28.

15. See Alberto Ferreiro, "The Siege of Barbastro, 1064–65: A Reassessment," *Journal of Medieval History* 9 (1983), 129–144. A number of relevant Iberian sources for the late eleventh and early twelfth centuries are now available in Olivia Remie Constable, ed., *Medieval Iberia: Readings from Christian, Muslim, and Jewish Sources* (Philadelphia, 1997), 109–151.

16. See Erdmann, *The Origin of the Idea of Crusade*, 118–147; H. E. J. Cowdrey, "The Genesis of the Crusades: The Springs of Western Ideas of Holy War," in *The Holy War*, 9–32, rept. in Cowdrey, *Popes, Monks, and Crusaders* (London, 1984), 13: 9–32; Riley-Smith, "Crusading as an Act of Love"; H. E. J. Cowdrey, "Bishop Ermenfrid of Sion and the Penitential Ordinance Following the Battle of Hastings," *Journal of Ecclesiastical History* 20 (1969), 225–242.

17. On Gregory VII and Byzantium, see H. E. J. Cowdrey, "The Gregorian Papacy, Byzantium, and the First Crusade," in *Byzantium and the West c. 850–c. 1200*, ed. J. D. Howard-Johnston, 145–169, and Cowdrey, "Pope Gregory VII's 'Crusading' Plans of 1074," in *Outremer*, 27–40, rept. in Cowdrey, *Popes, Monks, and Crusaders*, 10: 27–40.

tories, often with little concern for kings. They were capable of being mobilized for larger enterprises only by claims on their friendship and willing cooperation.[18] How and when the world of Carolingian kings gave way to that of territorial principalities and tough and stubborn castellans is still a matter of scholarly debate, but it is clear that the reality and imagery of a motley warrior group remaking itself into a knightly elite was a process well underway in the eleventh century, regardless of the differences among them in wealth and social rank. Many of these lords and lesser nobles, whose daily conduct was at best high-handed and brutal, also recognized their own interests and their spiritual well-being to be firmly linked to those of the ecclesiastical reformers.

One of the strongest links between lay warriors and the reforming clergy was the problem of sin, penance, and salvation. All humans, monks included, were prone to sin by virtue of their shared—and fallen—human nature. The warrior order was considered especially prone to the great sin of pride and its frequent companions, anger and violence. The Christian response to sin was penance. For warriors, penance might be expressed in almsgiving and the endowment of ecclesiastical institutions, fasting, penitential pilgrimage, and retirement to the monastic life for those capable of effecting such a drastic change in their way of living. These acts, however, regularly required a suspension of the warriors' most distinctive function, since they often required the prohibition of the bearing of arms for certain periods of time, expressions of penance after battles, or the design of a lifestyle that was generally incompatible with the life they were required to live. An excellent example of this last problem is found in the life of St. Gerald of Aurillac, written by Abbot Odo of Cluny in the tenth century.[19] But before the late eleventh century no one had worked out a doctrine whereby fighting itself might be considered a penitential and spiritually meritorious act.

Few members of the eleventh-century warrior order even remotely resembled later popular images of the saintly chivalric knight, although they were certainly his ancestors, and the complex process elevating the fighting man into this ideal social type began in their lifetimes and partly during the

---

18. There is a large literature, much of it summarized in the recent works of Jonathan Riley-Smith, Marcus Bull, and others cited throughout the notes to this introduction and in the bibliographical essay. Of particular interest are the review article by Timothy Reuter, "Pre-Gregorian Mentalities," *Journal of Ecclesiastical History* 45 (1994), 465–474, and John Howe, *Church Reform and Social Change.*

19. Odo of Cluny, "The Life of Saint Gerald of Aurillac," trans. Gerard Sitwell O.S.B., in *Soldiers of Christ: Saints and Saints' Lives from Late Antiquity and the Early Middle Ages*, ed. Thomas F. X. Noble and Thomas Head (University Park, Pa., 1995), 293–362. This volume is an invaluable introduction to one of the most important literary and devotional genres of early European history.

First Crusade.[20] They endowed reformed monasteries, learned the rudiments of lay piety from monastic-inspired prayerbooks, and stood in awe before the rich and intricate monastic liturgy. In their leisure moments, and sometimes in battle, they thought they could see the hand of God directing their actions: "It is in the presence of the miraculous," R. W. Southern has written of them, "that they become most human."[21] These were the lords who made long penitential pilgrimages to Santiago de Compostela, Rome, or Jerusalem—men like the terrible Fulk Nerra, Count of Anjou, who made three and perhaps four pilgrimages to Jerusalem, and Duke Robert I of Normandy, who in 1035 departed on a pilgrimage to Jerusalem from which he never returned, leaving his turbulent duchy in the hands of his six-year-old illegitimate son, William, later to become the conqueror of England.[22]

20. The relations among knighthood as a recognized status or order, the culture of chivalry that featured it, and the First Crusade have been and remain the matter of considerable scholarly debate. See Colin Morris, "*Equestris Ordo*: Chivalry as a Vocation in the Twelfth Century," *Studies in Church History* 15 (1978), 87–96; Janet Nelson, "Ninth-Century Knighthood: The Evidence of Nithard," in *Studies in Medieval History Presented to R. Allen Brown* (Woodbridge, 1989), 255–266; Maurice Keen, *Chivalry* (New Haven, Conn., 1984), 23–37; and C. Stephen Jaeger, *The Origins of Courtliness: Civilizing Trends and the Formation of Courtly Ideals, 939–1210* (Philadelphia, 1985). Two works by Jean Flori are important: *L'Idéologie du glaive: Préhistoire de la chevalerie* (Geneva, 1983), and *L'Essor de la chevalerie, XIe–XIIe siècles* (Geneva, 1986). Some of their results are incorporated in Flori's recent history of the First Crusade: *La Première croisade: L'Occident chrétien contre l'Islam (Aux origines des idéologies occidentales)* (Brussels, 1992), esp. 147–177. See also Karl J. Leyser, "Early Medieval Canon Law and the Beginnings of Knighthood," in Leyser, *Communications and Power in Medieval Europe: The Carolingian and Ottonian Centuries*, ed. Timothy Reuter (London-Rio Grande, 1994), 51–71; Marcus Bull, *Knightly Piety and the Lay Response to the First Crusade: The Limousin and Gascony, c. 970–c. 1130* (Oxford, 1993); and Bull, "The Roots of Lay Enthusiasm for the First Crusade," *History* 78 (1993), 353–372. Most recently, see Matthew Strickland, *War and Chivalry: The Conduct and Perception of War in England and Normandy, 1066–1217* (Cambridge, 1996).

21. R. W. Southern, *The Making of the Middle Ages* (New Haven, Conn., 1953), 87. See also Benedicta Ward, *Miracles and the Medieval Mind: Theory, Record, and Event, 1000–1215* (Philadelphia, 1982), and Thomas Head, *Hagiography and the Cult of Saints: The Diocese of Orléans, 800–1200* (Cambridge, 1990).

22. On Fulk Nerra, see Bernard Bachrach, *Fulk Nerra, the Neo-Roman Consul, 987–1040* (Berkeley-Los Angeles, 1993), and Bachrach, "The Pilgrimages of Fulk Nerra, Count of the Angevins, 987–1040," in *Religion, Culture, and Society in the Early Middle Ages: Studies in Honor of Richard E. Sullivan*, ed. Thomas F. X. Noble and John J. Contreni (Kalamazoo, Mich., 1987), 205–217. On Robert and William of Normandy see David C. Douglas, *William the Conqueror* (Berkeley-Los Angeles, 1967), 31–37. On the tactical as well as the spiritual motivation for Jerusalem pilgrimage, see Adriaan Bredero, "Jerusalem in the West," in Bredero, *Christendom and Christianity in the Middle Ages: The Relations Between Religion, Church, and Society*, trans. Reinder Bruinsma (Grand Rapids, Mich., 1994), 79–104. There are shrewd cautionary observations on overestimating western familiarity with Jerusalem and its eleventh-century history in John France, "The Destruction of Jerusalem and the First Crusade," *Journal of Ecclesiastical History* 47 (1996), 1–17; see also Sylvia Schein, "Jérusalem: Objectif originel de la Première Croisade?" *Autour de la Première Croisade*, 119–126, and Oleg Grabar, *The Shape of the Holy: Early Islamic Jerusalem* (Princeton, N.J., 1996). On pilgrimage generally, see Jonathan Sumption, *Pilgrimage:*

The centers of monastic reform, of which the Burgundian monastery of Cluny and its daughter houses are the best-known examples, urged men to undertake these pilgrimages and even helped them on the route. Although Cluniac support was denied to the visionary Pope Gregory VII (1073–1085) in his more extreme attacks on imperial authority in ecclesiastical affairs, it certainly shored up other aspects of reform, particularly the eleventh-century interest in pilgrimage.[23] A chain of Cluniac houses stretched across southern France and northern Spain providing way stations along the route to the popular shrine of Santiago Matamoros (St. James the Moor-Killer) at Compostela, the shrine that epitomized the spirit of Iberian reconquest of the peninsula from the Muslims.[24] It may have been Cluniac influence that attracted many French soldiers to the beginnings of the Spanish *reconquista*.[25]

After a short life of violence and temporary repentance, some eleventh-century lords chose to expiate their many sins by entering the monastic life — as did Hugh I, Duke of Burgundy, in 1078 — or by setting off on the pilgrim's route to Rome, Santiago, or Jerusalem.[26] The new cults of military saints like

An Image of Medieval Religion (London, 1975), and below, n. 24. For an English perspective, see Christopher Tyerman, *England and the Crusades, 1095–1588* (Chicago, 1988), 8–32.

23. On Cluny and the movement for ecclesiastical reform, see the works cited above, n. 1. On Cluny and Gregory VII, see H. E. J. Cowdrey, *The Cluniacs and the Gregorian Reform* (Oxford, 1970); on Cluny and the First Crusade, see Cowdrey, "Cluny and the First Crusade," rpt. in Cowdrey, *Popes, Monks, and Crusaders*, 15: 285–311.

24. On the topic generally, see John M. Howe, "The Conversion of the Physical World: The Creation of a Christian Landscape," in *Varieties of Religious Conversion in the Middle Ages*, ed. James Muldoon (Gainesville, Fl., 1997), 63–78. On Santiago, see Marilyn Stokstad, *Santiago de Compostela* (Norman, Okla., 1978); Marcelin Defourneaux, *Les français en Espagne aux XIe et XIIe siècles* (Paris, 1949); William Melczer, *The Pilgrim's Guide to Santiago de Compostela* (New York, 1993); Maryjane Dunn and Linda K. Davidson, *The Pilgrimage to Santiago de Compostela* (New York, 1994); Annie Shaver-Crandell and Paula Gerson, with the assistance of Alison Stones, *The Pilgrim's Guide to Santiago de Compostela: A Gazetteer* (London, 1995); Paula Gerson, Jeanne Krochalis, Annie Shaver-Crandell, and Alison Stones, *The Pilgrim's Guide to Santiago de Compostela: A Critical Edition* (London, 1996); Angus Mackay, *Spain in the Middle Ages: From Frontier to Empire, 1000–1500* (London, 1977); Bernard F. Reilly, *The Medieval Spains* (Cambridge, 1993), and the splendidly illustrated exhibition catalogue, *Santiago, camino de Europa: Culto y cultura en la peregrinación a Compostela* (Madrid, 1993). On Jerusalem, see J. Wilkinson, *Jerusalem Pilgrims Before the Crusades* (Warminster, 1977), and John Wilkinson, with Joyce Hill and W. F. Ryan, *Jerusalem Pilgrimage, 1099–1185* (London, 1988). On Rome, see Peter Llewellyn, *Rome in the Dark Ages* (New York, 1970), ch. 6, and Richard Krautheimer, *Rome: Profile of a City* (Princeton, N.J., 1980), chs. 2–6. On pilgrimage generally, see Linda Kay Davidson and Maryjane Dunn-Wood, *Pilgrimage in the Middle Ages: A Research Guide* (New York, 1994), and Robert Ousterhout, ed., *The Blessings of Pilgrimage* (Urbana, Ill., 1990).

25. R. A. Fletcher, *Saint James's Catapult: The Life and Times of Diego Gelmírez of Santiago de Compostela* (Oxford, 1984); Fletcher, "Reconquest and Crusade in Spain c. 1050–1150," *Transactions of the Royal Historical Society* 5th ser. 37 (1987), 31–47; Fletcher, *The Quest for El Cid* (New York, 1990).

26. On the admission of the duke and the pope's response, see I. S. Robinson, "Gregory VII and the Soldiers of Christ," *History* 58 (1973), 169–192, and Constance Brittain Bouchard,

St. Michael the Archangel, St. George, and St. Demetrius, no longer venerated and depicted because they had restrained their arms but because they
had used them in God's cause, sustained their journeys as exemplars of both
devotion and military prowess.[27]

Not only in Spain, however, were armed penitents welcome. The invasions of Europe by the Vikings, Magyars, and Muslims in the ninth and
tenth centuries had appeared to many as an attack on their lands and on
their faith.[28] Other enemies appeared in the eleventh century. In 1053 Pope
Leo X led an army in papal service against the Norman lords of south Italy.
Although Leo was ignominiously defeated at Benevento and the Normans
themselves became allies and then formal subjects of the popes in 1059, the
ecclesiastical approval and later encouragement of the use of force in defense
of the church and the faithful increased in frequency during this period. Normans in south Italy had themselves taken over their new lands after some of
them had been invited, while on a pilgrimage, to aid the Lombard princes in
their war against the Byzantines and Arabs. Although the invited Normans
returned home, the prince of Salerno appears to have gone looking for more
Normans, so impressed was he with the military prowess of the pilgrims. The
entry for the year 1017 in Amatus's *Chronicle of Monte Cassino* tells the story:

[In the year 999] forty Normans dressed as pilgrims, on their return from Jerusalem,
disembarked at Salerno. These were men of considerable bearing, impressive-looking,

---

Sword, Miter, and Cloister: Nobility and the Church in Burgundy, 980–1198 (Ithaca, N.Y.-London,
1987), 128–129.

27. See Jonathan Riley-Smith, "The First Crusade and St. Peter," in *Outremer*, 41–63.

28. See Simon Coupland, "The Rod of God's Wrath or the People of God's Wrath? The
Carolingian Theology of the Viking Invasions," *Journal of Ecclesiastical History* 42 (1991), 535–
554; J. M. Wallace-Hadrill, "War and Peace in the Early Middle Ages," rpt. in Wallace-Hadrill,
Early Medieval History (Oxford, 1975), 19–38; Friedrich E. Prinz, "King, Clergy, and War at the
Time of the Carolingians," in *Saints, Scholars, and Heroes: Studies in Medieval Culture in Honour
of Charles W. Jones*, 2 vols. (Collegeville, Minn., 1979), 2: 301–329; Janet Nelson, "The Church's
Military Service in the Ninth Century," rpt. in Nelson, *Politics and Ritual in Early Medieval Europe*
(London-Ronceverte, 1986), 117–132; Michael McCormick, "The Liturgy of War in the Early
Middle Ages: Crisis, Litanies, and the Carolingian Monarchy," *Viator* 15 (1984), 1–23; McCor-
mick, "A New Ninth-Century Witness to the Carolingian Mass Against the Pagans (Paris, B.N.,
Lat. 2812)," *Revue Bénédictine* 97 (1987), 68–86; McCormick, "Liturgie et guerre des Carolingiens
à la première croisade," in *"Militia Christi" e Crociata nei secoli XI–XIII*, Miscellanea del Centro
di studi medioevali 13 (Milan, 1992), 209–240. On the reflection in poetry, see Peter Godman,
The Poetry of the Carolingian Renaissance (Norman, Okla., 1985), 186–191, 312–315. An English
translation of a seventh-century Visigothic liturgical *ordo*, "The Order [of ceremony to be fol-
lowed] when the king with his army goes forth to battle," is given in J. N. Hillgarth, *Christianity
and Paganism, 350–750: The Conversion of Western Europe* (Philadelphia, 1986), 93–95. There is an
extensive discussion in the important book by Michael McCormick, *Eternal Victory: Triumphal
Rulership in Late Antiquity, Byzantium and the Early Medieval West* (Cambridge, 1986), 308–327,
and for the later Frankish period in general, 342–384.

men of the greatest experience in warfare. They found the city besieged by the Saracens. Their souls were inflamed with a call to God. They demanded arms and horses from Gaimar the prince of Salerno, got them, and threw themselves ferociously upon the enemy. They killed and captured many and put the rest to flight, achieving a miraculous victory with the help of God. They swore that they had done all this only out of love of God and of the Christian faith; they refused any reward and refused to remain in Salerno.[29]

By the late eleventh century the pope and others had need of the warriors, and the warriors needed a justification for their profession that only an ingenious pope might give. An excellent example of this reciprocal need is the change of heart attributed to the Norman warrior Tancred in Ralph of Caen's account of Tancred's crusade:

Day after day his prudent mind was in turmoil, and he burned with anxiety all the more because he saw that the warfare which flowed from his position of authority obstructed the Lord's commands. For the Lord enjoins that the struck cheek and the other one be offered to the striker, whereas secular authority requires that not even relatives' blood be spared. The Lord warns that one's tunic, and one's cloak, too, must be given to the man intending to take them away; but the imperatives of authority demand that a man who has been deprived of both should have whatever else remains taken from him. Thus, this incompatability dampened the courage of the wise man whenever he was given an opportunity for quiet reflection. But after the judgment of Pope Urban granted a remission of sins to every Christian setting out to overcome the gentiles, then at last the man's energies were aroused, as though he had earlier been asleep; his strength was renewed, his eyes opened, and his courage was redoubled. For until then . . . his mind was torn two ways, uncertain which path to follow, that of the Gospel, or that of the world.[30]

A similar idea is reflected in the observation of Guibert of Nogent:

God has instituted in our time holy wars, so that the order of knights and the crowd running in their wake, who following the example of the ancient pagans, have been engaged in slaughtering one another, might find a new way of gaining salvation. And so they are not forced to abandon secular affairs completely by choosing the monastic

---

29. *The Chronicle of Monte Cassino*, MGH SS VII, 651–652. On the chronicle and its author, see Cowdrey, *The Age of Abbot Desiderius*; Kenneth Baxter Wolf, *Making History: The Normans and Their Historians in Eleventh-Century Italy* (Philadelphia, 1995), 87–122; Barbara M. Kreutz, *Before the Normans: Southern Italy in the Ninth and Tenth Centuries* (Philadelphia, 1991); Donald Matthew, *The Norman Kingdom of Sicily* (Cambridge, 1992); David C. Douglas, *The Norman Achievement, 1050–1100* (London, 1969), ch. 5, "The Holy War," 89–109; John France, "The Occasion of the Coming of the Normans to Southern Italy, *Journal of Medieval History* 17 (1991), 185–205; G. A. Loud, "Norman Italy and the Holy Land," in *The Horns of Hattin*, 49–62; Loud, "Byzantine Italy and the Normans," in *Byzantium and the West c. 850–c. 1200*, ed. Howard-Johnston, 215–233.

30. Quoted in Bull, *Knightly Piety and the First Crusade*, 3–4.

life or any religious profession, as used to be the custom, but can attain in some measure God's grace while pursuing their own careers, with the liberty and dress to which they are accustomed.[31]

Here again God was thought to have created a way out of Tancred's dilemma. As Riley-Smith observes, Urban had taken a step along the road that would lead the Church to recognize the lay condition as a vocation in itself.

The Others

The incursions of the Turks and the growth of mature Jewish communities in western Europe became the focus of yet two other aspects of eleventh-century Christian consciousness: a sharpened awareness of the differences between Christianity and Judaism on the one hand and Christianity and Islam on the other—a new recognition of the "other" as "enemy"—and the legitimacy of the Holy War.

The history of Jews in Europe is long and complex. By the late eleventh century Jewish communities in western Europe were distinct from surrounding Christian communities—they indeed formed one of the most impressive early stages of the flowering of Ashkenazic Jewry, possessing synagogues, Torah scrolls, learned and eloquent rabbis (one of whom, Kalonymos of Mainz, could freely write to the emperor Henry IV and expect—and receive—an answer), *cohens*, cemeteries, and other features of mature Jewish communities.[32] They possessed local histories. They also possessed a religious identity that Christians recognized as distinct from Christianity and that Christians also came to believe was hostile to Christianity. Older Christian traditions of anti-Jewish sentiment grew sharper after the tenth century in both legal and devotional terms. Moreover, Christian attitudes toward Jews varied from one level of society and one locality to another. Although papal policy, for example, appears relatively tolerant, other manifestations of extreme hostility were expressed elsewhere and with greater consequences in Christian society.[33]

31. Guibert of Nogent, *Gesta Dei per Francos, RHC Occ.* IV, p. 124, cited in Riley-Smith, *The Crusades: A Short History*, 9.

32. The best introduction to the period and problem is that of Robert Chazan, *European Jewry and the First Crusade* (Berkeley-Los Angeles, 1987), with extensive references and material in translation. See also Chazan, *In the Year 1096: The First Crusade and the Jews* (Philadelphia-Jerusalem, 1996). For a broad social picture, see Irving A. Agus, *The Heroic Age of Franco-German Jewry*, 2 vols. (New York, 1969).

33. See Kenneth Stow, *The "1007 Anonymous" and Papal Sovereignty: Jewish Perceptions of the Papacy and Papal Policy in the High Middle Ages* (Cincinnati, Oh., 1984).

The language of tenth- and eleventh-century Latin Europe began to echo more distinctly with references to "enemies of God" and calls for vengeance on those "enemies," as well as eschatological calls for the conversion of the Jews.[34] The destruction of the Church of the Holy Sepulcher in Jerusalem by the mad Caliph al-Hakim in 1009 had triggered Christian accusations that the Jews in the kingdom of France had urged the caliph to this act and led a brief outburst of persecutions at the beginning of the eleventh century, particularly at the court of Robert the Pious of France, but also in such cities as Mainz.[35] New forms of Christian devotion, not only to the cross but to the crucified human figure on it, and the concurrent idea that Jews were somehow agents of the Muslim occupiers of the Holy Land made traditional anti-Jewish invective sharper and more immediate.[36] By the late eleventh century the Jews in Europe had come to be perceived by Christians as "other" in untraditional—and dangerous—ways.

The case of Islam was different, not in terms of the idea of "enemies of God," but in terms of Muslim power in Christian holy places and the threat of the extension of that power to other Christian places, real or perceived. The old allegations that the First Crusade was a response to actual Islamic persecutions and depredations in the Holy Land have long since been discredited, but the place of such accusations in eleventh-century crusade propaganda illustrates an important change in the Christian view of Islam.[37] The process of Christianization had, it appears, become sufficiently powerful an influence in Western society to have substantially altered not only forms of social organization but forms of social consciousness as well. These gains had been great, but the price for them may well have been a heightened sense

34. Most recently, see Ivan Marcus, "Christians and Jews Imagining the Other in Medieval Europe," *Prooftexts* 15 (1995), 209–226; H. Liebeschütz, "The Crusading Movement in Its Bearing on the Christian Attitude Toward Jewry," rpt. in *Essential Papers on Judaism and Christianity in Conflict from Late Antiquity to the Reformation*, ed. Jeremy Cohen (New York-London, 1991), 262–275; Jonathan Riley-Smith, "The First Crusade and the Persecution of the Jews," *Studies in Church History* 21 (1984), 51–72; and Jean Flori, "Une ou plusieurs 'première croisade'? Le message d'Urbain II et les plus anciens pogroms d'Occident," *Revue historique* 285 (1991), 3–27. On the crusaders' appropriation—and application to themselves—of the military imagery of the Old Testament, see Adolf Waas, "Volk Gottes und Militia Christi—Juden und Kreuzfahrer," in *Juden im Mittelalter: Beiträge zum christlich-jüdischen Gespräch* (Berlin, 1966), 410–434, and D. H. Green, *The Milstätter Exodus: A Crusading Epic* (Cambridge, 1966).

35. Robert Chazan, "1007–1012: Initial Crisis for Northern European Jewry," *Proceedings of the American Academy for Jewish Research* 38–39 (1970–71), 185–195, and below, Section X of the text.

36. Allan Harris Cutler and Helen Elmquist Cutler, *The Jew as Ally of the Muslim* (Notre Dame, 1986). See also the "Encyclical" of "Sergius IV," below, Section X.

37. See R. W. Southern, *Western Views of Islam in the Middle Ages* (Cambridge, Mass., 1962); Norman Daniel, *Islam and the West: The Making of an Image* (Edinburgh, 1966); E. Sivan,

of the differences between Christianity and Islam. Certainly the border areas of contact between the two religions—Spain, Sicily, south Italy, and Byzantium—do not appear to have generated these attitudes. The rough and ready tolerance of each other is a common phenomenon among border enemies in daily contact. The centers of this new opposition to Islam appear to have been those remote from this kind of contact—Burgundy, Lorraine, and France.

As a rationale for and effective vehicle of these attitudes, the eleventh-century concept of the Holy War is particularly striking. The term itself, along with "crusade" and "jihad" (the Arabic word for both spiritual struggle within the individual believer and war in the service of God), have had a long and repellent history and have come to be somewhat casually used.[38] In the first place, no direct connection has been established between the Muslim and Christian concepts of Holy War. Early Christianity, which had reluctantly accepted St. Augustine's justification for the *legitimacy* of war under certain specified conditions, had rarely regarded warfare as in any way virtuous and often expressed concern for the salvation of those who killed enemies in battle, regardless of the cause for which they fought.[39] The new perils of the ninth- and tenth-century invasions, however, the clearly acknowledged duty

---

L'Islam et la croisade: Idéologie et propagande dans les réactions musulmanes aux Croisades (Paris, 1968); Daniel, *The Arabs and Medieval Europe*, 3d ed. (London–Beirut, 1986); Daniel, "Crusade Propaganda," in *A History of the Crusades* (Madison, Wis., 1989), 6: 39–97, esp. 53–78; Philippe Sénac, *L'Image de l'autre: Histoire de l'Occident médiéval face à l'Islam* (Paris, 1983). In addition to the sources cited elsewhere in this introduction and in Sections VII and VIII below, see also Amin Maalouf, *The Crusades Through Arab Eyes*, trans. Jon Rothschild (London, 1984), and Penny J. Cole, "'O God, the heathen have come into your inheritance' (Ps. 78.1): The Theme of Religious Pollution in Crusade Documents, 1095–1188," in *Crusaders and Muslims*, 84–111.

38. On the Muslim term and idea, see W. Montgmery Watt, "Islamic Conceptions of the Holy War," *The Holy War*, 141–156; Peter Partner, "Holy War, Crusade, and Jihad: An Attempt to Define Some Problems," *Autour de la Première Croisade*, 333–343, and Benjamin Z. Kedar, "Croisade et Jihad vus par l'ennemi: Une étude des perceptions mutuelles des motivations," *Autour de la Première Croisade*, 345–355. For a Muslim perspective, see *The Sea of Precious Virtues (Bahr al-Fara'id): A Medieval Mirror for Princes*, trans. and ed. Julie Scott Meisami (Salt Lake City, 1991). On the protected status of Christians and Jews in Islamic territories, see C. E. Bosworth, "The 'Protected Peoples' (Christians and Jews) in Medieval Egypt and Syria," rpt. in Bosworth, *The Arabs, Byzantium, and Iran: Studies in Early Islamic History and Culture* (Aldershot-Brookfield, 1996), 7: 11–36.

39. See the work of Gilchrist, Brundage, and Cowdrey, cited above, as well as the essays in the volume *The Church and War*, *Studies in Church History* 20 (1983); Frederick H. Russell, *The Just War in the Middle Ages* (Cambridge, 1975), and Ernst-Dieter Hehl, *Kirche und Krieg im 12. Jahrhundert: Studien zu kanonischem Recht und politischer Wirklichkeit* (Stuttgart, 1980). On the crusaders as martyrs, see H. E. J. Cowdrey, "Martyrdom and the First Crusade," in *Crusade and Settlement*, 46–56; Jean Flori, "Mort et martyre des guerriers vers 1100: L'exemple de la première croisade," *Cahiers de Civilisation Médiévale* 34 (1991), 121–139; and Colin Morris, "Martyrs on the Field of Battle Before and During the First Crusade," *Studies in Church History* 30 (1993), 93–104. On the early tradition, see Louis J. Swift, *The Early Fathers on War and Military Service* (Wilmington, Del., 1983).

of the powerful to protect the poor and defenseless, and the new successes of
Christian armies in Spain, south Italy, and Sicily all represent a slow process
by which Christianity came to terms—but its own distinct terms—with war.
Armies in papal service, the papal benediction of military campaigns against
Muslims in Spain, new prayers for the blessing of weapons, and the literary
examples of warriors as instruments of God's will and even martyrs (as in *The
Song of Roland*) represent further stages of this process.[40]

The final step was the First Crusade itself. After its proclamation in 1095
and its success, the legal, liturgical, and theoretical links between warfare and
Christian thought quickly took shape: papal dispensation, benediction, and
the crusade vow and indulgence. As James Brundage has remarked:

By the late eleventh century, Western Christendom had arrived at a concept of war,
the Holy War, which was both novel and important. Although it was built upon the
Augustinian notion of the Just War, the Holy War went well beyond the positions
which Augustine had set forth. Not only was the Holy War considered not offensive
to God, but it was thought to be positively pleasing to Him. Participants were held
not merely to be acting in a morally acceptable fashion, but their fighting in a blessed
cause was believed to be a virtuous act which merited God's special favor, as embodied
in the commutation of penance granted by papal proclamations.[41]

Urban II and the popes who succeeded him regarded the crusade as an opportunity created by God that offered a new means of salvation to the laity
that had not existed earlier. Citing the verse from the Book of Daniel (2:21),
"[God] changes times and seasons, deposes kings and sets up kings," Urban
stated that God had indeed "changed the times" and offered a new remedy
for human sin.[42]

---

40. Gerald J. Brault, *The Song of Roland: An Analytical Edition*, 2 vols. (University Park,
Pa.-London, 1978), and Brault, *La Chanson de Roland: Student Edition* (University Park, Pa.-
London, 1984). See also the texts and references in Section X of the text below.

41. James A. Brundage, *Medieval Canon Law and the Crusader* (Madison, Wis., 1969),
29. See also Brundage, "Hierarchy of Violence in Twelfth and Thirteenth-Century Canonists,"
International History Review 17 (1995), 670–692, and Brundage's earlier collection of essays, *The
Crusades, Holy War, and Canon Law* (Aldershot-Brookfield, 1991).

42. The most extensive study is that of Ingrid Heike Ringel, "Ipse transfert regna et mutat tempora; Beobachtungen zur Herkunft von Dan. 2, 21 bei Urban II," in *Deus qui mutat
tempora: Menschen und Institutionen im Wandel des Mittelalters. Festschrift für Alfons Becker*, ed.
Ernst-Dieter Hehl, Hubertus Seibert, and Franz Staab (Sigmaringen, 1987), 137–156. See also the
observations in the important article by Ernst-Dieter Hehl, "Was ist eigentlich ein Kreuzzug?"
Historische Zeitschrift 259 (1994), 297–336, at 303, n. 24.

Pope and Warriors, Piacenza to Clermont, 1095

Pope, warriors, and the "enemies of God"—all of these, in addition to the great and continuing cause of ecclesiastical reform among laity and clergy in western Europe, as well as a growing concern for the protection of eastern Christians—came to a flashpoint in 1095. Among the most effective means for disseminating reform ideas and discipline was the use of papal legates, or representatives, in various parts of Europe, and church councils and synods, assemblies of senior churchmen from larger or more local areas, through which an increasingly legal claim to authority was expressed. Urban II, elected in 1088, had been Odo of Châtillon, former grand prior of Cluny, and since 1078 bishop of Ostia. Since Urban II was unable to remain in Rome for most of his early pontificate because of the city's occupation by the forces supporting the imperially designated antipope, Wibert of Ravenna, "Clement III," much of the early pontificate was spent in travel, and Urban could easily maintain diplomatic networks and personally preside at reform councils like those held at Melfi (1089), Benevento (1091), and Troia (1093) in the safe territory of Norman Italy.[43] By late 1093 Urban was finally able to enter Rome and occupy the Lateran. But he did not remain in Rome—he had diplomatic and mediatory work to do elsewhere. He moved through northern Italy, visiting a number of important cities and calling for a council to meet at Piacenza in March, 1095. The council's business concerned chiefly the problems of reform, the antipope, heresy, and the marital problems of Philip I of France, the latter an issue that was not resolved until 1108, well after the pontificate of Urban II. An unusual item on the conciliar agenda was the appearance of representatives sent by the Byzantine emperor Alexius I, who requested military aid against the Turks. According to the well-informed Swabian chronicler Bernold of St. Blasien, Urban inspired many soldiers to promise to enter the emperor's service and to aid him against the pagans.

From Piacenza, Urban traveled across the Alps into the kingdom of France, arriving at Valence in July and Le Puy in August, whence he called for

---

43. The standard work on Urban II is Alfons Becker, *Papst Urban II*, MGH, Schriften, 19: 1–2 (Stuttgart, 1964, 1988). The first volume treats the life and early pontificate; the second treats Urban's relations with Byzantium and the crusade. There is also a brief study by Becker in French: "Urbain II, pape de la croisade," in *Les champenois et la croisade*, ed. Yvonne Bellenger and Danielle Quéruel (Paris, 1989), 9–17. On the papal elections of 1086 and 1088, see Cowdrey, *The Age of Abbot Desiderius*, 177–217. There is also the recent short biography by Ivan Gobry, *Deux papes champenois: Urbain II, Urbain IV* (Troyes, 1994), 9–122. A nineteenth-century monumental statue of Urban II in Châtillon is reproduced in Gobry, *Deux papes*, 52. Although Urban II was widely venerated after his death, he was not beatified until 1881.

a council to meet at Clermont in the Auvergne later in the year. Among the calls to the council are indications that Urban wished that a number of prominent laymen also should appear at the council.[44] Apparently a journey to France had been on the pope's mind for several years, and Urban was the first reigning pope to visit France in nearly fifty years.[45] Besides scheduling a number of councils, Urban also exercised other papal functions—making judicial decisions, hearing cases of ecclesiastical privileges and confirming privileges, consecrating churches, and establishing or renewing personal contacts with important prelates and lay rulers. His path lay from Provence and Languedoc into Lyon and Burgundy, bringing him to his own former monastery at Cluny in late October. By November Urban had reached Clermont, and the council opened formally on Sunday, November 18, with the actual meetings beginning the following day. The twelfth-century Anglo-Norman chronicler Ordericus Vitalis has left a striking verbal portrait of Urban:

The Roman clergy met and elected Odo, bishop of Ostia and formerly a monk, as Roman pope with the name of Urban. The God of Israel appointed him as a mighty leader against the Moslems, and set him up as the tower of David with its armouries to oppose Damascus. He was French by race, of high birth and great courtesy, a citizen of Rheims and a monk of Cluny, middle-aged and tall in stature, unassuming in his modesty, of great piety, conspicuously learned and eloquent.[46]

Although Urban accomplished much else during his remarkable pontificate, Orderic and others remembered him chiefly for the Crusade.

Much of the council's business was similar to those of Urban's earlier councils, with the addition of a number of northern European affairs that Urban had postponed dealing with until he reached France. The actual work of the council, as well as its relation to the First Crusade, has been meticulously traced in the work of Alfons Becker, Robert Somerville, H. E. J. Cowdrey, and others.[47] On November 27, with the council's business com-

---

44. Robert Somerville, "The Council of Clermont (1095) and Latin Christian Society," *Archivum Historiae Pontificiae* 12 (1974), 55–90. On the councils of Gregory VII, see Somerville, "The Councils of Gregory VII," *La Riforma Gregoriana e l'Europa*, Studi Gregoriani 13 (1985), 33–53.

45. Robert Somerville, "The French Councils of Pope Urban II," *Annuarium Historiae Conciliorum* 2 (1970), 56–65. The most thorough and exact account of Urban's itinerary in France is that in Becker, *Papst Urban II*, vol. 2, 435–458. For one narrative text that gives some sense of Urban's journey, see the chronicle of the Count of Anjou in Section I of the text below.

46. *The Ecclesiastical History of Orderic Vitalis*, ed. and trans. Marjorie Chibnall (Oxford, 1973) IV, 8: 167. Orderic's account of the crusade is in book 9.

47. Becker, Cowdrey, and Somerville, as above, and Robert Somerville, *The Councils of Urban II*, vol. 1, *Decreta Claromontensia*, Annuarium Historiae Conciliorum, Supplementum, 1 (Amsterdam, 1972); Somerville, "The Council of Clermont and the First Crusade," *Mélanges Gérard Fransen*, vol. 2, *Studia Gratiana* 20 (1976), 325–337. The most recent collection of studies

pleted, Urban preached a sermon outside the city, since no building could be found that would hold the crowd of both clergy and laymen, although the actual size of Urban's audience is difficult to calculate.

The exact nature and content of the sermon has been a matter of debate since it was first remembered and recorded by chroniclers of the crusade.[48] Ecclesiastical reform, papal policy, lay devotion, and the theory of the Holy War—these formed the background to Pope Urban's remarkable speech to the assembled laymen and clergy at or just after the last session of the Council of Clermont on November 27, 1095. They formed the spirit behind the subsequent propagation of the appeal—which included a continuation of Urban's journey through France—and the recruitment of armies, the unforeseen "Crusade of the People" of Peter the Hermit and others, and the long march of the four armies of Christian knights who besieged and captured Jerusalem in July, 1099.[49] The events of those four years and the influences

---

on Clermont is that of fourth conference of the Society for the Study of the Crusades and the Latin East: *Autour de la Première Croisade*, with articles in English, French, and German. In this volume, Rudolf Hiestand argues for the existence of a further canon at the Council of Clermont, one based on recent events in Iberia and concerning the ecclesiastical territories reconquered from the Muslims: "Les canons de Clermont et d'Antioche sur l'organisation ecclésiastique des Etats croisés: Authentiques ou faux?" 29–37.

48. In addition to the works cited above, see Dana C. Munro, "The Speech of Pope Urban II at Clermont, 1095," *American Historical Review* 11 (1906), 231–242, long the classic analysis and reconstruction. More recently, see H. E. J. Cowdrey, "Pope Urban II's Preaching of the First Crusade," *History* 55 (1970), 177–188, rept. in Cowdrey, *Popes, Monks, and Crusaders*, 16: 177–188; Cowdrey, "Pope Urban II and the Idea of Crusade," *Studi Medievali* ser. III, 36 (1995), 721–742; Jean Richard, "Urbain II, la prédication de la croisade et la définition de l'indulgence," in *Deus Qui Mutat Tempora: Menschen und Institutionen im Wandel des Mittelalters. Festschrift für Alfons Becker* (Sigmaringen, 1987), 129–135. From the perspective of the tradition of preaching there is an important analysis of the sermon and its sources and different versions in Penny J. Cole, *The Preaching of Crusades to the Holy Land, 1095–1270* (Cambridge, Mass., 1991), 1–36. The most recent reassessment is that of John France, "Les origines de la Première Croisade: Un nouvel examen," *Autour de la Première Croisade*, 43–56.

49. On the composition of the armies, the journey, and the battles, see John France, *Victory in the East: A Military History of the First Crusade* (Cambridge, 1994), with extensive references; Charles R. Bowlus, "Tactical and Strategic Weaknesses of Horse Archers on the Eve of the First Crusade," *Autour de la Première Croisade*, 159–166; and Susan Edington, "The Doves of War: The Part Played by Carrier Pigeons in the Crusades," *Autour de la Première Croisade*, 167–175. See also Jonathan Riley-Smith, "Early Crusaders to the East and the Costs of Crusading, 1095–1130," in *Cross-Cultural Convergences in the Crusader Period*, 237–258, and Riley-Smith, *The First Crusaders, 1095–1131* (Cambridge, 1997); Christopher J. Tyerman, "Who Went on Crusades to the Holy Land?" in *The Horns of Hattin*, ed. B. Z. Kedar (Jerusalem-London, 1992), 13–26; John France, "Patronage and the Appeal of the First Crusade," *The First Crusade*, 5–20; R. C. Smail, *Crusading Warfare, 1097–1193*, 2nd ed. (Cambridge, 1995), and the Bibliographical Introduction by Christopher Marshall, xv–xxxiv. On the non-combatants, see W. Porges, "The Clergy, the Poor, and the Non-Combatants on the First Crusade," *Speculum* 21 (1946), 1–23, and Randall Rogers, "Peter Bartholomew and the Role of 'The Poor' in the First Crusade," *Warriors and Churchmen in the High Middle Ages: Essays Presented to Karl Leyser*, ed. Timothy Reuter (London-Rio Grande, 1992), 109–122.

On the significance of Jerusalem, see the studies by Bredero, France, and Schein, cited

that had directed them created in those who had participated a compelling impression of unity, purpose, and divine inspiration. As E. O. Blake has pointed out, the entire "Crusade Idea" was the product both of the forces that had shaped Pope Urban's appeal in the first place and of the actual experiences of those who participated in the crusade: "This pattern of events, seen progressively emerging into a coherent experience, established impressions, furnished the living proof, that this was indeed the army, in Albert of Aix's [Aachen's] recurrent phrase, of the living God."[50]

By the late twelfth century, as Blake and others have shown, the expedition that had captured Jerusalem and established a Christian kingdom in the East had assumed a distinct shape in the minds of men which not only defined the events of 1095–1099 but also constituted a model for later enterprises. The "First Crusade" was born, in effect, in the minds of men who had already lived through it. Blake remarks:

[These events] impressed upon some of their participants a group experience which was filtered back to their homelands by reports and histories and which received further shape and gloss in terms of Christian tradition at the hands of commentators. This growing view of a distinctive religious exercise was taken up in the planning of a repeat performance, deliberately based on precedent, thus sharpening the outline of the model into what was from then the First Crusade. After this it would be no longer necessary to appeal to the originally separate forms of lay devotion, "holy" war and pilgrimage in recruiting for a chosen campaign: the "crusade" had its own terms of reference—vocabulary of appeal, organization and conditioned response.[51]

Considered in these terms, the general label "First Crusade" should be used with a degree of caution. Changes in Christian attitudes to war and to Islam, the presence of a powerful, energetic, and, in its own way, devout lay aristocracy, and the wide distribution of centers of the reform movement contributed to both the preaching and the dispatch of the expedition to the Holy Land in 1095–1099. The shaping of the "Crusade Idea" out of the experience of that expedition and its role in subsequent appeals for new expeditions ought not to give the events of these years the character of an operatic set-piece in history which bears the comfortably vague label "Crusade" and

above, and Joshua Prawer, "The Jerusalem the Crusaders Captured: A Contribution to the Medieval Topography of the City," in *Crusade and Settlement*, 1–16; Norman Housley, "Jerusalem and the Development of the Crusade Idea, 1099–1128," in *The Horns of Hattin*, 26–40; Jonahan Riley-Smith, "The Motives of the Earliest Crusaders and the Settlement of Latin Palestine, 1095–1100," *English Historical Review* 98 (1983), 721–736; and Bernard Hamilton, "Ideals of Holiness: Crusaders, Contemplatives, and Mendicants," *International History Review* 17 (1995), 693–712.

50. Blake, "The Formation of the Crusade Idea," 20.
51. Ibid., 12.

the tidy numerical designation "First"—as if both terms taken together make them self-explanatory and account adequately for a sequence of numerically designated "crusades."[52] The study of the First Crusade must encompass eleventh-century reform ecclesiology, relations with East Rome, a heightened consciousness of the religious significance of the Holy Land, the appearance of new social groups and their attitudes, the institutional and literary evidence dealing with Holy War and pilgrimage, and, most important, the accounts of firsthand experiences by men who participated in the events of 1095–1099.

The First Crusade received its name and its shape late. To its participants, it was a journey or a pilgrimage, for which the Latin words *iter* and *expeditio* and *peregrinatio* sufficed; the later terms *crosata* and *croseria* to designate crusade do not appear until the late twelfth and thirteenth centuries. The men who went on this journey were *peregrini*—pilgrims—and not until much later *crucesignati*, "those signed with the Cross"—crusaders.[53] As Brundage says, the crusaders were "classed by Canon law as a specially privileged species of pilgrims," and the rite for taking the Cross developed "as an addendum to the service for blessing and bestowing the scrip and staff, the traditional insignia of pilgrims." But even such developments as these and the elaboration of crusaders' privileges did not occur until the late twelfth century, almost one hundred years after the events of the First Crusade.

The First Crusade had begun with the proclamation of the Peace and Truce of God, a universal peace for the first time proclaimed throughout Christendom, because, as one propaganda source said, "without peace no one is able to serve God."[54] Such a peace within Christendom, however, only signaled the possibility of a new kind of war with God's enemies. For a moment at the end of the eleventh century it may well have appeared that the first concerted effort of a single society, uniform in its Christianity, had indeed fulfilled Pope Urban's hope that the perils raised up by God's enemies had effectively been removed. God's peace and God's war had revealed once again

52. The broadest definition is that of Jonathan Riley-Smith: "A crusade was a holy war fought against those perceived to be the external or internal foes of Christendom for the recovery of Christian property or in defense of the Church or Christian people" (*The Crusades: A Short History*, xxviii). See also Hehl, "Was ist eigentlich ein Kreuzzug?" passim.

53. See James A. Brundage, "*Cruce Signari*: The Rite for Taking the Cross in England," *Traditio* 22 (1966), 289–310; Kenneth Pennington, "The Rite for Taking the Cross in the Twelfth Century," *Traditio* 30 (1974), 429–431; Michael Markowski, "*Crucesignatus*: Its Origins and Early Usage," *Journal of Medieval History* 10 (1984), 157–165. The development of a distinctive legal status for crusaders is described in James A. Brundage, *Medieval Canon Law and the Crusader*.

54. On the Peace, see now Thomas Head and Richard Landes, eds., *The Peace of God: Social Violence and Religious Response in France around the Year 1000* (Ithaca, N.Y.-London, 1992). In *Knightly Piety* Marcus Bull has expressed considerable skepticism about the role of the Peace movement in influencing the First Crusade.

the continuing divine concern with Christendom and the rewards in store for
those who understood that concern and acted on it. The complex series of
events and ideas which led up to the First Crusade and the interpretations that
men later placed on the crusade itself inform the student of history, as do few
other events, of the character of social and intellectual change and of the kind
of response men are able to make to such change. One of the major themes
in all versions of Pope Urban's speech at Clermont in 1095 was the turbulence of Christian society, a turbulence of which many men were acutely and
painfully aware. By invoking the only universal sanction that such a society
was willing or able to recognize, Pope Urban marshaled new forces of order
and momentarily strengthened the tenuous bonds of Christian society. His
speech at Clermont offered to a divisive and particularistic society a common
goal, and that society, or at least those of its members present at Clermont on
November 27, 1095, responded in kind. When Urban had finished his appeal,
so some of the sources tell us, all those present shouted as with a single voice.
"Deus vult," "Deus lo volt," they cried—"God wills it."

But not everyone thought that God willed it. A number of monastic
and clerical critics expressed considerable doubt as to the value of traveling to
Jerusalem, whether armed or not, and from their views there developed a consistent subtheme of criticism of the crusade movement that also ran through
the entire crusading period.[55] As later crusades proved less and less effective,
the theme of criticism became more pronounced, but throughout the next
few centuries it never overcame the memory of the events of 1095–1099.

Sources for the History of the First Crusade

In "A Note on Sources in Translation" in his *The Crusades: A Short History*,
Jonathan Riley-Smith expresses concern about readers reading a single narrative source without the essential comparative material that is the essence of

55. See Giles Constable, "Opposition to Pilgrimage in the Middle Ages," rpt. in Constable,
Religious Life and Thought (11th–12th Centuries) (London, 1979), 4: 125–146; James A. Brundage,
"Prostitution, Miscegenation and Sexual Purity in the First Crusade," in Edbury, ed., *Crusade
and Settlement*, 57–65, and Brundage, "St. Anselm, Ivo of Chartres, and the Ideology of the First
Crusade," in *Les mutations socio-cultureles au tournant des XIe–XIIe siècles, Études anselmiennes (IVe
session)*, Colloques Internationaux du Centre National de la Recherche Scientifique (Paris, 1984),
175–187; Jean Flori, "Pur eschalcier sainte chrestiénte: Croisade, guerre sainte et guerre juste dans
les chansons de geste françaises," *Le Moyen Age* 5 (1991), 171–187; and Elizabeth Siberry, *Criticism of Crusading, 1095–1274* (Oxford, 1985). The most detailed expression of scholarly skepticism
concerning the influence of the First Crusade on twelfth-century crusades is that of Christopher Tyerman, "Were There Any Crusades in the Twelfth Century?" *English Historical Review*
110 (1995), 553–577. See also Jonathan Riley-Smith, "Peace Never Established: The Case of the
Kingdom of Jerusalem," *Transactions of the Royal Historical Society* 5th ser. 28 (1978), 87–102.

historical research.[56] This book attempts to offer both: a single eyewitness narrative account, that of Fulcher of Chartres, in Section II, and a variety of sources for comparative purposes at key moments in the history of the First Crusade in Sections I and III–IX. The book begins with a section dealing with Urban II at the Council of Clermont and offering four versions of the Crusade sermon (the fifth is that of Fulcher of Chartres, given in Section II), the Crusade indulgence and Truce of God proclaimed at the Council, four letters of Urban II sent to various destinations and dealing with matters related to the Crusade, and an extract from the chronicle of the counts of Anjou describing the impression made by Urban during his journey through France after November, 1095.

The second section contains a single eyewitness narrative dealing with the events of 1095–1100, Book I of the chronicle of Fulcher of Chartres.

The following six sections (III through VIII) offer different versions of six key moments in the history of the First Crusade; the "Crusade of the People" (III), the journey from western Europe to Constantinople (IV), the brief stay of the main crusading armies at Constantinople and their dealings with Alexius I (V), the siege and capture of Nicaea (VI), the crucial siege and capture of Antioch and the discovery of the Holy Lance (VII), and the final siege and capture of Jerusalem (VIII).

The ninth section contains eight letters written during or shortly after the events of the First Crusade. Letters of the crusaders shed important light on attitudes, motives, and experiences.

The final section (X) offers a variety of sources that reflect the attitudes of both the crusaders and those in Europe who heard about the "liberation" of the Holy Land and the place that the Crusade came to acquire in their ideas of human history and its relation to God.

The book also includes a Bibliographical Essay.

The selections in this book from sources contemporary with and just following the First Crusade have been made with the intention of offering the reader both the unity of a single major work (in this case Book I of the *Historia Hierosolymitana* of Fulcher of Chartres, translated with notes by Martha E. McGinty) and the diversity of other views of some of the key events which Fulcher describes. Translated selections from the chronicles of Robert the Monk, Baldric of Dol, Guibert of Nogent, William of Tyre, Albert of Aix, Ekkehard of Aura, Anna Comnena, Raymond d'Aguilers, Peter Tudebode, and the anonymous author of the *Gesta francorum* have been chosen

56. Jonathan Riley-Smith, *The Crusades*, 271. There is an excellent discussion of the sources in John France, *Victory in the East*, 374–382, and in Susan Edington, "The First Crusade: Reviewing the Evidence," *The First Crusade*, 55–77.

from the following works: Dana C. Munro, *Urban and the Crusaders* (University of Pennsylvania, Translations and Reprints from the Original Sources of European History, vol. I, no. 2, Philadelphia, 1895); A. C. Krey, *The First Crusade: The Accounts of Eye-Witnesses and Participants* (copyright 1921 Princeton University Press); D. C. Munro, *Letters of the Crusaders* (University of Pennsylvania, Translations and Reprints from the Original Sources of European History, vol. I, no. 4, Philadelphia, 1896), as well as works cited in the Abbreviations above. Each author is introduced at the appearance of the first selection from his work. All translations not attributed to others are the work of the editor. From the different versions of Pope Urban II's speech at Clermont with which the book opens to the selections of chronicles and Crusaders' letters and the concluding documents, the book's purpose is to present clearly the broad variety of Crusaders' opinions and experiences as well as what was made of them by those who revised and rewrote them.

Because these sources have been translated at different times and in both England and the United States, there are variations of proper names and spellings throughout the book. These differences have been corrected where it has been possible and feasible, but many variations remain. In no case should these prove inconvenient to the reader.

I.

Pope Urban II at the Council of Clermont, November 27, 1095

There are five major versions of Urban's speech, or sermon, proclaiming the crusade. Four are reprinted in this section, and the version of Fulcher of Chartres appears in Book I of Fulcher's chronicle (below, Section II). Pope Urban II (1088–1099) was one of the most dynamic and probably the ablest of the reforming popes of the later eleventh and early twelfth centuries. His extensive administrative, judicial, diplomatic, and fiscal reforms substantially established the authority and effectiveness of the papacy after the diplomatic crises that followed the pontificate of Gregory VII (1073–1085). His own great skills as a diplomat restored papal relations with a number of individuals, clerical and lay, whom Gregory had alienated. The Council of Clermont was the first of three in France called to continue the work of ecclesiastical reform, and only at or after the final session were laymen and others given the great appeal for the defense of Christendom against both internal dissension and violence and the perceived menace posed by the Muslims in the Near East. On Urban and Clermont, see the works of Somervile, Becker, and Cowdrey cited in the notes to the introduction.

1. The Speech of Urban: The *Gesta* Version

The Gesta *(Gesta francorum et aliorum Hierosolymytanorum, "The Deeds of the Franks and Other Jerusalemers") was written by an anonymous crusader who followed Bohemund of Antioch and later continued on to Jerusalem with other crusader contingents when Bohemund remained at Antioch. He was not present at Clermont and must have reconstructed the sermon from the accounts of others that he heard. His work was probably written by 1100–1101, no later than 1103, and it was known in northern France by 1105 at the latest, since it was a major source for a number of other accounts of the First Crusade. Robert of Rheims, Guibert of*

*Nogent, Baldric of Dol, and Ekkehard of Aura all derive much of their material
from the* Gesta. *The work is edited, with a fine English translation, by Rosalind M.
Hill,* Gesta francorum et aliorum Hierosolymytanorum: The Deeds of the
Franks *(London, 1962). The English translation here is from Krey, 28–30. See also
Colin Morris, "The* Gesta francorum *as Narrative History," Reading Medieval
Studies 19 (1993), 55–71.*

When now that time was at hand which the Lord Jesus daily points out
to His faithful, especially in the Gospel, saying, "If any man would come after
me, let him deny himself and take up his cross and follow me," a mighty agi-
tation was carried on throughout all the region of Gaul. [Its tenor was] that
if anyone desired to follow the Lord zealously, with a pure heart and mind,
and wished faithfully to bear the cross after Him, he would no longer hesitate
to take up the way to the Holy Sepulcher.

And so Urban, Pope of the Roman see, with his archbishops, bishops,
abbots, and priests, set out as quickly as possible beyond the mountains and
began to deliver sermons and to preach eloquently, saying: "Whoever wishes
to save his soul should not hesitate humbly to take up the way of the Lord,
and if he lacks sufficient money, divine mercy will give him enough." Then the
apostolic lord continued, "Brethren, we ought to endure much suffering for
the name of Christ—misery, poverty, nakedness, persecution, want, illness,
hunger, thirst, and other [ills] of this kind, just as the Lord saith to His disciples: 'Ye must suffer much in My name,' and 'Be not ashamed to confess Me
before the faces of men; verily I will give you mouth and wisdom,' and finally,
'Great is your reward in Heaven.'" And when this speech had already begun
to be noised abroad, little by little, through all the regions and countries of
Gaul, the Franks, upon hearing such reports, forthwith caused crosses to be
sewed on their right shoulders, saying that they followed with one accord the
footsteps of Christ, by which they had been redeemed from the hand of hell.

2. The Speech of Urban: The Version of Robert of Rheims

Robert, the monk of Rheims, wrote his chronicle around 1107, using the Gesta *and
other sources. He may also have been present at Clermont. The* Historia Hierosolymitana, *"The Jerusalem History," is in* RHC, *Occ. III. The translation here
is from Munro,* Urban, *5–8.*

Oh, race of Franks, race from across the mountains, race chosen and beloved by God—as shines forth in very many of your works—set apart from

all nations by the situation of your country, as well as by your catholic faith and the honor of the holy church! To you our discourse is addressed and for you our exhortation is intended. We wish you to know what a grievous cause has led us to your country, what peril threatening you and all the faithful has brought us.

From the confines of Jerusalem and the city of Constantinople a horrible tale has gone forth and very frequently has been brought to our ears, namely, that a race from the kingdom of the Persians, an accursed race, a race utterly alienated from God, a generation forsooth which has not directed its heart and has not entrusted its spirit to God, has invaded the lands of those Christians and has depopulated them by the sword, pillage and fire; it has led away a part of the captives into its own country, and a part it has destroyed by cruel tortures; it has either entirely destroyed the churches of God or appropriated them for the rites of its own religion. They destroy the altars, after having defiled them with their uncleanness. They circumcise the Christians, and the blood of the circumcision they either spread upon the altars or pour into the vases of the baptismal font. When they wish to torture people by a base death, they perforate their navels, and dragging forth the extremity of the intestines, bind it to a stake; then with flogging they lead the victim around until the viscera having gushed forth the victim falls prostrate upon the ground. Others they bind to a post and pierce with arrows. Others they compel to extend their necks and then, attacking them with naked swords attempt to cut through the neck with a single blow. What shall I say of the abominable rape of the women? To speak of it is worse than to be silent. The kingdom of the Greeks is now dismembered by them and deprived of territory so vast in extent that it cannot be traversed in a march of two months. On whom therefore is the labor of avenging these wrongs and of recovering this territory incumbent, if not upon you? You, upon whom above other nations God has conferred remarkable glory in arms, great courage, bodily activity, and strength to humble the hairy scalp of those who resist you.

Let the deeds of your ancestors move you and incite your minds to manly achievements; the glory and greatness of king Charles the Great, and of his son Louis, and of your other kings, who have destroyed the kingdoms of the pagans, and have extended in these lands the territory of the holy church. Let the holy sepulchre of the Lord our Saviour, which is possessed by unclean nations, especially incite you, and the holy places which are now treated with ignominy and irreverently polluted with their filthiness. Oh, most valiant soldiers and descendants of invincible ancestors, be not degenerate, but recall the valor of your progenitors.

But if you are hindered by love of children, parents and wives, remember what the Lord says in the Gospel, "He that loveth father or mother more than me, is not worthy of me." "Every one that hath forsaken houses, or brethren, or sisters, or father, or mother, or wife, or children, or lands for my name's sake shall receive an hundred-fold and shall inherit everlasting life." Let none of your possessions detain you, no solicitude for your family affairs, since this land which you inhabit, shut in on all sides by the seas and surrounded by the mountain peaks, is too narrow for your large population; nor does it abound in wealth; and it furnishes scarcely food enough for its cultivators. Hence it is that you murder one another, that you wage war, and that frequently you perish by mutual wounds. Let therefore hatred depart from among you, let your quarrels end, let wars cease, and let all dissensions and controversies slumber. Enter upon the road to the Holy Sepulchre; wrest that land from the wicked race, and subject it to yourselves. That land which as the Scripture says "floweth with milk and honey," was given by God into the possession of the children of Israel.

Jerusalem is the navel of the world; the land is fruitful above others, like another paradise of delights. This the Redeemer of the human race has made illustrious by His advent, has beautified by residence, has consecrated by suffering, has redeemed by death, has glorified by burial. This royal city, therefore, situated at the centre of the world, is now held captive by His enemies, and is in subjection to those who do not know God, to the worship of the heathens. She seeks therefore and desires to be liberated, and does not cease to implore you to come to her aid. From you especially she asks succor, because, as we have already said, God has conferred upon you above all nations great glory in arms. Accordingly undertake this journey for the remission of your sins, with the assurance of the imperishable glory of the kingdom of heaven.

When Pope Urban had said these and very many similar things in his urbane discourse, he so influenced to one purpose the desires of all who were present, that they cried out, "It is the will of God! It is the will of God!" When the venerable Roman pontiff heard that, with eyes uplifted to heaven he gave thanks to God and, with his hand commanding silence, said:

Most beloved brethren, to-day is manifest in you what the Lord says in the Gospel, "Where two or three are gathered together in my name there am I in the midst of them." Unless the Lord God had been present in your spirits, all of you would not have uttered the same cry. For, although the cry issued from numerous mouths, yet the origin of the cry was one. Therefore I say to you that God, who implanted this in your breasts, has drawn it forth from you. Let this then be your war-cry in combats, because this word is given to you by God. When an armed attack is made upon the enemy, let this one cry be raised by all the soldiers of God: It is the will of God! It is the will of God!

And we do not command or advise that the old or feeble, or those unfit for bearing arms, undertake this journey; nor ought women to set out at all, without their husbands or brothers or legal guardians. For such are more of a hindrance than aid, more of a burden than advantage. Let the rich aid the needy; and according to their wealth, let them take with them experienced soldiers. The priests and clerks of any order are not to go without the consent of their bishop; for this journey would profit them nothing if they went without permission of these. Also, it is not fitting that laymen should enter upon the pilgrimage without the blessing of their priests.

Whoever, therefore, shall determine upon this holy pilgrimage and shall make his vow to God to that effect and shall offer himself to Him as a living sacrifice, holy, acceptable unto God, shall wear the sign of the cross of the Lord on his forehead or on his breast. When, truly, having fulfilled his vow he wishes to return, let him place the cross on his back between his shoulders. Such, indeed, by the two-fold action will fulfill the precept of the Lord, as He commands in the Gospel, "He that taketh not his cross and followeth after me, is not worthy of me."

3. The Speech of Urban: The Version of Baldric of Dol

Archbishop of Dol and formerly Abbot of Bourgueil in the early twelfth century, Baldric depended heavily on the Gesta. *His version indicates the theological rewriting and rethinking of the original sermon from a post-conquest perspective around 1108. Latin text in* RHC, *Occ. IV. The English version here is from Krey, 33–36.*

. . . "We have heard, most beloved brethren, and you have heard what we cannot recount without deep sorrow—how, with great hurt and dire sufferings our Christian brothers, members in Christ, are scourged, oppressed, and injured in Jerusalem, in Antioch, and the other cities of the East. Your own blood-brothers, your companions, your associates (for you are sons of the same Christ and the same Church) are either subjected in their inherited homes to other masters, or are driven from them, or they come as beggars among us; or, which is far worse, they are flogged and exiled as slaves for sale in their own land. Christian blood, redeemed by the blood of Christ, has been shed, and Christian flesh, akin to the flesh of Christ, has been subjected to unspeakable degradation and servitude. Everywhere in those cities there is sorrow, everywhere misery, everywhere groaning (I say it with a sigh).

The churches in which divine mysteries were celebrated in olden times are now, to our sorrow, used as stables for the animals of these people! Holy men do not possess those cities; nay, base and bastard Turks hold sway over our brothers. The blessed Peter first presided as Bishop at Antioch; behold, in his own church the Gentiles have established their superstitions, and the Christian religion, which they ought rather to cherish, they have basely shut out from the hall dedicated to God! The estates given for the support of the saints and the patrimony of nobles set aside for the sustenance of the poor are subject to pagan tyranny, while cruel masters abuse for their own purposes the returns from these lands. The priesthood of God has been ground down into the dust. The sanctuary of God (unspeakable shame!) is everywhere profaned. Whatever Christians still remain in hiding there are sought out with unheard of tortures.

"Of holy Jerusalem, brethren, we dare not speak, for we are exceedingly afraid and ashamed to speak of it. This very city, in which, as you all know, Christ Himself suffered for us, because our sins demanded it, has been reduced to the pollution of paganism and, I say it to our disgrace, withdrawn from the service of God. Such is the heap of reproach upon us who have so much deserved it! Who now serves the church of the Blessed Mary in the valley of Josaphat, in which church she herself was buried in body? But why do we pass over the Temple of Solomon, nay of the Lord, in which the barbarous nations placed their idols contrary to law, human and divine? Of the Lord's Sepulchre we have refrained from speaking, since some of you with your own eyes have seen to what abominations it has been given over. The Turks violently took from it the offerings which you brought there for alms in such vast amounts, and, in addition, they scoffed much and often at your religion. And yet in that place (I say only what you already know) rested the Lord; there He died for us; there He was buried. How precious would be the longed-for, incomparable place of the Lord's burial, even if God failed there to perform the yearly miracle! For in the days of His Passion all the lights in the Sepulchre and round about in the church, which have been extinguished, are relighted by divine command. Whose heart is so stony, brethren, that it is not touched by so great a miracle? Believe me, that man is bestial and senseless whose heart such divinely manifest grace does not move to faith! And yet the Gentiles see this in common with the Christians and are not turned from their ways! They are, indeed, afraid, but they are not converted to the faith; nor is it to be wondered at, for a blindness of mind rules over them. With what afflictions they wronged you who have returned and are now present, you yourselves know too well, you who there sacrificed your substance and your blood for God.

"This, beloved brethren, we shall say, that we may have you as witness of our words. More suffering of our brethren and devastation of churches remains than we can speak of one by one, for we are oppressed by tears and groans, sighs and sobs. We weep and wail, brethren, alas, like the Psalmist, in our inmost heart! We are wretched and unhappy, and in us is that prophecy fulfilled: 'God, the nations are come into thine inheritance; thy holy temple have they defiled; they have laid Jerusalem in heaps; the dead bodies of thy servants have been given to be food for the birds of the heaven, the flesh of thy saints unto the beasts of the earth. Their blood have they shed like water round about Jerusalem, and there was none to bury them.' Woe unto us, brethren! We who have already become a reproach to our neighbors, a scoffing, and derision to them round about us, let us at least with tears condone and have compassion upon our brothers! We who are become the scorn of all peoples, and worse than all, let us bewail the most monstrous devastation of the Holy Land! This land we have deservedly called holy in which there is not even a foot-step that the body or spirit of the Saviour did not render glorious and blessed; which embraced the holy presence of the mother of God, and the meetings of the apostles, and drank up the blood of the martyrs shed there. How blessed are the stones which crowned you, Stephen, the first martyr! How happy, O, John the Baptist, the waters of the Jordan which served you in baptizing the Saviour! The children of Israel, who were led out of Egypt, and who prefigured you in the crossing of the Red Sea, have taken that land by their arms, with Jesus as leader; they have driven out the Jebusites and other inhabitants and have themselves inhabited earthly Jerusalem, the image of celestial Jerusalem.

"What are we saying? Listen and learn! You, girt about with the badge of knighthood, are arrogant with great pride; you rage against your brothers and cut each other in pieces. This is not the [true] soldiery of Christ which rends asunder the sheep-fold of the Redeemer. The Holy Church has reserved a soldiery for herself to help her people, but you debase her wickedly to her hurt. Let us confess the truth, whose heralds we ought to be; truly, you are not holding to the way which leads to life. You, the oppressers of children, plunderers of widows; you, guilty of homicide, of sacrilege, robbers of another's rights; you who await the pay of thieves for the shedding of Christian blood—as vultures smell fetid corpses, so do you sense battles from afar and rush to them eagerly. Verily, this is the worst way, for it is utterly removed from God! If, forsooth, you wish to be mindful of your souls, either lay down the girdle of such knighthood, or advance boldly, as knights of Christ, and rush as quickly as you can to the defence of the Eastern Church.

For she it is from whom the joys of your whole salvation have come forth, who poured into your mouths the milk of divine wisdom, who set before you the holy teachings of the Gospels. We say this, brethren, that you may restrain your murderous hands from the destruction of your brothers, and in behalf of your relatives in the faith oppose yourselves to the Gentiles. Under Jesus Christ, our Leader, may you struggle for your Jerusalem, in Christian battle-line, most invincible line, even more successfully than did the sons of Jacob of old—struggle, that you may assail and drive out the Turks, more execrable than the Jebusites, who are in this land, and may you deem it a beautiful thing to die for Christ in that city in which He died for us. But if it befall you to die this side of it, be sure that to have died on the way is of equal value, if Christ shall find you in His army. God pays with the same shilling, whether at the first or eleventh hour. You should shudder, brethren, you should shudder at raising a violent hand against Christians; it is less wicked to brandish your sword against Saracens. It is the only warfare that is righteous, for it is charity to risk your life for your brothers. That you may not be troubled about the concerns of to-morrow, know that those who fear God want nothing, nor those who cherish Him in truth. The possessions of the enemy, too, will be yours, since you will make spoil of their treasures and return victorious to your own; or empurpled with your own blood, you will have gained everlasting glory. For such a Commander you ought to fight, for One who lacks neither might nor wealth with which to reward you. Short is the way, little the labor, which, nevertheless, will repay you with the crown that fadeth not away. Accordingly, we speak with the authority of the prophet: 'Gird thy sword upon thy thigh, O mighty one.' Gird yourselves, everyone of you, I say, and be valiant sons; for it is better for you to die in battle than to behold the sorrows of your race and of your holy places. Let neither property nor the alluring charms of your wives entice you from going; nor let the trials that are to be borne so deter you that you remain here."

And turning to the bishops, he said, "You, brothers and fellow bishops; you, fellow priests and sharers with us in Christ, make this same announcement through the churches committed to you, and with your whole soul vigorously preach the journey to Jerusalem. When they have confessed the disgrace of their sins, do you, secure in Christ, grant them speedy pardon. Moreover, you who are to go shall have us praying for you; we shall have you fighting for God's people. It is our duty to pray, yours to fight against the Amalekites. With Moses, we shall extend unwearied hands in prayer to Heaven, while you go forth and brandish the sword, like dauntless warriors, against Amalek."

As those present were thus clearly informed by these and other words of this kind from the apostolic lord, the eyes of some were bathed in tears; some trembled, and yet others discussed the matter. However, in the presence of all at that same council, and as we looked on, the Bishop of Puy, a man of great renown and of highest ability, went to the Pope with joyful countenance and on bended knee sought and entreated blessing and permission to go. Over and above this, he won from the Pope the command that all should obey him, and that he should hold sway over all the army in behalf of the Pope, since all knew him to be a prelate of unusual energy and industry. . . .

4. The Speech of Urban: The Version of Guibert of Nogent

Abbot of Nogent in the early twelfth century and an extensive commentator on the events and conditions of his own life and times, Guibert was not present at Clermont, but became very well informed about it and the events that followed. He reworked the Gesta and found other material. His history, the Historia quae dicitur Gesta Dei per Francos, *"The History That Is Called Deeds of God Done Through the Franks," is in* RHC, Occ. *IV. Guibert wrote between 1104 and 1108, making final revisions in 1111. Guibert is also an important figure in early twelfth-century intellectual and literary history generally. See John F. Benton,* Self and Society in Medieval France: The Memoirs of Abbot Guibert of Nogent (1064?–1125) *(New York, 1970); Benton, "Consciousness of Self and Perceptions of Individuality,"* in Renaissance and Renewal in the Twelfth Century, *ed. Robert L. Benson and Giles Constable, with Carol Lanham (Cambridge, Mass., 1982), 263–295; and R. I. Moore, "Guibert of Nogent and His World,"* in Studies in Medieval History Presented to R. H. C. Davis, *ed. Henry Mayr-Harting and R. I. Moore (London-Ronceverte, 1985), 107–118. The English translation here is from Krey, 36–40.*

"If among the churches scattered about over the whole world some, because of persons or location, deserve reverence above others (for persons, I say, since greater privileges are accorded to apostolic sees; for places, indeed, since the same dignity which is accorded to persons is also shown to regal cities, such as Constantinople), we owe most to that church from which we received the grace of redemption and the source of all Christianity. If what the Lord says—namely, 'Salvation is from the Jews—,' accords with the truth, and it is true that the Lord has left us Sabaoth as seed, that we may not become like Sodom and Gomorrah, and our seed is Christ, in whom is the salvation and benediction of all peoples, then, indeed, the very land and city in which

He dwelt and suffered is, by witnesses of the Scriptures, holy. If this land is spoken of in the sacred writings of the prophets as the inheritance and the holy temple of God before ever the Lord walked about in it, or was revealed, what sanctity, what reverence has it not acquired since God in His majesty was there clothed in the flesh, nourished, grew up, and in bodily form there walked about, or was carried about; and, to compress in fitting brevity all that might be told in a long series of words, since there the blood of the Son of God, more holy than heaven and earth, was poured forth, and His body, its quivering members dead, rested in the tomb. What veneration do we think it deserves? If, when the Lord had but just been crucified and the city was still held by the Jews, it was called holy by the evangelist when he says, 'Many bodies of the saints that had fallen asleep were raised; and coming forth out of the tombs after His resurrection, they entered into the holy city and appeared unto many,' and by the prophet Isaiah when he says, 'It shall be His glorious sepulchre,' then, surely, with this sanctity placed upon it by God the Sanctifier Himself, no evil that may befall it can destroy it, and in the same way glory is indivisibly fixed to His Sepulchre. Most beloved brethren, if you reverence the source of that holiness and glory, if you cherish these shrines which are the marks of His foot-prints on earth, if you seek [the way], God leading you, God fighting in your behalf, you should strive with your utmost efforts to cleanse the Holy City and the glory of the Sepulchre, now polluted by the concourse of the Gentiles, as much as is in their power.

"If in olden times the Maccabees attained to the highest praise of piety because they fought for the ceremonies and the Temple, it is also justly granted you, Christian soldiers, to defend the liberty of your country by armed endeavor. If you, likewise, consider that the abode of the holy apostles and any other saints should be striven for with such effort, why do you refuse to rescue the Cross, the Blood, the Tomb? Why do you refuse to visit them, to spend the price of your lives in rescuing them? You have thus far waged unjust wars, at one time and another; you have brandished mad weapons to your mutual destruction, for no other reason than covetousness and pride, as a result of which you have deserved eternal death and sure damnation. We now hold out to you wars which contain the glorious reward of martyrdom, which will retain that title of praise now and forever.

"Let us suppose, for the moment, that Christ was not dead and buried, and had never lived any length of time in Jerusalem. Surely, if all this were lacking, this fact alone ought still to arouse you to go to the aid of the land and city—the fact that 'Out of Zion shall go forth the law and the word of Jehovah from Jerusalem!' If all that there is of Christian preaching has flowed from the fountain of Jerusalem, its streams, whithersoever spread out over the whole world, encircle the hearts of the Catholic multitude, that they may consider wisely what they owe such a well-watered fountain. If rivers return to the place whence they have issued only to flow forth again, according to the saying of Solomon, it ought to seem glorious to you to be able to apply a new cleansing to this place, whence it is certain that you received the cleansing of baptism and the witness of your faith.

"And you ought, furthermore, to consider with the utmost deliberation, if by your labors, God working through you, it should occur that the Mother of churches should flourish anew to the worship of Christianity, whether, perchance, He may not wish other regions of the East to be restored to the faith against the approaching time of the Antichrist. For it is clear that Antichrist is to do battle not with the Jews, not with the Gentiles; but, according to the etymology of his name, He will attack Christians. And if Antichrist finds there no Christians (just as at present when scarcely any dwell there), no one will be there to oppose him, or whom he may rightly overcome. According to Daniel and Jerome, the interpreter of Daniel, he is to fix his tents on the Mount of Olives; and it is certain, for the apostle teaches it, that he will sit at Jerusalem in the Temple of the Lord, as though he were God. And according to the same prophet, he will first kill three kings of Egypt, Africa, and Ethiopia, without doubt for their Christian faith. This, indeed, could not at all be done unless Christianity was established where now is paganism. If, therefore, you are zealous in the practice of holy battles, in order that, just as you have received the seed of knowledge of God from Jerusalem, you may in the same way restore the borrowed grace, so that through you the Catholic name may be advanced to oppose the perfidy of the Antichrist and the Antichristians—then, who can not conjecture that God, who has exceeded the hope of all, will consume, in the abundance of your courage and through you as the spark, such a thicket of paganism as to include within His law Egypt, Africa, and Ethiopia, which have withdrawn from the communion of our belief? And the man of sin, the son of perdition, will find some to oppose him. Behold, the Gospel cries out, 'Jerusalem shall be trodden down by the Gentiles until the times of the Gentiles be fulfilled.' 'Times of the Gentiles" can be understood in two ways: Either that they have ruled over the Christians at their pleasure, and have gladly frequented the sloughs of all baseness for the satisfaction of their lusts, and in all this have had no obstacle (for they who have everything according to their wish are said to have their time; there is that saying: 'My time is not yet come, but your time is always ready,' whence the lustful are wont to say 'you are having your time'). Or, again, 'the times of the Gentiles' are the fulness of time for those Gentiles who shall have entered secretly before Israel shall be saved. These times, most beloved brothers, will now, forsooth, be fulfilled, provided the might of the pagans be repulsed through you, with the co-operation of God. With the end of the world already near, even though the Gentiles fail to be converted to the Lord (since according to the apostle there must be a withdrawal from the faith), it is first necessary, according to the prophecy, that the Christian sway be renewed in those regions, either through you, or others, whom it shall please God to send before the coming of Antichrist, so that the head of all evil, who is to occupy there the throne of the kingdom, shall find some support of the faith to fight against him.

"Consider, therefore, that the Almighty has provided you, perhaps, for this purpose, that through you He may restore Jerusalem from such debasement. Ponder, I beg you, how full of joy and delight our hearts will be when we shall see the Holy City restored with your little help, and the prophet's, nay divine, words fulfilled in our times. Let your memory be moved by what the Lord Himself says to the Church: 'I will bring thy seed from the East and gather thee from the West.' God has already brought our seed from the East, since in a double way that region of the East has given the first beginnings of the Church to us. But from the West He will also gather it, provided He repairs the wrongs of Jerusalem through those who have begun the witness of the final faith, that is the people of the West. With God's assistance, we think this can be done through you.

"If neither the words of the Scriptures arouse you, nor our admonitions penetrate your minds, at least let the great suffering of those who desired to go to the holy places stir you up. Think of those who made the pilgrimage across the sea! Even if they were more wealthy, consider what taxes, what violence they underwent, since they were forced to make payments and tributes almost every mile, to purchase release at every gate of the city, at the entrance of the churches and temples, at every side-journey from place to place: also, if any accusation whatsoever were made against them, they were compelled to purchase their release; but if they refused to pay money, the prefects of the Gentiles, according to their custom, urged them fiercely with blows. What shall we say of those who took up the journey without anything more than trust in their barren poverty, since they seemed to have nothing except their bodies to lose? They not only demanded money of them, which is not an unendurable punishment, but also examined the callouses of their heels, cutting them open and folding the skin back, lest, perchance, they had sewed something there. Their unspeakable cruelty was carried on even to the point of giving them scammony to drink until they vomited, or even burst their bowels, because they thought the wretches had swallowed gold or silver; or, horrible to say, they cut their bowels open with a sword and, spreading out the folds of the intestines, with frightful mutilation disclosed whatever nature held there in secret. Remember, I pray, the thousands who have perished vile deaths, and strive for the holy places from which the beginnings of your faith have come. Before you engage in His battles, believe without question that Christ will be your standard-bearer and inseparable fore-runner."

The most excellent man concluded his oration and by the power of the blessed Peter absolved all who vowed to go and confirmed those acts with apostolic blessing. He instituted a sign well suited to so honorable a profession by making the figure of the Cross, the stigma of the Lord's Passion, the emblem of the soldiery, or rather, of what was to be the soldiery of God. This, made of any kind of cloth, he ordered to be sewed upon the shirts, cloaks, and *byrra* of those who were about to go. He commanded that if anyone, after receiving this emblem, or after taking openly this vow, should shrink from his good intent through base change of heart, or any affection for his parents, he should be regarded an outlaw forever, unless he repented and again undertook whatever of his pledge he had omitted. Furthermore, the Pope condemned with a fearful anathema all those who dared to molest the wives, children, and possessions of these who were going on this journey for God. . . .

5. The Privilege of Urban to the Pilgrims

There is no single tradition of the canons of the Council of Clermont. The edition by Robert Somerville, The Councils of Urban II I, Decreta Claromontensia, Annuarium Historiae Conciliorum: Supplementum I *(Amsterdam, 1972), is a model of the method of reconstruction from a wide variety of partial sources. The text here is found in the northern French group of manuscripts containing Clermont material, particularly in the collection associated with Lambert, Bishop of Arras, one of Urban's closest associates in northern Europe. Latin text in Somerville,* Councils, *74.*

Whoever goes on the journey to free the church of God in Jerusalem out of devotion alone, and not for the gaining of glory or money, can substitute the journey for all penance for sin.

6. The Truce of God Proclaimed in the Diocese of Cologne

The great initial age of the movement known as the Peace and Truce of God stretched from the late tenth to the mid-eleventh century. It is best studied in the collection of essays edited by Thomas Head and Richard Landes, The Peace of God: Social Violence and Religious Response in France around the Year 1000 *(Ithaca, N.Y.-London, 1992). See also H. E. J. Cowdrey, "The Peace and Truce of God in the Eleventh Century," rpt. in Cowdrey,* Popes, Monks and Crusaders *(London, 1984), 7: 42–67; Aryeh Grabois, "De la trêve de Dieu à la paix du roi: Etude sur les transformations du mouvement de la paix à XII siècle," rpt. in Grabois,* Civilisation et société dans l'Occident médiéval *(London, 1983), 1: 585–596; and especially H. Hoffmann,* Gottesfriede und Treuga Dei, Monumenta Germaniae Historia, Schriften, Bd. 20 *(Stuttgart, 1964). The elaborate Truce proclaimed for Cologne in 1083 is a good example of the later form. In 1085 the emperor Henry IV modeled his own Truce on this one. English translations of the emperor's Truce may be found in J. F. Henderson,* Select Historical Documents *(London, 1892), 208–211, and in Jeremy Y. duQ. Adams,* Patterns of Medieval Society *(Englewood Cliffs, N.J., 1969), 17–21. This document has been preserved only in the form in which the bishop of Cologne communicated it to the bishop of Münster.*

Inasmuch as in our own times the church, through its members, has been extraordinarily afflicted by tribulations and difficulties, so that tranquility and peace were wholly despaired of, we have endeavored by God's help to aid it, suffering so many burdens and perils. And by the advice of our faithful subjects we have at length provided this remedy, so that we might to some extent re-establish, on certain days at least, the peace which, because of our sins, we could not make enduring. Accordingly we have enacted and set forth the following: having called together our parishioners to a legally summoned council, which was held at Cologne, the chief city of our province, in the Church of St. Peter, in the 1083d year of our Lord's Incarnation, in the sixth indiction, on the XII day before the Kalends of May, after arranging other business, we have caused to be read in public what we proposed to do in this matter. After this had been for some time fully discussed "pro and con" by all, it was unanimously agreed upon, both the clergy and the people consenting, and we declared in what manner and during what parts of the year it ought to be observed:

Namely, that from the first day of the Advent of our Lord through Epiphany, and from the beginning of Septuagesima to the eighth day after Pentecost and through that whole day, and throughout the year on every

Sunday, Friday and Saturday, and on the fast days of the four seasons, and on the eve and the day of all the apostles, and on all days canonically set apart— or which shall in the future be set apart—for fasts or feasts, this decree of peace shall be observed; so that both those who travel and those who remain at home may enjoy security and the most entire peace, so that no one may commit murder, arson, robbery or assault, no one may injure another with a sword, club or any kind of weapon, and so that no one irritated by any wrong, from the Advent of our Lord to the eighth day after Epiphany, and from Septuagesima to the eighth day after Pentecost, may presume to carry arms, shield, sword or lance, or moreover any kind of armor. On the remaining days indeed, viz., on Sundays, Fridays, apostles' days and the vigils of the apostles, and on every day set aside, or to be set aside, for fasts or feasts, bearing arms shall be legal, but on this condition, that no injury shall be done in any way to any one. If it shall be necessary for any one in the time of the decreed peace— *i.e.*, from the Advent of our Lord to the eighth day after Epiphany, and from Septuagesima to the eighth day after Pentecost—to go from one bishopric into another in which the peace is not observed, he may bear arms, but on the condition that he shall not injure any one, except in self-defence if he is attacked; and when he returns into our diocese he shall immediately lay aside his arms. If it shall happen that any castle is besieged during the days which are included within the peace the besiegers shall cease from attack unless they are set upon by the besieged and compelled to beat the latter back.

And in order that this statute of peace should not be violated by any one rashly or with impunity, a penalty was fixed by the common consent of all; if a free man or noble violates it, i.e., commits homicide or wounds any one or is at fault in any manner whatever, he shall be expelled from our territory, without any indulgence on account of the payment of money or the interces- sion of friends, and his heirs shall take all his property; if he holds a fief, the lord to whom it belongs shall receive it again. Moreover, if it is learned that his heirs after his expulsion have furnished him any support or aid, and if they are convicted of it, the estate shall be taken from them and given to the king. But if they wish to clear themselves of the charge against them, they shall take oath with twelve, who are equally free or equally noble. If a slave kills a man, he shall be beheaded; if he wounds a man, he shall lose a hand; if he does an injury in any other way with his fist or a club, or by striking with a stone, he shall be shorn and flogged. If, however, he is accused and wishes to prove his innocence, he shall clear himself by the ordeal of cold water, but he must himself be put into the water and no one else in his place; if, however, fear- ing the sentence decreed against him, he flees, he shall be under a perpetual excommunication; and if he is known to be in any place, letters shall be sent thither, in which it shall be announced to all that he is excommunicate, and that it is unlawful for any one to associate with him. In the case of boys who have not yet completed their twelfth year, the hand ought not to be cut off; but only in the case of those who are twelve years or more of age. Nevertheless if boys fight, they shall be whipped and deterred from fighting.

It is not an infringement of the peace, if any one orders his delinquent slave, pupil, or any one in any way under his charge to be chastised with rods or cudgels. It is also an exception to this constitution of peace, if the Lord King publicly orders an expedition to attack the enemies of the kingdom or is pleased to hold a council to judge the enemies of justice. The peace is not violated if, during the time, the duke or other counts, advocates or their substitutes hold courts and inflict punishment legally on thieves, robbers and other criminals.

The statute of this imperial peace is especially enacted for the security of those engaged in feuds; but after the end of the peace, they are not to dare to rob and plunder in the villages and houses, because the laws and penalties enacted before the institution of the peace are still legally valid to restrain them from crime, moreover because robbers and highwaymen are excluded from this divine peace and indeed from any peace.

If any one attempts to oppose this pious institution and is unwilling to promise peace to God with the others or to observe it, no priest in our diocese shall presume to say a mass for him or shall take any care for his salvation; if he is sick, no Christian shall dare to visit him; on his death-bed he shall not receive the Eucharist, unless he repents. The supreme authority of the peace promised to God and commonly extolled by all will be so great that it will be observed not only in our times, but forever among our posterity, because if any one shall presume to infringe, destroy or violate it, either now or ages hence, at the end of the world, he is irrevocably excommunicated by us.

The infliction of the above mentioned penalties on the violators of the peace is not more in the power of the counts, centenaries or officials, than in that of the whole people in common; and they are to be especially careful not to show friendship or hatred or do anything contrary to justice in punishing, and not to conceal the crimes, if they can be hidden, but to bring them to light. No one is to receive money for the release of those taken in fault, or to attempt to aid the guilty by any favor of any kind, because whoever does this incurs the intolerable damnation of his soul; and all the faithful ought to remember that this peace has not been promised to men, but to God, and therefore must be observed so much the more rigidly and firmly. Wherefore we exhort all in Christ to guard inviolably this necessary contract of peace, and if any one hereafter presumes to violate it, let him be damned by the ban of irrevocable excommunication and by the anathema of eternal perdition.

In the churches, however, and in the cemeteries of the churches, honor and reverence are to be paid to God, so that if any robber or thief flees thither, he is by no means to be killed or seized, but he is to remain there until by urgent hunger he is compelled to surrender. If any person presumes to furnish arms or food to the criminal or to aid him in flight, the same penalty shall be inflicted on him as on the criminal. Moreover, by our ban we interdict laymen from punishing the transgressions of the clergy and those living under this order; but if seized in open crime, they shall be handed over to their bishop. In cases in which laymen are to be executed, the clergy are to be degraded; in cases in which laymen are to be mutilated, the clergy are to be suspended from office, and with the consent of the laymen they are to suffer frequent fasts and floggings until they atone.

7. The Truce of God Proclaimed at the Council of Clermont

Although the Truce was not part of the crusade appeal, it indicates the extent to which Urban's thought linked the protection of the weak with the wider work of ecclesiastical reform. It is the first truce proclaimed by a pope and presumably extended to all Latin Christians. The text given here is from the manuscript associated with Lambert of Arras. Latin text in Somerville, Councils, 73.

It is enacted that monks, clerics, women, and those who may be with them shall remain in peace every day. And on three days, namely the second, third, and fourth days of the week, an injury inflicted by anyone on someone else will not be considered to be an infraction of the peace. However, on the four remaining days of the week, if anyone injures another, let him then be considered as a criminal violator of the peace and for that reason be punished in the manner prescribed.

8. Urban's Letter to the Faithful in Flanders, December 1095

The Latin text is in Hagenmeyer, 136. The English translation here is from Krey,
42–43.

Urban, bishop, servant of the servants of God, to all the faithful, both
princes and subjects, waiting in Flanders; greeting, apostolic grace, and
blessing.

Your brotherhood, we believe, has long since learned from many accounts that a barbaric fury has deplorably afflicted and laid waste the churches
of God in the regions of the Orient. More than this, blasphemous to say, it
has even grasped in intolerable servitude its churches and the Holy City of
Christ, glorified by His passion and resurrection. Grieving with pious concern
at this calamity, we visited the regions of Gaul and devoted ourselves largely
to urging the princes of the land and their subjects to free the churches of the
East. We solemnly enjoined upon them at the council of Auvergne [the ac-
complishment of] such an undertaking, as a preparation for the remission of
all their sins. And we have constituted our most beloved son, Ademar, Bishop
of Puy, leader of this expedition and undertaking in our stead, so that those
who, perchance, may wish to undertake this journey should comply with his
commands, as if they were our own, and submit fully to his loosings or bind-
ings, as far as shall seem to belong to such an office. If, moreover, there are
any of your people whom God has inspired to this vow, let them know that
he [Ademar] will set out with the aid of God on the day of the Assumption of
the Blessed Mary, and that they can then attach themselves to his following.

9. Urban in Anjou, Lent, 1096: The Chronicle of Fulk le Réchin

The chronicle of the house of Anjou was written by Count Fulk le Réchin, who ruled
from 1067 to 1109, in order to record his own deeds and those of his predecessors. Al-
though he was not at all a crusade historian, Fulk's testimony gives an important
glimpse of Urban II's tour of northern France in the months following Clermont,
especially in the combination of preaching, church dedications, and the cultivation
of local loyalties. Many of the cities and ecclesiastical institutions visited by Urban
had never been visited by a pope before, and these were occasions of great public cele-
bration. The chronicler of the bishops of Le Mans and other memorialists who noted
Urban's visits to their territories expressed sentiments similar to those of Fulk. For

another stop on Urban's French itinerary, see now George T. Beech, "Urban II, the Abbey of Saint-Florent of Saumur, and the First Crusade," Autour de la Première Croisade, 57–70. Urban's presentation of a golden rose to Fulk is the earliest instance of what later became a regular papal practice.

The text is published in Chroniques des comtes d'Anjou et des seigneurs d'Amboise, *ed. Louis Halphen and René Poupardin (Paris, 1913).*

I wish to recall certain signs and prodigies which occurred during the last year of this period [1068–1096] and which concerned not only our own land but the entire kingdom of Gaul, as the sequence of events later demonstrated. At this time stars fell from the heavens onto the earth like hailstones. This vision filled many people with wonder and struck them with a great terror. This sign was followed by a great wave of mortality throughout the kingdom of France and by a period of scarcity that was terrible. In our own city of Angers one hundred of our leading men perished and more than two thousand of the lesser folk.

Near the end of this same year [1096], near the approach of Lent, the Roman pope Urban came to Angers and exhorted our people to go to Jerusalem in order to hunt the pagan people who had occupied this city and all of the lands of the Christians as far as Constantinople. For this reason the pope consecrated the church of St. Nicholas on the day of Septuagesima [February 10, 1096] and translated the body of my uncle Geoffrey from the chapter house into this church. This same apostolic man decided and ordained by a papal privilege that every year, on the day of the anniversary of the consecration which he had performed, a public feast would be celebrated and that the seventh part of the penances of those who attended would be remitted.

Departing, he went to Le Mans [February 14, 1096] and from there to Tours. There he held a venerable council whose decrees were later published. During mid-Lent he was crowned and led a solemn procession from the church of St. Maurice to that of St. Martin [March 23, 1096]. He gave me a golden flower which he held in his hand, and I decided that I and my successors would always carry that flower on the feast of Palm Sunday in memory and for my love of him.* On the Palm Sunday that followed his departure, the church of St. Martin burned down. The pope moved on to Saintes and celebrated the feast of Easter there.

---

* On the Palm Sunday liturgy and processions, see Molly Lindner, "Topography and Iconography in Twelfth-Century Jerusalem," in *The Horns of Hattin*, 81–98.

10. Urban's Letter to His Supporters in Bologna, September 1096

The Latin text is in Hagenmeyer, 137–138.

Urban, bishop, servant of the servants of God, to his dear sons among the clergy and people of Bologna, greetings and apostolic benediction.

We give thanks for your goodness, that you remain always steadfast in the catholic faith, situated as you are in the midst of schismatics and heretics . . . and therefore we urge you, most beloved of the Lord, that you persist manfully along the path of truth and that your virtuous beginnings will lead to a better ending, since it is not he who begins a task, but he who perseveres in it until the end who will be saved. . . . We have heard that some of you have conceived the desire to go to Jerusalem, and you should know that this is pleasing to us, and you should also know that if any among you travel, not for the desire of the goods of this world, but only those who go for the good of their souls and the liberty of the churches, they will be relieved of the penance for all of their sins, for which they have made a full and perfect confession, by the mercy of Almighty God and the prayers of the catholic church, as much by our own authority as that of all the archbishops and bishops in Gaul, because they have exposed themselves and their property to danger out of their love of God and their neighbor. To neither clerics nor monks, however, do we concede permission to go without the permission of their bishops or abbots. Let it be the bishops' duty to permit their parishoners to go only with the advice and provision of the clergy. Nor should young married men rashly set out on the journey without the consent of their spouses.

11. Urban's Letter to the Monks of the Congregation of Vallombrosa, October 7, 1096

The source text is in Wilhelm Wiederhold, "Papsturkunden in Florenz," Nachrichten von der Gesellschaft der Wissenschaften zu Göttingen, Phil.-hist. Kl. (Göttingen, 1901), 313–314. The English translation is from Louise Riley-Smith and Jonathan Riley-Smith, The Crusades: Idea and Reality, 1095–1274 (London, 1981), 39–40.

We have heard that some of you want to set out with the knights who are making for Jerusalem with the good intention of liberating Christianity. This is the right kind of sacrifice, but it is planned by the wrong kind of person. For we were stimulating the minds of knights to go on this expedition, since they might be able to restrain the savagery of the Saracens by their arms and restore the Christians to their former freedom: we do not want those who have abandoned the world and have vowed themselves to spiritual warfare either to bear arms or to go on this journey; we go so far as to forbid them to do so. And we forbid religious—clerics or monks—to set out in this company without the permission of their bishops or abbots in accordance with the rule of the holy canons. The discretion of your religious profession must prevent you in this business from running the risk of either insulting the apostolic see or endangering your own souls. We have heard it said that your confrère, the abbot of the monastery of St. Reparata, is considering leaving the order shared by your congregation in common. And so in this present letter we send him an order, and by that we mean we forbid him to dare to rule the same monastery any longer without the permission of your common abbot, whom you call your major abbot. And if he does not obey, he or anyone else who perhaps dares to leave your congregation should be cut off with the sword of apostolic excommunication.

Given at Cremona on the seventh day of October. We want you to read this letter to the assembled monks and lay brothers and to let the other monasteries know its contents.

12. Urban's Letter to the Counts of Besalú, Empurias, Roussilon, and Cerdaña and Their Followers (between January 1096 and July 1099)

The source text is in Paul Kehr, Papsterkunden in Spanien. I Katalonien *(Berlin, 1926), 287–288. For the date, see Carl Erdmann,* The Origin of the Idea of Crusade *(Princeton, N.J., 1977), 317 n. 37. The English translation is from Louise Riley-Smith and Jonathan Riley-Smith,* The Crusades: Idea and Reality, 1095–1274 *(London, 1981), 40.*

We beseech most carefully your lordships on behalf of the city or rather the church of Tarragona and we order you to make a vigorous effort to restore it in every possible way for the remission of sins. For you know what a great defence it would be for Christ's people and what a terrible blow it would be to the Saracens if, by the goodness of God, the position of that famous city were restored. If the knights of other provinces have decided with one mind to go to the aid of the Asian Church and to liberate their brothers from the tyranny of the Saracens, so ought you with one mind and with our encouragement to work with greater endurance to help a church so near you resist the invasions of the Saracens. No one must doubt that if he dies on this expedition for the love of God and his brothers his sins will surely be forgiven and he will gain a share of eternal life through the most compassionate mercy of our God. So if any of you has made up his mind to go to Asia, it is here instead that he should try to fulfil his vow, because it is no virtue to rescue Christians from the Saracens in one place, only to expose them to the tyranny and oppression of the Saracens in another. May almighty God arouse in your hearts a love of your brothers and reward your bravery with victory over the enemy.

II.

The Chronicle of Fulcher
of Chartres, Book I
(1095–1100)

Fulcher was born in 1059 and was present at the Council of Clermont in 1095 when Pope Urban preached the Crusade. Fulcher, a cleric, left Europe with the army of Robert of Normandy, Stephen of Blois, and Robert of Flanders, accompanying it probably as far as Edessa, where he joined Baldwin, brother of Godfrey of Bouillon. In 1099, after the capture of Jerusalem, Fulcher visited the city and returned to Edessa, where he remained until Baldwin became King of Jerusalem in 1100. Fulcher remained Baldwin's chaplain until the king died in 1118, when Fulcher may have become Prior of the Mount of Olives. Fulcher's chronicle was probably begun in 1101, and the entire three books were not completed until 1127 or 1128. Fulcher's presence throughout most of the expedition, his close connection with the princes of northern France and later with Baldwin, and his ability to organize a maze of complex experiences and motives, make his chronicle perhaps the most reliable of all sources for the history of the First Crusade. The translation and notes printed here are those of Martha E. McGinty (originally published by the University of Pennsylvania Press in 1941). A valuable translation of Fulcher's entire chronicle is that of Frances Rita Ryan, S.S.J., Fulcher of Chartres, A History of the Expedition to Jerusalem, 1095–1127, *ed. with an introduction by Harold S. Fink (Knoxville, Tenn., 1969). The best individual study of Fulcher is Dana C. Munro, "A Crusader," Speculum 7 (1932), 321–335.*

Deeds of the Franks on Their Pilgrimage to Jerusalem

The Prologue of the Following Work of Fulcher the Cleric

1. It is especially pleasing to the living, and it is even beneficial to the dead, when the deeds of brave men (particularly of those serving as soldiers of God) are either read from writings or soberly recounted from memory among the faithful. For, after hearing of the deeds of faithful predecessors who rejected the beauties and pleasures of the world and clung to God, and in accordance with the precept of the Gospel, left their parents and wives and possessions, however great, to follow Him, those here on earth are inspired to serve Him more eagerly in that same spirit. It is beneficial to the dead, especially to those dead in the Lord, when the living, upon hearing of their good and devoted works, bless their faithful souls, and out of love bestow alms with prayers on their behalf whether they were known to them, or not.

2. Therefore, induced by the promptings of certain of my companions on several occasions, I carefully arranged the deeds, most distinguished in the Lord, of the armies of the Franks who, by God's ordination, made a pilgrimage to Jerusalem. I have recorded in my unpolished style, as truthfully as possible, what is worth remembering and what I saw with my own eyes on that journey.

3. Although I do not dare to compare this labor with that of the Israelites or Maccabees[1] or any other chosen people whom God has blessed with many and brilliant victories, yet I have taken care to record it, since it is not to be judged greatly inferior, because often, in this labor, too, God's miracles are evident. Indeed, these [Franks] are not unequal to those Israelites or Maccabees. In the very lands [of the Israelites and Maccabees], we ourselves actually saw, or heard, how the Franks were dismembered, crucified, excoriated, shot with arrows, cut to pieces, and consumed by diverse means of martyrdom. Neither could they be overcome by any threats or temptations; nay, rather, if the assassin's sword had been present, many of our people would not have refused to be destroyed out of love for Christ.

4. Oh, how many thousands met a martyr's blessed death on this expedition! Is there anyone with heart so stony who hears of these acts of God and is not moved by bowels of compassion to burst forth in praises to Him? Can there be anyone who does not marvel how we, a few people in the realms of so many of our enemies, could not only remain but could even thrive? Who has ever heard of such things? Here Egypt and Ethiopia, here Arabia and Chaldea and Syria, here Assyria and Medea, here Parthia and Mesopotamia, here Persia and Scythia,[2] here, even the great sea shut us off from Christianity; and just as God permitted it, enclosed us in the hands of the butchers. How-

---

1. A family of Jewish patriots, the five sons of Mattathias the Hasmonean, who headed a religious revolt in the reign of Antiochus IV, 175–164 B.C., which led to a period of freedom for Judea. The most important of the five sons was Judas Maccabeus.

2. Historical and biblical names; not accurate for this medieval period.

ever, out of pity, He protected us in His strong arm. "For blessed is the nation whose God is the Lord!"[3]

5. The history which follows will reveal how this work was begun, and how all the people of the West, aroused to perform such a great journey, very willingly extended hand and mind to it.

End of the Prologue

I. The Council of Clermont

1. In the year 1095 from the Lord's Incarnation, with Henry reigning in Germany as so-called emperor,[1] and with Philip as king in France,[2] manifold evils were growing in all parts of Europe because of wavering faith. In Rome ruled Pope Urban II,[3] a man distinguished in life and character, who always strove wisely and actively to raise the status of the Holy Church above all things.

2. He saw that the faith of Christianity was being destroyed to excess by everybody, by the clergy as well as by the laity. He saw that peace was altogether discarded by the princes of the world, who were engaged in incessant warlike contention and quarreling among themselves. He saw the wealth of the land being pillaged continuously. He saw many of the vanquished, wrongfully taken prisoner and very cruelly thrown into foulest dungeons, either ransomed for a high price or, tortured by the triple torments of hunger, thirst, and cold, blotted out by a death hidden from the world. He saw holy places violated; monasteries and villas burned. He saw that no one was spared of any human suffering, and that things divine and human alike were held in derision.

3. He heard, too, that the interior regions of Romania, where the Turks ruled over the Christians, had been perniciously subjected in a savage attack.[4]

---

3. Psalms 33:12.

---

1. Henry IV (1056–1106). Fulcher uses the term "so-called emperor," since Henry was not recognized as rightful emperor by adherents of Gregory VII and Urban II.

2. Philip I (1060–1108). One of the reasons Urban called the Council was to excommunicate Philip for his relationship with Bertrade de Montfort. Because he was excommunicated, Philip could not participate in the Crusade.

3. Urban II, Otho of Lagny, Bishop of Ostia, succeeded to the papal throne in 1088. The papacy was contested by Wibert, the anti-Pope, who had been made Clement III by Henry IV and whose adherents disputed the control of the Holy City.

4. This refers to the Seljuk conquest of Anatolia, probably to Manzikert, 1071.

Moved by long-suffering compassion and by love of God's will, he descended the mountains to Gaul, and in Auvergne he called for a council to congregate from all sides at a suitable time at a city called Clermont.[5] Three hundred and ten bishops and abbots,[6] who had been advised beforehand by messengers, were present.

4. Then, on the day set aside for it, he called them together to himself and, in an eloquent address, carefully made the cause of the meeting known to them. In the plaintive voice of an aggrieved Church, he expressed great lamentation, and held a long discourse with them about the raging tempests of the world, which have been mentioned, because faith was undermined.

5. One after another, he beseechingly exhorted them all, with renewed faith, to spur themselves in great earnestness to overcome the Devil's devices and to try to restore the Holy Church, most unmercifully weakened by the wicked, to its former honorable status.

II. The Decree of Pope Urban in the Council

1. "Most beloved brethren," he said, "by God's permission placed over the whole world with the papal crown, I, Urban, as the messenger of divine admonition, have been compelled by an unavoidable occasion to come here to you servants of God. I desired those whom I judged to be stewards of God's ministries to be true stewards and faithful, with all hypocrisy rejected.[1]

2. "But with temperance in reason and justice being remote, I, with divine aid, shall strive carefully to root out any crookedness or distortion which might obstruct God's law. For the Lord appointed you temporarily as stewards over His family to serve it nourishment seasoned with a modest savor. Moreover, blessed will you be if at last the Overseer find you faithful.[2]

3. "You are also called shepherds; see that you are not occupied after the manner of mercenaries. Be true shepherds, always holding your crooks in your hands; and sleeping not, guard on every side the flock entrusted to you.

4. "For if through your carelessness or negligence, some wolf seizes a

5. Clermont-Ferrand, Department of Puy de Dôme (Auvergne). Date of the Council was November 18–28, 1095. The great speech was delivered November 27.

6. Ferdinand Chalandon, *Histoire de la Première Croisade jusqu'à l'élection de Godefroi de Bouillon* (Paris, 1925), 75, states that the number of higher church officials present at the Council, as given by various accounts, ranged from 190 to 463. With a reminder that the number attending different sessions varied, Chalandon accepts as most nearly correct the number given by Urban in a Bull concerned with the Primacy at Lyons, which is the smallest, because it was an official statement, and because afterwards reporters of the Council were inclined to stress its importance by raising the figure.

1. Reference to 1 Corinthians 4:1, 2.
2. Reference to Matthew 24:45, 46.

sheep, you doubtless will lose the reward prepared for you by our Lord.[3] Nay, first most cruelly beaten by the whips of the lictors, you afterwards will be angrily cast into the keeping of a deadly place.

5. "Likewise, according to the evangelical sermon, you are the 'salt of the earth.'[4] But if you fail, it will be disputed wherewith it was salted. O how much saltiness, indeed, is necessary for you to salt the people in correcting them with the salt of wisdom, people who are ignorant and panting with desire after the wantonness of the world; so that, unsalted, they might not be rotten with sins and stink whenever the Lord might wish to exhort them.

6. "For if because of the sloth of your management, He should find in them worms, that is, sin, straightway, He will order that they, despised, be cast into the dungheap. And because you could not make restoration for such a great loss, He will banish you, utterly condemned in judgment, from the familiarity of His love.

7. "It behooves saltiness of this kind to be wise, provident, temperate, learned, peace-making, truth-seeking, pious, just, equitable, pure. For how will the unlearned be able to make men learned, the intemperate make temperate, the impure make them pure? If one despises peace, how will he appease? Or if one has dirty hands, how will he be able to wipe the filth off another one defiled? For it is read, 'If the blind lead the blind, both shall fall into a ditch.'[5]

8. "Set yourselves right before you do others, so that you can blamelessly correct your subjects. If you wish to be friends of God, gladly practise those things which you feel will please Him.

9. "Especially establish ecclesiastical affairs firm in their own right, so that no simoniac heresy will take root among you. Take care lest the vendors and moneychangers, flayed by the scourges of the Lord, be miserably driven out into the narrow streets of destruction.[6]

10. "Uphold the Church in its own ranks altogether free from all secular power. See that the tithes of all those who cultivate the earth are given faithfully to God; let them not be sold or held back.

11. "Let him who has seized a bishop be considered an outlaw. Let him who has seized or robbed monks, clerics, nuns and their servants, pilgrims, or merchants, be excommunicated. Let the robbers and burners of homes and their accomplices, banished from the Church, be smitten with excommunication.

3. Reference to John 10:12–16.
4. Matthew 5:13.
5. Matthew 15:14.
6. Reference to John 2:15.

12. "It must be considered very carefully, as Gregory says, by what penalty he must be punished who seizes other men's property, if he who does not bestow his own liberally is condemned to Hell. For so it happened to the rich man in the well-known Gospel, who on that account was not punished because he had taken away the property of others, but because he had misused that which he had received.

13. "And so by these iniquities, most beloved, you have seen the world disturbed too long; so long, as it was told to us by those reporting, that perhaps because of the weakness of your justice in some parts of your provinces, no one dares to walk in the streets with safety, lest he be kidnapped by robbers by day or thieves by night, either by force or trickery, at home or outside.

14. "Wherefore the Truce,[7] as it is commonly called, now for a long time established by the Holy Fathers, must be renewed. In admonition, I entreat you to adhere to it most firmly in your own bishopric. But if anyone affected by avarice or pride breaks it of his own free will, let him be excommunicated by God's authority and by the sanction of the decrees of this Holy Council."

III. The Pope's Exhortation Concerning the Expedition to Jerusalem

1. These and many other things having been suitably disposed of, all those present, both clergy and people, at the words of Lord Urban, the Pope, voluntarily gave thanks to God and confirmed by a faithful promise that his decrees would be well kept. But straightway he added that another thing not less than the tribulation already spoken of, but even greater and more oppressive, was injuring Christianity in another part of the world, saying:

2. "Now that you, O sons of God, have consecrated yourselves to God to maintain peace among yourselves more vigorously and to uphold the laws of the Church faithfully, there is work to do, for you must turn the strength of your sincerity, now that you are aroused by divine correction, to another affair that concerns you and God. Hastening to the way, you must help your brothers living in the Orient, who need your aid for which they have already cried out many times.[1]

3. "For, as most of you have been told, the Turks, a race of Persians,[2] who

---

7. Truce of God—Cessation of all feuds from Wednesday evening to Monday morning in every week and during church festivals, ordered by the Church in 1041. This was proclaimed anew at the Council of Clermont. Reference was made to this Truce in paragraph 11.

---

1. Alexius Comnenus called on Urban for help in January, 1095, and at the Council of Piacenza in March 1–7, 1095, where Alexius' legates asked Urban and Western Christians for help against the Infidels.
2. Really Seljuk Turks who conquered lands from east to west by way of Persia.

have penetrated within the boundaries of Romania[3] even to the Mediterranean to that point which they call the Arm of Saint George,[4] in occupying more and more of the lands of the Christians, have overcome them, already victims of seven battles, and have killed and captured them, have overthrown churches, and have laid waste God's kingdom. If you permit this supinely for very long, God's faithful ones will be still further subjected.

4. "Concerning this affair, I, with suppliant prayer—not I, but the Lord —exhort you, heralds of Christ, to persuade all of whatever class, both knights and footmen, both rich and poor, in numerous edicts, to strive to help expel that wicked race from our Christian lands before it is too late.

5. "I speak to those present, I send word to those not here; moreover, Christ commands it. Remission of sins will be granted for those going thither, if they end a shackled life either on land or in crossing the sea, or in struggling against the heathen. I, being vested with that gift from God, grant this to those who go.

6. "O what a shame, if a people, so despised, degenerate, and enslaved by demons would thus overcome a people endowed with the trust of almighty God, and shining in the name of Christ! O how many evils will be imputed to you by the Lord Himself, if you do not help those who, like you, profess Christianity!

7. "Let those," he said, "who are accustomed to wage private wars wastefully even against Believers, go forth against the Infidels in a battle worthy to be undertaken now and to be finished in victory. Now, let those, who until recently existed as plunderers, be soldiers of Christ; now, let those, who formerly contended against brothers and relations, rightly fight barbarians; now, let those, who recently were hired for a few pieces of silver, win their eternal reward. Let those, who wearied themselves to the detriment of body and soul, labor for a twofold honor. Nay, more, the sorrowful here will be glad there, the poor here will be rich there, and the enemies of the Lord here will be His friends there.

8. "Let no delay postpone the journey of those about to go, but when they have collected the money owed to them and the expenses for the journey, and when winter has ended and spring has come, let them enter the crossroads courageously with the Lord going on before."[5]

---

3. Fulcher uses the term *Romania* to refer to the Anatolian as well as to the European provinces of the Byzantine Empire, but here, of course, he means the Anatolian. The Seljuks called the state which they founded here *Rum*.

4. Brache de Saint George = Hellespont = Bosporus.

5. See D. C. Munro, "The Speech of Pope Urban II at Clermont, 1095," *American Historical Review* 11 (1906), 231–242, for a comparison of the versions of the speech.

IV. The Bishop of Puy and the Events After the Council

1. After these words were spoken, the hearers were fervently inspired. Thinking nothing more worthy than such an undertaking, many in the audience solemnly promised to go, and to urge diligently those who were absent. There was among them one Bishop of Puy, Ademar by name,[1] who afterwards, acting as vicar-apostolic, ruled the whole army of God wisely and thoughtfully, and spurred them to complete their undertaking vigorously.

2. So, the things that we have told you were well established and confirmed by everybody in the Council. With the blessing of absolution given, they departed; and after returning to their homes, they disclosed to those not knowing, what had taken place. As it was decreed far and wide throughout the provinces, they established the peace, which they call the Truce, to be upheld mutually by oath.

3. Many, one after another, of any and every occupation, after confession of their sins and with purified spirits, consecrated themselves to go where they were bidden.

4. Oh, how worthy and delightful to all of us who saw those beautiful crosses, either silken or woven of gold, or of any material, which the pilgrims sewed on the shoulders of their woolen cloaks or cassocks by the command of the Pope, after taking the vow to go. To be sure, God's soldiers, who were making themselves ready to battle for His honor, ought to have been marked and fortified with a sign of victory. And so by embroidering the symbol [of the cross] on their clothing in recognition of their faith, in the end they won the True Cross itself. They imprinted the ideal so that they might attain the reality of the ideal.

5. It is plain that good meditation leads to doing good work and that good work wins salvation of the soul. But, if it is good to mean well, it is better, after reflection, to carry out the good intention. So, it is best to win salvation through action worthy of the soul to be saved. Let each and everyone, therefore, reflect upon the good, that he makes better in fulfillment, so that, deserving it, he might finally receive the best, which does not diminish in eternity.

6. In such a manner Urban, a wise man and reverenced,
Meditated a labor, whereby the world florescenced.

1. Ademar de Monteil, Bishop of Puy, was the first to take the cross after Urban's crusading message. Having made a pilgrimage to Jerusalem in 1086–1087, he was the only person of any repute and experience to take the cross at this time, and thus Urban appointed him as leader of the expedition, November 27, 1095. He appointed him as his representative December, 1095, when he set August 15, 1096, as the day of departure.

For he renewed peace and restored the laws of the Church to their former standards; also he tried with vigorous instigation to expel the heathen from the lands of the Christians. And since he strove to exalt all things of God in every way, almost everyone gladly surrendered in obedience to his paternal care.

V. The Dissension Between Pope Urban and Wibert

1. But the Devil, who always persists in the detriment of man and goes about like a lion seeking to devour him, stirred up, to the confusion of the people, a certain man stimulated by pride, by the name of Wibert,[1] Urban's adversary. Recently supported by the impudence of the aforementioned emperor of the Bavarians,[2] while Urban's predecessor, Gregory,[3] who was Hildebrand,[4] was held on the throne rightly, this man began to usurp the papal office after that same Gregory was excluded from the threshold of Saint Peter's Church.

2. Because he acted thus perversely, the better people did not wish to recognize him. When Urban was lawfully elected and consecrated by bishops and cardinals after the death of Hildebrand, the greater and more pious part of the people favored obedience to him.

3. But Wibert, spurred by the support of the emperor and by the encouragement of most of the Roman citizens, forced Urban to become an exile from the monastery of Saint Peter's as long as he could. While Urban was thus separated from the Church, in going through the provinces, he united with God those people who had wandered somewhat astray.

4. Wibert, puffed up because of his preëminence in the Church, was inclined to favor sinners, and exercising the office of the Apostolate among his sympathizers, although unjustly, he disparaged the acts of Urban as vain.

5. However, in that year when the first Franks going to Jerusalem passed through Rome, Urban obtained the entire papal power with the aid of a cer-

---

1. Wibert, Archbishop of Ravenna, installed as Clement III, in 1084, by Henry IV in place of Gregory VII.
2. Henry IV was called emperor of the Bavarians, probably because the Saxons and many parts of Germany had revolted against him.
3. Urban did not immediately succeed Gregory. There was an eleven months' vacancy; then the short pontificate of Victor III in 1087; another vacancy of six months; then Urban II in 1088.
4. Hildebrand, Gregory VII, had plans to recapture the Holy Places, but was so involved in the struggle with Henry IV that it was left to Urban to launch the movement. Expelled from Rome by Henry in 1084, he was freed from the Castle of St. Angelo by Robert Guiscard. He died in Salerno in 1085.

tain most noble matron by the name of Mathilda,[5] who was then powerfully active in Rome.

6. Wibert was then in Germany. So two popes were over Rome; but whom to obey, or from whom to seek advice, or who cured illnesses was a question to many. Some favored this one; some, the other.

7. But it is evident to the minds of men that Urban was the more just; for he who subdues his passions as he would enemies, must rightly be considered the better man.

8. As Archbishop of Ravenna, Wibert, mighty in honor and riches, was exceedingly illustrious. It is a wonder that such an abundance was not sufficient for him. Why did he, a pompous one, who should have been considered by all as the model of justice, presume to usurp the scepter of the authority of God? Certainly this should not be seized with force, but accepted with fear and consecration.

9. Nor is it surprising that the whole world was disquieted and disturbed. When the Roman Church, from which all Christendom must obtain correction, is in disorder, it happens that all the subordinate members, being affected by the diseased fibers of the head, become weakened.

10. To be sure, the Church, our mother, on whose milk we were reared, by whose example instructed, and by whose prudence protected, was violently struck by that proud Wibert. Whenever the head is so bruised, at once the members of the body are hurt.

If the head ail, the rest of the members suffer pain.

11. The head was thus hurt, and already the members languished with pain, since in all parts of Europe, peace, goodness, and faith were forcibly trod upon by both the high and the low within the churches and without. But when all these evils had been renounced because of the warning of Pope Urban, it was necessary to substitute war against the pagans for wars between Christians.

12. I must now turn my pen to history: so that those who have not heard of them may learn about the deeds of those who made the journey to Jerusalem, what happened to them, how great was the enterprise, and how, little by little, the labor brilliantly progressed with the help of God. I, Fulcher of Chartres, going with the other pilgrims, afterwards collected it diligently and carefully in writing for posterity, just as I saw it with my own eyes.

---

5. Countess Mathilda of Tuscany, supporter of the Roman See, especially of Gregory VII and Urban II. It was at her favorite residence at Canossa that she persuaded Gregory to see Henry.

VI. The Departure of the Christians and the Names of the Chief Pilgrims

1. In March of the year 1096 from the Lord's Incarnation, after Pope Urban had held the Council, which has been described, at Auvergne in November, some people, earlier prepared than others, hastened to begin the holy journey. Others followed in April or May, June, or July, and also in August, September, or October, whenever the opportunity of securing expenses presented itself.

2. In that year, with God disposing, peace and a vast abundance of grain and wine overflowed through all the regions of the earth, so that they who chose to follow Him with their crosses according to His commands did not fail on the way for lack of bread.

3. Since it is appropriate that the names of the leaders of the pilgrims at that time be remembered, I name Hugh the Great,[1] brother of Philip, King of France. The first of the heroes crossing the sea, he landed at the city of Durazzo in Bulgaria[2] with his own men, but having imprudently departed with a scant army, he was seized by the citizens there and brought to the Emperor of Constantinople,[3] where he was detained for a considerable time not altogether free.

4. After him, Bohemond,[4] an Apulian of Norman race, the son of Robert Guiscard,[5] went along the same route with his army.

5. Next, Godfrey,[6] Duke of Lorraine, went through Hungary with many people.

6. Raymond, Count of the Provençals,[7] with Goths and Gascons; also, Ademar, Bishop of Puy, crossed through Dalmatia.

1. Hugh of Vermandois, leader of northern Franks, the younger son of Henry I. His influence on the Crusade was important, because Philip, being excommunicated, was unable to go. Hugh's route: Lyons, Turin, Genoa, Rome, Bari, Durazzo, Ochrida, Thessalonica, Constantinople.

2. Durazzo was not in Bulgaria but in the Byzantine Empire, commanded at this time by John, the son of Isaac, the Sebasticrator.

3. Alexius Comnenus, Emperor of Constantinople, 1081–1118. See Elizabeth A. S. Dawes, *Alexiad of the Princess Anna Comnena* (London, 1928).

4. Bohemond, son of Robert Guiscard by Alberade. See R. B. Yewdale, *Bohemond I, Prince of Antioch* (Princeton University, 1924). Bohemond's route: Brindisi, Devol, Ochrida, Thessalonica, Constantinople.

5. Robert Guiscard, son of Tancred de Hauteville and father of Bohemond. He was the founder of the Norman principality in Apulia and the ally of Gregory.

6. Godfrey, Duke of Lower Lorraine, was accompanied by his brothers, Baldwin and Eustace. They led the contingent from the lower Rhine. Godfrey's route: Hungary, Semlin, Belgrade, Nissa, Sardica, Philippopolis, Adrianople, Constantinople. Departed August 15, 1096.

7. Raymond of Saint Gilles, Count of Toulouse, had considerable experience with wars in Spain. Raymond's route: Lyons, Geneva, Milan, Aquilaea, Spalata, Ragusa, Durazzo, Ochrida, Thessalonica, Constantinople.

7. A certain Peter the Hermit,[8] after many people on foot and a few knights had joined him, first made his way through Hungary. Afterwards, Walter, called the Penniless,[9] certainly a very good soldier, who later with many of his companions was slain by the Turks between Nicomedia and Nicaea, was the commander of these people.

8. In October, Robert, Count of the Normans,[10] son of William, King of the English, began the journey, after collecting a great army composed of people of Normandy, England, and Brittany; and with him went Stephen, the noble Count of Blois,[11] his brother-in-law, and Robert, Count of Flanders,[12] with many other nobles.[13]

9. So with such a great band proceeding from western parts, gradually from day to day on the way there grew armies of innumerable people coming together from everywhere. Thus a countless multitude speaking many languages and coming from many regions was to be seen. However, all were not assembled into one army until we arrived at the city of Nicaea.

10. What more shall I tell? The islands of the seas and all the kingdoms of the earth were so agitated that one believed that the prophecy of David was fulfilled, who said in his Psalm: "All nations whom Thou hast made shall come and worship before Thee, O Lord";[14] and what those going all the way there later said with good reason: "We shall worship in the place where His feet have stood."[15] We have read much about this in the Prophets which it is tedious to repeat.

11. Oh, how much grief there was! How many sighs! How much sorrow! How much weeping among loved ones when the husband left his wife so dear to him, as well as his children, father and mother, brothers and grandparents, and possessions however great!

12. But however so many tears those remaining shed for those going,

---

8. Peter of Amiens preached the Crusade and was one of the leaders of the Peasants' Crusade. Hagenmeyer's biography reduced the legendary Peter to the historical.

9. Walter of Perejo. The standard treatment of this expedition is Frederic Duncalf, "The Peasants' Crusade," *American Historical Review* 26, 440–453.

10. See David, *Robert Curthose*.

11. Stephen, husband of Adèle of Normandy, daughter of William the Conqueror, father of Stephen of Boulogne who became King of England. Stephen's letters to his wife are the most human documents of the First Crusade. See Heinrich Hagenmeyer, *Die Kreuzzugsbriefe aus den Jahren 1088–1100* (Innsbruck, 1901).

12. For the crusading career of Robert of Flanders, see M. M. Knappen, "Robert II of Flanders in the First Crusade," in *The Crusades and Other Historical Essays*, ed. L. J. Paetow (New York, 1928).

13. As Fulcher went on this expedition, its route will be given in detail in the text below.

14. Psalms 86:9.

15. Psalms 132:7.

these were not swayed by such tears from leaving all that they possessed; without doubt believing that they would receive an hundredfold what the Lord promised to those loving him.[16]

13. Then the wife reckoned the time of her husband's return, because if God permitted him to live, he would come home to her. He commended her to the Lord, kissed her, and promised as she wept that he would return. She, fearing that she would never see him again, not able to hold up, fell senseless to the ground; mourning her living beloved as though he were dead. He, having compassion, it seems, neither for the weeping of his wife, nor feeling pain for the grief of any friends, and yet having it, for he secretly suffered severely, unchanging, went away with a determined mind.

14. Sadness to those remaining, however, was joy to those going away. What, then, can we say? "This is the Lord's doing; it is marvelous in our eyes."[17]

VII. The Journey of the Count of Normandy,[1] and the Events at Rome at That Time

1. After leaving Gaul and going through Italy, we Western Franks came as far as Lucca, a most renowned city. Near there we met Pope Urban; and Robert the Norman and Stephen, Count of Blois, and others of us who wished spoke with him. Having received his blessing,[2] we went on our way joyfully to Rome.

2. When we had entered the Church of Saint Peter, we met, before the altar, men of Wibert, the pseudo-Pope, who, with swords in their hands, wrongly snatched the offerings placed on the altar. Others ran up and down on the roof of the church itself, and from there threw stones at us as we were prostrate praying. For when they saw anyone faithful to Urban, they straightway wished to slay him.

3. In one of the towers of the church were Lord Urban's men, who carefully guarded it in fidelity to him, and withstood their adversaries as well as they could. We were very grieved when we saw such a great atrocity com-

---

16. Compare this statement with that of Guilelmis Monachi Malmesburiensis, *De Gestis regum Anglorum*, adapted translation by John Sharpe (London, 1815), bk. 4, ch. 2, 416: "Then the Welshman abandoned his forests and neglected his hunting; the Scotchman deserted the fleas with which he is so familiar; the Dane ceased to swallow his intoxicating draughts; and the Norwegian turned his back upon his raw fish."

17. Psalms 118:23.

---

1. Date of departure was 1096, September or October.

2. October 25, 1096.

mitted there, but we earnestly wished for nothing to be done except as punishment by the Lord. Thereupon, without hesitation, many who had come this far with us, now weak with cowardice, returned to their homes.

4. We, on the other hand, going through the middle of Campania, came to Bari,[3] a wealthy town situated on the edge of the sea. There in the Church of Saint Nicholas, we prayed to God effusively. Then, approaching the harbor, we thought to cross the sea at that time. But since opposition of the sailors, fickle fortune, and winter weather, even then bearing down upon us, all exposed us to danger, it was necessary that Count Robert of Normandy withdraw to Calabria and spend the severe winter weather there. Yet, at that time, Count Robert of Flanders with his cohort crossed the sea.

5. Many of the people, deserted by their leaders and fearing future want, sold their bows, took up their pilgrims' staves, and returned to their homes as cowards. For this, they were held worthless by God as well as by man, and they became utterly disgraced.

VIII. The Drowning of the Pilgrims and the Divinely Manifest Miracle

1. In the year of the Lord 1097, with spring weather accompanying March, immediately Robert the Norman and Count Stephen of Blois, who had been waiting for favorable weather, accompanied by their men, again turned seaward. The fleet was prepared, and on the Nones of April, which at that time fell on the Holy Day of Easter, they embarked at the port of Brindisi.

2. "How unsearchable are His judgments, and His ways past finding out!"[1] For we saw one boat among the others, which, while near the shore and apparently unhindered, suddenly cracked apart in the middle. Whereby four hundred of both sexes perished by drowning, concerning whom joyful praise to God immediately sounded.

3. For when those who were standing around had collected as many of the dead bodies as they could, they discovered crosses actually imprinted in the flesh on the shoulders of some of them. For what those living bore on their garments, it was fitting, with the Lord willing, that the same victorious sign remain with them thus preoccupied in His service under a pledge of faith. And at the same time, reason made it plain to those reflecting on it, that it was appropriate that, by such a miracle, those dead had already by God's mercy obtained the peace of everlasting life in the clearly evident ful-

---

3. Arrived at the end of November or the beginning of December, 1096.

1. Romans 11:33.

fillment of the prophecy which had been written: "The just, though taken prematurely by death, shall find peace."[2]

4. Of the others now wrestling with death, only a few lived. Horses and mules were destroyed by the waves, and much money was lost, too. When we saw this misfortune, we were confused with so great a fear that very many of the weak-hearted ones, not yet aboard the vessels, went back to their homes, having abandoned the pilgrimage, and saying that never would they place themselves on the deceptive water.

5. But placing our hope on almighty God deep within us, with topsails raised again, and with a great trumpet sound, we thrust ourselves upon the sea, when the wind was blowing slightly. After we had been detained on the high seas for three days by the failing wind, on the fourth day[3] we reached land about ten miles, I judge, from the city of Durazzo. Two harbors received our fleet.[4] Then, joyfully we resumed our dry-land journey, and we approached the aforementioned city.

6. We proceeded over the land of the Bulgars, over mountain precipices and rather desert places. Then all of us came to the rapid river which is called the Demon by the inhabitants of the place, and deservedly. For there we saw many people, submerged unexpectedly by the strong current, perish when they hoped to wade through it step by step, and not one of the onlookers could help them. There we shed many tears out of pity over this, and if knights with dexterous horses had not brought assistance to those on foot, many others would have lost life in like manner. Then our camp was laid out close to the bank of the river, where we stopped for one night. Vast mountains on which no inhabitant was visible, towered over us on all sides.

7. In the early morning at daybreak, with the trumpet signals sounding, we began to climb the mountains which they call the Bagulatus [Bagora]. After passing the mountainous cities of Lucretia, Botella, Bonfinat, and Stella, we reached a river which was called Bardarius [Vardar]. It was customary to cross it only in boats, but with God's aid we forded it, and rejoiced. Having crossed it, we pitched our tents on the following day before Thessalonica, a city abounding in all goods.

8. After a delay of four days there,[5] and from there going over into Macedonia, through the Valley of Philippi[6] and through Crisopolis, we

---

2. Wisdom of Solomon 4:7.
3. April 9, 1097.
4. The other harbor was ancient Epidamnus. Both of these harbors are in modern Albania.
5. April 22 to 26.
6. Valley of the Strymon River.

came to Christopolis, Praetoria, Messinopolis, Macra, Traianopolis, Neapolis, Panadox, Rodosto, Heraclea, Salumbria, Natura, and Constantinople.[7] After stretching our tents before this city, we rested for fourteen days.

9. Because we were not able to enter that city, since it was not pleasing to the emperor (for he feared that by chance we might plot some injury to him), it was necessary that we buy outside the walls our daily supplies, which the citizens brought to us by his order. Only five or six of us at the same time were permitted to go into the city each hour; thus some were coming out and others were going in to pray in the churches.

IX. The City of Constantinople and the Journey of the Pilgrims to Nicaea

1. Oh, what an excellent and beautiful city! How many monasteries, and how many palaces there are in it, of wonderful work skilfully fashioned! How many marvelous works are to be seen in the streets and districts of the town! It is a great nuisance to recite what an opulence of all kinds of goods are found there; of gold, of silver, of many kinds of mantles, and of holy relics. In every season, merchants, in frequent sailings, bring to that place everything that man might need. Almost twenty thousand eunuchs, I judge, are kept there continuously.

2. When we had sufficiently refreshed our fatigued selves, then our leaders, after counsel, agreed upon a contract under oath with the Emperor, upon his demand. Already Lord Bohemond and Duke Godfrey, who had preceded us, had taken it. However, Count Raymond at that time refused to do so. The Count of Flanders, just as the others did, took that same oath.[1]

3. It was necessary for all to confirm friendship with the Emperor, without whose counsel and aid we could not have completed our journey, nor could those who were to follow us on that same road. To these, then, the Emperor himself offered as many coins and silken garments as he pleased; also some horses and some money, which they needed to complete such a great journey.

4. After this was completed, we crossed the sea which they call the Arm

---

7. Arrived in Constantinople, May 14, 1097.

---

1. Raymond's refusal to take the oath is attested by both the *Gesta* and Raymond of Aguilers, but it is not mentioned by Anna, who talks of the close relation between Raymond and her father. On the whole matter of the oath, see A. C. Krey, "A Neglected Passage in the *Gesta* and Its Bearing on the Literature of the First Crusade," in Paetow, *The Crusades and Other Historical Essays*, 57–58.

Bohemond took the oath November 1096; Godfrey, January 21, 1097; and Raymond's refusal but assurance of peace was given April 26, 1097.

of Saint George. We hastened then to the city of Nicaea, which Lord Bohemond, Duke Godfrey, Count Raymond, and the Count of Flanders had
already surrounded in siege by the middle of May. The Oriental Turks,[2] very
keen archers and bowmen, then possessed this city. These Turks from Persia,
after they had crossed the Euphrates River fifty years before, subjugated the
whole land of Romania for themselves as far as the city of Nicomedia.[3]

5. Oh, how many severed heads and bones of the dead lying on the plains
did we then find beyond Nicomedia near that sea! In the preceding year, the
Turks destroyed those who were ignorant of and new to the use of the arrow.
Moved to compassion by this, we shed many tears there.[4]

X. The Siege of Nicaea[1] and the Surrender of That City

1. When those who were besieging Nicaea had heard, as it was told, that
our princes, the Count of the Normans and Stephen of Blois, had come,[2]
they came joyfully to meet them and us on the way, and escorted us to the
place where we stretched our tents before the city on the south side.

2. Once already, the Turks had gathered in force and had prepared either
to break the blockade if they could, or to better fortify the city with their soldiers. But repulsed fiercely by our men, almost two hundred of theirs were
killed. When they had seen the Franks so furious and mighty in strength, they
fled into the interior of Romania, until they should feel that the time was opportune to attack them.

3. We, who were the last to come, arrived at the siege in the first week
of June.

4. Then the many armies there were united into one, which those who
were skilled in reckoning estimated at six hundred thousand strong for war.
Of these, there were one hundred thousand full-armed with corselets and helmets, not counting the unarmed, that is, the clerics, monks, women, and little
children.

5. And what more? If all those, who had departed from their homes on
the consecrated journey, had been present at one time, without doubt six

2. Oriental Turks: This is not, as might be expected, a reference to the Sultanate of Bagdad
to distinguish it from that of Iconium, but merely a reference to the eastern origin of the Seljuks.
3. In the Seljuk conquest, they crossed the Euphrates in 1047, but did not reach Nicomedia
until 1081.
4. Here the Turks had killed many of the followers of Peter the Hermit: the people of the
Peasants' Crusade who had met disaster in October, 1096.

1. The siege was begun May 14, 1097.
2. June 3, 1097.

million warriors would have been there. But some, refusing hardships, had returned to their homes at Rome, Apulia, Hungary, or Dalmatia, and thousands had been killed on the way. Others, going on with us, though weak, died upon arrival. You could see the many cemeteries where our pilgrims were buried along the footpaths, on the plains, and in the woods.

6. It must be explained, since we besieged the city of Nicaea for a long time, that we could buy food which with the Emperor's permission was brought to us by boat. Then our heroes had machines made: battering-rams, sows, wooden towers, and petrariae.³ Arrows were stretched on bows, and stones were hurled by the tormenta. Our enemy and we retaliated alternately with all our might in the struggle. Often, armed with our machines, we dashed on the city, but with the strong wall obstructing us, the assault was brought to nought. Often, some of the Turks; often, some of the Franks, struck by arrows or by stones, died.

7. Truly, you would have grieved and sighed with compassion, to see them let down iron hooks, which they lowered and raised by ropes, and seize the body of any of our men that they had slaughtered in some way near the wall. None of our men dared, nor could, take the body from them. Having robbed the corpse, they threw the carcass outside.

8. Then we drew some large skiffs overland with oxen and ropes from Civetot as far as Nicaea.⁴ We placed them on a lake⁵ near the city to guard the entrance, so that the city might not be supplied with food.

9. We had harassed the city in siege for five weeks,⁶ and many times had terrified the Turks by assaults. Meanwhile, they parleyed with the Emperor through mediators, and slyly returned the city to him, when already it had been greatly encompassed by force and cleverness.

10. Then the Turks let in the Turcoples,⁷ sent there by the Emperor, who guarded the city with the money in it on behalf of the Emperor just as he had commanded them. Because he kept all of that money in his possession, the

---

3. The *battering-ram* was a large beam or log suspended from perpendicular beams. By swinging it, the wall was shaken down or a hole was made through it. A *sow* was a machine for undermining the wall and served as a cover for the manipulators also. The *tower* was made of wood and equipped with wheels or rollers which made it movable; generally it was two-storied, the lower one containing a battering-ram, and the upper serving as a platform for archers and hurling machines. Sometimes the tower was covered with skins to protect the manipulators. Usually a drawbridge was attached to the tower, which enabled the warriors to have access to the wall. The *petraria* was a machine for throwing stones, and the *tormentum* hurled missiles by the use of twisted cords. (Duncalf, *The Capture of Jerusalem*, 17, n. 5 and 20, nn. 11 and 12.)

4. June 17, 1097.

5. Lake Isnik.

6. May 14 to June 18.

7. Greek mercenary soldiers, light-armed cavalry, recruited from half-breeds and natives.

Emperor gave some of his own gold and silver and mantles to our nobles; he also distributed some of his copper coins, which they call *tartarons*,[8] to the footsoldiers.

11. The summer solstice came on the day in June when Nicaea was thus seized or restored.[9]

XI. The Fatal Battle of the Christians with the Turks[1]

1. When our soldiers had received permission from the Emperor to leave, three days before the Kalends of July,[2] we left Nicaea to go into the interior regions of Romania. But when we had proceeded on our journey for two days, it was announced that the Turks, after laying ambushes for us on the plains over which they thought we would go, awaited battle.

2. When we had heard this, we lost no courage. But on that evening, when our scouts had seen many of them from a distance, they immediately warned us; because of that, we had our tents guarded on all sides that night by watchmen. In the early morning, which fell on the Kalends of July,[3] after arms were taken up, and being arranged in wings facing them with the tribunes and centurions properly leading the cohorts and centuries, with a warning horn and with banners flying, we began to advance in battle formation.

3. In the second hour of the day, lo, their advance guards approached our scouts! When we heard this, we pitched our tents near a certain marsh, so that having removed the pack saddles, we should be more readily prepared for fighting.

4. After this was done, behold! there were the Turks whose emir and prince[4] was Sulaiman[5] who held Nicaea and Romania under his power. The Turks, heathen Persians, who, commanded by him, had come for a journey of thirty days and more to his aid, were with him; also many emirs or princes, namely, Admircaradigum and Miriathos, and many others.[6] All of

---

8. Tartarons: Eastern cheap copper coin of varying value.
9. June 19, 1097.

---

1. Battle of Dorylaeum.
2. June 29.
3. July 1, 1097.
4. *Emir* was the commander of a regiment and incorrectly translated *prince* by the Westerners, according to H. A. R. Gibb, *Damascus Chronicles of the Crusades*, extracted and translated from the *Chronicle of Ibn Al-Qualānist* (London, 1932), 33.
5. Sulaiman II, Kiliz Arslan Daud, Sultan of Iconium or Rum, 1092–1107.
6. Admircaradigum = al amîr Korâdja; Miriathos = mîr Atsiz. The identification of these rather obscure Turkish emirs is discussed at length by Hagenmeyer, *Historia, bk. I*, ch. 11, 4, n. 16.

these together numbered three hundred and sixty thousand warriors, that is, archers.[7] For it is their custom to use such arms. They were all cavalry. We, on the other hand, were both infantry and cavalry.

5. At that time, Duke Godfrey and Count Raymond and Hugh the Great were not with us. For two days, I know not for what reason, they, with a large number of our people, had withdrawn from us at a forked crossroad. On account of this, irreparable harm befell us, because our men were slain, and because the Turks were not killed nor repulsed. Since they received our messengers late, they brought aid to us late.

6. The Turks, with clashing of weapons and shrieking, fiercely let loose a shower of arrows. Stunned and almost dead and with many injured, we straightway turned our backs in flight. Nor is this to be wondered at since such fighting was unknown to any of us.

7. Directly from another part of the marsh, a large band of them fiercely forced their way as far as our tents. Having entered, they were snatching our things and were killing some of our people, when, with God arranging, the advance guards of Hugh the Great, of Count Raymond, and of Duke Godfrey came upon this disaster from the rear. When our men had retreated to our tents, the Turks, who had entered them, left, for they thought our men had returned to fight them. But what they took for boldness and courage, was, if they had been able to know, really great fear.

8. What shall I tell next? All of us, huddled together like sheep in a fold, trembling and terrified, were fenced in by the enemy on all sides, so that we could not turn in any direction. It was evident that this had befallen us because of our sins. For dissipation had polluted certain ones, and avarice or some other iniquity had corrupted others. There was a vast cry smiting the heavens, of men and women and little children, and also of the heathens who rushed in upon us. No hope of life remained.

9. Then we confessed that we were culprits and sinners, humbly begging mercy from God. The Bishop of Puy, our Protector, and four other bishops were there. There were many priests present, clothed in white vestments, who besought the Lord most humbly to overthrow the strength of our enemy and pour gifts of His mercy on us. They sang weeping; they wept singing. Many, fearing immediate death, ran to them and confessed their sins.

10. Our leaders, Robert, Count of Normandy, Stephen, Count of Blois, Robert, Count of Flanders, and also Bohemond, resisted them with all their

---

7. *'Askar* is the term used for these mounted archers, according to Gibb, *Damascus Chronicles of the Crusades*, 33.

might, and often strove to attack them. These, likewise, were strongly asailed by the Turks.

XII. The Flight of the Turks and the Victory of the Christians

1. The Lord does not give victory to the pomp of nobility nor to brilliance in arms, but out of pity He aids the pure in heart who are fortified by divine strength in time of need. Therefore the Lord, perhaps pleased with our supplication, little by litlte restored vigor to us, and more and more weakened the Turks. When our allies, who were hastening to help us, were seen, praising God we resumed our courage and in troops and cohorts we strove to resist further.

2. Alas! How many of our men straggling slowly behind us did they kill that day! Even from the first hour of the day, as I have said, up to the sixth, difficulties encompassed us; but then, little by little, after we were spurred on and strengthened by union with some of our allies, divine grace was miraculously present. Suddenly, we saw the backs of the Turks as they turned in flight.[1]

3. Shouting fiercely, we pursued them over mountains and through valleys. Nor did we cease to rout them, until our swiftest men came to their tents. There, some of them loaded camels and many horses with the Turks' possessions and the tents themselves which they, out of fright, had left. Others followed the fleeing Turks until nightfall. Because our horses were hungry and tired, we kept a few of theirs.

4. It was a great miracle of God that on the morrow and on the third day they never stopped their flight, although no one except God put them to flight any longer.

5. Happy over this outcome, we unloosed our thanks to God, because He was not willing that our journey be altogether brought to nought, but had indicated that it would succeed more honorably than usual and would bring honor to His Christianity. As a result, the story shall sound from East to West forever.

6. Then, we pressed on our journey carefully. One day, we endured a very severe thirst, which so oppressed some men and women that they died. The Turks, fleeing before us in troops, sought hiding places for themselves all over Romania.

---

1. For other accounts of Dorylaeum, see Charles W. C. Oman, *History of the Art of War, Middle Ages from the Fourth to the Fourteenth Century* (London, 1898), 271–275.

XIII. The Want of the Christians

1. Then we came to Antioch, which they called the Lesser,[1] in the province of Pisidia; thence to Iconium.[2] We very often suffered the lack of enough bread and other food in these places; for we found Romania, which is very good land and especially fertile for all crops, excessively devastated and ravaged by the Turks.

2. Yet ever so many times, you would see such a great multitude of people well refreshed by what was found on the scattered farms, which we found here and there in this region, with the aid of God who fed five thousand men with two loaves and five fishes. We were very glad for this and, rejoicing, acknowledged that these were gifts of the mercy of God.

3. Truly, either you would laugh or perhaps shed tears out of compassion, when many of our people lacking beasts of burden, because many had died, loaded wethers, she-goats, sows, or dogs with their possessions, such as garments, loaves of bread, or whatever pack is necessary for the use of pilgrims. We saw the backs of these small beasts chafed by the heavy loads. Occasionally armed knights even used oxen as mounts.

4. Who ever heard of such a mixture of languages in one army, since there were French, Flemings, Frisians, Gauls, Allobroges, Lotharingians, Allemani, Bavarians, Normans, English, Scots, Aquitanians, Italians, Dacians, Apulians, Iberians, Bretons, Greeks, and Armenians? If any Breton or Teuton wished to question me, I could neither understand nor answer.

5. But we who were diverse in languages, nevertheless seemed to be brothers in the love of God and very close to being of one mind. For if one lost any of his possessions, he who found it would keep it carefully for many days, until by inquiry he found the loser and returned the article to him. This is fit and proper for those who make the pilgrimage in the right spirit.

XIV. The Acts and Courage of Count Baldwin, Brother of Godfrey, and the Return of the City of Edessa, Which Was Called Rohas

1. When we approached the city of Heraclea,[1] we saw a certain sign in the sky shining with a whitish brilliance, which appeared in the shape of a sword with the point stretching toward the East. We knew not what it promised for the future, but committed things present and things future to the Lord.

1. July 31, 1097.
2. August 15, 1097.

---

1. September 10, 1097.

2. Next we came to a certain very good city, which was named Marasch,[2] where we rested for three days. When we had trudged a day's march from this place and were no more than three days from Antioch of Syria,[3] I, Fulcher, departed from the army and with lord Count Baldwin,[4] brother of Duke Godfrey, turned into the country on the left.

3. He was, to be sure, as good a soldier as possible. Having left the army earlier, accompanied by those whom he had brought with him, he had captured with great daring the city which they call Tarsus, in Cilicia. He took it away from Tancred,[5] who by agreement with the Turks had already put his own men in the city. Having left a garrison there, he returned to the army.[6]

4. Then, trusting in the Lord and in his own strength, he collected a few soldiers, and set out toward the Euphrates River, and there seized many forts both by force and cleverness. Among these, he took the very best one, which was called Turbezel.[7] The Armenians who lived there granted it to him peaceably, and many others were subjected to him.

5. When the report of this had already been spread far and wide, the prince of the city of Edessa[8] sent a legation to him.[9] This city is most renowned and is in a very fertile region. It is in Mesopotamia of Syria, nearly twenty miles across the Euphrates River, and about a hundred or more from Antioch.

6. Baldwin was invited to go there, so that they would become mutual friends like father and son as long as both should live. If, by chance, the Edessan duke should die, immediately Baldwin, as if he were his son, would possess the city and his whole land in inheritance forever. For he had neither son nor daughter. And because they were unable to defend themselves from the Turks, that Greek[10] wished to have himself and his land defended by Baldwin and his soldiers, who he had heard were very brave warriors.[11]

7. After hearing this and believing it on the oath of the ambassadors,

2. October 13, 1097.
3. October 17, 1097.
4. Baldwin appears for the first time in Fulcher's chronicle.
5. See Robert Nicholson, *Tancred* (University of Chicago, 1940).
6. Tancred and Baldwin were both sent to Tarsus as scouts. Tancred arrived first, but Baldwin came during the night. By morning, natives of the city had fled, and the question arose as to whose capture it was. It was ceded to Baldwin, because he had the larger army. See Krey, *First Crusade*, 291, n. 8, and Nicholson, *Tancred*, 38–56.
7. Tell bashir.
8. The prince was Thoros (Theodorus), son of Hethun, an Armenian, who held the city in fief from the Byzantine emperor. For a good study of these Armenian principalities, see René Grousset, *Histoire des Croisades et du Royaume Franc de Jérusalem* (Paris, 1936), volume 1, introduction.
9. Beginning of February, 1098.
10. Armenian, although a vassal of the Greek Empire as noted above.
11. Matthew of Edessa, *Recueil des Historiens des Croisades, Documents Arméniens* (Paris, 1869), 1: 35–36, confirms the account in this part of the story, but says sixty knights.

with his very small army (actually eighty soldiers), he continued across the Euphrates. Having crossed it, we very hastily proceeded all night in great fear close to the camps of the Saracens, but avoided them here and there.

8. When those who lived in Samosata,[12] a strong town, had heard this, they set ambushes before us on the way over which they thought we would go. But the next night, a certain Armenian carefully lodged us in his castle, and he warned us to beware of those enemies lying in ambush. Because of this, we concealed ourselves there for two days.

9. On the third day, wearied by such a long delay, they suddenly rushed forth from the place of ambush and, with their banners aloft, ran before the castle where we were, and before our eyes drove off the cattle which they found there in the pastures for booty.

10. We went out against them, but since we were few, were not able to fight them. They shot arrows at us, yet wounded none of us. They left one of their men, slain by a lance, on the field. The man who unseated him kept the horse. Then they went away, but we remained there.

11. On the following day, we resumed our journey. When we passed by the villages of the Armenians, it was astonishing to see them advancing toward us with crosses and standards, kissing our feet and our garments most humbly for love of God, because they had heard there that we would defend them from the Turks under whose yoke they had been oppressed for a long time.

12. Finally we arrived at Edessa,[13] where the aforementioned prince of the city and his wife, together with his subjects, received us joyfully, and they fulfilled their promise to Baldwin without delay.

13. After we had been there fifteen days, the citizens of the city wickedly plotted to kill their prince, whom they hated, and to elevate Baldwin in the palace to rule the land. It was said, and it was done. Because of this, Baldwin and his men were especially saddened, for they were unable to obtain mercy for him.[14]

14. Once Baldwin had received as the gift of the citizens the power of this man who had been so basely killed, he immediately made war on the Turks who were in the country. He either conquered or killed many of them. It happened, too, that many of ours were slain by the Turks.

15. I, Fulcher of Chartres, was chaplain of this Baldwin. I wish now to resume the discourse, which I stopped, about the army of God.

12. About five miles northwest of Edessa.
13. February 20, 1098.
14. Cf. Matthew of Edessa, 37–48, who says that Baldwin was a party to the plot against Thoros, and lays much of the blame for the rebellion on him.

XV. The Arrival of the Franks at Antioch and the Siege of that City

1. In the month of October,[1] after crossing the river which they call the Fernus or Orontes, the Franks came to Antioch in Syria, the city which Seleucus,[2] son of Antiochus, founded and made the capital of Syria. It was formerly called Reblata.[3] Tents were ordered to be pitched within the first milestone before the city, where later fierce encounters were often made by both sides. For when the Turks darted forth from that city, they killed many of our men. But retaliation having been made, they mourned for the men they had lost also.

2. Antioch is an extensive city, has a strong wall, and is well situated for defense. It could never be captured by outside enemies if the inhabitants, supplied with bread, wished to defend it long enough. In the city there is a church worthy to be revered, dedicated to the Apostle Peter. Elevated to the episcopate, he sat on the throne here after he had received dominion of the Church and the keys of the Kingdom of Heaven from the Lord Jesus.

3. Also there is another church, round in form, built in honor of the Blessed Mary, and several others fittingly constructed. Although these had long been under the Turks, yet God, knowing all things beforehand, saved them intact for us, so that at some time or other He would be magnified by us in them.

4. The sea is about thirteen miles, I judge, from Antioch. Since the Fernus [Orontes] River happens to flow into the sea, boats loaded with all goods come from far distant parts almost to Antioch through the channel of this river. Thus the city, fortified by sea as well as by land, abounds in manifold riches.

5. When our princes had seen the great difficulty of overcoming it, they swore mutually by oath to work together in siege until, with God favoring, they would capture it either by force or by ruse.[4]

6. They found some boats on the aforementioned river, which they seized, and out of them fashioned a bridge for themselves. They were able to cross over this to carry on their work, whereas before they had to wade over with difficulty.

7. When the Turks saw that they were besieged by such a great Christian

1. October 20, 1097.

2. Antioch was founded on the Orontes c. 300 B.C. by Seleucus Nicator (312–280 B.C.), the general of Alexander the Great. The new city was named after Antiochus, Seleucus's father, who had been an officer of Philip of Macedon.

3. Reblata or Ribleth was confused with Antioch by St. Jerome in his *Onomastikon*, and Fulcher followed Jerome in this error. Reblata is actually a little south of Homs.

4. Siege of Antioch lasted from October 20, 1097, to June 3, 1098.

multitude, they feared that they could in no way shake them off. After a plan was mutually formed, Aoxian, prince and emir of Antioch,[5] sent his son, Sensadolus by name,[6] to the Sultan,[7] that is, the emperor, of Persia, to get his help most quickly, since they held hope for aid from no other except Mohammed, their advocate. Thus directed, he conducted this legation there very hastily.

8. Meanwhile, those who remained, awaiting the requested aid, guarded the city, and frequently plotted many kinds of harm to the Franks. Nevertheless the Franks resisted their cunning with all their power.

9. It happened on a certain day that the Franks killed seven hundred Turks; and the Turks, who set ambushes for the Franks, were overcome by the Franks lying in ambush. The strength of God was present there. All of our men retreated uninjured, with the exception of one whom they wounded.

10. Alas! how many Christians, Greeks, Syrians, and Armenians, who lived in the city, were killed by the maddened Turks. With the Franks looking on, they threw outside the walls the heads of those killed, with their petrariae and slings. This especially grieved our people. Holding these Christians in hatred, the Turks feared lest by some chance they give the Franks information to their own detriment.

11. When the Franks had besieged the city for some time, and had pillaged the surrounding region for food necessary for themselves and had devastated it on all sides, bread could be bought nowhere, and they endured excessive hunger. As a result, everybody was especially desolate and many secretly considered withdrawal from the siege in flight, either by land or by sea.

12. They had no supplies on which they could live. It was with great fear that they sought food far away, in going distances of forty or fifty miles from the siege, that is, in the mountains, where they were often killed by the Turks lying in ambush.

13. We believed that these misfortunes befell the Franks, and that they were not able for so long a time to take the city because of their sins. Not only dissipation, but also avarice or pride or rapaciousness corrupted them.

14. After holding council, they drove out the women from the army, both married and unmarried, lest they, stained by the defilement of dissipation, displease the Lord. Those women then found places to live in the neighboring camps.

15. Both the rich and the poor were desolate from hunger as well as from

---

5. *Aoxian* is Fulcher's version of Yagi Siyan of Antioch, 1086–1098, formerly sent by Sultan Malik Shah as governor of Antioch.

6. Sensadolus, Shams-ad-Daula.

7. Sultan of Persia, Bark-yarok (1094–1104), son of Malik Shah.

the daily slaughtering. It seemed that unless God, like a Good Shepherd, would bind His sheep together in flocks, then without doubt all of them would flee, even though they had sworn to maintain the siege. Because of the lack of bread for many days, many sought those things necessary for their nourishment in the neighboring castles; and not returning to the army afterwards, they entirely deserted the siege.

16. At that time,[8] we saw an astonishing glow in the sky, and, in addition, we felt a great movement of the earth, which made us all quake. Many at that time also saw a certain sign in the shape of a cross, whitish in color, advancing toward the East in a straight path.

XVI. The Wretched Poverty of the Christians and the Flight of the Count of Blois

1. In the year of the Lord 1098, after the region all around Antioch had been wholly devastated by the multitude of our people, the strong as well as the weak were more and more harassed by famine.

2. At that time, the famished ate the shoots of beanseeds growing in the fields and many kinds of herbs unseasoned with salt; also thistles, which, being not well cooked because of the deficiency of firewood, pricked the tongues of those eating them; also horses, asses, and camels, and dogs and rats. The poorer ones ate even the skins of the beasts and seeds of grain found in manure.

3. They endured winter's cold, summer's heat, and heavy rains for God. Their tents became old and torn and rotten from the continuation of rains. Because of this, many of them were covered by only the sky.

4. So like gold thrice proved and purified sevenfold by fire, long predestined by God, I believe, and weighed by such a great calamity, they were cleansed of their sins. For even if the assassin's sword had not failed, many, long agonizing, would have voluntarily completed a martyr's course. Perhaps they borrowed the grace of such a great example from Saint Job, who, purifying his soul by the torments of his body, ever held God fast in mind. Those who fight with the heathen, labor because of God.

5. Granting that God—who creates everything, regulates everything created, sustains everything regulated, and rules by virtue—can destroy or renew whatsoever He wishes, I feel that He assented to the destruction of the heathen after the scourging of the Christians. He permitted it, and the people deserved it, because so many times they cheaply destroyed all things of God.

8. December 30, 1097.

He permitted the Christians to be killed by the Turks, so that the Christians would have the assurance of salvation; the Turks, the perdition of their souls. It pleased God that certain Turks, already predestined for salvation, were baptized by priests. "For those whom He predestined, He also called and glorified."[1]

6. So what then? There were some of our men, as you heard before, who left the siege because it brought so much anguish; others, because of poverty; others, because of cowardice; others, because of fear of death; first the poor and then the rich.

7. Stephen, Count of Blois, withdrew from the siege and returned home to France by sea.[2] Therefore all of us grieved, since he was a very noble man and valiant in arms. On the day following his departure, the city of Antioch was surrendered to the Franks.[3] If he had perserved, he would have rejoiced much in the victory with the rest. This act disgraced him. For a good beginning is not beneficial to anyone unless it be well consummated.[4] I shall cut short many things in the Lord's affairs lest I wander from the truth, because lying about them must be especially guarded against.

8. The siege lasted continuously from this same month of October, as it was mentioned, through the following winter and spring until June. The Turks and Franks alternately staged many attacks and counter-attacks; they overcame and were overcome. Our men, however, triumphed more often than theirs. Once it happened that many of the fleeing Turks fell into the Fernus River, and being submerged in it, they drowned. On the near side of the river, and on the far side, both forces often waged war alternately.

9. Our leaders constructed castles before the city, from which they often rushed forth vigorously to keep the Turks from coming out [of the city]. By this means, the Franks took the pastures from their animals.[5] Nor did they get any help from Armenians outside the city, although these Armenians often did injury to our men.

XVII. The Surrender of the City of Antioch

1. When it pleased God that the labor of His people should be consummated, perhaps pleased by the prayers of those who daily poured out

1. Romans 8:30.
2. June 2, 1098.
3. June 3, 1098.
4. Fulcher here ignores Stephen's return in 1101 when he met delayed martyrdom.
5. One of these fortresses was constructed on a bridge over which the Turks were accustomed to lead their animals to pasture.

supplications and entreaties to Him, out of His compassion He granted that through a fraud of the Turks the city be returned to the Christians in a secret surrender. Hear, therefore, of a fraud, and yet not a fraud.

2. Our Lord appeared to a certain Turk,[1] chosen beforehand by His grace, and said to him: "Arise, thou who sleepest! I command thee to return the city to the Christians." The astonished man concealed that vision in silence.

3. However, a second time, the Lord appeared to him: "Return the city to the Christians," He said, "for I am Christ who command this of thee." Meditating what to do, he went away to his ruler, the prince of Antioch, and made that vision known to him. To him the ruler responded: "You do not wish to obey the phantom, do you, stupid?" Returning, he was afterwards silent.

4. The Lord again appeared to him, saying: "Why hast thou not fulfilled what I ordered thee? Thou must not hesitate, for I, who command this, am Lord of all." No longer doubting, he discreetly negotiated with our men, so that by his zealous plotting they might receive the city.

5. He finished speaking, and gave his son as hostage to Lord Bohemond, to whom he first directed that discourse, and whom he first persuaded.[2] On a certain night, he sent twenty of our men over the wall by means of ladders made of ropes. Without delay, the gate was opened. The Franks, already prepared, entered the city. Forty of our soldiers, who had previously entered by ropes, killed sixty Turks found there, guards of the tower. In a loud voice, altogether the Franks shouted: "God wills it! God wills it!" For this was our signal cry, when we were about to press forward on any enterprise.

6. After hearing this, all the Turks were extremely terrified. Then, when the redness of dawn had paled, the Franks began to go forward to attack the city. When the Turks had first seen Bohemond's red banner on high, furling and unfurling, and the great tumult aroused on all sides, and the Franks running far and wide through the streets with their naked swords and wildly killing people, and had heard their horns sounding on the top of the wall, they began to flee here and there, bewildered. From this scene, many who were able fled into the citadel situated on a cliff.

7. Our rabble wildly seized everything that they found in the streets and houses. But the proved soldiers kept to warfare, in following and killing the Turks.

1. This was Pirus or Firouz whom the Christian sources call a Turk, although the Muslims prefer to consider him as an Armenian.

2. According to other accounts, Bohemond secretly contrived with Firouz to hand over the towers of the city, promising him rewards. Then Bohemond asked the other Christian leaders to let the one who took the city first be given control over it.

8. The fleeing emir of Antioch, Aoxian, was beheaded by a certain rustic Armenian.

He, thereupon, brought the severed head to the Franks.

XVIII. The Finding of the Lance [1]

1. After the city was taken, it happened that a Lance was found by a certain man.[2] When it was discovered in a pit in the ground of Saint Peter's Church, he asserted confidently that, according to the Scriptures, it was the one with which Longinus pierced Christ in the right side. He said that this had been revealed by Saint Andrew the Apostle.

2. When it had been found, and he himself had told this to the Bishop of Puy and to Count Raymond, the Bishop thought it was false, but the Count hoped it was true.

3. Upon hearing this, all the people, rejoicing, glorified God for it, and for almost a hundred days it was held in great veneration by all, and handled gloriously by Count Raymond, who guarded it. Then it happened that many of the clergy and the people hesitated, thinking it was not the Lord's Lance, but another one deceitfully found by that foolish man.

4. A plan was formed, and a three-day fast was fixed and executed with a supplication in prayer to God. After this, they set fire to a heap of wood in the middle of the plain before the town of Archas. This was in the eighth month after the capture of Antioch. After an invocation asking for judgment was made over the fire by priests, the finder of the Lance spontaneously crossed quickly through the middle of the blazing pyre, as he himself had earnestly requested to prove his own truthfulness. After he crossed it, they saw him going forth from the flames as a culprit, burned on the skin, and they knew that he was mortally injured within, just as the end of the affair showed, for on the twelfth day, being burned, he died in anguish.[3]

5. Since everybody had venerated that Lance for the honor and love of God, after judgment was thus accomplished, those who formerly appeared credulous of this culprit, now especially saddened, remained incredulous. Nevertheless, Count Raymond kept it for a long time after that.

---

1. For a detailed study of this question of the Lance, see L. F. Sheffy, "The Use of the Holy Lance in the First Crusade" (unpublished master's thesis, University of Texas, Austin, 1915).

2. Peter Bartholomew.

3. The trial of Peter Bartholomew did not occur until April, 1099. Fulcher anticipates in order to finish the episode of the Lance.

XIX. The Siege of the Christians by the Turks in the City of Antioch

1. On the day after Antioch had been taken, as has been told, an innumerable multitude of Turks surrounded the city in siege. The Sultan, that is, the King of the Persians, had been told by a legation that the Franks were besieging Antioch, and after collecting many people, immediately he sent an army against the Franks. Corbagath[1] was the leader and commander of this people.

2. He had besieged the city of Edessa, which Lord Baldwin possessed at that time, for three weeks;[2] but accomplishing nothing there, he hastened to Antioch to aid Prince Aoxian.

3. Seeing this army, the Franks were more desolate than ever, because punishment for their sins was doubled. For when they had entered the city, many of them had sought out unlawful women without delay.

4. Almost sixty thousand Turks entered by way of a fort on the top of a cliff. These exerted pressure on our men most fiercely in repeated attacks. There was not a pause; filled with great trembling, after leaving the city, they went forth to the siege. The Franks, shut in, remained unbelievably anxious.[3]

XX. The Visions Appearing Below the City

1. Yet the Lord, not unmindful of the Franks, appeared to many. Often they asserted this. Being present, in comforting them, He promised that the people would rejoice in victory. The Lord appeared to a certain cleric fleeing away in fear of death, saying: "Whither, brother, dost thou run?" "I flee," he responded, "lest being unfortunate, I perish. Many flee thus, lest they perish in cruel death."

To him the Lord said: "Flee not, but hasten back and tell the others that I shall be present with them in battle. For, pleased by the prayers of My Mother, I shall propitiate them; but because they have sinned, they shall nearly perish. However, let their hope be strong in Me, and I shall make them to triumph over the Turks. Let them repent and be saved. I am the Lord, who speak to thee." Soon the cleric, having returned, told what he had heard.

2. Meanwhile, many wished to descend by ropes from the wall during the night, and to flee, since many who feared to perish either from starva-

---

1. Kiwam ed-Daula Kerboga, Atabek of Mosul, was the lieutenant of Bark-yarok-Ibn-Malik-Shah, and seems to have exercised a vague suzerainty over the other lesser Turkish emirs of northwestern Syria.

2. May 4 to 25, 1098.

3. The terror of the Turks and Franks was caused by a meteor that Fulcher neglects to mention.

tion or from the sword did this. A certain man, descending, envisioned his dead brother standing near and saying to him: "Whither do you flee, brother? Wait; fear not; for the Lord will be with you in your battle; and your comrades, who have already died on this journey, will fight with you against the Turks." He, astonished at the words of the dead man, stopped and recounted to the others what he had heard.

3. They could no longer bear such anguish. They now had nothing to eat, and they, as well as their horses, were excessively weakened by this. When it pleased the Lord to consummate the labor of His servants, they agreed upon a three-day fast to be carried out with prayers and offerings, so that God might be propitiated by their being penitent and suppliant.

XXI. The Battle Which the Franks Asked of the Turks

1. Meanwhile, after holding council, they announced to the Turks through a certain Peter the Hermit, that unless they peacefully evacuated the region which at one time belonged to the Christians, they would surely begin war against them on the following day. But if they wished it to be done otherwise, war could be waged by five or ten or twenty or by one hundred soldiers chosen from each side, so that with not all fighting at the same time, such a great multitude of people would not die, and the party which overcame the other would take the city and kingdom freely without controversy.

2. This was proposed, but not accepted by the Turks, who, confident in the large number of their people and in their courage, thought that they could overcome and destroy ours.

3. In number, they were estimated to be three hundred thousand altogether, both cavalry and infantry. They knew our knights had been forced to become footmen, weak and helpless.

4. After Peter, the ambassador, returned, the answer was given. After they heard it, the Franks prepared to fight, stopping at nothing, but placing their hope wholly in God.

5. There were many Turkish princes whom they called emirs present. These are Corbagath,[1] Maleducat,[2] Amisoliman,[3] and many others whom it takes too long to name.

---

1. Kerboga of Mosul.
2. Shams el-Muluk Dukak of Damascus.
3. Emir Sulaiman, governor of Aleppo and son of Ilgazi.

XXII. The Preparation for Battle

1. The Frankish princes were: Hugh the Great, Robert, Count of the Normans, Robert, Count of Flanders, Duke Godfrey, Count Raymond, Bohemond, and others of lesser rank. May God bless the soul of Ademar, Bishop of Puy, an apostolic man, who always kindly comforted the people and strengthened them in the Lord.

2. Oh, pious circumstance! On the preceding evening, he ordered by heralds to all the soldiers of the army of God, that each one lay out as much grain as he could, considering the dearness of it, to supply his horse, so that those carrying the riders on the morrow might not become weak from hunger in the hour of battle. It was ordered, and it was done.

3. All having been thus prepared, they went forth to battle from the city in the early morning, which fell four days before the Kalends of July.[1] The banners of the squadrons and lines, conveniently divided into troops and phalanges, went first. Among these were the priests clothed in white vestments, who, weeping for all the people, sang hymns to God, and poured out many prayers devoutly.

4. When a certain Turk, Amirdal by name,[2] a well-proven soldier had seen our people with standards raised coming forth against them, he was exceedingly astonished. And when he had carefully regarded our nobles' standards, which he saw advancing one by one in order, he supposed that the battle would shortly ensue.

5. He had reconnoitred frequently in Antioch, where he had learned this about the Franks. He immediately hastened to Corbagath, and informed him what he had seen, saying: "Why do you amuse yourself with chess? Behold, the Franks are coming!" Corbagath responded to him: "Are they coming to fight?" Amirdal responded: "Up to the present time, I do not know, but wait a little while."

6. When Corbagath also saw the banners of our nobles carried before them in order and the divisions of men, properly ordered, following them, returning quickly, he said: "Behold, the Franks! What do you think?" Amirdal responded: "It is war, I believe, but it is still doubtful. I shall soon recognize to whom these standards, which I see, belong."

7. Looking more closely, he recognized the standard of the Bishop of Puy advancing in the third squadron.

---

1. June 28, 1098.
2. Probably merely emir and not personally identifiable.

Without waiting any longer, he told Corbagath:

"Behold, the Franks are coming; either flee now, or fight well; for I see the standard of the great Pope advancing. Today you may fear to be overcome by those whom you thought could be entirely annihilated."

8. Corbagath said: "I shall send word to the Franks, that what they asked of me yesterday, today I shall grant." Amirdal said, "You have spoken too late." Although he demanded it, he did not obtain what he asked. Amirdal presently

Withdrawing from that place, drove his horse with spurs.

He reflected whether or not to flee; yet he told his comrades

That everybody should fight bravely and hurl arrows.

XXIII. The Battle and the Victory of the Christians and the Flight of the Turks

1. Behold, Hugh the Great and Count Robert the Norman, and also Robert, Count of Flanders, were stationed in the first line of battle for the attack. In the second, Duke Godfrey followed with the Germans and Lotharingians. After those marched the Bishop of Puy and the people of Count Raymond, Gascons and Provençals. Count Raymond himself remained in the city to guard it. Bohemond skilfully led the last division.

2. When the Turks saw that they were being fiercely attacked by the whole army of the Franks, they began to dart out in a scattered fashion, as was their custom, and to hurl arrows. But fear having been let loose from heaven against them, as if the whole world had fallen, all of them took to unrestrained flight, and the Franks chased them with all their might.

3. But because the Franks had few horses and these weak from hunger, they did not take as much booty as they should have. Nevertheless, all the tents remained on the plains, and they found many kinds of things in them, such as gold, silver, coverlets, clothing, utensils, and many other things, which the Turks, in great flight, had left or flung away in their flight, namely, horses, mules, camels, asses, the best helmets, and bows and arrows with quivers.

4. Corbagath, who had slain the Franks many times with such cruel words and threats, fled more swiftly than a deer. But why did he, who had a people so great and so well equipped with horses, flee? Because he strove to fight against God, and the Lord seeing him afar, entirely broke his pomp and strength.

5. Because they had good and swift horses, they escaped, although the slower ones fell into the hands of the Franks. Many of them and of the Saracen infantry were killed. A few of ours were injured. When their women were found in the tents, the Franks did nothing evil to them except pierce their bellies with their lances.

6. Everybody, placed in such great need and distress, blessed and glorified God in a voice of exultation, God, who in the righteousness of His compassion liberated those trusting in Him from such savage enemies. He powerfully scattered them in defeat, after the Christians were almost conquered first. Made wealthy with the substance of those people, they returned pleased to the city.

7. When the venerable city of Antioch was taken,

Eleven times a hundred, if you subtract therefrom twice one,
Then so many were the years of our Lord born of the Virgin
Under the star of Phoebus, twice nine times risen from Gemini.

8. At that time Ademar the Bishop, may his soul enjoy eternal rest, died on the Kalends of August.[1] Amen! Then Hugh the Great, with the good will of the princes, went away to Constantinople; thence to France.[2]

XXIV. The Letter of the Princes Addressed to the Roman Pontiff[1]

1. To the Venerable Urban, Lord and Pope: Bohemond; Raymond, Count of Saint Gilles; Godfrey, Duke of Lorraine; Robert, Count of Normandy; Robert, Count of Flanders; and Eustace, Count of Boulogne, in true subjection to Christ send greetings as faithful servants and sons to their spiritual father.

2. We desire that everything be made known to you: how with the great mercy of God and His most evident support, Antioch was captured by us; how the Turks who had brought many insults on our Lord Jesus Christ, were captured and killed; how we pilgrims of Jesus Christ avenged the harm to Highest God; how we, who besieged the Turks first, were afterwards besieged by Turks coming from Khorassan, Jerusalem, Damascus, and from many other places;[2] and how we were liberated through the mercy of Jesus Christ.

3. After the capture of Nicaea, we subjugated that very great multitude of Turks, as you have heard, on the Kalends of July, as they met us in the Valley of Dorylaeum. We put to flight that great Sulaiman and plundered everything of his, both land and possessions, and all of Romania was acquired and pacified. After these things were done, we came to besiege Antioch. We endured many evils in the siege. Because of the battles with the neighboring Turks and

1. August 1, 1098.
2. Beginning of July, 1098.

---

1. The letter was written September 11, 1098.
2. Pure rhetoric. They never fought the Turks of Khorassan and had little dealings with the Damascenes, and as yet they had had no fighting with the Egyptians of Jerusalem.

heathen rushing in on us so frequently in great numbers, we were more truly said to be besieged by those whom we had besieged in Antioch.

4. At length, after all the battles were over, the Christian faith was exalted at their fortunate outcome in this manner: I, Bohemond, after a compact was made with a certain Turk, who handed over that city to me, placed the ladders on the wall shortly before daybreak three days before the Nones of June. Thus we took the city which had formerly resisted Christ. We killed Aoxian, the tyrant of that city, with many of his soldiers, and kept their wives, sons, and households, along with their gold and silver and all their possessions.

5. However, we were not able to take possession of the citadel of Antioch fortified by the Turks. When, on the morrow, we had wished to attack that citadel, we saw the countless multitude of Turks that we had awaited outside the city for many days to come to wage war with us, running to and fro across the plains. On the third day, they besieged us, and more than a hundred thousand of them entered the aforementioned citadel. From the gate of the citadel, they hoped to get down into the city, part of which was held by them, and part by us.

6. We, however, by standing on another height opposite this citadel, guarded the path descending to the city between both armies, so that they, far more numerous than we, might not break through, and by fighting within and without by night and day, forced them to reënter the citadel gates and return to camp.

7. When they had seen that they were not able to injure us from that side, they so surrounded us on every side that none of our men could leave nor come to us. We were all desolate and discouraged about this. Dying from hunger and many other worries, many of our men killed our famished horses and asses, and ate them.

8. Meanwhile, with the kindest mercy of almighty God coming to our aid and watching over us, we found in the Church of Saint Peter, the first of the Apostles, the Lord's Lance by which our Savior's side was pierced by the hands of Longinus. Saint Andrew, the Apostle, thrice revealed it to a certain servant of God, even showing the place where the Lance lay. We were so comforted and strengthened by his discovery and by so many other divine revelations that some of us who had been discouraged and fearful beforehand, then became courageous and resolute to fight, and encouraged others.

9. Besieged for three weeks and four days, on the eve of the feast day of Apostles Peter and Paul,[3] trusting in God, and confessing all our sins, we went

3. June 28.

out of the gates of the city with all our war equipment. We were so few that they were assured that we were not fighting against them, but were fleeing.

10. All of our men having been prepared, and certain ranks both of foot-soldiers and knights have been arranged in order for battle, with the Lord's Lance we boldly sought where their greater courage and strength lay, and forced them to flee from their most advanced positions. As was their custom, they began to scatter on all sides, occupying hills and paths, and wherever they could they wished to surround us. For they thought they could kill all of us in this manner. But our men having been trained in many battles against their trickery and cleverness, God's grace and mercy so came to our aid that we, who were very few in comparison to them, drove them all close together. Then with God's right hand fighting with us, we forced them so driven together to flee, and to leave their camps with everything in them.

11. Having totally conquered them, having put them to flight for a whole day, and having killed many thousands of their soldiers, we returned to the city glad and cheerful. A certain emir,[4] who was in the citadel with a thousand men, surrendered it to Bohemond, and by his own hand cordially yoked himself to the Christian faith. And so our Lord Jesus Christ transferred all Antioch to the Roman religion and faith.

12. Since it is always customary for some gloom to intervene on happy occasions, that Bishop of Puy, whom you committed to us as your vicar, died on the Kalends of August, after the battle, in which he nobly participated, was finished, and after the city was restored to peace.

13. Now, we, thy sons, deprived of the father committed to us, ask of you, our spiritual father, who initiated this enterprise, and by your sermons made us leave everything, both our lands and whatever was in them, and bade us take up our crosses to follow Christ, and charged us to exalt the Christian name above every name; in order to complete what you urged, we ask you to come to us, and urge whomsoever you can to come with you. For it was here that the name Christian was first employed. After Saint Peter was enthroned in his church which we see daily, those who formerly were called Galileans here first and originally were called Christians. Therefore, what in the world would seem more appropriate than that you, who stand as the head and father of the Christian religion, should come to the principal city and capital of the Christian name, and that you should finish the war, which is yours, in person?

14. We have overcome the Turks and heathens; heretics, however, Greeks

---

4. Ahmed ibn Meruan ("Chronologie," 292.)

and Armenians, Syrians, and Jacobites,[5] we have not been able to overcome. Therefore we enjoin you again and again, our dearest father, that you, the father and head, come to the place of your fatherhood; that you, who are the vicar of Saint Peter, sit on his throne; that you keep us, thy sons, obedient in doing all things rightly; and that you eradicate and destroy all heresies, of whatever nature they be, with your authority and with our strength. And thus with us may you bring about the way of Jesus Christ begun by us and suggested first by you; may you even open the gates both to Jerusalem and to the liberated Sepulchre of the Lord for us; and may you make the Christian name be exalted above every name. If you come to us and accomplish with us the course begun through you, the whole world will be obedient to you. May God who lives and reigns in ages without end suffer you to do it. Amen.

XXV. The Invasion of the Cities. The Siege Undertaken at Archas and the Journey and Arrival of the Franks at Jerusalem

1. When our men and their horses, who had been wearied by much labor for many days, were refreshed by food and rest for four months at Antioch, they resumed their former strength. Having arranged a plan, one part of the army went into inner Syria, desiring to delay the march to Jerusalem. In this, Bohemond and Count Raymond were the leaders.[1] Other princes remained in the vicinity of Antioch.

2. These two men, with their people, seized Barra[2] and Marra,[3] by a courageous attack. After the former city had been captured quickly and completely depopulated by the slaughter of its citizens and everything which they found there had been seized, they hastened to the other city. Here, when the siege had lasted twenty days,[4] our people suffered excessive hunger. I shudder to tell that many of our people, harassed by the madness of excessive hunger, cut pieces from the buttocks of the Saracens already dead there, which they cooked, but when it was not yet roasted enough by the fire, they devoured it with savage mouth. So the besiegers rather than the besieged were tormented.

3. Meanwhile, after they had made what machines they could, and moved them to the wall, in an assault of great boldness, with God favoring, the

---

5. Syrians are Greek Orthodox who celebrate service in Syriac. Jacobites are a monophysite sect in Syria, much like the Copts of Egypt, and are named for their founder Jacobus Baradaeus.

---

1. According to the *Gesta*, chapter 30, this expedition was begun by Raymond Pilet, one of Count Raymond's men, but Count Raymond had to rescue him.

2. Barra (Albara) was taken September 25, 1098.

3. The Franks arrived at Marra (Ma'arrat al-Nu'man) November 27, 1098.

4. The siege ended December 11, 1098, but the Franks remained there until January 13, 1099.

Franks entered over the top of the wall. On that day and the following, they killed all the Saracens from the greatest to the least, and plundered all their substance.

4. This city having been thus destroyed, Bohemond returned to Antioch, from which he drove out the men whom Count Raymond had left there to guard his section of the city. Afterwards he possessed this city with the whole province. For he said that it was through his promises and through his negotiations that it had been acquired.

5. Count Raymond, after Tancred joined him, continued the journey to Jerusalem already begun. Also the Norman Count joined this army on the second day after the departure from captured Marra.

6. In the year 1099 from the Incarnation of the Lord, they set out to the aforementioned town of Archas,[5] situated at the foot of Mount Lebanon, which Aracaeus, the son of Canaan, the nephew of Noah,[6] founded. But because it was most difficult to take, after laboring for almost five weeks in its siege, they accomplished nothing.

7. Duke Godfrey and Robert, Count of Flanders, followed not far after the army. They were besieging Gibellum,[7] when, upon the arrival of messengers, they had to hasten to the others. For this reason, they left Gibellum immediately, and because of the call for aid, they hastened to join the army. But the battle for which they had been summoned did not materialize. They stayed to take part in the siege [of Archas].[8]

8. In that siege, Anselm of Ribemont,[9] a vigorous soldier, died of a blow from a stone.

9. Having held council, they decided that to stay there and not take the town would do great harm to the whole army. It would be advantageous, some said, to abandon the siege and take up the march at a time when the road was not crowded with merchants, and during the harvest season. For as they marched along, they could live on the ripened harvests prepared for their subsistence by God, under Whose leadership they would reach the much desired end of their pilgrimage. This plan was accepted and undertaken.

10. The tents having been packed, they went away and crossed through

5. February 14, 1099.

6. Reference to Genesis 10:15–17.

7. Gibellum = Gabala, port in Northern Syria near St. Simeon, and not to be confused with Gibelet (Djubail) south of Tripoli.

8. While besieging Archas, Raymond and Robert of Normandy heard that a Turkish army was coming to attack them; so they requested Godfrey to come to their aid. The alarm turned out to be a false rumor, and Godfrey was angry because he had given up the siege of Gibellum for nothing.

9. Anselm of Ribemont, vassal of the Archbishop of Rheims; his letters to his lord Manasses are among the most important sources for the Crusades. He died February 25, 1099.

the city of Tripoli. After they had passed through this city, they came to the town of Gibelet.[10] It was April, and already they were living off the harvests. Thence, going forward and passing near the city of Beirut,[11] they came upon another city which we read as Sidon[12] by its name in the land of Phoenicia; which Sidon, a son of Canaan, founded, whence came the Sidonians. From Sidon to Sarepta. From here, they came to Tyre,[13] a very excellent city, from which Apollo came, about whom we have read. About these two cities, the Gospel says: "into the provinces of Tyre and Sidon."[14] Now, the inhabitants of the region called the former Sagitta, and the other Sur. For it was called Soor in Hebrew.

11. Thence to the fortress named Ziph, in the sixth mile from Ptolemais. After this, they crossed over to Ptolemais, formerly called Accon,[15] which certain mistaken ones of our men thought to be Acharon. But the city of Acharon is in the land of the Philistines near Ascalon, between Jamnia[16] and Azot. In truth Accon, that is Ptolemais, has Mount Carmel on the south. Crossing next to it, they left to the right the city called Caypha.[17] After these, we came close to Dora, then to Caesarea of Palestine, which in ancient times was called by another name of Turris Stratonis. Here Herod, named Agrippa, the nephew of that Herod in whose time Christ was born, died unhappily, consumed by worms.

12. Then they left the maritime region on the right and the town of Arsur, and they proceeded through a city, Rama or Aramathea by name, from which the Saracen inhabitants had fled on the day before the Franks arrived. Here they found much grain which they loaded on their beasts of burden and carried all the way to Jerusalem.

13. After a delay of four days there,[18] when they had appointed the bishop of the Church of Saint George,[19] and had placed men on guard in the citadels of the city, they went forward on their journey to Jerusalem. On that day they marched as far as the fortress, which was called Emmaus,[20] near which was Modin, the city of the Maccabees.

10. They arrived in Gibelet (Djubail), ancient Byblos (whence Bible), March 2, and the siege lasted until March 11.

11. The Franks arrived in Beirut, ancient Berytus, May 18 or 19, 1099.

12. They came to Sidon (Saida), ancient Phoenician city, May 20.

13. Tyre = Tyr, Sur, Phoenician city.

14. Matthew 15:21.

15. The Franks stayed May 24–25 in Acre (Accon), St. Jean d'Acre, ancient Ptolemais.

16. Jamnia = Ibelin.

17. Caypha = Haifa.

18. The Franks remained from June 2 to June 6, 1099, in Rama (Ramleh). Fulcher errs in identifying Rama as Aramathea. (Hagenmeyer, *Historia*, Bk. 1, Ch. 25, 12, n. 41.)

19. Robert de Rouen. ("Chronologie," 382.)

20. Emmaus = Amwas.

14. On the following night, one hundred of the truest soldiers mounted their horses. When the dawn grew bright, they came close to Jerusalem, and hastened all the way to Bethlehem. Of these, one was Tancred, and another one was Baldwin.[21] When the Christians, evidently Greeks and Syrians, who frequently reconnoitred there, found that the Franks had come, they were especially filled with great joy. Yet at first they did not know what race they were, thinking them to be either Turks or Arabs.

15. But when they looked at them more closely face to face, they did not doubt that they were Franks. Immediately, when they had gladly taken up their crosses and banners, they proceeded to meet the Franks with weeping and pious singing: with weeping, because they feared lest such a small number of people at one time or other would be very easily slain by such a great multitude of heathen, whom they knew to be in their own land; with singing, because they wished joy to those whom they had desired to come for a long time, those who they knew would raise Christianity again to its proper and former honor, after it had been ruined by the wicked for such a long time.

16. A consecrated public thanksgiving to God was performed there in the Church of the Blessed Mary. When they had visited the place where Christ was born, and after they had given the kiss of peace to the Syrians, they returned quickly to the holy city of Jerusalem.

17. Behold! there was the army following. Gabaon,[22] which was about five and three-quarters miles from Jerusalem, had been passed on the left. Here Joshua had commanded the sun and the moon. They approached the city. When the advance guard bearing the banners aloft had shown them to the citizens, straightway the enemy within came out against them. But those who had so hastily come out, were soon driven hastily back into the city.

June was now warmed by the heat of its seventh sun,
When the Franks surrounded Jerusalem in siege.

XXVI. *The Situation of Jerusalem*

1. The city of Jerusalem is situated in a mountainous region, lacking in streams, woods, and springs, with the exception of the Pool of Siloam, which is a bowshot from the city. Here there is sufficient water sometimes, but occasionally the supply is reduced by drawing off the water.[1] This little pool is in the valley at the foot of Mount Zion, in the course of the brook Cedron

21. Baldwin de Bourg, cousin of Godfrey, later became Baldwin II.
22. Gabaon = Gibeon.

---

1. Concerning the Pool of Siloam, see Duncalf, *Capture of Jerusalem*, 19, n. 9.

which, in the winter time, is accustomed to flow through the middle of the Valley of Jehosophat.

2. Many cisterns in the city, which are reserved for winter rains, are kept filled with an abundance of water. Many, from which man and beast are refreshed, are found outside the city also.

3. This city was made of modest size in its extent, so that neither because of its smallness nor because of its magnitude does it offend anyone. Within, it is as wide from wall to wall as a bow can shoot an arrow four times. On the west there is the Tower of David, at the angle of two walls of the city; on the south is Mount Zion, a little closer than a bowshot; to the east is the Mount of Olives, a mile from the city.

4. The Tower of David is of solid masonry up to the middle, constructed of large square stones sealed with molten lead. If it were well supplied with rations for soldiers, fifteen or twenty men could defend it from every attack of the enemy.

5. In this city is the Temple of the Lord, a round structure, at the place where Solomon had formerly built one which was more wonderful. Although in no wise can this Temple be compared to that former one, yet it is most beautifully made and of marvelous workmanship.

6. The Church of the Lord's Sepulchre, also round in form, was never covered, but through a wide opening which was skilfully devised by a wise architect, the Sepulchre can always be seen from above.[2]

7. I am not able, nor do I dare to assert, nor am I wise enough to tell many things that are kept therein, some of which are there now, and others already gone, lest I mislead those who hear of or read about these things. In the middle of the Temple, when we first entered it, and for almost fifteen years afterward, we saw kept a certain native rock. They claimed to know by divination that the Ark of the Covenant of the Lord with the urn and with the tablets of Moses were inclosed and sealed in it. Josiah, King of Judah, ordered it to be placed there, saying: "You will in no wise carry it from that place." For he saw its future captivity.

8. But that is contrary to what we read in the writings of Jeremiah in the second book of the Maccabees, because Jeremiah himself hid it in Arabia, saying that it was in no wise to be found, until many nations were gathered together. He was a contemporary of the King Josiah; although the king's life came to an end before Jeremiah died.

9. They also said that an Angel of the Lord had stood on the aforemen-

---

2. The Church of the Lord's Sepulchre was the most important church in all Christendom. For a description of it, see "Felix Fabri," I, part 2, *Palestine Pilgrims' Text Society*, ed. Aubrey Stewart (London, 1896).

tioned rock and that people had perished because of an enumeration foolishly made by David and displeasing to the Lord. Since that rock disfigured the Temple of the Lord, afterwards it was entirely covered and encased in marble. Its present position is under the altar where the priest performs the rituals. All the Saracens had greatly revered this Temple of the Lord. Here they made their prayers more gladly than elsewhere, although they wasted them, since in idolatry they made them in the name of Mohammed. They permitted no Christian to enter there.

10. Another temple, which is said to be Solomon's, is large and marvelous. However, it is not that same one which Solomon built. Because of our poverty, it could not be maintained in the state in which we found it; and because of this, it is now destroyed in great part.

11. They had gutters in the streets of the city, in which all dirt was washed away in the rainy season.

12. The Emperor Aelius Hadrian decorated this city wonderfully, and adorned the streets beautifully with pavements. Jerusalem was called Aelia in his honor. Because of these and other such things, it is a venerated and glorious city.

XXVII. The Siege of the City of Jerusalem

1. When the Franks viewed the city, and saw that it would be difficult to take, our princes ordered wooden ladders to be made. By erecting them against the wall they hoped to scale it, and by a fierce attack enter the city, with God helping.

2. After they had done this, when the leaders gave the signal and the trumpets sounded, in morning's bright light of the seventh day following[1] they rushed upon the city from all sides in an astonishing attack. But when they had rushed upon it until the sixth hour of the day, and were unable to enter by means of the scaling ladders because there were few of them, they sadly abandoned the assault.

3. After consultation,[2] craftsmen were ordered to make machines, so that by moving them to the walls they might, with God's aid, obtain the desired end. So this was done.

4. Meanwhile they suffered lack of neither bread nor meat; but, because that place was dry, unirrigated, and without rivers, both the men and the beasts of burden were very much in need of water to drink. This necessity

1. June 13, 1099.
2. June 15.

forced them to seek water at a distance, and daily they laboriously carried it in skins from four or five miles to the siege.

5. After the machines were prepared, namely, the battering-rams and the sows, they again prepared to assail the city. In addition to other kinds of siege craft, they constructed a tower from small pieces of wood, because large pieces could not be secured in those regions. When the order was given, they carried the tower piecemeal to a corner of the city. Early in the same morning, when they had gathered the machines and other auxiliary weapons, they very quickly erected the tower in compact shape not far from the wall. After it was set up and well covered by hides on the outside, by pushing it they slowly moved it nearer to the wall.

6. Then a few but brave soldiers, at a signal from the horn, climbed on the tower. Nevertheless the Saracens defended themselves from these soldiers and, with slings, hurled firebrands dipped in oil and grease at the tower and at the soldiers, who were in it. Thereafter death was present and sudden for many on both sides.

7. From their position on Mount Zion, Count Raymond and his men likewise made a great assault with their machines. From another position, where Duke Godfrey, Robert, Count of the Normans, and Robert of Flanders, were situated, an even greater assault was made on the wall. This was what was done on that day.

8. On the following day, at the blast of the trumpets, they undertook the same work more vigorously, so that by hammering in one place with the battering-rams, they breached the wall. The Saracens had suspended two beams before the battlement and secured them by ropes as a protection against the stones hurled at them by their assailants. But what they did for their advantage later turned to their detriment, with God's providence. For when the tower was moved to the wall, the ropes, by which the aforesaid beams were suspended, were cut by falchions, and the Franks constructed a bridge for themselves out of the same timber, which they cleverly extended from the tower to the wall.

9. Already one stone tower on the wall, at which those working our machines had thrown flaming firebrands, was afire. The fire, little by little replenished by the wooden material in the tower, produced so much smoke and flame that not one of the citizens on guard could remain near it.

10. Then the Franks entered the city magnificently at the noonday hour on Friday,[3] the day of the week when Christ redeemed the whole world on the

3. July 15, 1099.

cross. With trumpets sounding and with everything in an uproar, exclaiming: "Help, God!" they vigorously pushed into the city, and straightway raised the banner on the top of the wall. All the heathen, completely terrified, changed their boldness to swift flight through the narrow streets of the quarters. The more quickly they fled, the more quickly were they put to flight.

11. Count Raymond and his men, who were bravely assailing the city in another section, did not perceive this until they saw the Saracens jumping from the top of the wall. Seeing this, they joyfully ran to the city as quickly as they could, and helped the others pursue and kill the wicked enemy.

12. Then some, both Arabs and Ethiopians, fled into the Tower of David; others shut themselves in the Temple of the Lord and of Solomon, where in the halls a very great attack was made on them. Nowhere was there a place where the Saracens could escape the swordsmen.

13. On the top of Solomon's Temple, to which they had climbed in fleeing, many were shot to death with arrows and cast down headlong from the roof. Within this Temple about ten thousand[4] were beheaded. If you had been there, your feet would have been stained up to the ankles with the blood of the slain. What more shall I tell? Not one of them was allowed to live. They did not spare the women and children.

XXVIII. The Spoils Which the Christians Took

1. After they had discovered the cleverness of the Saracens, it was an extraordinary thing to see our squires and poorer people split the bellies of those dead Saracens, so that they might pick out besants[1] from their intestines, which they had swallowed down their horrible gullets while alive. After several days, they made a great heap of their bodies and burned them to ashes, and in these ashes they found the gold more easily.

2. Tancred rushed into the Temple of the Lord, and seized much of the gold and silver and precious stones. But he restored it, and returned everything or something of equal value to its holy place. I say "holy," although nothing divine was practised there at the time when the Saracens exercised their form of idolatry in religious ritual and never allowed a single Christian to enter.

3. With drawn swords, our people ran through the city;

---

4. Albert of Aix says three hundred, and Hagenmeyer accepts this number, not Fulcher's.

---

1. Besants: gold coins, so called because they were originally Byzantine. Saracen besants were dinars of the same value as the Byzantine coins.

Nor did they spare anyone, not even those pleading for mercy.
The crowd was struck to the ground, just as rotten fruit
Falls from shaken branches, and acorns from a wind-blown oak.

XXIX. The Sojourn of the Christians in the City

1. After this great massacre, they entered the homes of the citizens, seizing whatever they found in them. It was done systematically, so that whoever had entered the home first, whether he was rich or poor, was not to be harmed by anyone else in any way. He was to have and to hold the house or palace and whatever he had found in it entirely as his own. Since they mutually agreed to maintain this rule, many poor men became rich.

2. Then, going to the Sepulchre of the Lord and His glorious Temple, the clerics and also the laity, singing a new song[1] unto the Lord in a high-sounding voice of exultation, and making offerings and most humble supplications, joyously visited the Holy Place as they had so long desired to do.

3. Oh, time so longed for! Oh, time remembered among all others! Oh, deed to be preferred before all deeds! Truly longed for, since it had always been desired by all worshippers of the Catholic faith with an inward yearning of the soul. This was the place, where the Creator of all creatures, God made man, in His manifold mercy for the human race, brought the gift of spiritual rebirth. Here He was born, died, and rose. Cleansed from the contagion of the heathen inhabiting it at one time or another, so long contaminated by their superstition, it was restored to its former rank by those believing and trusting in Him.

4. And truly memorable and rightly remembered, because those things which the Lord God our Jesus Christ, as a man abiding among men on earth, practised and taught have often been recalled and repeated in doctrines. And, likewise, what the Lord wished to be fulfilled, I believe, by this people so dear, both His disciple and servant and predestined for this task, will resound and continue in a memorial of all the languages of the universe to the end of the ages.

XXX. The Creation of King and Patriarch of Jerusalem and the Finding of the Lord's Cross

1. In the thousand and one hundred year less one
From the illustrious Lord's birth of the Virgin,

---

1. Reference to Psalms 33:3, 96:1.

When Phoebus had lighted July fifteen times,[1]
The Franks captured Jerusalem by strength of power;
And soon made Godfrey the ruler of the land.

All the people of the army of the Lord elected him because of his noble excellence, the proven worth of his military service, his patient temperance, and also the elegance of his manners, as the ruler of the kingdom in the Holy City, to preserve and govern it.

2. At that time canons were appointed to serve in the Church of the Lord's Sepulchre and in His Temple. Then they decided not to elect a patriarch until they had asked the Roman Pope whom he wished to nominate.[2]

3. Meanwhile about five hundred Turks, Arabs, and black Ethiopians, who had fled into the Tower of David, requested Count Raymond, who sojourned near that tower, to permit as many as were alive to go away provided they leave their money in the tower. He granted this, and from that place they went to Ascalon.

4. It was pleasing to God at that time, that a small piece of the Lord's Cross was found in a hidden place.[3] From ancient times until now it had been concealed by religious men, and now, God being willing, it was revealed by a certain Syrian. He, with his father as conspirator, had carefully concealed and guarded it there. This particle, reshaped in the style of a cross and artistically decorated with gold and silver, was first carried to the Lord's Sepulchre and then to the Temple joyfully, with singing and giving thanks to God, who for so many days had preserved this treasure, His own and ours.

XXXI. The Arrival and Attack of the Pagans and the Victory of the Christians

1. The king of Babylon[1] and the leader of his army, Lavedal by name,[2] heard that the Franks already had come into their territory, and were subduing the Babylonian kingdom for themselves. After a multitude of Turks, Arabs, and Ethiopians had assembled, they came to wage war on the Franks. When messengers reported that Jerusalem had been so fiercely captured, the

1. The date Fulcher gives here is that of the capture of Jerusalem; Godfrey was made prince on July 22.
2. Arnulf of Chocques, the chaplain of Robert of Normandy, was elected Patriarch pro tem. (See David, *Robert Curthose*, 217–220.)
3. The particle was found August 5, 1099.

1. Babylon always means Cairo, but according to Beatrice A. Lees, *Anonymi Gesta Francorum et Aliorum Hierosolymitanorum* (Oxford, 1924), p. 117, the name, strictly speaking, refers to the old fortress at some distance from modern Cairo, which is said to have been built by one of the later Pharaohs to receive the Babylonian mercenaries in the Egyptian service.
2. Lavedal = Shah-an-Shah el-Afdal (1094–1121), Emir or Vizier of the Egyptian Caliph, Mustali.

unworthy Babylonian leader hastened either to do battle with them or to besiege them while they were within that city.

2. When the Franks learned this, they undertook a plan of great boldness. Turning toward Ascalon and carrying with them the wood of the aforementioned life-giving Cross, they directed their army against the usurpers [of the land rightfully belonging to the Christians].

3. On a certain day when the Franks were awaiting battle in the vicinity of Ascalon, they found there a considerable booty of oxen, camels, sheep, and goats. And with the sunset, when they had assembled this quarry close to the tents, our leaders, under edict, ordered them not to take it with them on the morrow, when they thought the battle would take place, so that they would be relieved of any burden and ready to fight.

4. Morning came, and through scouts they learned that the heathen were approaching. After knowing this, the tribunes and centurions, with their men formed in wings and phalanges, so as to carry on battle most skilfully, advanced boldly, with banners aloft, against the enemy.

5. You should have seen the animals which had been captured, as if at a signal from the leaders, march in a straight line on the left and right of the battle lines, although herded by no one, so that many of the heathens from a distance, seeing them marching with our soldiers, thought all were the Frankish army.

6. Our foes were countless. When they advanced toward our lines, the Arabs were spread out in a two-pointed formation like the horns of a stag, for they intended to surround us in the rear. Later, Duke Godfrey protected the rear guard by going to its aid with a band of knights in close formation. The other leaders went ahead, some in the first, some in the second line.

7. But when on both sides enemy had approached enemy within a stone's throw or less, our footsoldiers shot arrows into their extended lines. Most fittingly, lances soon followed the arrows, and our horsemen, as if all had mutually agreed on it under oath, rushed upon them in fierce attack. Their beasts were not swift enough in the race, and they constantly overturned on their riders, so that in the space of a few hours many corpses were white in death.

8. Many of their frightened men climbed to the tops of the trees. But there, too, they were shot with arrows and mortally wounded, and unhappily fell to the ground. By penetrating thrusts from all sides, the Saracens were annihilated. Their tents were rent. Those who escaped fled as far as the walls of Ascalon, which lies seven hundred and twenty stadia from Jerusalem.

9. In the first line their leader, Lavedal, although he had previously held the Franks in contempt, turned his back in swift flight. Against his will, he left

them his tent, which was pitched like the others and contained much money. The Franks, pleased with victory, returned and joined in giving thanks to the Lord.[3]

10. They entered the tents of the Saracens and found in them great riches, gold, silver, mantles, clothes, and precious stones. Twelve of these are named as follows: jasper, sapphire, chalcedony, emerald, sardonyx, sardius, chrysolite, beryl, topaz, chrysoprase, jacinth, and amethyst. They also found vessels and many kinds of useful things, such as golden helmets, the finest rings, wonderful swords, grain, flour, and many other things.

11. They spent the night there and, always on watch, guarded themselves well. For on the following day they thought the fighting would be renewed by the Saracens, but these, exceedingly terrified, had fled on the same night. The next morning, when scouts had discovered this, in voices filled with praise they blessed and glorified God, who permitted so many thousands of the heathen to be routed by a scant army of Christians. "Blessed be the Lord, who hath not given us as a prey to their teeth!"[4] "Blessed is the nation whose God is the Lord!"[5]

12. Had not those same Babylonians threatened, saying: "Let us go and seize Jerusalem with the Franks enclosed therein! After all of them have been killed, let us wipe out that Sepulchre so precious to them and hurl the very stones of the building outside the city, so that no further deceit can ever come from that place!" But with God's mercy, this was turned to nought. The Franks loaded the horses and camels with the money of the Saracens. Since they could not carry the tents and the many javelins and bows and arrows thrown on the fields, they put them all in the fire. Thereafter, they returned to Jerusalem rejoicing.

XXXII. The Return of the Princes to Their Native Lands

1. After these things were done, it pleased certain men to return to their native lands. And after they had been immersed in the Jordan River and had gathered branches of palms from Jericho, in what was said to be Abraham's garden, Robert, Count of the Normans, and Robert, Count of Flanders, sailed to Constantinople. From there, they returned to France to their own people.[1] Raymond returned as far as Laodicaea of Syria, and leaving his

3. August 12, 1099.
4. Psalms 124:6.
5. Psalms 33:12.

1. This was the end of August, 1099.

wife[2] there, went on to Constantinople. Duke Godfrey, keeping Tancred and several others with himself, ruled the kingdom of Jerusalem, which he had undertaken to maintain with the general consent of all.

XXXIII. Bohemond and Baldwin and Their Sojourn in Other Parts

1. When Lord Bohemond, the prince of Antioch, who was a wise and active man, and Lord Baldwin, brother of Godfrey, who ruled the city of Edessa and the neighboring land across the Euphrates River, had heard that Jerusalem had been captured by their colleagues who had preceded them, they were very happy and gave praise and prayers to God.

2. Those who had preceded them with speed on the journey had worked well and usefully, but there is no doubt that Bohemond and Baldwin and their comrades, although they would follow them later, would share the same glory.

3. It was now necessary for the land and the cities taken from the Turks to be carefully guarded, because if everybody, in going to Jerusalem, abandoned the land, it, perchance, might be retaken in a surprise attack by the Turks, now driven back as far as Persia. If this should happen, great harm would befall all the Franks, both those going and those returning. Perhaps divine providence delayed Bohemond and Baldwin, judging that they would be more useful in what they were to do than in what they had already done.

4. Oh, how often, meanwhile, was that same Baldwin wearied in battles with the Turks in the regions of Mesopotamia! How many of their heads had been cut off there none could say. Often it happened that with a few of his own people, he fought against a great multitude of theirs and with the aid of God rejoiced in triumph.

5. But when Bohemond had sent messengers to him suggesting that both of them with their men finish the unfulfilled journey to Jerusalem, Baldwin disposed of his affairs at the first opportunity and prepared to go.[1]

6. Hearing that the Turks had invaded one corner of his country, he put off the undertaking, and as he had not yet assembled his small army, he approached the enemy with only a few men. Thinking that he had departed on the journey, the enemy were unconcerned in their tents on a certain day, when they saw the white standard which Baldwin carried. They were terrified

2. This was Raymond's third wife, who was Elvira, daughter of Alfonse VI of Leon and Castile and his mistress, Ximene.

1. This was in November 1099.

and fled as quickly as possible. When he saw that he had put them to flight
with so few men, he returned to the former undertaking.

7. Beginning the journey, with Antioch on the right, Baldwin came to
Laodicaea, where the supplies for the journey were bought, and the pack
saddles were reloaded. We went away in the month of November. When we
had passed by Gibellum, we came upon Bohemond lodged in his tents before
a certain town, named Valenia.

8. There was with him a certain Archbishop of Pisa, Daimbert by name,[2]
who had sailed to the port of Laodicaea with certain Tuscans and Italians,
and there they were waiting to go with us. There was present a certain bishop
from Apulia.[3] With Lord Baldwin, there was a third bishop.[4] We estimated
these gathered together in a friendly manner to be twenty-five thousand of
both sexes; both footsoldiers and knights.

9. When we had entered the lands of the Saracens, we could secure
neither bread nor anything edible from the inhabitants, who were hostile to
us. There was no one who would give or sell, and because more and more
of our supplies were consumed, many were distressed by hunger. Also the
horses and beasts of burden, with insufficient grain, were especially troubled
with double pain—they were moving, but were not eating.

10. Then we found certain crops, on the cultivated fields through which
we passed, that the people called "honey-cane" [sugar-cane], almost like reeds.
The name was composed of "cane" and "honey"; whence came wood-honey
(I think it was called), because it was ingeniously procured from this crop.
We hungry people chewed these stalks all day because of their taste of honey,
but with little satisfaction.

11. So, for love of God, we suffered these things and many others, such
as hunger, cold, and excessive rains. Some wanting food ate even horses,
asses, and camels. Also, we were very often racked by excessive cold and frequent rainstorms. The sun's heat was not great enough to dry thoroughly our
drenched, shabby clothes, since a continuation of rainstorms would harass us
for four or five days.

12. I saw many, without tents, die from the coldness of the rainstorms. I,
Fulcher of Chartres, who was present with them, saw some of both sexes and

2. Daimbert was ordained by the anti-Pope, Wibert, but soon returned to the side of
Urban. Bohemond favored him, because he wished to win the favor of the Pope against Alexius.
Daimbert was the first Archbishop of Pisa.

3. For a discussion of his identity, see Hagenmeyer, *Historia*, bk. 1, ch. 33, 8, n. 24.

4. This third bishop was Benedict, Archbishop of Edessa.

very many beasts die from this most frigid rain. It is long to tell and perhaps tedious to hear, since no grief nor pain escaped the people of God.

13. Often some were killed by the Saracens lying in ambush around the narrow passages, or were abducted by them when they were seeking victuals. You would see soldiers of noble birth become footsoldiers, their horses having been lost in some way. Since they needed beasts of burden, you would see goats and wethers, which they had taken from the Saracens, become very tired from the packs placed on them and their backs chafed from the weight of the load.

14. Only twice on the way, from the Tripolitans and the Caesareans, did we have grain, and that at a very dear price. It is evident that no one can achieve anything great without tremendous effort. It was a great event when we came to Jerusalem.

15. With the visit to this city, our labor of long duration was consummated. When we had looked at the most desired Holy of Holies, we were filled with an immense joy. Oh, how many times we recalled to memory that prophecy of David in which he said: "We shall worship in the place where His feet have stood!"[5] Doubtless the satisfaction which we enjoyed was likewise experienced by ever so many others. Truly, we went up "whither the tribes go up, the tribes of the Lord to testify in His name, in His sanctuary."[6]

16. On that day when we entered Jerusalem, its winter descent being completed, the sun resumed its upward course.[7]

17. After we had visited the Sepulchre of the Lord and His glorious Temple and all the other holy places, on the fourth day[8] we went to Bethlehem, so that on the same night of the annual celebration of the Lord's Nativity we might be present and keep vigil with prayers in the stall where the reverend Mary Mother gave birth to Jesus.

18. After the appropriate religious rites had been performed that night and the third mass observed, in the third hour of the day we left for Jerusalem.

19. Oh, what a stench there was at that time around the walls of the city, within and without, from the dead bodies of the Saracens rotting there until then. Our colleagues had massacred them in the captured city, and wherever they had followed them.

20. When we and our beasts of burden had been refreshed for a rather long time with the necessary rest,[9] and when the Duke and the other leaders had chosen the patriarch, that is, the aforementioned Lord Daimbert, in the

5. Psalms 132:7.
6. Psalms 122:4.
7. December 21, 1099.
8. December 24.
9. December 26 to 31, 1099. Again, Fulcher fails to mention Arnulf, provisional patriarch.

Church of the Holy Sepulchre, our supplies were replenished and our beasts of burden reloaded. On our way back, we went down to the Jordan River.

21. It pleased certain ones in the army lately arrived to remain in Jerusalem, and certain ones of the first army to go with us. Duke Godfrey, as formerly, actively governed the land of Jerusalem.

22. Urban, the venerated pontiff of Rome,

When he was so ill on the third of the Ides of August, passed away.[10]

XXXIV. The Return of Duke Bohemond and Count Baldwin to Their Own People

1. In the year 1100 from the Lord's Incarnation, on the first day of the year, we cut palm branches in Jericho to carry with us, as is the custom, and on the second day we commenced the return journey.

2. It pleased our leaders to go through the city of Tiberias close to the sea. This sea of fresh water is eighteen miles long and five miles wide. Then we went through Caesarea Philippi, which is called Banyas in the Syrian language, situated at the foot of Mount Lebanon. Here two springs emerge, from which the Jordan River rises, whose course runs through the Sea of Galilee into the Dead Sea.

3. This sea, called Genesareth,[1] is forty stadia in breadth and one hundred stadia in length, according to Josephus. The bed of the Jordan River carries it to the sea which is called the Dead, because it produces no living thing. This sea, called Asphaltites, is believed to be without a bottom, because cities, such as Sodom and Gomorrha, were thrown into the abyss there.

4. I was making conjectures about these springs rather shrewdly, in the manner of Saint Jerome, whose book on the Prophet Amos I have read, and I concluded that Dan is in the borders of the land of Judah, where Banyas is now, and that the tribe of Dan built the city there, which they called Dan in his honor. For this reason, I believe that that spring is called Dan and the other, which joins it, Jor.

5. We came to a very strong city, surrounded by remarkable walls, which they called Baalbek,[2] founded by Solomon and called Thadmor by him.[3] It is

---

10. Fulcher is in error here; most authoritative sources cite July 29 as the day of Urban's death.

---

1. Sea of Galilee.

2. They arrived at Baalbek January 18, 1100.

3. As Krey, *First Crusade*, 298 n. 26, points out, Fulcher's identifying Baalbek as Thadmor is an error. Thadmor is Palmyra, east from Damascus. Krey says that Fulcher applied to Baalbek the descriptions he had heard of Palmyra.

located a two days' journey from upper Syria and six days' journey from the great Babylon and about a day's journey from the Euphrates. The Greeks call it Palmyra. Springs and wells are especially abundant in that place, but on the land below water is found nowhere.

6. Here, nearly four hundred Damascene Turkish soldiers came to meet us. And when they learned that we were unarmed and especially weary from labor, they thought that we were weak. If Lord Baldwin had not wisely and cautiously commanded the rear guard on that day, they would have killed many of our men. On account of excessive rains, both bows and arrows had failed them because, in those places, they were fitted together with glue. Bohemond commanded the first phalanx. With God helping, they gained nothing from us.

7. Then we pitched our camp before Baalbek. On the following day,[4] approaching the sea more closely, we passed through the cities of Tortosa and Laodicaea. We again met Count Raymond, whom we had left there. Since grain was dear, we found nothing there to buy on which we could live. Because of this, we hastened without delay to Edessa.[5]

XXXV. The Capture of Duke Bohemond

1. Bohemond first came to Antioch, where he was joyously received by his own people. Then for six months he occupied his kingdom, as formerly.

2. In the following month of July, with a few of his men, he arrived at the city called Melitene, which Gabriel[1] gave to him as its defender, after a compact of mutual friendship between them was already made through messengers. There a certain emir, Danisman by name,[2] met him with a great tribe of Turks and strove to intercept Bohemond as he marched undefended.

3. Not far from Melitene these wicked people, concealed in ambush, sprang on him from all sides. Our men, not daring to fight, because they were few, immediately scattered and fled. The Turks killed many of them and took all their money. They also seized Bohemond and carried him into captivity.[3]

4. When this misfortune was disclosed by those who had escaped, the desolation of our people waxed great. But Duke Baldwin of the city of Edessa,

---

4. January 26, 1100.
5. They arrived at Edessa February 10, 1100.

---

1. Gabriel of Melitene, father-in-law of Baldwin I.
2. Malik Gasi Ahmed Kumushtakin ibn Danishmend, emir of Sivas, lord of Paphlygonia and Cappadocia.
3. August 15, 1100.

with as many Franks as he could gather together from Edessa and Antioch, went off to find these enemies at the place where he heard they were.

5. Having cut off a lock of his hair, a prearranged symbol of identification between them, Bohemond entreated Baldwin for love of God to help him as quickly as possible. When Danisman had heard this, fearing the animosity of these Franks, he dared not stay before the city of Melitene, which he had surrounded in siege, and fleeing before us little by little, he managed to return to his own people. We, who had struggled so willingly against them for those three days, were greatly grieved when they escaped, after we had pursued them beyond the aforementioned city.

6. When we had returned, Gabriel gave the city of Melitene to Baldwin. After making an amicable arrangement and putting his own guards there, Baldwin returned to Edessa, and the people of Antioch, sad about their lord, returned to their homes.

XXXVI. The Death of Godfrey

1. When Baldwin was enjoying good fortune, lo, a messenger coming from the people of Jerusalem told him that Duke Godfrey, his own brother, had ended his last day on July eighteenth at Jerusalem.

2. It is the end of the year since the capture of the city,
When the Lord bestowed on you, Duke Godfrey, the
highest reward, the rule of the city.
But not for long did you discharge this function,
For by nature's command, you passed away.
With the sun arising under Leo's sign, you, happy, rose
to Heaven with Michael coming to meet you.

III.

Peter the Hermit and the "Crusade of the People" (March–October, 1096)

From the early twelfth to the mid-nineteenth century, Peter the Hermit, leader of the so-called Crusade of the Poor, or the Crusade of the People, was thought to epitomize the popular spirituality that responded enthusiastically and quickly to the appeal of Urban II, indeed, to have conceived the idea of crusade himself. Urban had stated that he expected the organized crusading armies to leave Europe in August, 1096, but by March, unorganized groups of nobles, fighting men, and others, not all—or even many of them—the "poor" in a modern sense, had begun to move through Europe toward Hungary and Constantinople. Although Heinrich von Sybel's study of 1841 demolished most of the myths surrounding the figure of Peter the Hermit, and Heinrich Hagenmeyer's study of 1879 demolished the rest, Peter nevertheless is an interesting example of popular preaching in the late eleventh century and of the response to Urban's appeal from unexpected quarters. The "Crusade of the People" ultimately ended in disaster, cut to pieces by the Turks soon after leaving Constantinople, but its chief significance is to indicate the range of hostility that many Christians felt toward Jews as well as the dangers that a badly organized military campaign entailed.

See now E. O. Blake and Colin Morris, *"A Hermit Goes to War: Peter and the Origins of the First Crusade,"* Studies in Church History 22 (1985), 79–107; M. D. Coupe, *"Peter the Hermit—Reassessment,"* Nottingham Medieval Studies 31 (1987), 37–45; Jean Flori, *"Faut-il réhabiliter Pierre l'Ermite? Une réévaluation des sources de la première croisade,"* Cahiers de Civilisation Médiévale 38 (1995), 35–54; *and* Colin Morris, *"Peter the Hermit and the Chroniclers,"* in The First Crusade, 21–34.

1. Peter the Hermit: The Version of Guibert of Nogent

Guibert, who once saw Peter, here characterizes him in a manner typical of a number of wandering preachers in the late eleventh and early twelfth centuries. Elsewhere Guibert is more skeptical of Peter's appeal and the intense devotion to him that his followers expressed. This translation is from Munro, Urban, 20.

Therefore, while the princes, who felt the need of many expenses and great services from their attendants, made their preparations slowly and carefully; the common people who had little property, but were very numerous, joined a certain Peter the Hermit, and obeyed him as a master while these affairs were going on among us.

He was, if I am not mistaken, from the city of Amiens, and we have learned that he had lived as a hermit, dressed as a monk, somewhere in Upper Gaul. After he had departed from there—I do not know with what intention—we saw him going through the cities and towns under a pretense of preaching. He was surrounded by so great throngs of people, he received such enormous gifts, his holiness was lauded so highly, that no one within my memory has been held in such honor.

He was very liberal in the distribution to the poor of what he had received. He restored prostitutes to their husbands with gifts. By his wonderful authority he restored everywhere peace and concord, in place of discord. For in whatever he did or said it seemed as if there was something divine, especially when the hairs were snatched from his mule for relics. We do not report this as true, but for the common people who love novelties. He wore a woolen shirt, and over it a mantle reaching to his ankles; his arms and feet were bare. He lived on wine and fish; he hardly ever, or never, ate bread.

2. Peter the Hermit: The Version of Albert of Aachen

Albert was a canon at Aix-la-Chapelle/Aachen in the mid-twelfth century. He neither went on the crusade nor ever visited the East; he compiled his chronicle, which tells of the First Crusade and the establishment of the Kingdom of Jerusalem down to 1120, from surviving witnesses and other literary sources, but not from the Gesta *or the work of Fulcher of Chartres. Scholars have suggested that Albert may have had access to a now-lost "Lorraine Chronicle" of the crusade, one that paralleled the northern French emphasis of Fulcher of Chartres, the Provençal emphasis of Raymond of Aguilers (see below), and the south Italian, Norman emphasis of the* Gesta.

See Colin Morris, "The Aims and Spirituality of the First Crusade as Seen Through the Eyes of Albert of Aachen," Reading Medieval Studies *16 (1990), 99–117. Susan Edington is preparing a new edition and translation of Albert's work. There is a brief discussion in John France,* Victory in the East, *379–380, in which France suggests that Edington will disprove the existence of the "Lost Lorraine Chronicle."*

English translation is from Krey, 48–52.

There was a priest, Peter by name, formerly a hermit. He was born in the city of Amiens, which is in the western part of the kingdom of the Franks, and he was appointed preacher in Berri in the aforesaid kingdom. In every admonition and sermon, with all the persuasion of which he was capable, he urged seting out on the journey as soon as possible. In response to his constant admonition and call, bishops, abbots, clerics, and monks set out; next, most noble laymen, and princes of the different kingdoms; then, all the common people, the chaste as well as the sinful, adulterers, homicides, thieves, perjurers, and robbers; indeed, every class of the Christian profession, nay, also, women and those influenced by the spirit of penance—all joyfully entered upon this expedition. . . .

In the year of the Incarnation of the Lord, 1096, in the fourth Indiction, in the thirteenth year of the reign of Henry IV, third august Emperor of the Romans, and in the forty-third year of the Empire, in the reign of Pope Urban II, formerly Odoard, on the eighth day of March, Walter, surnamed the Penniless, a well-known soldier, set out, as a result of the preaching of Peter the Hermit, with a great company of Frankish foot-soldiers and only about eight knights. On the beginning of the journey to Jerusalem he entered into the kingdom of Hungary. When his intention, and the reason for his taking this journey became known to Lord Coloman, most Christian king of Hungary, he was kindly received and was given peaceful transit across the entire realm, with permission to trade. And so without giving offence, and without being attacked, he set out even to Belgrade, a Bulgarian city, passing over to *Malevilla*, where the realm of the king of Hungary ends. Thence he peacefully crossed the Morava river.

But sixteen of Walter's company remained in *Malevilla*, that they might purchase arms. Of this Walter was ignorant, for he had crossed long before. Then some of the Hungarians of perverse minds, seeing the absence of Walter and his army, laid hands upon those sixteen and robbed them of arms, garments, gold and silver and so let them depart, naked and empty-handed. Then these distressed pilgrims, deprived of arms and other things, hastened on their way to Belgrade, which has been mentioned before, where Walter with all his band had pitched tents for camp. They reported to him the misfortune which had befallen them, but Walter heard this with equanimity, because it would take too long to return for vengeance.

On the very night when those comrades, naked and empty-handed, were received, Walter sought to buy the necessaries of life from a chief of the Bulgarians and the magistrate of the city; but these men, thinking it a pretense, and regarding them as spies, forbade the sale of any thing to them. Wherefore, Walter and his companions, greatly angered, began forcibly to seize and lead away the herds of cattle and sheep, which were wandering here and there through the fields in search of pasture. As a result, a serious strife arose between the Bulgarians and the pilgrims who were driving away the flocks, and the came to blows. However, while the strength of the Bulgarians was growing even to one hundred and forty, some of the pilgrim army, cut off from the multitude of their companions, arrived in flight at a chapel. But the Bulgarians, their army growing in number, while the band of Walter was weakening and his entire company scattered, besieged the chapel and burned sixty who were within; on most of the others, who escaped from the enemy and the chapel in defense of their lives, the Bulgarians inflicted grave wounds.

After this calamity and the loss of his people, and after he had passed eight days as a fugitive in the forests of Bulgaria, Walter, leaving his men scattered everywhere, withdrew to Nish, a very wealthy city in the midst of the Bulgarian realm. There he found the duke and prince of the land and reported to him the injury and damage which had been done him. From the duke he obtained justice for all; nay, more, in reconciliation the duke bestowed upon him arms and money, and the same lord of the land gave him peaceful conduct through the cities of Bulgaria, Sofia, Philippopolis, and Adrianople, and also license to trade.

He went down with all his band, even to the imperial city, Constantinople, which is the capital of the entire Greek empire. And when he arrived there, with all possible earnestness and most humble petition he implored from the Lord Emperor himself permission to delay peacefully in his kingdom, with license to buy the necessaries of life, until he should have as his companion Peter the Hermit, upon whose admonition and persuasion he had begun this journey. And he also begged that, when the troops were united, they might cross in ships over the arm of the sea called the Strait of St. George, and thus they would be able to resist more safely the squadrons of the Turks and the Gentiles. The outcome was that the requests made of the Lord Emperor, Alexius by name, were granted.

Not long after these events, Peter and his large army, innumerable as the sands of the sea—an army which he had brought together from the various realms of the nations of the Franks, Swabians, Bavarians, and Lotharingians—

were making their way to Jerusalem. Descending on that march into the kingdom of Hungary, he and his army pitched their tents before the gate of Oedenburg. . . .

Peter heard this report and, because the Hungarians and Bulgarians were fellow Christians, absolutely refused to believe so great crime of them, until his men, coming to *Malevilla*, saw hanging from the walls the arms and spoils of the sixteen companions of Walter who had stayed behind a short time before, and whom the Hungarians had treacherously presumed to rob. But when Peter recognized the injury to his brethren, at the sight of their arms and spoils, he urged his companions to avenge their wrongs.

These sounded the trumpet loudly, and with upraised banners they rushed to the walls and attacked the enemy with a hail of arrows. In such quick succession and in such incredible numbers did they hurl them in the face of those standing on the walls that the Hungarians, in no wise able to resist the force of the besieging Franks, left the walls, hoping that within the city they might be able to withstand the strength of the Gauls. Godfrey, surnamed Burel—a native of the city Etampes, master and standard-bearer of two hundred foot-soldiers, himself a foot-soldier, and a man of great strength—seeing the flight of the Hungarians away from the walls, then quickly crossed over the walls by means of a ladder he chanced to find there. Reinald of Broyes, a distinguished knight, clad in helmet and coat of mail, ascended just after Godfrey; soon all the knights, as well as the foot-soldiers, hastened to enter the city. The Hungarians, seeing their own imminent peril, gathered seven thousand strong for defense; and, having passed out through another gate which looked toward the east, they stationed themselves on the summit of a lofty crag, beyond which flowed the Danube, where they were invincibly fortified. A very large part of these were unable to escape quickly through the narrow passage, and they fell before the gate. Some who hoped to find refuge on the top of the mountain were cut down by the pursuing pilgrims; still others, thrown headlong from the summit of the mountain, were buried in the waves of the Danube, but many escaped by boat. About four thousand Hungarians fell there, but only a hundred pilgrims, not counting the wounded, were killed at that same place.

This victory won, Peter remained with all his followers in the same citadel five days, for he found there an abundance of grain, flocks of sheep, herds of cattle, a plentiful supply of wine, and an infinite number of horses. . . .

When Peter learned of the wrath of the King and his very formidable gathering of troops, he deserted *Malevilla* with all his followers and planned to cross the Morava with all spoils and flocks and herds of horses. But on the whole bank he found very few boats, only one hundred and fifty, in which the great multitude must pass quickly over and escape, lest the King should overtake them with a great force. Hence many who were unable to cross in boats tried to cross on rafts made by fastening poles together with twigs. But driven hither and thither in these rafts without rudders, and at times separated from their companions, many perished, pierced with arrows from the bows of the Patzinaks, who inhabited Bulgaria. As Peter saw the drowning and destruction which was befalling his men, he commanded the Bavarians, the Alemanni, and the other Teutons, by their promise of obedience to come to the aid of their Frankish brethren. They were carried to that place by seven rafts; then they sank seven small boats of the Patzinaks with their occupants, but took only seven men captive. They led these seven captives into the presence of Peter and killed them by his order.

When he had thus avenged his men, Peter crossed the Morava river and entered the large and spacious forests of the Bulgarians with supplies of food, with every necessary, and with the spoils from Belgrade. And after a delay of eight days in those vast woods and pastures, he and his followers approached Nish, a city very strongly fortified with walls. After crossing the river before the city by a stone bridge, they occupied the field, pleasing in its verdure and extent, and pitched their tents on the banks of the river. . . .

Peter, obedient to the mandate of the Emperor, advanced from the city of Sofia and withdrew with all his people to the city Philippopolis. When he had related the entire story of his misfortune in the hearing of all the Greek citizens, he received, in the name of Jesus and in fear of God, very many gifts for him. Next, the third day after, he withdrew to Adrianople, cheerful and joyful in the abundance of all necessaries. There he tarried in camp outside the walls of the city only two days, and then withdrew after sunrise on the third day. A second message of the Emperor was urging him to hasten his march to Constantinople, for, on account of the reports about him, the Emperor was burning with desire to see this same Peter. When they had come to Constantinople, the army of Peter was ordered to encampe at a distance from the city, and license to trade was fully granted. . . .

3. Peter the Hermit: The Version of William of Tyre

William, born in the Holy Land of French parents, was educated in Syria and France, later returning to Jerusalem, where he became Archbishop of Tyre and Chancellor of the Latin Kingdom of Jerusalem. Writing in the late twelfth century, he is the greatest of the crusade historians, and his History of Deeds Done Beyond the Sea *(translated, with an introduction, by E. A. Babcock and A. C. Krey [New*

York, 1943]) is one of the greatest of all histories written during the Middle Ages. William is cited here as evidence for the growth of the legend of Peter the Hermit within a century after the First Crusade. Some scholars suggest that both Albert of Aachen and William drew on the lost "Lorraine Chronicle" independently of each other. See also Peter Edbury and John Gordon Rowe, William of Tyre, Historian of Tyre, Historian of the Latin East *(Cambridge, 1981).*

The English translation is from Munro, Urban, *20.*

A certain priest named Peter, from the kingdom of the Franks and the bishopric of Amiens, a hermit both in deed and name, led by the same ardor, arrived at Jerusalem. He was small in stature and his external appearance contemptible, but greater valor ruled in his slight frame. For he was sharp witted, his glance was bright and captivating, and he spoke with ease and eloquence. Having paid the tax which was exacted from all Christians who wished to enter, he went into the city and was entertained by a trusty man who was also a confessor of Christ. He diligently questioned his host, as he was a zealous man, and learned more fully from him not only the existing perils, but also the persecutions which their ancestors had suffered long before. And if in what he heard any details were lacking, he completed the account from the witness of his own eyes. For remaining in the city and visiting the churches he learned more fully the truth of what had been told to him by others.

Hearing also that the Patriarch of the city was a devout and God-fearing man, he wished to confer with him and to learn more fully from him the truth concerning some matters. Accordingly he went to him, and having been presented by a trustworthy man, both he and the Patriarch mutually enjoyed their conferences.

The name of the Patriarch was Simeon. As he learned from Peter's conversation that the latter was prudent, able and eloquent, and a man of great experience, he began to disclose to him more confidentially all the evils which the people of God had suffered while dwelling in Jerusalem.

To whom Peter replied: "You may be assured, holy father, that if the Roman church and the princes of the West should learn from a zealous and a reliable witness the calamities which you suffer, there is not the slightest doubt that they would hasten to remedy the evil, both by words and deeds. Write them zealously both to the lord Pope and the Roman church and to the kings and princes of the West, and confirm your letter by the authority of your seal. I, truly, for the sake of the salvation of my soul, do not hesitate to undertake this task. And I am prepared under God's guidance to visit them all, to exhort them all, zealously to inform them of the greatness of your sufferings and to urge them to hasten to your relief."

Of a truth, Thou art great, O Lord our God, and to thy mercy there is no end! Of a truth, blessed Jesus, those who trust in Thee shall not be brought to confusion! How did this poor pilgrim, destitute of all resources and far from his native land, have so great confidence that he dared to undertake an enterprise so much beyond his strength and to hope to accomplish his vow, unless it was that he turned all his thoughts to Thee, his protector, and filled with charity, pitying the misfortunes of his brethren, loving his neighbor as himself, he was content to fulfill the law? Strength is a vain thing, but charity overcometh. What his brethren prescribed might appear difficult and even impossible, but the love of God and of his neighbor rendered it easy for him, for love is strong as death. Faith which worketh by love availeth with Thee, and the good deeds near Thee do not remain without fruit. Accordingly Thou didst not permit Thy servant long to remain in doubt. Thou didst manifest Thyself to him. Thou didst fortify him by Thy revelation that he might not hesitate, and breathing into him Thy hidden spirit, Thou madest him arise with greater strength to accomplish the work of charity.

Therefore, after performing the usual prayers, taking leave of the lord Patriarch and receiving his blessing, he went to the seacoast. There he found a vessel belonging to some merchants who were preparing to cross to Apulia. He went on board, and after a successful journey arrived at Bari. Thence he proceeded to Rome, and found the lord Pope Urban in the vicinity. He presented the letters of the Patriarch and of the Christians who dwelt at Jerusalem, and showed their misery and the abominations which the unclean races wrought in the holy places. Thus faithfully and prudently he performed the commission entrusted to him.

4. The Slaughter of the Jews:
The Version of Albert of Aachen

This narrative is the most sensitive of the Christian accounts of the massacres of the Jews in the Rhineland and southeastern Europe that marked the beginning of the "Crusade of the People." On the Christian sources for the slaughter see Robert Chazan, European Jewry and the First Crusade *(Berkeley-Los Angeles, 1987), 38–40, and Jonathan Riley-Smith, "The First Crusade and the Persecution of the Jews,"* Studies in Church History *21 (1984), 51–72.*

The English translation here is from Krey, 54–56.

At the beginning of summer in the same year in which Peter and Gottschalk, after collecting an army, had set out, there assembled in like fashion a large and innumerable host of Christians from diverse kingdoms and lands; namely, from the realms of France, England, Flanders, and Lorraine. . . . I know not whether by a judgment of the Lord, or by some error of mind, they rose in a spirit of cruelty against the Jewish people scattered throughout these cities and slaughtered them without mercy, especially in the Kingdom of Lorraine, asserting it to be the beginning of their expedition and their duty against the enemies of the Christian faith. This slaughter of Jews was done first by citizens of Cologne. These suddenly fell upon a small band of Jews and severely wounded and killed many; they destroyed the houses and synagogues of the Jews and divided among themselves a very large amount of money. When the Jews saw this cruelty, about two hundred in the silence of the night began flight by boat to Neuss. The pilgrims and crusaders discovered them, and after taking away all their possessions, inflicted on them similar slaughter, leaving not even one alive.

Not long after this, they started upon their journey, as they had vowed, and arrived in a great multitude at the city of Mainz. There Count Emico, a nobleman, a very mighty man in this region, was awaiting, with a large band of Teutons, the arrival of the pilgrims who were coming thither from diverse lands by the King's highway.

The Jews of this city, knowing of the slaughter of their brethren, and that they themselves could not escape the hands of so many, fled in hope of safety to Bishop Rothard. They put an infinite treasure in his guard and trust, having much faith in his protection, because he was Bishop of the city. Then that excellent Bishop of the city cautiously set aside the incredible amount of money received from them. He placed the Jews in the very spacious hall of his own house, away from the sight of Count Emico and his followers, that they might remain safe and sound in a very secure and strong place.

But Emico and the rest of his band held a council and, after sunrise, attacked the Jews in the hall with arrows and lances. Breaking the bolts and doors, they killed the Jews, about seven hundred in number, who in vain resisted the force and attack of so many thousands. They killed the women, also, and with their swords pierced tender children of whatever age and sex. The Jews, seeing that their Christian enemies were attacking them and their children, and that they were sparing no age, likewise fell upon one another, brother, children, wives, and sisters, and thus they perished at each other's hands. Horrible to say, mothers cut the throats of nursing children with knives and stabbed others, preferring them to perish thus by their own hands rather than to be killed by the weapons of the uncircumcised.

From this cruel slaughter of the Jews a few escaped; and a few because of fear, rather than because of love of the Christian faith, were baptized. With very great spoils taken from these people, Count Emico, Clarebold, Thomas, and all that intolerable company of men and women then continued on their way to Jerusalem, directing their course towards the Kingdom of Hungary, where passage along the royal highway was usually not denied the pilgrims. But on arriving at *Wieselburg*, the fortress of the King, which the rivers Danube and Leytha protect with marshes, the bridge and gate of the fortress were found closed by command of the King of Hungary, for great fear had entered all the Hungarians because of the slaughter which had happened to their brethren. . . .

But while almost everything had turned out favorably for the Christians, and while they had penetrated the walls with great openings, by some chance or misfortune, I know not what, such great fear entered the whole army that they turned in flight, just as sheep are scattered and alarmed when wolves rush upon them. And seeking a refuge here and there, they forgot their companions. . . .

Emico and some of his followers continued in their flight along the way by which they had come. Thomas, Clarebold, and several of their men escaped in flight toward Carinthia and Italy. So the hand of the Lord is believed to have been against the pilgrims, who had sinned by excessive impurity and fornication, and who had slaughtered the exiled Jews through greed of money, rather than for the sake of God's justice, although the Jews were opposed to Christ. The Lord is a just judge and orders no one unwillingly, or under compulsion, to come under the yoke of the Catholic faith.

There was another detestable crime in this assemblage of wayfaring people, who were foolish and insanely fickle. That the crime was hateful to the Lord and incredible to the faithful is not to be doubted. They asserted that a certain goose was inspired by the Holy Spirit, and that a she-goat was not less filled by the same Spirit. These they made their guides on this holy journey to Jerusalem; these they worshipped excessively; and most of the people following them, like beasts, believed with their whole minds that this was the true course. May the hearts of the faithful be free from the thought that the Lord Jesus wished the Sepulchre of His most sacred body to be visited by brutish and insensate animals, or that He wished these to become the guides of Christian souls, which by the price of His own blood He deigned to redeem from the filth of idols! . . .

5. The Slaughter of the Jews:
The Version of Ekkehard of Aura

Ekkehard was a monk of Corvey who later went to the Holy Land on the Crusade of 1101. His world chronicle is widely admired although it is derivative for the period considered here. Compare his account with that of Albert of Aachen. The translation here is from Krey, 53.

Just at that time, there appeared a certain soldier, Emico, Count of the lands around the Rhine, a man long of very ill repute on account of his tyrannical mode of life. Called by divine revelation, like another Saul, as he maintained, to the practice of religion of this kind, he usurped to himself the command of almost twelve thousand cross bearers. As they were led through the cities of the Rhine and the Main and also the Danube, they either utterly destroyed the execrable race of the Jews wherever they found them (being even in this matter zealously devoted to the Christian religion) or forced them into the bosom of the Church.

6. *Gezerot Tatnu* 4856/1096:
The Version of the Anonymous of Mainz

Several chronicles in Hebrew survive from the end of the eleventh century and give accounts of the slaughters in the cities of northern and southeastern Europe in 1096–97. The literature is discussed above in the introduction. Of the Hebrew chronicles, that of the Anonymous of Mainz is the most vivid and eloquent. He wrote shortly after 1096 and probably used firsthand accounts by Jewish survivors and information from Christian informants as well. The Hebrew chronicles are available in English in Schlomo Eidelberg, The Jews and the Crusaders: The Hebrew Chronicles of the First and Second Crusades *(Madison, Wis., 1977). See the review of the literature by Anna Sapir Abulafia, "The Interrelationship Between the Hebrew Chronicles of the First Crusade,"* Journal of Semitic Studies *27 (1982), 221–239, and Abulafia, "Invectives Against Christianity in the Hebrew Chronicles of the First Crusade," in* Crusade and Settlement, *66–72. The English translation here is from Robert Chazan,* European Jewry and the First Crusade *(Berkeley-Los Angeles, 1987), 226–242.*

I shall begin the account of the former persecution. May the Lord protect us and all Israel from persecution.

It came to pass in the year one thousand twenty-eight after the destruction of the Temple that this evil befell Israel. There first arose the princes and nobles and common folk in France, who took counsel and set plans to ascend and "to rise up like eagles" and to do battle and "to clear a way" for journeying to Jerusalem, the Holy City, and for reaching the sepulcher of the Crucified, "a trampled corpse" "who cannot profit and cannot save for he is worthless." They said to one another: "Behold we travel to a distant land to do battle with the kings of that land. 'We take our souls in our hands' in order to kill and to subjugate all those kingdoms that do not believe in the Crucified. How much more so [should we kill and subjugate] the Jews, who killed and crucified him." They taunted us from every direction. They took counsel, ordering that either we turn to their abominable faith or they would destroy us "from infant to suckling." They—both princes and common folk—placed an evil sign upon their garments, a cross, and helmets upon their heads.

When the [Jewish] communities in France heard, they were seized by consternation, fear, and trembling. . . . They wrote letters and sent emissaries to all the [Jewish] communities along the Rhine River, [asking that they] fast and deprive themselves and seek mercy from [God "who"] dwells on high," so that he deliver them [the Jews] from their [the crusaders'] hands. When the letters reached the saintly ones who were in that land, they—those men of God, "the pillars of the universe," who were in Mainz—wrote in reply to France. Thus was it written in them [their letters]: "All the [Jewish] communities have decreed a fast. We have done our part. May God save us and save you from 'all distress and hardship.' We are greatly fearful for you. We, however, have less reason to fear [for ourselves], for we have heard not even a rumor [of such developments]." Indeed we did not hear that a decree had been issued and that "a sword was to afflict us mortally."

When the crusaders began to reach this land, they sought funds with which to purchase bread. We gave them, considering ourselves to be fulfilling the verse: "Serve the king of Babylon, and live." All this, however, was of no avail, for our sins brought it about that the burghers in every city to which the crusaders came were hostile to us, for their [the burghers'] hands were also with them [the crusaders] to destroy vine and stock all along the way to Jerusalem.

It came to pass that, when the crusaders came, battalion after battalion, like the army of Sennacherib, some of the princes in the empire said: "Why do we sit thus? Let us also go with them. For every man who sets forth on this journey and undertakes to ascend to the impure sepulcher dedicated to the Crucified will be assured paradise." Then the crusaders along with them [the princes] gathered from all the provinces until they became as numerous "as the sands of the sea," including both princes and common folk. They circulated a report . . . "Anyone who kills a single Jew will have all his sins absolved." Indeed there was a certain nobleman, Ditmar by name, who announced that he would not depart from this empire until he would kill one Jew—then he would depart. Now when the holy community in Mainz heard this, they decreed a fast. "They cried out mightily to the Lord" and they passed night and day in fasting. Likewise they recited dirges both morning and evening, both small and great. Nonetheless our God "did not turn away from his awesome wrath" against us. For the crusaders with their insignia came, with their standards before our houses. When they saw one of us, they ran after him and pierced him with a spear, to the point that we were afraid even to cross our thresholds.

It came to pass on the eighth of the month of Iyyar, on the Sabbath, the measure of justice began to manifest itself against us. The crusaders and burghers arose first against the saintly ones, the pious of the Almighty in Speyer. They took counsel against them, [planning] to seize them together in the synagogue. But it was revealed to them and they arose [early] on the Sabbath morning and prayed rapidly and left the synagogue. When they [the crusaders and burghers] saw that their plan for seizing them together was foiled, they rose against them [the Jews] and killed eleven of them. From there the decree began, to fulfill that which is said: "Begin at my sanctuary." When Bishop John heard, he came with a large force and helped the [Jewish] community wholeheartedly and brought them indoors and saved them from their [the crusaders' and burghers'] hands. He seized some of the burghers and "cut off their hands." He was a pious one among the nations. Indeed God brought about well-being and salvation through him. R. Moses ben Yekutiel the *parnas* "stood on the breach" and extended himself on their behalf. Through him all those forcibly converted who remained "here and there" in the empire of Henry returned [to Judaism]. Through the emperor, Bishop John removed the remnant of the community of Speyer to his fortified towns, and the Lord turned to them, for the sake of his great Name. The bishop hid them until the enemies of the Lord passed. They [the Jews] remained there, fasting and weeping and mourning. "They despaired deeply," for every day the crusaders and the gentiles and Emicho—may his bones be ground up—and the common folk gathered against them, to seize them and to destroy them. Through R. Moses the *parnas*, Bishop John saved them, for the Lord inclined his heart to save them without bribery. This was from the Lord, in order to give us there "a remnant and a residue" through him.

It came to pass that, when the sad report that some of the community of Speyer had been killed reached Worms, they [the Jews of Worms] cried out to the Lord and wept loudly and bitterly, for they saw that a decree had been issued from heaven and that there was no place to flee, neither forward nor backward. Then the community divided itself into two groups. Some of them fled to the bishop in his towers; some of them remained in their homes, for the burghers promised them vainly and cunningly. They are "splintered reeds," for evil and not for good, for their hand was with the crusaders in order to destroy our name and remnant. They gave us vain and meaningless encouragement, [saying]: "Do not fear them, for anyone who kills one of you—'his life will be forfeit for yours.'" They [the burghers] did not give them [the Jews] anywhere to flee, for [the members of] the community deposited all their money in their [the burghers'] hands. Therefore they surrendered them.

It came to pass on the tenth of Iyyar, on Sunday, "they plotted craftily against them." They took "a trampled corpse" of theirs, that had been buried thirty days previously and carried it through the city, saying: "Behold what the Jews have done to our comrade. They took a gentile and boiled him in water. They then poured the water into our wells in order to kill us." When the crusaders and burghers heard this, they cried out and gathered—all who bore and unsheated [a sword], from great to small—saying: "Behold the time has come to avenge him who was crucified, whom their ancestors slew. Now let not 'a remnant or a residue' escape, even 'an infant or a suckling' in the cradle." They then came and struck those who had remained in their houses—comely young men and comely and lovely young women along with elders. All of them stretched forth their necks. Even manumitted servingmen and servingwomen were killed along with them for the sanctification of the Name which is awesome and sublime, . . . who rules above and below, who was and will be. Indeed the Lord of Hosts is his Name. He is crowned with the splendor of seventy-two names; he created the Torah nine hundred and seventy-four generations prior to the creation of the world. There were twenty-six generations from the creation of the world to Moses, the father of the prophets, through whom [God] gave the holy Torah. Moses came and wrote in it: "The Lord has affirmed this day that you are, as he promised you, his treasured people which shall observe all his commandments." For him and his Torah they were killed like oxen and were dragged through the market places and streets "like sheep to the slaughter" and lay naked, for they [the attackers] stripped them and left them naked.

It came to pass that, when those who remained saw their brethren naked and the modest daughters of Israel naked, they then acceded to them [the attackers] under great duress, for the crusaders intended to leave not "a remnant or a residue." There were those of them who said: "Let us do their will for the time being, and let us go and bury our brethren and save our children from them." For they had seized the children that remained, "a small number," saying that perhaps they would remain in their pseudo-faith. They [the Jews who converted] did not desert their Creator, nor did their hearts incline after the Crucified. Rather they cleaved to the God on high. Moreover, the rest of the community, those who remained in the chambers of the bishop, sent garments with which to clothe those who had been killed through those who had been saved. For they were charitable. Indeed the heads of the community remained there [in the bishop's chambers] and most of the community was saved during the first incident. They sent to those forcibly converted messages of consolation: "Fear not and do not take to heart that which you have done. For if the Holy One, blessed be he, saves us from the hands of our enemies, then we shall be with you 'for both death and life.' 'However do not desert the Lord.' "

It came to pass on the twenty-fifth of Iyyar that the crusaders and the burghers said: "Behold those who remain in the courtyard of the bishop and in his chambers. Let us take vengeance on them as well." They gathered from all the villages in the vicinity, along with the crusaders and the burghers; they beseiged them [the Jews]; and they did battle against them. There took place a very great battle, one side against the other, until they seized the chambers in which the children of the sacred covenant were. When they saw the battle raging to and fro, the decree of the King of kings, then they accepted divine judgment and expressed faith in their Creator and "offered up true sacrifices." They took their children and slaughtered them unreservedly for the unity of the revered and awesome Name. There were killed the notables of the community.

There was a certain young man, named R. Meshullam ben R. Isaac. He called out loudly to all those standing there and to Zipporah his helpmate: "Listen to me both great and small. This son God gave me. My wife Zipporah bore him in her old age and his name is Isaac. Now I shall offer him up as did our ancestor Abraham with his son Isaac." Zipporah replied: "My lord, my lord. Wait a bit. Do not stretch forth your hand against the lad whom I have raised and brought up and whom I bore in my old age. Slaughter me first, so that I not witness the death of the child." He then replied: "I shall not delay even a moment. He who gave him to us will take him as his portion. He will place him in the bosom of Abraham our ancestor." He then bound Isaac his son and took in his hand the knife with which to slaughter his son and made the benediction for slaughtering. The lad answered amen. He then slaughtered the lad. He took his screaming wife. The two of them departed together from the chamber and the crusaders killed them. "At such things will you restrain yourself, O Lord?" Nevertheless "he did not turn away from his great wrath" against us.

There was a certain young man, named Isaac ben Daniel. They asked him, saying: "Do you wish to exchange your God for 'a wretched idol?'" He said: "Heaven forfend that I deny him; in him shall I trust. Thus shall I commend to him my soul." They put a rope around his neck and dragged him throughout the entire city, through the mud of the streets, up to the place of their idolatry. His soul was still bound up in his body. They said to him: "You may still be saved. Do you wish to convert?" He signaled with his finger—for he was unable to utter a word with his mouth, for he had been strangled—saying: "Cut off my head!" and they severed his neck.

There was still another young man, named R. Simhah the *cohen*, son of our teacher R. Isaac the *cohen*. They sought to sully him with their fetid waters. They said to him: "Behold, all of them have already been killed and they lie naked." Then the young man answered them cleverly: "I shall fulfill all your desires, but take me with you to the bishop." They took him and led him to the chamber of the bishop. The nephew of the bishop was there with them. They began designating him with the name of "the loathsome offshoot," leaving him in the chamber of the bishop. Then the young man took out his knife and "gnashed his teeth" in anger against the prince, the relative of the bishop, as does the lion over its prey. He . . . and sank the knife in his belly, and he fell and died. He turned and stabbed two more until the knife broke in his hand. They all fled "to and fro." But when they saw that the knife had broken, they assaulted him and killed him. There was killed the young man who sanctified the [Divine] Name and who did what the rest of the community did not do, for he killed three of the uncircumcised with his knife. The rest had devoted themselves and had fasted daily. Previously they had wept, each for his family and friends, to the point where their strength dissipated. They were unable to do battle against them [the enemy]; rather they said: "It is the decree of the King. 'Let us fall into the hands of the Lord.' Then we shall come and see the great light." There they all fell for the unity of the [Divine] Name.

There was also a respected woman there, named Minna, hidden in a house underground, outside the city. All the men of the city gathered and said to her: "Behold you are 'a capable woman.' Know and see that God does not wish to save you, for 'they lie naked at the corner of every street,' unburied. Sully yourself [with the waters of baptism]." They fell before her to the ground, for they did not wish to kill her. Her reputation was known widely, for all the notables of the city and the princes of the land were found in her circle. She responded and said: "Heaven forfend that I deny the God on high. For him and his holy Torah kill me and do not tarry any longer." There the woman "whose praises were sung at the gates" was killed. All of them were killed and sanctified the Divine Name unreservedly and willingly. All of them slaughtered one another together—young men and young women, old men and old women, even infants slaughtered themselves for the sanctification of the [Divine] Name. Those who have been designated by name did so; the rest who have not been designated by name did so all the more. They behaved in a way never seen by the human eye. With regard to them and those like them it is said: "[Rescue me from the wicked with your sword,] from men, O Lord, by your hand, from men whose share in life is fleeting. [But as to your treasured ones, fill their bellies. Their sons too shall be satisfied, and have something left over for their young.]" "[Such things have never been heard or noted.] No eye has seen [them], O God, but you, who act for those who trust in you." They all fell by the hand of the Lord and returned to their rest, to the great light in paradise. Behold their souls are bound up in the bond of life, with the God who created them, to the end of days.

It came to pass that, when the saintly ones, the pious of the Almighty, the holy community in Mainz, heard that some of the community of Speyer had been killed and the community of Worms [had been attacked] twice, then their spirit collapsed and "their hearts melted and turned to water." They cried out to the Lord and said: " 'Ah Lord God of Israel! Are you wiping out the remnant of Israel?' 'Where are all your wondrous deeds about which our ancestors told us, saying: "Truly the Lord brought you up from Egypt." But now you have abandoned us, delivering us into the hands of the gentiles for destruction.' " Then all the leaders of Israel gathered from the community and came to the archbishop and his ministers and servants and said to them: "What are we to do with regard to the report which we have heard concerning our brethren in Speyer and Worms who have been killed?" They said to them: "Heed our advice and bring all your moneys into our treasury and into the treasury of the archbishop. Then you and your wives and your children and all your retinue bring into the courtyard of the archbishop. Thus will you be able to be saved from the crusaders." They contrived and gave this counsel in order to surrender us and to gather us up and to seize us "like fish enmeshed in a fatal net." In addition, the archbishop gathered his ministers and servants—exalted ministers, nobles, and grandees—in order to assist us and to save us from the crusaders. For at the outset it was his desire to save us, but ultimately he failed.

It came to pass on a certain day that a gentile woman came and brought with her a goose that she had raised since it was a gosling. This goose went everywhere that the gentile woman went. She said to all passersby: "Behold this goose understands that I intend to go on the crusade and wishes to go with me." Then the crusaders and burghers gathered against us, saying to us: "Where is your source of trust? How will you be saved? Behold the wonders that the Crucified does for us!" Then all of them came with swords and spears to destroy us. Some of the burghers came and would not allow them [to do so]. At that time they stood . . . and killed along the Rhine River, until they killed one of the crusaders. Then they said: "All these things the Jews have caused." Then they almost gathered [against us]. When the saintly ones saw all these things, their hearts melted. They [the Christians] spoke harshly with them, [threatening] to assault and attack us. When they [the Jews] heard their words, they said—from great to small: "If only we might die by the hand of the Lord," rather than die at the hands of the enemies of the Lord. For he is a merciful God, the only king in his universe."

They left their houses empty and came to the synagogue only on the sabbath, that last sabbath prior to our disaster, when "a few" entered to pray. R. Judah ben R. Isaac entered there to pray on that Sabbath. They wept copiously, to the point of exhaustion, for they saw that this was the decree of the King of kings. There was a venerable scholar, R. Baruch ben R. Isaac, and he said to us: "Know that a decree has truly and surely been enacted against us, and we will not be able to be saved. For tonight we—I and my son-in-law Judah—heard the souls praying here loudly, [with a sound] like weeping. When we heard the sound, we thought that perhaps they [those praying] came from the courtyard of the archbishop and that some of the community had returned to pray in the synagogue at midnight out of pain and anguish. We ran to the door of the synagogue, but it was closed. We heard the sound, but we comprehended nothing. We returned home shaken, for our house was close to the synagogue." When we heard these words, we fell on our faces and said: " 'Ah Lord God! Are you wiping out the remnant of Israel?' " They went and recounted these incidents to their brethren in the courtyard of the burgrave and in the courtyard of the archbishop. They likewise wept copiously.

It came to pass on the new moon of Sivan that the wicked Emicho—may his bones be ground up on iron millstones—came with a large army outside the city, with crusaders and common folk. For he also said: "It is my desire to go on the crusade." He was our chief persecutor. He had no mercy on the elderly, on young men and young women, on infants and sucklings, nor on the ill. He made the people of the Lord "like dust to be trampled." "Their young men he put to the sword and their pregnant women he ripped open." They camped outside the city for two days. Then the heads of the [Jewish] community said: "Let us send him money, along with our letters, so that the [Jewish] communities along the way will honor him. Perhaps the Lord will treat us with his great loving-kindness." For previously they had liberally spent their moneys, giving the archbishop and the burgrave and their ministers and their servants and the burghers approximately four hundred marks, so that they might aid them. It availed them nothing. We were unlike Sodom and Gomorrah, for in their case ten [righteous] were sought in order to save them. For us neither twenty nor ten were sought.

It came to pass on the third of the month of Sivan, on that very day when Moses said: "Be ready for the third day." On that very day the crown of Israel fell. Then the students of Torah fell and the scholars disappeared. The honor of the Torah fell. "He threw down from heaven to earth the glory of Israel." Fear of sin and humility came to an end. Men of deeds, the luster of wisdom and purity, those who turn back [evil] decrees and the anger of their Creator disappeared. The givers of charity in secret diminished. Truth was eclipsed; the preachers disappeared; the revered fell and the arrogant multiplied. Woe for all these! From the day that the Second Temple was destroyed, there have been none like them; after them there will be no more. For they sanctified the [Divine] Name "with all their hearts and with all their souls and with all their might." They are blessed.

It came to pass at midday that the wicked Emicho—may his bones be ground up—he and all his army—came, and the burghers opened up to him the gates. Then the enemies of the Lord said one to another: "Behold the gates have been opened by themselves. All this the Crucified has done for us, so that we might avenge his blood on the Jews." They came with their standards to the archbishop's gate, where the children of the sacred covenant were—an army as numerous "as the sands on the seashore." When the saintly and God-fearing saw the huge multitude, they trusted in and cleaved to their Creator. They donned armor and strapped on weapons—great and small—with R. Kalonymous ben Meshullam at their head.

There was a pious one, one of the great men of the generation, Rabbi Menahem ben Rabbi David the *levi*. He said: "All the congregation, sanctify the revered and awesome Name unreservedly." They all replied: . . . [He said]: "All of you must do as did the sons of our ancestor Jacob when he sought to reveal to them the time of redemption, at which point the Divine Presence left him. [Jacob said]: 'Perhaps I too am sullied as was my grandfather Abraham [from whom proceeded Ishmael] or like my father Isaac [from whom proceeded Esau.'] [His sons said to him: 'Hear O Israel! The Lord is our God; the Lord is one.'] [Do] as did our ancestors when they answered and said, as they received the Torah at this very time on Mount Sinai: 'We shall do and hear.'" They then called out loudly: "Hear O Israel! The Lord is our God, the Lord is one." They all then drew near to the gate to do battle with the crusaders and with the burghers. They did battle one with another around the gate. Our sins brought it about that the enemy overcame them and captured the gate. The men of the archbishop, who had promised to assist, fled immediately, in order to turn them over to the enemy, for they are "splintered reeds." Then the enemy came into the courtyard and found R. Isaac ben R. Moses [and others and struck them] a mortal sword blow. Not so for the fifty-three souls who fled with R. Kalonymous through the chambers of the archbishop, exiting into a long room called . . . and remaining there.

The enemy entered the courtyard on the third of Sivan, on the third day of the week, "a day of darkness and gloom, a day of densest clouds." May darkness and day gloom reclaim it." "May God above have no concern for it; may light never shine upon it." O sun and moon! Why did you not hide your light? And you stars, to whom Israel has been compared, and you twelve constellations, like the number of the tribes of Israel, the sons of Jacob, how was it that your light not cease to provide illumination to the enemy who intended to blot out the name of Israel? Ask and see—was there ever so numerous a set of sacrifices from the days of Adam?

When the children of the sacred covenant saw that the decree had been issued and that the enemy had overcome them, they all cried out—young men and old men, young women and children, menservants and maidservants—and wept for themselves and their lives. They said: "We shall suffer the yoke of awe of the sacred. For the moment the enemy will kill us with the easiest of the four deaths—by the sword. But we shall remain alive; our souls [will repose] in paradise, in the radiance of the great light, forever." They all said acceptingly and willingly: "Ultimately one must not question the ways of the Holy One blessed be he and blessed be his Name, who gave us his Torah and commanded us to put to death and to kill ourselves for the unity of his holy Name. Blessed are we if we do his will and blessed are all those who are killed and slaughtered and who die for the unity of his Name. Not only are they privileged to enter the world to come and sit in the circle of the saintly, 'the pillars of the universe.' What is more, they exchange a world of darkness for a world of light, a world of pain for a world of happiness, a transitory world for a world that is eternal and everlasting." They all cried out loudly and in unison: "Ultimately we must not tarry. For the enemy has come upon us suddenly. Let us offer ourselves up before our Father in heaven. Anyone who has a knife should come and slaughter us for the sanctification of the unique Name [of God] who lives forever. Subsequently let him pierce himself with his sword either in his throat or in his belly or let him slaughter himself." They all stood—men and women—and slaughtered one another. The young women and the brides and bridegrooms looked through the windows and cried out loudly and said: "Look and see, God, what we do for the sanctification of your great Name, rather than to abandon your divinity for a crucified one, a trampled and wretched and abominable offshoot . . . , a bastard and a child of menstruation and lust." They were all slaughtered. The blood of this slaughter flowed through the chambers in which the children of the sacred covenant were. They lay in slaughtered rows—the infant with the elderly. . . . [making sounds] like those made by slaughtered sheep. "At such things will you restrain yourself, O Lord; will you stand idly by and let us suffer so heavily?" Avenge the blood of your servants that has been spilled. Behold, has such a thing ever happened before? For they jostled one another, saying: "I shall sanctify first the Name of the King of kings." The pious women threw money outside, in order to deter them [the enemy] a bit, until they might slaughter their children, in order to fulfill the will of the Creator. . . .

It came to pass that, when the enemy came to the chambers and broke down the doors and found them convulsing, still writhing in their blood, they took their money and stripped them naked. They struck those remaining and left not "a remnant or a residue." Thus they did in all the chambers where there were children of Israel, [children of] the sacred covenant, with the exception of one chamber which was too strong. The enemy did battle against it till evening. When the saintly ones [in that chamber] saw that the enemy was mightier than they were, the men and the women rose up and slaughtered the children. Subsequently, they slaughtered one another. Some fell on their swords or knives. The saintly women threw rocks through the windows. The enemy in turn struck them with rocks. They [the Jewish women] endured all these rocks, until their flesh and faces became shredded. They cursed and blasphemed the crusaders in the name of the Crucified, the profane and despise, the son of lust: "Upon whom do you rely? 'Upon a trampled corpse!'" Then the crusaders advanced to break down the door.

There was a notable lady, Rachel the daughter of R. Isaac ben R. Asher. She said to her companions: "I have four children. On them as well have no mercy, lest these uncircumcised come and seize them and they remain in their pseudo-faith. With them as well you must sanctify the holy Name." One of her companions came and took the knife. When she saw the knife, she cried loudly and bitterly. She beat her face, crying and saying: "'Where is your steadfast love, O Lord?'" She took Isaac her small son—indeed he was very lovely—and slaughtered him. She . . . said to her companions: "Wait! Do not slaughter Isaac before Aaron." But the lad Aaron, when he saw that his brother had been slaughtered, cried out: "Mother, Mother, do not slaughter me!" He then went and hid himself under a bureau. She took her two daughters, Bella and Matrona, and sacrificed them to the Lord God of Hosts, who commanded us not to abandon pure awe of him and to remain loyal to him. When the saintly one finished sacrificing her three children before our Creator, she then lifted her voice and called out to her son: "Aaron, Aaron, where are you? I shall not have pity or mercy on you either." She pulled him by the leg from under the bureau, where he had hidden, and sacrificed him before the sublime and exalted God. She then put them under her two sleeves, two on one side and two on the other, near her heart. They convulsed near her, until the crusaders seized the chamber. They found her sitting and mourning them. They said to her: "Show us the money which you have under your sleeves." When they saw the slaughtered children, they smote her and killed her. With regard to them and to her it is said: "Mother and babes were dashed to death together." She died with them, as did the [earlier] saintly one with her seven sons. With regard to her it is said: "The mother of the child is happy." The crusaders killed all those in the chamber and stripped them naked. They were still writhing and convulsing in their blood, as they stripped them. "See, O Lord, and behold, how abject I have become."

Subsequently they threw them from the chambers through the windows naked, heap upon heap and mound upon mound, until they formed a high heap. Many of the children of the sacred covenant, as they were thrown, still had life and would signal with their fingers: "Give us water that we might drink." When the crusaders saw this, they would ask them: "Do you wish to sully yourselves [with the waters of the baptism]?" They would shake their heads and would look at their Father in heaven as a means of saying no and would point with their fingers to the Holy One blessed be he. The crusaders then killed them.

All these things were done by those whom we have designated by name. The rest of the community all the more proclaimed the unity of the sacred Name, and all fell in the hands of the Lord.

Then the crusaders began to exult in the name of the Crucified. They lifted their standards and came to the remnant of the community, to the courtyard of the burgrave. They besieged them as well and did battle against them and seized the entranceway to the courtyard and smote them also.

There was a certain man, named Moses ben Helbo. He called to his sons and said to them: "My sons Simon and Helbo. At this moment hell and paradise are open [before you]. Into which do you wish to enter?" They answered him and said: "Bring us into paradise." They stretched forth their necks. The enemy smote them, the father along with the sons.

There was a Torah scroll there in the chamber. The crusaders came into the chamber, found it, and tore it to shreds. When the saintly and pure daughters of royalty [the Jewish women] saw that the Torah had been torn, they called out loudly to their husbands: "Behold, behold the holy Torah. The enemy is tearing it." Then they all, the men and the women, said together: "Woe for the holy Torah, 'perfect in beauty,' 'the delight of our eyes.' We used to bow before it in the synagogue; we used to kiss it; we used to honor it. How has it now fallen into the hands of the unclean and uncircumcised." When the men heard the words of the saintly women, "they became exceedingly zealous" for the Lord our God and for the holy and beloved Torah. There was there a young man named R. David ben Rabbi Menahem. He said to them: "My brethren, rend your garments over the honor of the Torah." They rent their garments as our teacher commanded. They then found a crusader in a chamber and they all—both men and women—rose up and stoned him. He fell and died. Now when the burghers and crusaders saw that he had died, they did battle against them. They went up on the roof over the place where the children of the covenant were, broke the roof, shot at them with arrows, and pierced them with spears.

There was a certain man named Jacob ben Sullam. He was not from a family of notables. Indeed his mother was not Jewish. He called out loudly to all standing near him: "All the days of my life till now, you have despised me. Now I shall slaughter myself." He slaughtered himself for the Name which is most sublime, which is the Name of the Lord of Hosts.

There was, in addition, a certain man named Samuel the elder ben R. Mordechai. He also sanctified the [Divine] Name. He took his knife and plunged it into his belly, spilling his innards upon the ground. He called to all standing near him and said to them: "Behold my brethren what I do for the sanctification of the Eternal." There the elder fell for the unity of the [Divine] Name and sanctified his awesome God.

The crusaders and burghers turned from there and came to the center of the city, to a certain courtyard. There was hidden David the *gabbai* ben R. Nathaniel—he, his wife, his children, and all the members of his household—in the courtyard of a certain priest. The priest said to him: "Behold there remains in the courtyard of the archbishop and in the courtyard of the burgrave 'neither a remnant nor a residue.' They have all been killed, cast out, and trampled in the streets, with the exception of a few whom they baptized. Do likewise and you will be able to be saved—you and your wealth and all the members of your household—from the hands of the crusaders." The God-fearing man replied: "Indeed go to the crusaders and to the burghers and tell them to come to me." When the priest heard the words of David the *gabbai*, he was very happy over his words, for he thought: "This distinguished Jew has agreed to heed us." He ran to meet them and told them the words of the saintly one. They likewise were very happy. They gathered around the house by the thousands and the ten thousands. When the saintly one saw them, he trusted in his Creator and called to them saying: "Lo you are the children of lust. You believe in one who was born of lust. But I believe in the God who lives forever, who dwells in the highest heaven. In him have I trusted to this day, to the point of death. If you kill me, my soul will repose in paradise, in the light of life. But 'you will descend to the nethermost pit,' 'to everlasting abhorrence,' to hell, where you will be judged along with your deity, who was a child of lust and was crucified." When they heard the pious one, they were enraged. They raised their standards and camped about the house and began to call and shout in the name of the Crucified. They assaulted him and killed him and his saintly wife and his children and his son-in-law and all the members of his household and his maidservant. All were killed there for the sanctification of the [Divine] Name. There fell the saintly one and the members of his household.

They turned and came to the house of R. Samuel ben R. Naaman. He likewise sanctified the [Divine] Name. They gathered around his house, for he alone of all the community had remained in his house. They asked him and sought to baptise him with fetid and impure waters. He put his trust in his Creator—he and all those with him. They [the Jews] did not heed them [the crusaders and burghers]. They killed all of them and threw them all from the windows.

All these things were done by those whom we have singled out by name. The rest of the community and the notables of the congregation—what they did for the unity of the Name of the King of kings, the Holy One blessed be he and blessed be his Name, like R. Akiba and his associates. . . .

I know not how much is missing here. May God save us from this exile. The end of the former persecutions.

7. *Gezerot Tatnu* 4856/1096:
The Version of Solomon ben Simson

The account attributed to Solomon ben Simson is part of a longer chronicle written in Speyer later in the twelfth century. English translation from Chazan, European Jewry and the First Crusade, *243–261.*

Now I shall recount the development of the persecution in the rest of the [Jewish] communities that were killed for the sake of his unique Name and how they cleaved to the Lord God of their ancestors and declared his unity unto death itself.

It came to pass in the year 4856, the year 1028 of our exile, in the eleventh year of the two hundred and fifty-sixth cycle, during which we had hoped for salvation and comfort according to the prophecy of the prophet Jeremiah: "Cry out in joy for Jacob, shout at the crossroads of the nations!" Instead it was turned into "agony and sighing," weeping and crying. Many evils designated in all the [passages of] rebuke—written and unwritten—passed over us. For then rose up initially the arrogant, "the barbaric," "a fierce and impetuous people," both French and German. They set their hearts to journey to the Holy City, which had been defiled by "a ruffian people," in order to seek there the sepulcher of the crucified bastard and to drive out the Muslims who dwell in the land and to conquer the land. "They put on their insignia" and placed an idolatrous sign on their clothing—the cross—all the men and women whose hearts impelled them to undertake the pilgrimage to the sepulcher of their messiah, to the point where they exceeded the locusts on the land—men, women, and children. With regard to them it is said: "The locusts have no king."

It came to pass that, when they traversed towns where there were Jews, they said to one another: "Behold we journey a long way to seek the idolatrous shrine and to take vengeance upon the Muslims. But here are the Jews dwelling among us, whose ancestors killed him and crucified him groundlessly. Let us take vengeance first upon them. 'Let us wipe them out as a nation; Israel's name will be mentioned no more.' Or else let them be like us and acknowledge the son born of menstruation."

Now when the [Jewish] communities heard their words, they reverted to the arts of our ancestors—repentance, prayer, and charity. The hands of the holy people fell weak and their hearts melted and their strength flagged. They hid themselves in innermost chambers before "the ever turning sword." They afflicted themselves with fasting. They fasted three consecutive days—both night and day, in addition to daily fasts, until "their skin shriveled on their bones and became dry as wood." They cried out and gave forth a loud and bitter shriek. But their Father did not answer them. "He shut out their prayer" and "screened himself off with a cloud, that no prayer might pass through." "The tent [of prayer] was rejected" and he banished them from his presence." For a decree had been enacted before him from [the time when God had spoken] of a day of accounting, and this generation had been chosen as his portion, for they had the strength and valor to stand in his sanctuary and to fulfill his command and to sanctify his great Name in his world. Concerning them David said: "Bless the Lord, O his messengers, mighty men who do his bidding, ever obedient to his bidding."

That year Passover fell on Thursday and the new moon of Iyyar on Friday. On the eighth of Iyyar, on the Sabbath, the enemy arose against the [Jewish] community of Speyer and killed eleven saintly souls who sanctified their Creator on the holy Sabbath day and refused to be baptized. There was a notable and pious woman who slaughtered herself for the sanctification of the [Divine] Name. She was the first of those who slaughtered themselves in all the communities. The rest were saved by the bishop without baptism, as has been written above.

On the twenty-third of Iyyar, they rose up against the [Jewish] community of Worms. The community divided into two groups. Some stayed in their homes and some fled to the bishop. Then "the wolves of the steppes" rose up against those that were in their homes and pillaged them—men, women, and children; young and old. They tore down the stairways and destroyed the houses. They plundered and ravaged. They took the Torah and trampled it in the mud and tore it and burned it. "They devoured Israel with a greedy mouth."

Seven days later, on the new moon of Sivan, the day of the arrival of Israel at Sinai in order to receive the Torah, those who still remained in the chambers of the bishop were subjected to terror. The enemy assaulted them, as they had done to the earlier group, and put them to the sword. They [the Jews] held firm to the example of their brethren and were killed and sanctified the [Divine] Name publicly. They stretched forth their necks, so that their heads might be cut off for the Name of their Creator. There were some of them that took their own lives. They fulfilled the verse: "Mothers and babes were dashed together." Indeed fathers also fell with their children, for they were slaughtered together. They slaughtered brethren, relatives, wives, and children. Bridegrooms [slaughtered] their intended and merciful mothers their only children. All of them accepted the heavenly decree unreservedly. As they commended their souls to their Creator, they cried out: "Hear O Israel! The Lord is our God; the Lord is one." The enemy stripped them and dragged them about. There remained only "a small number" whom they converted forcibly and baptized against their will in their baptismal waters. Approximately eight hundred was the number killed, who were killed on these two days. All of them were buried naked. With regard to them Jeremiah laments: "Those who were reared in purple have embraced refuse heaps." I have mentioned their names above. May God recall them beneficently.

When the saintly ones, the pious of the Almighty, the holy community in Mainz—"a shield and buckler" for all the [Jewish] communities, whose reputation spread throughout all the provinces—heard that some of the community in Speyer had been killed and that the community in Worms [had been attacked] twice and that the sword had reached them, their hands fell weak and "their hearts melted and turned to water." They cried out to the Lord with all their heart and said: " 'Lord God of Israel, are you wiping out the remnant of Israel?' 'Where are all your awesome wonders about which our ancestors told us, saying, "Truly the Lord brought you up from Egypt and from Babylonia?" ' How many times have you saved us? How have you now abandoned and forsaken us, O Lord, leaving us in the hands of wicked Christendom that they might destroy us? 'Do not distance yourself from us, for tragedy is near and there is none to aid us.' "

The notables of Israel gathered together to give them good counsel, so that they might be able to be saved. They said to one another: "Let us choose of our elders and let us decide what we shall do, for this great evil will swallow us up." They agreed on the counsel of redeeming their souls by spending their moneys and bribing the princes and officers and bishops and burghers. The leaders of the community, notable in the eyes of the archbishop, then rose and came to the archbishop and to his ministers and servants to speak with them. They said to them: "What shall we do about the report which we have heard concerning our brethren in Speyer and in Worms who have been killed?" They said to them: "Listen to our advice and bring all your moneys to our treasury. Then you, your wives, your sons and daughters, and all that you have bring into the chamber of the archbishop until these bands pass by. Thus will you be able to be saved from the crusaders." They contrived and gave this counsel in order to gather us and to surrender us into their hands and to seize us "like fish enmeshed in a fatal net" and to take our moneys, as they ultimately did. The end result proves the original intention. In addition, the archbishop gathered his ministers and servants—exalted ministers, nobles—in order to assist us. For at the outset it was his desire to save us with all his strength. Indeed we gave him great bribes to this end, along with his ministers and servants, since they intended to save us. Ultimately all the bribery and all the diplomacy did not avail in protecting us "on the day of wrath" from catastrophe.

At that time a duke arose, Godfrey by name—may his bones be ground up—harsh in spirit. "A fickle spirit moved him" to go with those journeying to their idolatrous shrine. He swore wickedly that he would not depart on his journey without avenging the blood of the Crucified with the blood of Israel and that he would not leave "a remnant or residue" among those bearing the name Jew. His anger waxed against us. To be sure, "a protector" arose—the exemplar of the generation, the God-fearing, offered up on the innermost altar, R. Kalonymous the *parnas* of the community of Mainz—who immediately sent an emissary to Emperor Henry in the kingdom of Apulia, where he had tarried for nine years. He told him of all these events. Then the anger of the emperor was aroused, and he sent letters throughout all the provinces of his empire, to the princes and bishops, to the nobles and to Duke Godfrey— messages of peace and [orders] with regard to the Jews that they protect them so that no one harm them physically and that they provide aid and refuge to them. The wicked duke swore that it had never occurred to him to do them any harm. Nonetheless we bribed him in Cologne with five hundred silver *zekukim*. They likewise bribed him in Mainz. He swore on his staff to behave peacefully toward them. But [God] "who truly makes peace" turned away from them and hid his eyes from his people and consigned them to the sword. No prophet or seer nor any man of wisdom or understanding can fathom the essential issue—how could the sin of "the innumerable people" be so heavy and how could the souls of these saintly communities be so destructive, as though shedding blood. Except that surely [God] is "a just judge" and we bear the shortcomings.

Then "the seething waters" gathered. "They heaped up unfounded charges" against the people of God. They said: "You are the descendants of those who killed our deity and crucified him. Indeed he said: 'A day will surely arrive when my children will come and avenge my blood.' We are his children and it is our responsibility to avenge him upon you, for you are the ones who rebelled and transgressed against him. Indeed your God was never pleased with you. While he sought to do well by you, you did evil before him. Therefore he has forgotten you and no longer desires you, for you have been "stiff-necked" with him. He has separated himself from you and has shown favor to us and has taken us as his portion." When we heard this, "our hearts quaked and were distressed." "We were struck silent." We sat in darkness "like those long dead," until "the Lord might look down and see from heaven."

"Then Satan also came"—the pope of wicked Rome—and circulated a pronouncement along all the gentiles who believe in the offshoot of adultery, the children of Seir, that they congregate together and ascend to Jerusalem and conquer the city "on a way built up" for pilgrims and that they go to the sepulcher . . . whom they accepted as a deity over them. Satan came and mingled among the nations. They all gathered as one man to fulfill the commandment. They came "as the sand on the seashore," with a noise like the rumbling of "a storm or a tempest." It came to pass that, when the embittered and poor had gathered, they took evil counsel against the people of God.

They said: "Why are they occupied with doing battle against the Muslims in the vicinity of Jerusalem? Indeed among them is a people which does not acknowledge their deity. What is more, their ancestors crucified their god. Why should we let them live? Why should they dwell among us? Let our swords begin with their heads. After that we shall go on the way of our pilgrimage." "The hearts of the people of God went numb" and "their spirits departed". . . .

They came and pressed their entreaty before the Lord. They fasted and diminished their blood and flesh. "The hearts of Israel melted inside them." Indeed "God did as he had said, for we sinned before him." He forsook "the tabernacle of Shiloh," "the diminished sanctuary," which he had placed among his people in the midst of the nations. His anger waxed against them and "he unsheathed the sword against them," until "what was left of them was like a mast on a hilltop, like a pole upon a mountain." "He let his might go into captivity" and trampled it underfoot. "Look O Lord, and behold, to whom have you done thus?" Is not Israel, "a people plundered and despoiled," your special portion? Why have you lifted the shield before his enemies? Why have they become mighty? "They hear how I sigh." All those who hear about me . . . "both their ears will tingle." "Alas the strong rod is broken, the lordly staff," the saintly congregation "valued as gold," the community of Mainz. For there was a divine edict in order to test those who fear him, that they suffer the yoke of his pure awe.

It came to pass on a certain day that a gentile woman came and brought with her a goose that she had raised since it was a gosling. This goose went everywhere that the gentile woman went. She said to all passersby: "Behold this goose understands that I intend to go on the crusade and wishes to go with me." Then the crusaders and burghers and common folk gathered against us, saying to us: "Where is your source of trust? How will you be saved? Behold the signs that the Crucified does for them publicly in order to take vengeance on their enemies." Then all of them came with swords to destroy us. Some of the high-ranking burghers came and stood opposite and would not allow them to harm us. At that moment the crusaders stood united against the burghers and one side smote the other until they killed one of the crusaders. Then they said: "All these things the Jews have caused." Then they almost gathered against us. They spoke harshly, [threatening] to assault and attack us. When the saintly ones saw all these things, their hearts melted. When they heard their words, they said, both great and small: "'If only we might die by the hand of the Lord,' rather than die by the hands of the enemies of the Lord. For he is a merciful God, unique in his universe."

They left their houses empty and came to the synagogue only on the

Sabbath before the new moon of Sivan, the last Sabbath prior to our destruction, when "a few" entered to pray. R. Judah ben R. Isaac entered there to pray as part of that quorum. They wept copiously, to the point of exhaustion, for they saw that this was the decree of the King of all kings and that no one might annul it. There was there a venerable scholar, R. Baruch ben R. Isaac, and he said to us: "Know truly and surely that a decree has been enacted against us from heaven and we will not be able to be saved. For tonight we—I and my son-in-law Judah—heard the souls which were praying at night in the synagogue loudly, like a cry. When we heard the sound, we thought that perhaps some of the community came from the courtyard of the archbishop to pray in the synagogue at midnight, in anguish and bitterness. We ran to the door of the synagogue to see who was praying. The door was closed. We heard the sound and the loud wail, but we could comprehend nothing of what they were saying. We returned home shaken, for our house was close to the synagogue." When we heard these words, we fell on our faces and said: "You, O Lord God—are you wiping out the remnant of Israel?" They went and recounted these events to their brethren in the courtyard of the burgrave and in the chambers of the archbishop. They too knew that a decree had been issued by the Lord and they wept copiously and accepted divine judgment and said: "You are righteous, O Lord, and your rulings are just."

It came to pass on the new moon of Sivan that Count Emicho, the persecutor of all the Jews—may his bones be ground up between iron millstones—came with a large army outside the city, with crusaders and common folk in tents. The gates of the city were locked before him. He also had said: "It is my desire to go on the crusade." He became head of the bands and concocted the story that an emissary of the Crucified had come to him and had given him a sign in his flesh indicating that, when he would reach Byzantium, then he [Jesus] would come to him [Emicho] himself and crown him with royal diadem and that he would overcome his enemies. He was our chief persecutor. He had no mercy on the elderly or on young women; he had no pity on the infant and the suckling and the sickly. He made the people of the Lord "like dust to be trampled." "Their young men he put to the sword and their pregnant women he ripped open." They camped outside the city for two days.

At the time when the wicked one came to Mainz on his way to Jerusalem, the elders of the people came to their archbishop, Ruthard, and bribed him with two hundred silver *zekukim*. It had been his intention to go to the villages which belonged to the archbishops. But the [Jewish] community came, when they bribed him, and begged him, so that he stayed with them in Mainz. He brought all the community into his inner chambers and said:

"I have agreed to aid you. Likewise the burgrave has said that he wishes to remain here for your sakes, to assist you. You must therefore supply all our needs until the crusaders pass through." The [Jewish] community agreed to do so. The two—the archbishop and the burgrave—agreed and said: "We shall either die with you or live with you." Then the community said: "Since those who are our neighbors and acquaintances have agreed to save us, let us also send to the wicked Emicho our moneys and our letters, so that the [Jewish] communities along the way will honor him. Perhaps the Lord will behave in accord with his great loving-kindness and will relent against us. For this purpose we have disbursed our moneys, giving the archbishop and his ministers and his servants and the burghers approximately four hundred silver *zekukim*." We gave the wicked Emicho seven gold pounds so that he might assist us. It was of no avail, and to this point no balm has been given for our affliction. For we were unlike Sodom and Gomorrah. For them ten [righteous] were sought in order to save them. For us neither twenty nor ten were sought.

It came to pass on the third day of Sivan, which had been a day of sanctity and setting apart for Israel at the time of the giving of the Torah— on that day when Moses our teacher, may his memory be blessed, said: "Be ready for the third day"—on that day the [Jewish] community of Mainz, the pious of the Almighty, were set apart in holiness and purity and were sanctified to ascend to God all together. "Cherished in life, in death they were not parted." For all of them were in the courtyard of the archbishop. The wrath of the Lord was kindled against his people and he fulfilled the counsel of the crusaders and they were successful. All wealth was unavailing, along with fasting, self-affliction, wailing, and charity. There was no one "to stand in the breach"—neither a teacher nor a prince. Even the holy Torah did not protect those who study it. "Gone from Zion are all that were her glory," namely Mainz. The sound of "the lords of the flock" ceased, along with the sound of "the valorous who repel attacks," "who lead the many to righteousness." "The glorious city, the citadel of joy," which had distributed untold sums to the poor. One could not write with "an iron stylus" on a whole book the multitude of good deeds that were done in it of yore. In one place [were found] Torah and power and wealth and honor and wisdom and humility and good deeds, taking innumerable precautions against transgression. But now their wisdom had been swallowed up and turned into destruction, like the children of Jerusalem in their destruction.

It came to pass at midday that the wicked Emicho, persecutor of the Jews, came—he and all his army—to the gate. The burghers opened the gate to him. Then the enemies of the Lord said to one another: "Behold the gate has been opened before us. Now let us avenge the blood of the Crucified." When the children of the holy covenant—the saintly ones, the God-fearing—who were there saw the huge multitude, the army as large "as the sand on the seashore," they cleaved to their Creator. They donned armor and strapped on weapons— great and small—with R. Kalonymous ben R. Meshullam the *parnas* at their head. But from their great anguish and from the many fasts undertaken, they did not have sufficient strength to stand up before the enemy. They then came in battalions and companies, sweeping down like a river, until Mainz was filled completely. The enemy Emicho made an announcement to the citizenry that they surrender and remove the enemy [the Jews] from the city. "A great panic from the Lord fell upon them." The men of Israel strapped on their weapons in the innermost courtyard of the archbishop and all of them approached the gate [of the courtyard] to do battle with the crusaders and the burghers. They did battle against one another at the gate. Our sins brought it about that the enemy overcame them and captured the gate. "The hand of the Lord lay heavy" upon his people. Then all the gentiles gathered against the Jews in the courtyard, in order to destroy them totally. The hands of our people wavered, when they saw that the hand of wicked Edom had overcome them. Indeed the men of the archbishop, who had promised to help them, fled immediately, in order to turn them over to their enemies, for they were "splintered reeds." Even the archbishop himself fled from his church, for they intended to kill him as well, since he had spoken up on behalf of Israel.

The enemy entered the courtyard on the third of Sivan, on the third day of the week, "a day of darkness and gloom, a day of densest clouds." "May darkness and day gloom reclaim it"; "may God above have no concern for it; may light never shine upon it." Woe for the day when we saw the anguish of our souls. Stars, why did you not cover your light—was not Israel compared to the stars? The twelve constellations, like the number of the tribes of Jacob, why did you not extinguish your light from shining on the enemy that intended to blot out the name of Israel?

When the children of the sacred covenant saw that the decree had been enacted and that the enemy had overcome them, they entered the courtyard and all cried out together—elders, young men and young women, children, menservants and maidservants—to their Father in heaven. They wept for themselves and their lives. They accepted upon themselves the judgment of heaven. They said to one another: "Let us be strong and suffer the yoke of the sacred awe. For the moment the enemy will kill us, but the easiest of the four deaths is by sword. We shall, however, remain alive; our souls [shall be] in paradise, in the radiance of the great light forever." They said unreservedly and willingly: "Ultimately one must not question the ways of the Holy One, blessed be he and blessed be his Name, who gave us his Torah and the commandment to put to death and to kill ourselves for the unity of his holy Name. Blessed are we if we do his will. Blessed are all those who are killed and slaughtered and die for the unity of his name. They are destined for the world to come and shall sit in the circle of the righteous, R. Akiba and his associates, "the pillars of the universe," who were killed for his Name. What is more, a world of darkness will be exchanged for a world of light, a world of pain for a world of happiness, a transitory world for a world that is eternal and everlasting." Then they all cried out loudly, saying in unison: "Now let us tarry no longer, for the enemy has already come upon us. Let us go quickly and sacrifice ourselves before the Lord. Anyone who has a knife should inspect it, that it not be defective. Then he should come and slaughter us for the sanctification of the unique [God] who lives forever. Subsequently he should slaughter himself by his throat or should thrust the knife into his belly.

The enemy, immediately upon entering the courtyard, found there some of the perfectly pious with Rabbi Isaac ben R. Moses the dialectician. He stretched out his neck and they cut off his head immediately. They had clothed themselves in their fringed garments and had seated themselves in the midst of the courtyard in order to do speedily the will of their Creator. They did not wish to flee to the chambers in order to go on living briefly. Rather, with love they accepted upon themselves the judgment of heaven. The enemy rained stones and arrows upon them, but they did not deign to flee. They struck down all those whom they found there, with "blows of sword, death, and destruction."

Those in the chambers, when they saw this behavior on the part of those saintly ones and that the enemy had come upon them, all cried out: "There is nothing better than to offer ourselves as a sacrifice." There women girded themselves with strength and slaughtered their sons and daughters, along with themselves. Many men likewise gathered strength and slaughtered their wives and their children and their little ones. "The tenderest and daintiest" slaughtered "their beloved children." They all stood—men and women—and slaughtered one another. The young women and the brides and the bridegrooms gazed through the windows and cried out loudly: "Behold and see, our God, what we do for the sanctification of your holy Name, rather than deny you for a crucified one, a trampled and wretched and abominable offshoot, a bastard and a child of menstruation and lust." "The precious children of Zion," the children of Mainz, were tested ten times, like our ancestor Abraham and like Hananiah, Mishael, and Azariah. They offered up their children as did Abraham with his son Isaac. They accepted upon themselves the yoke of the fear of heaven, of the King of kings, the Holy One, blessed be he, willingly. They did not wish to deny the awe of our King or to exchange it for [that of] "a loathsome offshoot," a bastard born of menstruation and lust. They stretched forth their necks for the slaughter and commended their pure souls to their Father in heaven. The saintly and pious women stretched forth their necks one to another, to be sacrificed for the unity of the [Divine] Name. Likewise men to their children and brothers, brothers to sisters, women to their sons and daughters, and neighbor to neighbor and friend, bridegroom to bride, and betrothed to his betrothed. They sacrificed each other until the blood flowed together. The blood of husbands mingled with that of their wives, the blood of parents with that of their children, the blood of brothers with that of their sisters, the blood of teachers with that of their students, the blood of bridegrooms with that of their brides, the blood of cantors with that of their scribes, the blood of infants and sucklings with that of their mothers. They were killed and slaughtered for the unity of the revered and awesome Name. At such reports "the ears of those who hear must surely tingle." "For who has heard the like? Who has ever witnessed such events?" "Ask and see." Were there ever so many sacrifices like these from the days of Adam? Were there ever a thousand one hundred sacrifices on one day, all of them like the sacrifice of Isaac the son of Abraham? For one the world shook, when he was offered up on Mount Moriah, as is said: "Hark! The angels cried aloud!" The heavens darkened. What has been done [this time]? "Why did the heavens not darken? Why did the stars not withdraw their brightness?" . . . and light— "why did they not darken in their cloud cover," when one thousand one hundred holy souls were killed and slaughtered on one day, on the third day of Sivan, a Tuesday—infants and sucklings who never transgressed and never sinned and poor and innocent souls? "At such things will you restrain yourself, O Lord?" "For your sake they were killed"—innumerable souls. "Avenge the blood of your servants that has been spilled" in our days and before our eyes speedily. Amen.

That day the crown of Israel fell. Then the students of Torah fell and the scholars disappeared. The honor of the Torah fell, as is written: "He threw down from heaven to earth the glory of Israel." Those who fear sin ceased. Men of good deeds disappeared, along with the splendor of wisdom and purity and abstinence and the splendor of the priesthood and men of trust and "those who repair the breach" and those who turn back evil decrees and the anger of their Creator. Those who give charity in secret diminished. "Truth was absent" and preachers ceased, along with the revered and the luster of old age. [Woe for] the day upon which many troubles befell us. "There was nowhere to turn, either right or left," "because of the rage of the oppressor." For from the day that the Second Temple was destroyed there were none like them in Israel and after them there will be no more. For they sanctified and declared the unity of the [Divine] Name with all their heart and with all their soul and with all their might. Blessed are they and blessed is their portion, for all of them are destined for the life of the world to come. May my portion be with them.

"He has increased within fair Judah mourning and moaning." The enemy arose against them and killed youngsters and women, lads and elders on one day. "They showed no regard for the priests, no favor to elders." They had no pity on infants or on sucklings nor on pregnant women. They left no remnant, like a date, like "two or three berries." For all of them wished to sanctify the Name of their Creator. Indeed when the enemy came upon them, they all cried out loudly with one heart and mouth: "Hear O Israel! The Lord is our God; the Lord is one."

There was a pious and righteous man—one of the great men of the generation—Rabbi Menahem ben R. Judah. He spoke to the people and expounded before them. [He said: "All of you must do as did the son of our ancestor Jacob] when he sought to reveal to them the time of redemption, at which point the Divine Presence left him. He said: 'Perhaps just as unworthiness proceeded from Isaac our father, so too am I sullied with unworthiness.' They [his sons] answered and said: 'Hear O Israel! The Lord is our God; the Lord is one.' [Do also] as did our ancestors on Mount Sinai, at this very time, when they said: 'We shall do and hear.' They said loudly: 'Hear O Israel! The Lord is our God; the Lord is one.' You likewise must do so today." They declared his unity wholeheartedly and did as the leader of the land said. They called out with one mouth and heart: "Hear O Israel! The Lord is our God; the Lord is one." Rabbi Isaac ben R. Moses and the rest of the rabbis and notables were with him. They sat in the courtyard of the archbishop and wept, with their necks stretched out. They said: "When will the ravager come, so that we may accept upon ourselves the judgment of heaven. We have already set forth the sacrifice and constructed the altar for his Name."

Now I shall recount and tell the great wonders that were done that day by these saintly ones. Behold has such a thing ever happened before, from the earliest days? For they jostled one another saying: "I shall sanctify first the Name of the King of kings, the Holy One, blessed be he." The pious women, the daughters of kings, threw coins and silver out the windows at the enemy, so that they would be occupied with gathering the money, in order to impede them slightly until they might finish slaughtering their sons and daughters. The hands of merciful mothers slaughtered their children, in order to do the will of their Creator.

When the enemy came to the chambers and broke down the doors and found them still convulsing and writhing in blood, they took their money and stripped them naked and smote those who remained. They did not leave "a remnant or a residue." Thus they did in all the chambers where the children of the holy covenant were, with the exception of one chamber that was somewhat stronger. The enemy did battle against them till evening. When the saintly ones saw that the enemy was stronger than they and that they would be unable to withstand them any longer, they bestirred themselves and rose up— men and women—and slaughtered the children first. Subsequently the saintly women threw stones through the windows against the enemy. The enemy threw stones against them. They took the stones, until their flesh and faces became shredded. They cursed and blasphemed the crusaders in the name of the Crucified, the impure and foul, the son of lust: "Upon whom do you trust? Upon a rotting corpse!" The crusaders advanced to break down the door.

"Who has seen anything like this; who has heard anything" like that which the saintly and pious woman, Rachel daughter of R. Isaac ben R. Asher, wife of R. Judah, did? She said to her companions: "I have four children. On them as well have no mercy, lest these uncircumcised come and seize them alive and they remain in their pseudo-faith. With them as well you must sanctify the Name of the holy God." One of her companions came and took the knife to slaughter her son. When the mother of the children saw the knife, she shouted loudly and bitterly and smote her face and breast and said: "Where is your steadfast love, O Lord?" Then the woman said to her companions in her bitterness: "Do not slaughter Isaac before his brother Aaron, so that he not see the death of his brother and take flight." The women took the lad and slaughtered him—he was small and exceedingly comely. The mother spread her sleeve to receive the blood; she received the blood in her sleeves instead of in the [Temple] vessel for blood. The lad Aaron, when he saw that his brother had been slaughtered, cried out: "Mother, do not slaughter me!" He went and hid under a bureau. She still had two daughters, Bella and Matrona, comely and beautiful young women, the daughters of R. Judah her husband. The girls took the knife and sharpened it, so that it not be defective. They stretched forth their necks and she sacrificed them to the Lord God of Hosts, who commanded us not to renounce pure awe of him and to remain faithful to him, as it is written: "You must be wholehearted with the Lord your God." When the saintly one completed sacrificing her three children before the Creator, then she raised her voice and called to her son: "Aaron, Aaron, where are you? I shall not have mercy nor pity on you as well." She pulled him by the leg from under the bureau where he was hidden and she sacrificed him before the sublime and exalted God. She placed them under her two sleeves, two on each side, near her heart. They convulsed near her, until the enemy seized the chamber and found her sitting and mourning them. They said to her: "Show us the moneys which you have in your sleeves." When they saw the children and saw that they were slaughtered, they smote her and killed her along with them. With regard to her it is said: "Mothers and babes were dashed to death together." She [died] with her four children as did the saintly woman with her seven sons. With regard to them it is said: "The mother of the children is happy." The father wailed and cried out when he saw the death of his four children, "comely and beautiful." He went and threw himself on the sword in his hand. His innards flowed forth and he writhed in blood on the roadway along with those who had been killed, who had been convulsing and writhing in their blood. The enemy killed all those that remained in the chamber and stripped them naked. "See, O Lord, and behold, how abject I have become."

Then the crusaders began to exult in the name of the crucified, for they had done their will upon all those found in the chambers of the archbishop, and there remained not a remnant. They raised their standards and came "with their tumult" against the rest of the community, before the courtyard of the burgrave. They besieged them as well, until they seized the entrance to the gate of the courtyard and smote those found there. There was a pious man named Moses ben R. Helbo. He had two sons. He called to his sons and said to them: "My sons, Helbo and Simon. At this moment hell and paradise are open [before you]. Into which of them do you wish to enter now?" They answered and said to him: "We wish to enter paradise." They stretched forth their necks and the enemy smote them, father along with sons. May their souls reside in paradise, in the light of life.

There was a Torah scroll there in the chamber. The crusaders came into the chamber, found it, and tore it to shreds. When the saintly and pious women, the daughters of kings, saw that the Torah had been torn, they called out loudly to their husbands: "Behold, behold the holy Torah, for the enemy is tearing it." The women said all together: "Woe for the holy Torah, 'perfect in beauty,' 'the delight of our eyes.' We would bow down to it in the synagogue and our little children kissed it. We honored it, yet how has it now fallen into the hands of these uncircumcised and impure." When the men heard the words of the saintly women, "they became exceedingly zealous" for the Lord our God and for his holy and beloved Torah. There was there a lad named R. David ben Rabbi Menachem. He said to them: "My brethren, rend your garments over the honor of the Torah." They rent their garments. They found in the chamber a crusader and they all—men and women—arose and stoned him and he died. When the burghers and the crusaders saw that the crusader had died, they did battle with them. They went up on the roof [over the place] where children of the sacred covenant were and shot arrows at them and threw stones at them and pierced them, until they destroyed them.

8. Folcmar and Gottschalk in Hungary: The Version of Albert of Aachen

The English translation here is from Krey, 52–53.

Not long after the passage of Peter, a certain priest Gottschalk by name, a Teuton in race, an inhabitant of the Rhine country, inflamed by the preaching of Peter with a love and a desire for that same journey to Jerusalem, by his own preachings likewise stirred the hearts of very many peoples of diverse nations to go on that journey. He assembled from the various regions of Lorraine, eastern France, Bavaria, and Alemannia more than fifteen thousand persons of military station, as well as ordinary foot soldiers, who, having collected an inexpressible amount of money, together with other necessaries, are said to have continued on their way peacefully, even to the kingdom of Hungary.

When they arrived at the gate of *Wieselburg* and its fortress, they were honorably received by the favor of King Coloman. They were likewise granted permission to buy the necessaries of life, and peace was commanded on both sides by an order of the King, lest any outbreak should arise from so large an army. But as they delayed there for several days, they began to roam about, and the Bavarians and Swabians, spirited peoples, together with other thoughtless persons, drank beyond measure and violated the peace which had been commanded. Little by little they took away from the Hungarians wine, grain, and all other necessaries; finally, they devastated the fields, killing sheep and cattle, and also destroying those who resisted, or who wished to drive them out. Like a rough people, rude in manners, undisciplined and haughty, they committed very many other crimes, all of which we cannot relate. As some who were present say, they transfixed a certain Hungarian youth in the market place with a stake through his body. Complaints of this matter and of other wrongs were brought to the ears of the King and their own leaders. . . .

When Gottschalk and the other sensible men heard this, they trusted with, pure faith in these words, and also because the Hungarians were of the Christian profession, they counselled the entire assembly to give their arms in satisfaction to the King, according to this command. Thus everything would return to peace and concord. . . .

And yet, when all their arms had been placed under lock and key, the Hungarians proved false regarding all the faith and clemency which they had promised that the King would show to the people; nay, rather they fell upon them with cruel slaughter, cut down the defenceless and unarmed and inflicted upon them frightful slaughter, to such an extent (as those affirm for a truth who were present and barely escaped) that the entire plain of Belgrade was filled by the bodies of the slain and was covered with their blood. Few escaped from that martyrdom.

9. Folcmar and Gottschalk in Hungary: The Version of Ekkehard of Aura

The English translation here is from Krey, 53.

Now, as has been said, a band followed Folcmar through Bohemia. At the city of Neitra, in Pannonia, an uprising took place, in which a part were killed, and a part were taken prisoners, while the very few survivors are wont to testify that the sign of the cross, appearing in the heavens above them, delivered them from imminent death.

Then Gottschalk, not a true, but a false servant of God, entered Hungary with his followers, and that not without injury to East Noricum. Next, under an astonishing glamour of false piety, he fortified a certain town situated on a height and placed a garrison there and began, with the rest of his company, to ravage Pannonia round about. This town, forsooth, was captured by the natives without delay, and great numbers of the band having been killed or taken prisoners, the rest were dispersed, and he himself, a hireling, not the shepherd of the flock, was driven away from there in disgrace.

10. The Crusaders in Hungary: The Version of Solomon ben Simson

Solomon ben Simson did not fail to note the savage behavior of the crusaders after they had left western Europe. English translation from Chazan, European Jewry and the First Crusade, 294–297.

It came to pass after these events, in which they did their desire and will, that they turned and went on the way of their pseudo-pilgrimage to Jerusalem. The first band was that of the priest from France, and with him a very great army. He came to the borders of the kingdom of Hungary. He sent emissaries to the king of Hungary, saying: "Let us pass through your land. We shall travel on the royal road. We shall eat and drink only [by purchase of goods] with money." The king gave permission to cross through his borders—he and all his army. However, they must travel peacefully and not harm his people in all the cities. They came to a fortified city, a large city, in which there were many people. They [the crusaders] were already seized with hunger pangs, and they bought a bit of bread for a denarius. One of the crusaders carried in his hand woolen leg wrappers in order to sell them in the market and to purchase with the proceeds bread. One of the townspeople came and mocked him. Satan came between them, to the point they rose up to kill each other. An evil spirit circulated among them. The crusaders arose and killed all the townspeople, "from infant to suckling." The report reached the king. The enemies of the Lord traveled from there and came to a certain river, named the Danube. The river was full on all its banks. There were no boats with which to cross the river. Near the river was a village. They came and destroyed the village and took the wood of the houses. They fashioned the wood and made with it a bridge and crossed the river. They came to a city fortified with "wall, gates, and bars." The townspeople closed the gate in their faces and did not wish to allow them entry into the city, for the king was already aware and had commanded that they not allow entry into their fortifications; so that they not destroy the kingdom. They did so. The priest Peter saw that he could not enter the city. He sent messengers to the city—a certain priest. [He said]: "Since you do not permit us to enter the city, send us bread outside the city and we shall buy it." The townspeople did not wish to do so, for thus was the command of the king. He sent further messengers to the town ruler to sell them bread at a double price. They answered him, saying: "Even to avoid endangerment to your lives we shall not sell to you." That night the enemies of the Lord fasted and all came before the priest Peter and took counsel with him as to what they should do. They said: "On the morrow let us take vengeance upon them." Peter answered them and said: "It is certainly true that there is nothing of substance in this people and in its faith, for they are lesser in faith than the Muslims. Indeed they are worthy of stoning, for they are openly unconcerned with sustaining us." He called to the people and said: "Surround the city." The enemy came into the city, broke down the gates, and killed all those found in it. They remained in the city for three days and consumed everything in it. They plundered the city and went on their way. The king of Hungary heard what the crusaders had done—that they had made desolate two of his towns—and his heart melted. He gathered all his army to do battle with the crusaders—it was a very mighty army, a people "like the sand on the seashore." Then the king commanded his servants to tell the people that they should return to their homes and be prepared to come to the king at any time that he might command. On the morrow, the king called his ministers, nobles, and officials alone. They took counsel with the king to close the gates of the border at the periphery of the kingdom of Hungary, so that henceforth no more crusaders might enter. With regard to those who had already entered, they began "to cut down all the stragglers." When they seized a hundred crusaders together, they would kill them. On the next day they would do likewise and on the next day likewise, until they killed them all—those traveling with the priest Peter. The Holy One blessed be he avenged the blood of his servants upon them. There remained of them not one man.

The kingdom of Hungary "was shut up tight" in the face of the enemy. Then came the Rhinelanders, the inhabitants of the Rhineland, a very mighty army, along with the army of Swabia and the army of France and the army of Austria—they are the children of Seir the Horite—an army as numerous as the sand on the shore of the sea. The head of them all was the wicked Count Emicho of Leinigen, may his bones be ground up. They came to the perimeter of the kingdom of Hungary, to the city of. . . . Around the walls were pits of clay. They proceeded against it to do battle and could not overcome it. Then the leaders and nobles agreed upon the counsel of sending to the king of Hungary that he behave generously on behalf of the Crucified and give them a place for crossing. They would put aside their weapons. They took four noblemen from among them and sent him [a message] in these terms. The king came and ordered that they be imprisoned for three days. On the third day the four noblemen swore to him that they would bring him the head of Count Emicho. He then dismissed them with booty. The matter was told to Emicho and he fled during the night. Those remaining fled and the army of the king of Hungary pursued them. They struck them a great blow. More died in "the slimy clay" than were killed by sword. When one fled, he fell into the clay up to his knees and could not move from there till he died. The Greeks pursued them from all sides up to the Danube River. They fled on the bridge which the priest Peter had made. They broke the bridges and there drowned in the Danube River more than a thousand thousands and ten thousand myriads, to the point where they walked on the back [of the drowned] as one walks on dry land. The remnant came. Our hearts heard and were gladdened, for the Lord showed us vengeance upon our enemies. On these days

the sun was eclipsed. On that day God "broke the proud glory" of our enemies and their name was uprooted. But the enemy has not yet repented of
their evil thoughts. Every day they set forth for Jerusalem. The Lord has consigned them to slaughter "like sheep to slaughter and has set them aside for
a day of slaying." "Pay back our neighbors sevenfold." "Give them, O Lord,
their deserts according to their deeds. Give them anguish of heart; your curse
be upon them. Oh, pursue them in anger and destroy them from under the
heavens of the Lord." "For it is the Lord's day of retribution, the year of vindication for Zion's cause." "But Israel has won through the Lord triumph
everlasting. You shall not be ashamed or disgraced in all the ages to come."

11. The End of the "Crusade of the People": The Version of Anna Comnena

*Anna Comnena was the daughter of the Emperor Alexius I and wrote her history
of her father's reign in the 1130s and 1140s. Thus her memories of the crusaders in
Constantinople date from the time when she was thirteen years old, although she supplemented her own memories substantially with records from the imperial archives,
to which she had access, and with conversations with members of her father's surviving entourage. See Georgina Buckler,* Anna Comnena *(London, 1929); J. Chryso-
stomides, "A Byzantine Historian: Anna Comnena," in* Medieval Historical
Writing in the Christian and Islamic Worlds, *ed. D. O. Morgan (London, 1982),
30–46; John France, "Anna Comnena, the Alexiad, and the First Crusade,"* Reading Medieval Studies *10 (1984), 20–38; and F. E. Schlosser, "Byzantine Studies
and the History of the Crusades: The* Alexiad *of Anna Comnena as a Source for
the Crusades,"* Byzantinische Forschungen *15 (1990), 397–406. English translation
here is from Krey, 70–71.*

. . . Moreover, Alexius was not yet, or very slightly, rested from his
labors when he heard rumors of the arrival of innumerable Frankish armies.
He feared the incursions of these people, for he had already experienced the
savage fury of their attack, their fickleness of mind, and their readiness to approach anything with violence. . . .

And finally, he kept ever in mind this information, which was often repeated and most true—that they were known to be always immoderately
covetous of anything they strove after and to break very easily, for any reason
whatsoever, treaties which they had made. Accordingly, he did not indulge in
any rest, but made ready his forces in every way, so that when occasion should

demand he would be ready for battle. For it was a matter greater and more terrible than famine which was then reported. Forsooth, the whole West, and as much of the land of barbarian peoples as lies beyond the Adriatic Sea up to the Pillars of Hercules—all this, changing its seat, was bursting forth into Asia in a solid mass, with all its belongings, taking its march through the intervening portion of Europe.

A certain Gaul, Peter by name, surnamed Kuku-Peter, had set out from his home to adore the Holy Sepulchre. After suffering many dangers and wrongs from the Turks and Saracens, who were devastating all Asia, he returned to his own country most sorrowfully. He could not bear to see himself thus cut off from his proposed pilgrimage and intended to undertake the expedition a second time. . . .

After Peter had promoted the expedition, he, with 80,000 foot soldiers and 100,000 knights, was the first of all to cross the Lombard strait. Then passing through the territory of Hungary, he arrived at the queenly city. For, as anyone may conjecture from the outcome, the race of the Gauls is not only very passionate and impetuous in other ways, but, also, when urged on by an impulse, cannot thereafter be checked. Our Emperor, aware of what Peter had suffered from the Turks before, urged him to await the arrival of the other counts.

12. The End of the "Crusade of the People": The *Gesta* Version

The English translation here is from Krey, 71–72.

But the above-mentioned Peter was the first to reach Constantinople, on the Kalends of August, and with him was a very large host of Alemanni. There he found assembled Lombards, and Longobards, and many others. The Emperor had ordered such a market as was in the city to be given to these people. And he said to them, "Do not cross the Strait until the chief host of the Christians has come, for you are not so strong that you can do battle with the Turks." The Christians conducted themselves badly, inasmuch as they tore down and burned buildings of the city and carried off the lead with which the churches were constructed and sold it to the Greeks. The Emperor was enraged thereat and ordered them to cross the Strait. After they had crossed, they did not cease doing all manner of evil, burning and plundering houses and churches. At length they reached Nicomedia, where the

Lombards and Longobards and Alemanni separated from the Franks because the Franks were constantly swelled with arrogance.

The Lombards and Longobards chose a leader over themselves whose name was Reinald. The Alemanni did likewise. They entered Romania and proceeded for four days beyond the city of Nicaea. They found a certain fortress, *Xerogord* by name, which was empty of people, and they seized it. In it they found an ample supply of grain, wine, and meat, and an abundance of all goods. The Turks, accordingly, hearing that the Christians were in the fortress, came to besiege it. Before the gate of the fortress was a cistern, and at the foot of the fortress was a fountain of running water, near which Reinald went out to trap the Turks. But the Turks, who came on the day of the Dedication of St. Michael, found Reinald and those who were with him and killed many of them. Those who remained alive fled to the fortress, which the Turks straightway besieged, thus depriving them of water. Our people were in such distress from thirst that they bled their horses and asses and drank the blood; others let their girdles and handkerchiefs down into the cistern and squeezed out the water from them into their mouths; some urinated into one another's hollowed hands and drank; and others dug up the moist ground and lay down on their backs and spread the earth over their breasts to relieve the excessive dryness of thirst. The bishops and priests, indeed, continued to comfort our people, and to admonish them not to yield, saying, "Be everywhere strong in the faith of Christ, and do not fear those who persecute you, just as the Lord saith, 'Be not afraid of them that kill the body, but are not able to kill the soul.'" This distress lasted for eight days. Then the lord of the Alemanni made an agreement with the Turks to surrender his companions to them; and, feigning to go out to fight, he fled to them, and many with him. Those, however, who were unwilling to deny the Lord received the sentence of death; some, whom they took alive, they divided among themselves, like sheep; some they placed as a target and shot with arrows; others they sold and gave away, like animals. Some they took captive to their own home, some to Chorosan, some to Antioch, others to Aleppo, or wherever they themselves lived. These were the first to receive a happy martyrdom in the name of the Lord Jesus.

Next, the Turks, hearing that Peter the Hermit and Walter the Penniless were in Civitote, which is located above the city of Nicaea, went there with great joy to kill them and those who were with them. And when they had come, they encountered Walter with his men [all of] whom the Turks soon killed. But Peter the Hermit had gone to Constantinople a short while before because he was unable to restrain that varied host, which was not willing to listen either to him or to his words. The Turks, indeed, rushed upon these people and killed many of them. Some they found sleeping, some lying down, others naked—all of whom they killed. With these people they found a certain priest celebrating mass, whom they straightway martyred upon the altar. Those who could escape fled to Civitote; others hurled themselves headlong into the sea, while some hid in the forests and mountains. But the Turks, pursuing them to the fortress, collected wood to burn them with the fort. The Christians who were in the fort, therefore, set fire to the wood that had been collected, and the fire, turning in the direction of the Turks, cremated some of them; but from the fire the Lord delivered our people at that time. Nevertheless, the Turks took them alive and divided them, just as they had done the others, and scattered them through all these regions, some to Chorosan, and others to Persia. This all happened in the month of October. The Emperor, upon hearing that the Turks had so scattered our people, was exceedingly glad and sent for them (the Turks) and had them cross the Strait. After they were across, he purchased all their arms. . . .

13. The End of the "Crusade of the People": The Version of Albert of Aachen

The English translation here is from Krey, 73–76.

The Emperor was moved by compassion on hearing this humble narrative and ordered two hundred gold besants to be given to Peter; of that money which was called tartaron he disbursed one measure for his army. After that, Peter retired from the conference and from the palace of the Emperor. Although under the kind protection of the Emperor, he rested only five days in the fields and lands near Constantinople, where Walter the Penniless had likewise pitched his tents. Becoming companions from that very day, thereafter their troops, arms, and all necessary provisions were joined together. Next, after five days, they moved their tents and, with the aid of the Emperor, passed by boat over the Strait of St. George. Entering the confines of Cappadocia, they advanced through mountainous country into Nicomedia and there passed the night. After this, they pitched camp at the port called Civitote. There merchants were constantly bringing ships laden with supplies of wine, corn, oil, and barley, and with abundance of cheese, selling all to the pilgrims with just measure.

While they were rejoicing in this abundance of necessities and were resting their tired bodies, there came messengers from the most Christian Emperor. Because of the danger of ambushes and attacks from the Turks, they forbade Peter and his whole army from marching towards the mountainous region of the city of Nicaea, until a greater number of Christians should be added to their number. Peter heard the message, and he with all the Christian people assented to the counsel of the Emperor. They tarried there for the course of two months, feasting in peace and joy, and sleeping secure from all hostile attacks.

And so two months later, having become wanton and unrestrained because of ease and an inestimable abundance of food, heeding not the voice of Peter, but against his will, they entered into the region of the city of Nicaea and the realms of Soliman. They took as plunder cattle, sheep, goats, the herds of the Greek servants of the Turks, and carried them off to their fellows. Peter, seeing this, was sorrowful in heart, knowing that they did it not with impunity. Whereupon he often admonished them not to seize any more booty contrary to the counsel of the Emperor, but in vain did he speak to a foolish and rebellious people. . . .

But the Teutons, seeing that affairs turned out so well for the Romans and the Franks, and that they returned unhindered so many times with their booty, were inflamed with an inordinate desire for plunder. About three thousand foot-soldiers were collected and about two hundred knights. . . .

And thus, after all the stronghold had been captured and its inhabitants driven out, they rejoiced in the abundance of food found there. And exulting in that victory, they in turn gave counsel that, by remaining in that fortress, they could easily obtain, through their own valor, the lands and principality of Soliman; that they would gather from all sides booty and food, and thus could easily weaken Soliman, until the promised army of the great leaders should approach. Soliman, the leader and chief of the army of the Turks, having heard of the arrival of the Christians, and of their plunder and booty, assembled from all Romania and the territory of Chorosan fifteen thousand of his Turks, most agile archers, very skilful in the use of bows of horn and bone. . . . Next, it is said, that after sunrise on the third day, Soliman with his followers arrived from Nicaea at the fortress which the Teutons had invaded. . . .

Therefore, the Turks, unable to drive out the Alemanni with this assault and shower of arrows, gathered all kinds of wood at the very gate of the fortress. They set fire to it and burned the gate and very many buildings which were within the citadel. As the heat of the flames became greater, some were burned to death; others, hoping for safety, leaped from the walls. But the Turks who were outside the walls cut down with swords those who were fleeing and took captive about two hundred who were pleasing in appearance and youthful in body; all the others they destroyed with sword and arrow. . . .

In the meantime, the truth was discovered and tumult arose among the people. The foot-soldiers came in a body to Reinald of Broyes, Walter the Penniless, to Walter of Breteuil, also, and to Folker of Orleans, who were leaders of Peter's army, to urge them to rise in a body in vindication of their brethren and against the audacity of the Turks. But they positively refused to go without the presence and the counsel of Peter. Then Godfrey Burel, master of the foot-soldiers, upon hearing their response, asserted that the timid by no means avail so much in war as the bold; and in sharp words he frequently reproached those men who prevented their other companions from pursuing the Turks to avenge their brethren. On the other hand, the leaders of the legion, unable to endure his insults and reproaches any longer, or those of their own followers, were deeply moved by wrath and indignation and promised that they would go against the strength and wiles of the Turks, even if it should happen that they died in battle.

Nor was there delay; at dawn on the fourth day, all the knights and foot-soldiers throughout the entire camp were ordered to arm themselves, to sound the trumpets, and to assemble for battle. Only the unarmed, the countless sick, and the women remained in camp. But all the armed men, to the number of 25,000 foot-soldiers and 500 knights in armor, pressed on their way together toward Nicaea, in order to avenge their brethren by provoking Soliman and the rest of the Turks to engage in battle. And so, divided and arrayed in six battle lines, with standards uplifted in each, they advanced on the right and on the left.

Boasting and shouting with vehement tumult and great clamor, they had scarcely advanced through the aforesaid forest and mountain region three miles from the port of Civitote, their halting place, (Peter being absent and unaware of all this), when lo! Soliman, with all his intolerable following, entered that same forest from the opposite side. He was coming down from the city of Nicaea to fall suddenly upon the Gauls in camp, intending at the point of the sword to wipe out and destroy them, unaware and unprepared. Upon hearing the approach and the violent outcry of the Christians, he marvelled greatly what this tumult meant, for all that the Christians had decided was unknown to him. Finding out straightway that they were pilgrims, Soliman addressed his men as follows, "Behold the Franks, against whom we were marching, are at hand. Let us withdraw from the forest and the mountains into the open plain, where we may freely engage in battle with them, and they can find no refuge." Accordingly, this was done without delay, at Soliman's command, and in deep silence they withdrew from the forest and the mountains.

But the Franks, unaware of Soliman's approach, advanced from the forest and the mountains with shouting and loud clamor. There they first beheld the battle lines of Soliman in the midst of the field, awaiting them for battle. When they had seen the Turks, they began to encourage one another in the name of the Lord. . . .

There Walter the Penniless fell, pierced by seven arrows which had penetrated his coat of mail. Reinald of Broyes and Folker of Chartres, men of the greatest renown in their own lands, fell in like martyrdom, destroyed by the enemy, though not without great slaughter of the Turks. But Walter of Breuteuil, son of Waleramnus, and Godfrey Burel, master of the foot-soldiers, having slipped away in flight through briars and thickets, turned back along the narrow path where the entire band, withdrawn from battle, had gathered together. When the flight and desertion of these men became known, all turned in flight, hastening their course towards Civitote along the same route by which they had come, but with little defense against the enemy.

And so the Turks, rejoicing in the pleasing success of victory, were destroying the wretched band of pilgrims, whom they followed for a distance of three miles, killing them even at the camp of Peter. And going within the tents, they destroyed with the sword whomever they found, the weak and the feeble, clerics, monks, old women, nursing children, persons of every age. But they led away young girls whose face and form was pleasing in their eyes, and beardless youths of comely countenance. They carried off to Nicaea money, garments, mules, horses, and all valuable things, as well as the tents themselves.

But above the shore of the sea, near the aforesaid Civitote, was an ancient, deserted fortress. Towards that fortress three thousand pilgrims rushed in flight. They entered the ruined fortress in hope of defense. But finding no gates or other obstacles, and anxious and deprived of aid, they piled up their shields for a gate, along with a huge pile of rocks; and with lances, wooden bows, and slingstones, they bravely defended themselves from the enemy. But the Turks, seeing that they were having little success in killing those inside, surrounded the fortress, which was without a roof, on all sides. They aimed their arrows high, so that, as they fell from the air in a shower, they would strike the bodies of the enclosed Christians, destroying the poor wretches; and that all the others, at the sight of this, might be compelled to surrender. In this way very many are said to have been wounded and killed there; but the rest, fearing yet more cruel treatment from the impious enemy, could not be compelled to come out either by force or by arms. . . .

The Emperor was moved with pity when he had heard from Peter about the siege and the fall of his men. So he summoned the Turcopoles and all the nations of his kingdom, and commanded them to go in all haste across the Strait to the aid of the fugitive and besieged Christians, and to drive the assaulting Turks from the siege. But the Turks, having learned of the Emperor's edict, moved from the fortress at midnight with their Christian captives and very great spoils, and so the pilgrim soldiers who had been shut up and besieged by the impious (Turks) were freed. . . .

14. The Byzantines Save Peter the Hermit: The Version of Anna Comnena

The English translation here is from Krey, 76–78.

But relying on the multitude of those who followed him, Peter did not heed the warning and, after crossing the strait, pitched camp at a little town called *Helenopolis*.

But since there were also Normans in his army, estimated at about ten thousand men, these, separating themselves from the rest of the body, devastated the region lying around the city of Nicaea, rioting most cruelly in every way. For they tore some of the children apart, limb from limb and, piercing others through with wooden stakes, roasted them in fire; likewise, upon those advanced in years they inflicted every kind of torture. When those in the city saw this being done, they opened the gates and went out against them. As a result, a fierce battle took place, in which, since the Normans fought ferociously, the citizens were hurled back into the fortress. The Normans, after gathering up all the plunder, again returned to *Helenopolis*. There a quarrel arose between themselves and the other pilgrims who had not gone off with them, a thing which usually happens in an affair of this kind, envy inflaming the wrath of those left behind, and a riotous fight followed the quarrel. The fierce Normans again separated [from the others] and captured *Xerogord* on their way at the first attack.

When this was learned, the Sultan sent Elchanes against them with a suitable number of troops. When he reached them, he recaptured *Xerogord*, killed some of the Normans with the sword, and carried off the rest as captives, planning at the same time, also, an attack upon those who had remained with Kuku-Peter. And he set ambushes at opportune places into which, when they left for Nicaea, they would unexpectedly fall and be killed. But knowing also of the avarice of the Gauls, he had summoned two men of bold spirit and ordered them to go to the camp of Kuku-Peter to announce that the Normans had captured Nicaea and were now sacking it to the utmost. This report, brought to the camp of Peter, excited all violently; for when the mention of plunder and riches was heard, they straightway set out in tumult on the road which leads to Nicaea, forgetful of their military training and of observing discipline in going out to battle. For the Latins are not only most fond of riches, as we said above, but when they give themselves to raiding any region for plunder, are also no longer obedient to reason, or any other check. Accordingly, since they were neither keeping order nor forming into lines, they fell into the ambush of the Turks around *Draco* and were wretchedly cut to pieces. Indeed, so great a multitude of Gauls and Normans were cut down by the Ishmaelite sword that when the dead bodies of the killed, which were lying all about in the place, were brought together, they made a very great mound, or hill, or look-out place, lofty as a mountain, and occupying a space very conspicuous for its width and depth. So high did that mound of bones tower, that some barbarians of the same race as the killed later used the bones of the slain instead of stones in constructing a wall, thus making that fortress a sort of sepulchre for them. It stands to this day, an enclosure of walls built with mixed rocks and bones.

And thus, after all had been wiped out in the slaughter, Peter returned with only a few to *Helenopolis*. The Turks, in their desire to get him into their power, again beset him with an ambush. But when the Emperor heard of the whole affair and learned how great was the slaughter of men, he held it very wrong that Peter should also be taken. Immediately, therefore, he summoned Catacalon Constantine Euphorbenus, of whom mention has often been made in this history, and sent him with suitable forces on war-vessels across the sea as a succour to Peter. When the Turks saw him approach, they fled. . . .

IV.

The Journey to Constantinople (August, 1096–May, 1097)

The arrival at Constantinople was an important moment. The emperor knew of the armies' coming and of their need for supplies and cooperation on his part, but he also knew his own interests. Memories of this encounter lasted long, and some of the anti-Byzantine attitudes of later western Europeans can be traced to the first meetings in the fall of 1096. On the rates of march, see John W. Nesbitt, "The Rate of March of Crusading Armies in Europe: A Study and Computation," Traditio 19 (1963), 167–182, and John France, Victory in the East: A Military History of the First Crusade (Cambridge, 1994).

1. The *Gesta* Version

The English translation here is from Krey, 57.

Soon they departed from their homes in Gaul, and then formed three groups. One party of Franks, namely, Peter, the Hermit, Duke Godfrey, Baldwin, his brother, and Baldwin, Count of the Mount, entered the region of Hungary. These most powerful knights, and many others whom I do not know, went by the way which Charles the Great, wonder-working king of France, long ago had made, even to Constantinople. . . .

The second party—to wit, Raymond, Count of St. Gilles, and the Bishop of Puy—entered the region of Slavonia. The third division, however, went by the ancient road to Rome. In this division were Bohemund, Richard of Principati, Robert, Count of Flanders, Robert the Norman, Hugh the Great, Everard of Puiset, Achard of Montmerle, Ysoard of Mousson, and many others. Next, they went to the port of Brindisi, or Bari, or Otranto. Then

Hugh the Great, and William, son of Marchisus, took to the sea at the port of Bari and, crossing the strait, came to Durazzo. But the governor of this place, his heart touched with evil design, took these most renowned men captive immediately upon hearing that they had landed there and ordered them to be conducted carefully to the Emperor at Constantinople, where they should pledge loyalty to him.

2. The Deserters: The Version of Albert of Aachen

The English translation here is from Krey, 57.

After the departure of Peter the Hermit and the most dire destruction of his army; after the killing of the distinguished soldier Walter the Penniless, and the grievous disaster to his army; shortly after the cruel slaughter of the priest, Gottschalk, and of his army; after the misfortune of Hartmann, Count of Alemannia, of Emico, and all the other brave men and leaders from the land of Gaul (to wit, Drogo of Nesle and Clarebold of Vendeuil); . . . taking up again their pilgrim's staves, the remnants of the crusading army ignominiously returned to their homes. This desertion debased them before God and man, and it redounded to their shame.

3. Bohemund: The *Gesta* Version

Bohemund* was one of the leaders of the crusade, and the Gesta *author admired him greatly. Others, however, found him overbearing and dangerous.*
The English translation here is from Krey, 62–64.

But Bohemund, powerful in battle, who was engaged in the siege of Amalfi on the sea of Salerno, heard that a countless host of Christians from among the Franks had come to go to the Sepulchre of the Lord, and that they were prepared for battle against the pagan horde. He then began to inquire closely what fighting arms these people bore, and what sign of Christ they carried on the way, or what battle-cry they shouted. The following replies were made to him in order: "They bear arms suitable for battle; on the right shoulder, or between both shoulders, they wear the cross of Christ; the

---

* For Bohemund, see above, p. 57, n. 4.

cry, 'God wills it! God wills it! God wills it!' they shout in truth with one voice." Moved straighway by the Holy Spirit, he ordered the most precious cloak which he had with him cut to pieces, and straightway he had the whole of it made into crosses. Thereupon, most of the knights engaged in that siege rushed eagerly to him, so that Count Roger remained almost alone.

Returning again to his own land, Lord Bohemund diligently prepared himself to undertake in true earnest the journey to the Holy Sepulchre. At length, he crossed the sea with his army. With him were Tancred, son of Marchisus, Richard of Principati, and Rainulf, his brother, Robert of Anse, Herman of Cannae, Robert of *Surda* Valley, Robert, son of *Tostanus*, Hunfred, son of Raoul, Richard, son of Count Rainulf, the Count of *Roscignolo*, with his brothers, Boellus of Chartres, Albered of Cagnano, and Hunfred of Mt. Scaglioso. All of these crossed the sea to do service for Bohemund and landed in the region of Bulgaria, where they found a very great abundance of grain, wine, and bodily nourishment. Thence descending into the valley of *Andronopoli*, they waited for his forces, until all had likewise crossed the sea. Then the wise Bohemund ordered a council with his people, comforting and admonishing all [with these words]: "Seignors, take heed all of you, for we are pilgrims of God. We ought, therefore, to be better and more humble than before. Do not plunder this land, since it belongs to Christians, and let no one, at the cost of blessing, take more than he needs to eat."

Departing thence, we journeyed through great plenty from villa to villa, city to city, fortress to fortress, until we reached Castoria. There we solemnly celebrated the nativity of the Lord. We remained there for several days and sought a market, but the people were unwilling to accord it to us, because they feared us greatly, thinking that we came not as pilgrims, but to devastate their land and to kill them. Wherefore we took their cattle, horses, asses, and everything that we found. Leaving Castoria, we entered Pelagonia, in which there was a certain fortified town of heretics. This we attacked from all sides and it soon yielded to our sway. Thereupon, we set it on fire and burned the camp with its inhabitants, that is, the congregation of heretics. Later, we reached the river Vardar. And then Lord Bohemund went across with his people, but not with all, for the Count of *Roscignolo* with his brothers remained behind.

Thereupon, an army of the Emperor came and attacked the Count with his brothers and all who were with them. Tancred, hearing of this, went back and, hurling himself into the river, reached the others by swimming; and two thousand went into the river following Tancred. At length, they came upon the Turcopoles and Patzinaks struggling with our men. They [Tancred and his men] charged the enemy suddenly and bravely and overcame them gloriously.

Several of them they seized and led them, bound, into the presence of Bohemund, who spoke to them as follows: "Wherefore, miserable men, do you
kill Christ's people and mine? I have no quarrel with your Emperor." They replied, "We cannot do otherwise; we have been placed in the service of the Emperor, and whatever he commands we must fulfill." Bohemund allowed them
to depart unpunished. This battle was fought in the fourth day of the week,
which is the beginning of the fast. Through all, blessed is the Lord! Amen.

The unhappy Emperor sent one of his own men, whom he greatly loved,
and whom they call *Corpalatius*, together with our envoys, to conduct us in
security through his land until we should come to Constantinople. And as
we paused before their cities, he ordered the inhabitants to offer us a market,
just as those also did of whom we have spoken. Indeed, they feared the most
brave host of Lord Bohemund so greatly that they permitted none of us to
enter the walls of the city. Our men wanted to attack and seize a certain fortified town because it was full of all kinds of goods. But the renowned man,
Bohemund, refused to consent not only in justice to the land, but also because of his pledge to the Emperor. Therefore, he was greatly angered on this
account with Tancred and all the rest. This happened toward evening. When
morning came, the inhabitants of the town came out, and, in procession,
bearing crosses in their hands, they came into the presence of Bohemund.
Delighted, he received them; and with gladness he permitted them to depart.
Next we came to a certain town, which is called Serrhae, where we fixed our
tents and had a market sufficient for that time. There the learned Bohemund
made a very cordial agreement with two *Corpalatii*; and out of regard for
their friendship, as well as in justice to the land, he ordered all the stolen animals which our men had to be returned. The *Corpalatius* promised him that
he would despatch messengers to return the animals to their owners in order.
Then we proceeded from castle to castle and from villa to villa to the city of
Rusa. The people of the Greeks came out, bringing us the greatest market,
and went joyfully to meet Lord Bohemund. There we pitched our tents in
the fourth day of the week before the feast of the Lord.

There, also, the learned Bohemund left all his host and went on ahead to
speak with the Emperor at Constantinople. He gave commands to his vassals,
saying, "Approach the city gradually. I, however, will go on in advance." And
he took with him a few knights. Tancred remained at the head of the army
of Christ, and, seeing the pilgrims buying food, he said to himself that he
would go off the road and lead his people where they would live happily. At
length he entered a certain valley, filled with goods of all kinds that are suitable nourishment for the body, and in it we most devoutly celebrated Easter.

4. Raymond of Toulouse and Ademar of Le Puy: The Version of Raymond d'Aguilers

Raymond of Aguilers was the chaplain of Raymond of St. Gilles, Count of Toulouse and leader of the Provençal contingent on the First Crusade. Raymond of Saint-Gilles had been one of the first warriors to take the cross, and he evidently knew of Urban's plans well before the Council of Clermont. Ademar of Le Puy was urban's legate on the crusade, and hence its ecclesiastical leader.* The chronicle of Raymond d'Aguilers, written before 1105, becomes especially important once the crusaders reached Antioch. Raymond's history has been translated by John H. Hill and Laurita L. Hill, Raymond d'Aguilers, Historia Francorum qui ceperunt Iherusalem *(Philadelphia, 1968), with an excellent introduction and bibliography.*
The English translation here is from Krey, 64–67.

While advancing into the land of Slavonia they suffered many losses on the way, especially because it was then winter. For Slavonia was such a desert and so pathless and mountainous that we saw in it neither wild animals, nor birds for three weeks. The inhabitants of the region were so boorish and rude that they were unwilling to trade with us, or to furnish us guidance, but instead fled from their villages and their castles. Indeed, they even butchered like cattle, or, as if they had done much harm, the feeble aged and the weak poor, who, because of their weakness, followed our army at a distance. Nor was it easy amidst steep mountains and thick woods for our armed knights to pursue the unarmed brigands who were acquainted with the country. But they suffered them constantly, unable either to fight or to keep from fighting. Let us not pass over a certain illustrious act of the Count. When the Count with some of his knights had been hedged about for some little time by the Slavonians, he made a charge upon them and captured as many as six of them. And when, on this account, the Slavonians pressed upon him the more violently, and the Count was compelled to follow the army, he ordered the eyes of some of them [the prisoners] to be torn out, the feet of others cut off, and the nose and hands of still others to be slashed, so that while the pursuers were thus moved at the sight and preoccupied with their sorrow, the Count could safely escape with his companions. And thus, by the grace of God he was delivered from the straits of death and this difficult situation.

Indeed, what courage and wisdom the Count displayed in this region is not easy to relate! For we were in Slavonia for almost forty days, during which time we encountered clouds so dense that we could feel them and push

---

* For Raymond of Toulouse, see above, p. 57, n. 7, for Ademar, see above, p. 54, n. 1.

them before us with a slight movement. Amidst all this, the Count was fighting constantly at the rear and ever defending his people. He was never the
first, but always the last, to encamp, and though the others went to rest at
midday, or at evening, the Count often did so at midnight, or at cockcrow.
At length, through the compassion of God, the labor of the Count, and the
advice of the Bishop, the army so crossed [Slavonia] that we lost no one there
from hunger, and no one in open battle. On that account, I bear witness,
God wanted his army to cross Slavonia, in order that the boorish men who
did not know God, upon recognizing the valor and patience of His knights,
might either lose something of their wildness or be brought without excuse
to God's judgment. And then, after many labors, we came to the king of the
Slavonians at Scutari. The Count swore friendship with him and gave him
a large tribute, so that the army might buy or seek necessaries in security.
But this was a [vain] expectation, for we did penance enough for the peace
we had sought when thereafter the Slavonians, raging in their usual manner,
killed our men and took from the unarmed what they could. We sought not
vengeance, but a place of refuge. So much about Slavonia.

We came to Durazzo. We believed we were in our own country, thinking that the Emperor and his satellites were our brothers and helpmates.
They, indeed, raging in the manner of lions, attacked a peaceful people who
thought of nothing less than arms. They butchered them in secret places; they
stole what they could by night, in the woods, and in villages remote from
the camp. Although they raged thus, their leader promised peace. But during
the intervals of peace, they killed Pontius Reinald and mortally wounded his
brother, Peter, and these were most noble princes. However, when an opportunity was presented to us for revenge, we chose to continue the journey, not
to avenge our wrongs. On the way, we had letters from the Emperor about
peace, brotherhood, and, as I may also say, about alliance; this, however, was
a snare in words. For in front and behind, to right and to left, Turks and Cumans, Uzi, *Tanaces*, Patzinaks, and Bulgarians were lying in ambush for us.

On a certain day, moreover, when we were in the valley of Pelagonia, the
Bishop of Puy, who, in order to find a comfortable resting place, had withdrawn a little distance from the camp, was captured by the Patzinaks. They
knocked him down from his mule, robbed him, and beat him severely on the
head. But since so great a pontiff was still necessary to the people of God,
through God's mercy he was saved to life. For one of the Patzinaks, in order
to obtain gold from him, protected him from the others. Meanwhile, the
noise was heard in the camp; and so, between the delay of the enemy and the
attack of his friends, he was rescued.

When we had come amidst treachery of this fashion to a certain fortress called *Bucinat*, the Count learned that the Patzinaks intended to attack our army in the passes of a certain mountain. Staying in hiding with some of his knights, he came upon the Patzinaks, and, after killing several of them, he turned the rest to flight. Meanwhile, pacifying letters from the Emperor reached us, [and yet] by his evil design the enemy surrounded us on all sides. When we came to Thessalonica, the Bishop was ill and remained in the city with a few men.

After this, we came to a certain city, Rusa by name, where, since its citizens were plainly disposed to do us evil, our usual patience was somewhat disturbed. So, taking up arms, we destroyed the outer walls, seized great plunder, and forced the city to surrender; then, having taken our standards into the city and shouted "Toulouse!" which was the battle cry of the Count, we departed.

We came to another city, called Rodosto. When knights in the pay of the Emperor there sought to carry out his vengeance upon us, many of them were killed and a quantity of plunder taken. There, also, the envoys whom we had sent ahead to the Emperor came to us and, having received money from him, promised that everything boded well for us with the Emperor. What more? The message [brought] by our envoys and those of the Emperor was that the Count, leaving his army behind, should hasten unarmed and with a few men to the Emperor. For they said that Bohemund, the Duke of Lorraine, the Count of Flanders, and other princes made this prayer: that the Count should hasten to agree with the Emperor about the march to Jerusalem; that the Emperor, having taken the cross, should also become leader in the army of God. In addition to this, they reported that the Emperor had said that he would make all arrangements with the Count, both about themselves and whatever else should be necessary for the journey. They announced, furthermore, that a battle was imminent, and that without the support of so great a man it would probably be unfavorable; that the Count should therefore go ahead with a few men, so that when his army should arrive, everything would have been arranged with the Emperor, and there would be no delay for anyone. At length, the Count was persuaded to go ahead of his army, in this instance, alone, leaving his guard behind him in the camp. And thus he went unarmed to Constantinople.

V.

The Crusaders at Constantinople (October, 1096–May, 1097)

Alexius I had probably not anticipated a force as large as that which the crusaders brought. Although he provided them with food and shelter and promised them guides, he also attempted to extract oaths of loyalty from them and exerted considerable pressure on those who would not comply. The visit of the crusaders to Constantinople marked the beginning of that Western distrust of Byzantium that greatly hampered the Second Crusade in 1147 and helped provide a rationale for the later diversion of the Fourth Crusade to the capture of Constantinople itself in 1204.

1. Hugh of Vermandois of France: The Version of Anna Comnena

Hugh (the Great) * of Vermandois was the brother of King Philip VI of France and thus in a sense represented the Capetian dynasty as a crusader at the very beginning of the crusades, a movement which later reigning French kings virtually made their own.

The English translation here is from Krey, 78–79.

As we said above, there were among the Latins such men as Bohemund and his fellow counsellors, who, eager to obtain the Roman Empire for themselves, had been looking with avarice upon it for a long time. Seeing an opening for their plans in the expedition which was promoted by Peter, they stirred up this huge movement; and, in order to deceive the more simple, they feigned a crusade against the Turks to regain the Holy Sepulchre and

---

* For Hugh of France, see above, p. 57, n. 1.

sold all their possessions. Moreover, a certain Hugh, brother of the King of France, who conducted himself with the spirit of a *navatus* on account of his wealth and power and the nobility of his birth, decided to leave his fatherland, as if to set out for the Holy Sepulchre. Upon reaching this decision, he looked forward to a most glorious meeting and announced in letters full of swollen insolence to the Emperor:

"Know, O King, that I am King of Kings, and superior to all who are under the sky. You are now permitted to greet me, on my arrival, and to receive me with magnificence, as befits my nobility."

At this time the Governor of Durazzo was John, son of Isaac, the *Sebastocrator*, of whom we have spoken above. Nicolaus Maurocatacalon, in command of the fleet, had arranged his ships at stations around the port of Durazzo, so that he could make excursions and watch the seas, lest, perchance, pirate ships might secretly approach. To each of these men, therefore, the Emperor, after hearing this letter [from Hugh], immediately sent a message, bidding the Governor of Durazzo watch closely by land and sea for the arrival of this man, upon whose coming a messenger was to be sent quickly to the Emperor. Hugh, however, was to be received magnificently. He further ordered the commander of the fleet to be constantly alert and on the watch with every faculty awake, not with his usual negligence.

Meanwhile Hugh reached the seacoast of Longobardy; there he sent envoys to the Governor of Durazzo, twenty-four in number, each decorated with gold and red breastplates. Along with them went Count Carpenter and that Helia who had fled from the Emperor at Thessalonica. These men addressed the following message to the Governor:

"Be it known to you, O Governor, that our lord, Hugh, will soon be here, bringing with him from Rome the golden banner of St. Peter; moreover, know that he is the highest leader of all the armies of France. Prepare yourself, therefore, to receive him and the army obeying him according to the dignity of his power; and gird yourself about to meet him."

While they were thus commanding the Governor, Hugh, as it is said, came from Rome into Longobardy; and leaving Bari toward Illyricum, he was caught by a most awful storm and lost the greater number of his ships, together with their oarsmen and passengers. The little boat in which he saved himself was cast up by the waves, as though they spewed it forth, on the seacoast which lies half way between Durazzo and another place called *Palus*. It, too, was half cut to pieces. Two men, who were on the watch for his arrival, met him after he had been saved and pressed him with these words: "The Governor is awaiting your arrival, desiring very much to enjoy your coming." Thereupon, Hugh immediately asked for a horse, and one of those men, dismounting from his horse, very dutifully gave it over to him. As a result, the Governor, after seeing that Hugh was safe, was the first to greet him and asked whither, and whence, and what dangers and evils had befallen him in sailing. And when he had been set upon his feet and refreshed with kind words, the Governor then put before him a well-prepared feast. After dinner he loosed him, but did not yet permit him to walk about freely, for all these things had been quickly announced to the Emperor, and the Governor was waiting to find out his commands from him.

When the Emperor was informed, he quickly sent Butumites to Epidamnus, which we have often called Durazzo, with orders to bring Hugh back with him and not to return by the direct road, but, by turning aside, to bring him to Constantinople through Philippopolis; for he was afraid of the forces and throngs of Gauls who followed. The Emperor treated him honorably with all kindness and gave him, in addition, considerable sums of money. He immediately urged the man to attach himself to him [the Emperor], and to bind himself by the customary oaths of the Latins. . . .

2. Godfrey of Bouillon: The *Gesta* Version

Godfrey of Bouillon, Duke of Lower Lorraine and the most prestigious of the "German" contingent on the First Crusade, became the Guardian of the Holy Sepulcher after the capture of Jerusalem in July, 1099, and thus the first ruler of what became the Latin Kingdom of Jerusalem. See J. C. Andressohn, The Ancestry and Life of Godfrey of Bouillon *(Bloomington, Ind., 1947), and P. Aube,* Godfroi de Bouillon *(Paris, 1985).*

The English translation here is from Krey, 80.

Duke Godfrey was the first of all the seignors to come to Constantinople with a great army. He arrived two days before the Nativity of Our Lord and camped outside the city, until the iniquitous Emperor ordered him to be lodged in a suburb of the city. And when the Duke had been so lodged, he used to send his squires, under pledge, day by day to fetch hay and other necessities for the horses. When now they planned to go wherever they wished, on the strength of their pledge, the evil Emperor placed a watch upon them and commanded his Turcopoles and Patzinaks to attack and kill them. Thereupon, when Baldwin, brother of the Duke, heard of this, he placed himself in ambush and then found them killing his people. He attacked them in great anger and, God helping, overcame them. Capturing sixty of them, he killed some and presented the rest to the Duke, his brother. When the Emperor had heard of this, he was exceedingly angry. Then the Duke, seeing that the Emperor was enraged, went with his men out of the suburb and encamped outside the city. Moreover, toward evening the Emperor ordered his forces to attack the Duke and the people of Christ. The unconquered Duke and the knights of Christ pursued these, killed seven of them, and drove the rest even to the gates of the city. The Duke, returning to his tents, remained there for five days, until he had entered into an agreement with the Emperor. The Emperor told him to cross the Strait of St. George, and promised to have every kind of market there, just as at Constantinople, and to distribute alms to the poor, upon which they could live.

3. Godfrey of Bouillon: The Version of Albert of Aachen

The English translation here is from Krey, 80–86.

With his entire band of pilgrims Godfrey withdrew to the city of Constantinople itself. There, after pitching their tents, they lodged, a strong and powerful band, protected by armor and all warlike equipment. And, behold, at the meeting Hugh, Drogo, William Carpenter, and Clarebold, set free by the Emperor, were present, rejoicing because of the arrival of the Duke and of his multitudes, and meeting the embrace of the Duke and of the others with many a kiss. And, likewise, the above mentioned messenger of the Emperor met the Duke, asking him to come to the palace of the Emperor with some of the chiefs of his army, that he might hear the word of the King. The rest of his multitude should remain outside the walls of the city. Scarcely had the Duke received the message when, behold, some strangers from the land of the Franks appeared by stealth in his camp. The strangers cautioned the Duke very strongly to beware of the wiles and alluring appearance of the Emperor, and by no means to go to the Emperor because of some flattering promise, but to sit outside the walls and listen carefully to all which the Emperor should propose to him. Thereupon, the Duke, so warned by the strangers, and caught by the deception of the Greeks, did not go to the Emperor.

For this reason, the Emperor, moved by a violent indignation towards the Duke and all his army, refused them the privilege of buying and selling. But when Baldwin, brother of the Duke, learned of the wrath of the Emperor and saw the need of the people and their very great lack of necessaries, he pleaded with the Duke and the leaders to plunder again the region and lands of the Greeks, and to collect spoils and food, until the Emperor, compelled by this damage, should again grant the privilege of buying and selling. Therefore, when the Emperor saw devastation and misfortune befalling the lands of his kingdom, he once more gave to all the privilege of buying and selling.

It was the time of the Nativity of the Lord. At that festal time, and in those days of peace and joy, it seemed to all praiseworthy, good, and acceptable before God that peace should be restored on both sides between the household of the Emperor and the Duke and all the mighty ones of the army. And so, when peace had been made, they withheld their hands from all plunder and hurt. Accordingly, during those four holy days they rested in all quiet and happiness before the walls of the city Constantinople.

Four days after, the legation of the Emperor went to the Duke asking, for the sake of the Emperor and his entreaties, that he would move his camp, and with his army lodge in the houses situated on the shore of the Straight, so that their tents might not become wet and worn from wintry cold and snow, which was threatening in that rainy season. Finally, the Duke and all the other leaders yielded to the will of the Emperor, and, after moving their tents, they, with all the Christian army, lodged in the castles and turreted buildings which were along the shore for a distance of thirty miles. From that day on successively they found and bought every abundance of food and necessities by order of the Emperor.

Shortly after, an embassy of the Emperor again appeared before the Duke, urging him to go and learn what the Emperor had to say. This the Duke absolutely refused to do, having been warned by the strangers of the craftiness of the Emperor. But he sent to him as messengers the distinguished men Conon, Count of Montaigu, Baldwin of Burg, and Godfrey of Ascha, who were to make excuses for him, speaking in this manner: "Duke Godfrey to the Emperor; trust and obedience. Willingly and eagerly would I come before you to look upon the wealth and glory of your household, were it not that many evil rumors, which have come to my ears regarding you, have terrified me. However, I know not whether these reports have been invented and spread about from envy or malice towards you." The Emperor, hearing this, warmly protested his innocence of all these charges, saying that never should the Duke or any of his followers fear any artifice on his part, but that he would serve and honor the Duke as his son, and the Duke's associates as his friends. Then the messengers of the Duke, on their return, reported favorably on all the good and faithful promises which they had heard from the Emperor's lips. But the Duke, still placing little faith in the honeyed promises of the Emperor, again refused him a conference. And so, between these messages back and forth, fifteen days rolled away.

Therefore the Emperor, recognizing the firmness of the Duke and that he could not be lured before him, again took offense and withdrew the privilege of buying barley, and fish, and then bread, so that the Duke, thus coerced, could not refuse to enter the presence of the Emperor. The Emperor, unsuccessful in changing the Duke's mind, one day had five hundred Turcopoles armed with bows and quivers taken in ships across the strait. Early in the morning, they shot the soldiers of the Duke with arrows; some they killed, others they wounded, keeping them all from the shore, so that they could not there buy the usual food.

This cruel report was carried immediately to the chair of the Duke. He thereupon ordered the trumpets to be sounded and all the people to arm themselves and return to the city of Constantinople itself, and there to replace their tents. After the trumpets had been sounded at this command of the Duke, all rushed to arms. They laid waste the buildings and towers in which they had been lodged, setting fire to some, pulling others to pieces, thus causing irreparable damage to Constantinople.

Finally, when the report of this great fire and destruction had reached the palace, the Duke became excessively alarmed, fearing that when the flaming buildings and the noise of a moving army had been noticed, the knights and archers of the Emperor would suddenly seize the bridge over which they had come from the city of Constantinople to the palatial residences. Therefore, without delay he sent Baldwin, his brother, with five hundred armored knights to seize the bridge, lest any force of the Emperor, anticipating him, should destroy it, and thus deny the pilgrims passage back and forth.

Baldwin had scarcely taken a stand on the middle of the bridge, when, behold, from right and left, Turcopoles [the soldiers of the Emperor brought over on the ships] rushed upon them from all sides with arrows and fiercely attacked them. Baldwin, unable to resist from the bridge, hastened to escape their arrows by going across the bridge. Along the dry shore he swiftly betook himself to the other side of the bridge, [hoping] to hold it and keep watch upon the walls of the lord and master of the city while the entire army passed over that bridge, and the Duke with his men kept guard from the rear. In the meantime, from the gates opposite *St. Argenteus* an infinite band of Turcopoles and soldiers of every kind, equipped with bows and arms of every description, ran forward to attack Baldwin and the whole band of Christian people. But in the appointed place Baldwin, immovable and unconquered, withstood their every attack from early morning even to vespers, until the people were taken across the bridge and lodged in the camps placed before the walls of the city. Baldwin, with his five hundred knights, advanced fiercely upon these same Turcopoles who had come out from the gates and were attacking the people. Both sides having engaged in heavy battle, very many fell on this side and that, and very many horses of the Franks perished by arrows. But Baldwin, conquering at last, forced these harried and fleeing soldiers of the Emperor to go inside the gates. Then the Turcopoles and soldiers of the Emperor, indignant that they had been beaten and put to flight in war, rushed forth again from the gates in larger numbers to harass and attack the army.

Then the Duke arrived and, since it was night, brought an end to the fight, advising his brother to return to camp with all his forces, and to keep his men from fighting during the night. Likewise, the Emperor himself, fearing that the tempest of war would become more and more violent, and that his soldiers would fail and perish in the darkness of evening, commanded peace to be made, rejoicing that the Duke had been willing to withdraw his army from battle.

But after sunrise the next day, the people, surging forth at the command of the Duke, wandered about plundering the lands and kingdom of the Emperor for six days, so that, to say the least, the pride of the Emperor and his men seemed to be humbled. When this became known, the Emperor began to grieve and lament because his lands and kingdom were being thus devastated. Taking counsel immediately, he sent a message to the Duke to the effect that he should prohibit plunder and fire, and that he himself would give satisfaction in every respect to the Duke. The message ran as follows: "Let enmity between you and us cease. Let the Duke, upon receiving hostages as a pledge from me, advance without any doubt that he will come and return unharmed, assured of all the honor and glory which we are able to give him and his people." The Duke graciously agreed, provided hostages were given to whom he could trust his life and safety; then without doubt he would come to the Emperor, freely to speak by word of mouth.

Hardly had the legates of the Emperor departed after this response of the Duke, when, behold, certain other legates, coming to the same Duke from Bohemund, greeted him, speaking thus: "Bohemund, the most wealthy prince of Sicily and Calabria, asks that you by no means enter into peace with the Emperor; but that you withdraw to Adrianople and Philippopolis, cities of the Bulgarians, and pass the winter there. You may be certain that this same Bohemund will come to your aid with all his troops early in the month of March, to attack the Emperor and to invade his kingdom." After he had heard the message of Bohemund, the Duke put off answering it until the next day. Then, upon the counsel of his followers, he replied that neither for gain nor for the destruction of Christians had he left his country and kindred, but, rather, in the name of Christ to pursue the way to Jerusalem. He wished to accomplish this and to fight the designs of the Emperor, provided he could regain and keep his favor and good will. The messengers of Bohemund, upon learning the reply and intention of the Duke, were graciously commended by him and returned to the country of Apulia, reporting all as they had heard it from the lips of the Duke.

Learning of this new embassy and suggestion from Bohemund, the Emperor yet more earnestly urged the Duke and his friends to enter upon an agreement with him; he would give his most beloved son, John, as hostage, on condition that they would make peace, would pass through the country quietly, and would meet him in conference face to face. Furthermore, he would favor Godfrey and his followers with the privilege of buying all necessaries. When the Duke learned that these promises of the Emperor had been made in the form of a decree, he moved his camp from the wall of the city by the advice of his council and again withdrew across the bridge to take lodging in the fortified dwellings on the strait. He admonished all his people to remain at peace, and to purchase whatever was necessary without disturbance.

On the following day, he commanded Conon, Count of Montaigu, and Baldwin of Burg, most noble men and skilled in speaking, to come before him. He then confidently directed them to receive as hostage the Emperor's son, which was done. When, therefore, the Emperor's son had been brought and placed in faithful custody under the power of the Duke and his men, the Duke was carried at once by boat through the Strait to Constantinople. Accompanied by the distinguished men, Werner of Grez, Peter of Dampierre, and the other leaders, he boldly advanced to the Court of the Emperor and stood before him, that he might hear his word and reply to him by word of mouth. Baldwin, however, by no means entered then into the palace of the Emperor, but remained on the shore with the multitude.

Upon seeing the magnificence of the Duke and all his men, honorably clad, as they were, in splendid and rich apparel of purple and gold, bordered with ermine white as snow, with martin, and other kinds of fur, such as the princes of Gaul, especially, wear, the Emperor heartily admired their pomp and splendor. He first graciously received the Duke, then all his chiefs and companions, whom he honored with the kiss of peace. Moreover, the Emperor sat in majesty upon his throne, according to his custom, and did not rise to give the kiss to the Duke, or anyone. But the Duke, together with his men, bowed with bended knees to kiss so glorious and great an Emperor.

When at last all had received the kiss, according to their rank, he spoke to the Duke in these words: "I have heard that you are the most mighty knight and prince in your land, a man most prudent and of perfect trust. In the presence of this multitude and more to come, I, therefore, take you for my adopted son; and all that I possess I place in your power, that through you my empire and lands may be saved and freed."

The Duke, appeased and seduced by these friendly and lofty words of the Emperor, not only recognized himself as his son, according to the custom of the country, but, likewise, giving him his hand, declared himself his vassal, together with the princes then present, who followed the Duke in the ceremony. Nor was there delay. Invaluable gifts of all kinds were brought from the treasury of the Emperor, both gold and silver, purples, mules, and horses, and all that he held valuable. So, indeed, the Emperor and the Duke were bound by the indissoluble bond of perfect faith and friendship, from the time of the Nativity of the Lord, when the agreement took place, even to a few days before Pentecost. Every week, four men, bearing gold besants, with ten measures of money called tartaron, were sent from the palace of the Emperor to the Duke to provide sustenance for the soldiers. Wonderful to relate! All that the Duke distributed to his men from the gifts of the Emperor was forthwith returned to the treasury of the Emperor in exchange for food. Nor is this to be wondered at, for none but the Emperor's wares (such as wine, and oil, as well as grain, barley, and every kind of food) were in that whole kingdom. And thus the treasury of the Emperor was always filled with gold and could not be emptied by any extravagance.

After peace and concord between the Emperor and the Duke had been made on the conditions we have named, the Duke, still more certain of the Emperor's faith and friendship, returned to lodge in the buildings on the Strait and sent back with honor the Emperor's son, who had remained a hostage up to this time. On the day following, it was announced through the entire army, by order of the Duke, that peace and honor should be shown to the Emperor and to all in his command, and that justice should be preserved in transactions of buying and selling. Similarly, the Emperor proclaimed in all his realm that no one, under penalty of death, should harm or defraud any one of the army, but that they should sell all things with just weight and measure to the pilgrims, and, indeed, should lessen the price.

After these events, at the beginning of Lent, the Emperor summoned the Duke into his presence and begged him, on his pledge of friendship, to cross the sea and pitch his tents in Cappadocia, on account of the buildings which his incorrigible people were destroying. The Duke graciously assented to this, and, after crossing the river and pitching camp, he and his people tar-ried on the plains of Cappadocia.

After this, everything was gradually sold more dearly to the pilgrims, but, nevertheless, the gifts of the Emperor to the Duke were not at all dimin-ished, for he feared him greatly. But the Duke, seeing the difficulty of buying necessaries and unable to endure the clamor of his people, went often by ship to the Emperor and complained to him about the high price of food stuffs. Then the Emperor, as though unaware of this, and unwilling to have it occur, again lightened the burden for all the pilgrims.

4. Godfrey of Bouillon: The Version of Anna Comnena

The English translation here is from Krey, 86–90.

At that time, too, came Count Godfrey, who had crossed the sea with the other counts and was accompanied by an army of 10,000 knights and 70,000 foot-soldiers. He established his force about the Propontis, his camp extending from the bridge which was opposite Cosmidion up to *St. Phocas.* While the Emperor urged him to cross the strait of the Propontis, he went on from day to day contriving one excuse or another and put off the matter. The real reason, to state the matter simply, was that he was awaiting the ar-rival of Bohemund and the other counts. For, though in the beginning Peter had aroused this great expedition to adore the Holy Sepulchre, the other counts, Bohemund above all, were cherishing in mind the old grudge against the Emperor and were awaiting a favorite opportunity to take vengeance on him for the splendid victory which he had gained over Bohemund when the latter engaged him in battle at Larissa. And dreaming that if they were of one mind they could take Constantinople itself, they had combined with the same thought and purpose of which we have often made mention above. Thus, ap-parently they were making an expedition to Jerusalem; in reality, however, they wanted to divest the Emperor of his kingdom and take Constantinople. But the Emperor, long since acquainted with their wiles, by letter ordered forces of Gentiles with their leaders to be stationed by squadrons from the Athyras river up to Philea, a seaport on the Black Sea. [He also ordered them] to watch in ambush for anyone sent, perchance, by Godfrey to Bohemund and the rest of the counts who were following, or by these, in turn, to him, and to deny these messengers all passage.

In the meantime, while this was going on, the following incident oc-curred, somewhat in this way. The Emperor had summoned before him some of the counts who had come with Godfrey, in order to urge that they consent to persuade Godfrey to carry out the promise which he had made under oath. While the time was thus being dragged out longer [than expected], for the reason that the Latin race is by nature exceedingly garrulous and wordy, there was reported to these people the false rumor that the counts had been taken into custody at the Emperor's command. Thereupon, the Latin legions surged together in a huge crowd and moved upon Byzantium and without delay utterly destroyed the palaces which are situated toward the swamp called *Argyra*. At the same time they tried the walls of the city, not with siege machines, for they were not at hand, but, trusting in their multitude, they resorted to a piece of insolence: they dared to set fire to the lower gate of the palace located near the Temple, which had been built in olden times by one of the Emperors under the invocation of Nicolaus, the greatest of the holy pontiffs.

At the sight of the Latin legions, not only did all of the basest class, the foolish and the unwarlike, groan, cry out, and beat their breasts in their fear, not knowing what else to do; but even the zealous adherents of the Emperor, mindful of that Friday on which the seizure of the city had formerly taken place, feared the present day lest vengeance should fall violently upon them for the deeds committed at that time. However, all who had any acquaintance with military practice and skill poured in at the regal palace, each man coming by himself. But the Emperor neither armed his sides with breastplate of scale-armor, his left hand with a shield, his right with a spear, nor girded himself about with a sword; but, clothed in royal raiment, he seated himself upon the imperial throne, as though secure. Thus, on the one hand, he reassured all, injecting courage into their hearts by his happy look, and, on the other, he discussed with his advisers and military leaders plans for coming events. First of all, he absolutely refused to have any armed band led outside of the walls against the Latins, this for a twofold reason: First, because this was the most sacred of days, for it was Friday of the greatest, of Holy, Week, when the Saviour had undergone ignominious death for all. In the second place, he refused to engage in civil war between Christians. Therefore, by means of frequent messengers to the Latins he wished to bring about the cessation of the undertaking which they had begun, saying: "Remember that on this day there died for us the Lord, who for the sake of our salvation did not fear to endure the cross, nails and the lance, punishments befitting criminals. But if your desire for a fight is so great, we, too, will stand ready after the coming day of the Lord's resurrection."

But the Latins were so far from yielding to him that they closed their ranks and threw missiles in such profusion that they struck across the chest one of the men standing near the Emperor's throne. At the sight of this, most of those who were standing near fell back, here and there, from the Emperor, while he, meanwhile, remained on his throne, not only without any sign of fear, but likewise reassuring them and chiding them greatly for their fear. All admired his presence of mind.

Finally, when he saw that the Latins, bereft of all shame, were invading the walls of the city and scorning his useful counsel, he first summoned his son-in-law, Nicephorus, and commanded him to take with him the strongest men and those skilled in shooting arrows and go to the top of the wall. He advised him, at the same time, to hurl down weapons on the Latins as frequently as possible, but, for the most part, harmlessly, with bad aim, in order to frighten them, not to kill them. For, as was said above, the Emperor respected the religious significance of the day and did not wish to engage in civil war between Christians. At the same time, he ordered some other chosen leaders (each with his cohorts, most of them provided with bows, but some armed with long lances) to charge forth suddenly from the gate which is close to St. Romanus, thus presenting the appearance of violence to the enemy. The battle line was so arranged that each spearman should march protected on each side by bowmen armed with shields. Thus arrayed, they were ordered to advance against the enemy at a slow pace, and archers, instructed to turn about frequently here and there, were sent ahead to wound the Gauls at close quarters. Now, when the two lines were a slight distance apart, they were then to order those bowmen who had spearmen at their side to use their bows carefully, aiming at the horses of the enemy, sparing the riders; and it was further ordered that the spearmen should charge with loose reins upon the Latins and with the full weight of their horses. He gave that order with this in mind, that when their horses were wounded, the violence of the Gallic attack would languish and the Romans would not easily be pursued by the knights; and this, also, which he especially desired, that as little Christian blood as possible should be shed. These men with ready courage did what they had been commanded by the Emperor, and, after the gates had been suddenly opened, they rushed against the enemy, now giving free rein to their horses, now checking them. Thus they killed many of the enemy; a few of our men were wounded in this affair that day. . . . At length the Emperor sent in his own forces and scattered and routed the legions of the Latins.

On the next day, Hugh set out to meet Godfrey and counselled him to make peace with the Emperor, if he did not want to try the warlike skill of the latter anew, to his own hurt, but especially to pledge that he would keep inviolate his faith to the Emperor. Godfrey received him very bitterly saying, "Have not you, who came from home in the spirit and surroundings of a king, with great forces and wealth, now debased yourself from highest dignity to the condition and lot of a humble client? And then, as if this were some great and distinguished deed, you have come to urge me, too, to this same fate!" In reply to him Hugh said, "In the first place, we ought not to have departed from our own lands, and we ought to have stayed away from those of others; but after we have come hither to this place, where we may have necessities by the benevolent care and providence of him who rules here, our business will not turn out happily unless we accede to his counsels and demands."

When Hugh had returned, the matter only made worse, the Emperor, informed through other sources that the rest of the counts who were following Godfrey at a distance were already near, sent chosen leaders with their forces to the army of Godfrey with orders to persuade him, but, if necessary, to compel him to cross the Strait. When the Latins saw them coming, without delay or even questions of what was wanted, they sprang up immediately to blows and battle. There occurred a most bitter conflict between them, in which many on both sides fell. Those of our men who rushed too boldly into the fray were wounded, but, as the Romans were conducting themselves valiantly, the Latins turned their backs. And thus, at length, Godfrey after a short time obeyed the Emperor. He came to him and in solemn manner took the oath which was demanded of him: that whatever cities, lands, or fortresses he should thenceforth capture from the barbarians (which cities, lands, or fortresses had formerly belonged to the Emperor) he would in good faith hand over to the military leaders or prefects who should be sent by the Emperor for this very purpose. When this had been confirmed by oath, Godfrey was enriched with great gifts by the Emperor; he was received in the imperial palace and magnificently dined at the royal table. He then crossed the Strait and pitched his camp at *Pelecanum*, the Emperor seeing to it that an ample supply of necessities was provided everywhere.

5. The Byzantines: The Version of Peter Tudebode

Peter Tudebode was a French priest who went on the crusade but wrote his account considerably later than several of the others (around 1110) and used other materials, particularly the Gesta. *His* Historia de Hierosolymitano Itinere, *"The History of the Journey to Jerusalem," has been edited and translated by John Hugh Hill and Laurita L. Hill, as Peter Tudebode,* Historia de Hierosolymitano Itinere *(Philadelphia, 1974).*

The English translation here is from Hill and Hill, 28–30.

Then the Provençal army journeyed to another town, Rodosto; and following their arrival, the imperials attacked them. In a rear guard action, the count killed thirty of the mercenaries and captured forty horses. Our ambassadors, who had been in Constantinople, came to Rodosto saying that Alexius promised to reimburse carefully all losses of the Crusaders after their arrival in Constantinople. They further stated that Duke Godfrey, Bohemond, Count Robert of Flanders, and all the other princes prayed Raymond to leave the main force, and unarmed and accompanied by a few knights to hasten to Constantinople. Since the emperor had taken the Cross, he said he would take the Jerusalem journey as their commander-in-chief and head. After these reports were delivered, Raymond left his army and hastened to Constantinople where he began discussions.

The Basileus informed him that he must pay homage and swear fealty to him as Bohemond and other princes had done. The count replied, "God forbid!" and further stated: "Surely, I shall pledge no lord allegiance on this journey other than the One for whom I have, out of love, come all the way to Constantinople. But, if you go crusading enthusiastically and come with us to Jerusalem, I and all of my men, as well as all I possess through God's mercy, shall voluntarily be in your trust."

While the count was in Constantinople, the army of the emperor arrived secretly and found the forces of Raymond leaderless and so attacked the Provençals forcefully and inflicted as much damage as possible. When Raymond heard that the emperor's army had struck his soldiers, he was saddened and deplored it very much. He immediately summoned Bohemond and the other princes and asked Alexius whether he had invited him to Constantinople for expediting his treachery and had he given personal orders to attack his men.

Alexius, openly admitting the attack, replied: "Yet this was not done by my orders and the damage done to your forces was unknown to me. But this I know full well—your army has inflicted widespread damage to me and has struck castles and towns in my empire. But I shall faithfully make amends, and I give Lord Bohemond to you as my pledge."

When they came to judgment, the count first freed his hostage; after he had released Bohemond, the Provençal army came to Constantinople. Alexius, as we stated above, demanded that Raymond pay homage and fealty to him as the other leaders had done. While the emperor made these demands, the count thought of ways to get revenge on the imperial army. However, Duke Godfrey, the Count of Flanders, and other leaders said that it would be unjust for him to fight Christians. Furthermore, Bohemond stated that if the count was unfair to the emperor and refused to swear fealty, he, himself, would side with Alexius. Consequently, after accepting the advice of his men, Raymond swore that he would not, either through himself or through others, take away the emperor's life and possessions. When he was questioned concerning homage, he replied that he would not pay homage because of peril to his rights.

Alexius, who secretly feared Bohemond very much because he had often routed his forces, told that most valiant Norman that if he would freely swear to him, in return he would give him lands equivalent to fifteen days journey in length and eight such days in width from Antioch. In a like manner Alexius swore that, if Bohemond faithfully held to his oath, he, in turn, would not violate his obligations. Then the army of Bohemond came to Constantinople and so completed the arrival of all of the Latins.

6. Bohemund: The *Gesta* Version

The English translation here is from Krey, 93–94.

When the Emperor heard that the most honorable man, Bohemund, had come to him, he commanded that he be received with honor and carefully lodged outside the city. When he had been so lodged, the evil Emperor sent for him to come to speak with him in secret. Thither, also, came Duke Godfrey with his brother, and at length the Count of St. Gilles approached the city. Then the Emperor in anxious and fervid rage was pondering some way by which they might seize these knights of Christ adroitly and by fraud. But Divine Grace disclosing [his plans], neither time nor place was found by him, or his men, to do them ill. At last, all the noble leaders who were at Constantinople were assembled. Fearing lest they should be deprived of their country, they decided in their counsels and ingenious calculations that our dukes, counts, or all the leaders, ought to make an oath of fealty to the Emperor. These absolutely refused and said: "It is indeed unworthy of us, and, furthermore, it seems to us unjust to swear an oath to him." Perchance we shall yet often be deceived by our leaders. In the end, what were they to do? They say that under the force of necessity they humiliated themselves, willy-nilly, to the will of the most unjust Emperor. To that most mighty man Bohemund, however, whom he greatly feared because in times past he [Bohemund] had often driven him from the field with his army, the Emperor said that, if he willingly took the oath to him, he would give him, in return, land in extent from Antioch fifteen days journey, and eight in width. And he [the

Emperor] swore to him in such wise that, if he loyally observed that oath, he would never pass beyond his own land. Knights, so brave and so sturdy, why did they do this? For the reason that they were constrained by much necessity. The Emperor also gave to all our men a pledge of security. He likewise took oath that he, together with his army, would come with us, by land and by sea; that he would afford us faithfully a market by land and sea, and that he would diligently make good our losses; in addition, that he did not wish, and would not permit, any of our pilgrims to be disturbed or come to grief on their way to the Holy Sepulchre.

7. Bohemund: The Version of Anna Comnena

The English translation here is from Krey, 94–97.

But when Bohemund had arrived at Apri with his companions, realizing both that he was not of noble birth, and that for lack of money he had not brought with him a large enough army, he hastened, with only ten Gauls, ahead of the other counts and arrived at Constantinople. He did this to win the favor of the Emperor for himself, and to conceal more safely the plans which he was concocting against him. Indeed, the Emperor, to whom the schemes of the man were known, for he had long since become acquainted with the hidden and deceitful dealings of this same Bohemund, took great pains to arrange it so that before the other counts should come he would speak with him alone. Thus having heard what Bohemund had to say, he hoped to persuade him to cross before the others came, lest, joined with them after their coming, he might pervert their minds.

When Bohemund had come to him, the Emperor greeted him with gladness and inquired anxiously about the journey and where he had left his companions. Bohemund responded to all these things as he thought best for his own interests, affably and in a friendly way, while the Emperor recalled in a familiar talk his bold undertakings long ago around Durazzo and Larissa and the hostilities between them at that time. Bohemund answered, "Then I confess I was your enemy, then I was hostile. But, behold, I now stand before you like a deserter to the ranks of the enemy! I am a friend of your Majesty." The Emperor proceeded to scrutinize the man, considering him cautiously and carefully and drawing out what was in his mind. As soon as he saw that Bohemund was ready to consent to swear an oath of fealty to him, he said, "You must be tired from the journey and should retire to rest. We will talk tomorrow about anything else."

So Bohemund departed to Cosmidion, where hospitality was prepared for him, and he found a table richly laden with an abundance of food and condiments of all kinds. Then the cooks came and showed him the uncooked flesh of animals and birds, saying: "We have prepared this food which you see on the table according to our skill and the custom of this region; but if, perchance, these please you less, here is food, still uncooked, which can be prepared just as you order." The Emperor, because of his almost incredible tact in handling men, had commanded that this be done and said by them. For, since he was especially expert in penetrating the secrets of minds and in discovering the disposition of a man, he very readily understood that Bohemund was of a shrewd and suspicious nature; and he foresaw what happened. For, lest Bohemund should conceive any suspicion against him, the Emperor had ordered that raw meats be placed before him, together with the cooked, thus easily removing suspicion. Neither did his conjecture fail, for the very shrewd Bohemund took the prepared food, without even touching it with the tips of his fingers, or tasting it, and immediately turned around, concealing, nevertheless, the suspicion which occurred to him by the following ostentatious show of liberality. For under the pretext of courtesy he distributed all the food to those standing around; in reality, if one understood rightly, he was dividing the cup of death among them. Nor did he conceal his cunning, so much did he hold his subjects in contempt; for he this day used the raw meat which had been offered to him and had it prepared by his own cooks after the manner of his country. On the next day he asked his men whether they were well. Upon their answering in the affirmative, that they were indeed very well, that not even one felt even the least indisposed, he disclosed his secret in his reply: "Remembering a war, once carried on by me against the Emperor, and that strife, I feared lest perchance he had intended to kill me by putting deadly poison in my food."

Such a man was Bohemund. Never, indeed, have I seen a man so dishonest. In everything, in his words as well as in his deeds, he never chose the right path; and when anyone deviates from the moderation of virtue, it makes little difference to whatsoever extreme he goes, for he is always far from honesty.

For the rest, the Emperor then summoned Bohemund and exacted from him the usual oath of the Latins. The latter, knowing well his own resources, and realizing that he was neither of noble birth nor well supplied by fortune with wealth, for he had no great force, but only a moderate number of Gauls with him, and being, besides, dishonest in character, readily submitted himself to the will of the Emperor.

After this, the Emperor saw to it that a room in the palace was so filled with a collection of riches of all kinds that the very floor was covered with costly raiment, and with gold and silver coins, and certain other less valuable things, so much so that one was not able even to walk there, so hindered was he by the abundance of these things. The Emperor ordered the guide suddenly and unexpectedly to open the doors, thus revealing all this to Bohemund. Amazed at the spectacle, Bohemund exclaimed: "If such riches were mine, long ago I would have been lord of many lands!" The guide answered, "And all these things the Emperor bestows upon you today as a gift." Most gladly Bohemund received them and with many gracious thanks he left, intending to return to his rest in the inn. But changing his mind when they were brought to him, he, who a little before had admired them, said: "Never can I let myself be treated with such ignominy by the Emperor. Go, take those things and carry them back to him who sent them." The Emperor, knowing the base fickleness of the Latins, quoted this common saying, "Let the evil return to its author." Bohemund having heard this, and seeing that the messengers were busily bringing these things back to him, decided anew about the goods which he had sent back with regret, and, like a polypus, changed in a moment, he now showed a joyous countenance to the bearers. For he was quick, and a man of very dishonest disposition, as much surpassing in malice and intrepidity all the Latins who had crossed over as he was inferior to them in power and wealth. But even though he thus excelled all in great cunning, the inconstant character of the Latins was also in him. Verily, the riches which he spurned at first, he now gladly accepted. For when this man of evil design had left his country in which he possessed no wealth at all (under the pretext, indeed, of adoring at the Lord's Sepulchre, but in reality endeavoring to acquire for himself a kingdom), he found himself in need of much money, especially, indeed, if he was to seize the Roman power. In this he followed the advice of his father and, so to speak, was leaving no stone unturned.

Moreover, the Emperor, who understood fully his wicked intention and perverse mind, skillfully managed carefully to remove whatever might further Bohemund's ambitious designs. Wherefore, Bohemund, seeking a home for himself in the East and using Cretan scheming against Cretans, did not obtain it. For the Emperor feared lest, after obtaining power, he would use it to place the Latin counts under obligation to him, finally thus accomplishing easily what he wished. But since he did not want Bohemund to surmise that he was already discovered, the Emperor misled him by this hope: "Not yet," he said, "has the time come for the thing which you say; but after a little it shall come about by your fortitude and trust in me."

After the Emperor had bestowed upon the Gauls promises, gifts, and honors of every kind, the next day he solemnly took his seat on the imperial throne. Summoning Bohemund and all the counts, he talked about the things which would happen to them on the journey. He wanted, likewise, to show what methods and means of warfare the Turks were wont to employ, and to give directions how the line of battle should be drawn up against them, how ambushes should be set, and how they ought not to follow the fleeing Turks too far. And so, both by gifts of money and by flattering speeches, he soothed the rude nature of the people, and, after giving useful advice, he persuaded them to pass over the sea. . . .

8. Raymond of Toulouse and Ademar of Le Puy: The Version of Raymond d'Aguilers

The English translation here is from Krey, 97–98.

Although events have lightly accompanied the writer so far with happy and favorable step, they now follow with so great a weight of bitterness and sorrow that it grieves me to have begun what I have vowed to finish. What, indeed; is the most important and first matter that I shall proceed to mention? The most false and detestable deceit of the Emperor's admonition? Or the most base flight and unthinkable desperation of our army? Or shall I leave a monument of perpetual sorrow by enumerating the deaths of such great princes? Let any one who desires to know this, however, seek it rather from others than from me. This one very memorable event I consider to merit excuse from silence. When our men thought of abandoning the camp, taking flight, deserting their fellows, and leaving everything that they had brought along from such distant regions, they were brought back by the saving deeds of penance and fast to such staunch fortitude that only shame at their former desperate condition and flight most deeply affected them. So much may be said about this.

Accordingly, when the Count had been received most honorably by the Emperor and his princes, the Emperor demanded of the Count homage and the oath which the other princes had made to him. The Count replied that he had not come hither to make another his lord or to fight for any other than the One for whom he had left his country and his possessions. Nevertheless, if the Emperor would go to Jerusalem with the army, he would commit himself and his men and all his goods to him. But the Emperor excused himself from the journey by saying that he greatly feared lest the Germans, Hungarians, Cumans, and other wild peoples would devastate his empire, if he made the journey with the pilgrims. Meanwhile the Count, upon hearing of the flight and death of his men, believed that he had been betrayed, and through certain

of our princes he vehemently charged the Emperor with having committed
treason. But Alexius said that he did not know that our men had devastated
his kingdom, and that he and his men had suffered many injuries; that there
was nothing of which the Count could complain, except that while the army
of the Count in its usual manner was devastating the villages and towns, it
took to flight upon seeing his [the Emperor's] army. Nevertheless, he promised that he would give satisfaction to the Count and offered Bohemund as a
hostage for the satisfaction. They went to trial; the Count, according to law,
was compelled to give up his hostage.

Meanwhile, our army came to Constantinople; and after this the Bishop,
whom the army had left ill at Durazzo, followed us with his brother. Alexius
asked [homage] again and again and promised that he would give much to
the Count if he would do him the desired homage as the other princes had
done. The Count, however, was constantly meditating how he might avenge
the injury to his men, and drive away from himself and his followers the disgrace of such great infamy. But the Duke of Lorraine, the Count of Flanders,
and the other princes deprecated such action, saying that it would be very
foolish to fight with Christians when the Turks were threatening. Bohemund,
indeed, promised that he would aid the Emperor, if the Count made any
attempt against the Emperor, or if he no longer refused homage and oath.
Thereupon, the Count took counsel with his men and swore that neither in
person nor through another would he sully the life or honor of Alexius. And
when asked about homage, he replied that he would not do it at the risk of
his head, wherefore the Emperor gave him few gifts.

9. Raymond of Toulouse: The *Gesta* Version

The English translation here is from Krey, 98–99.

The Count of St. Gilles, however, was lodged outside the city in a suburb, and his force had remained behind. Accordingly, the Emperor bade the
Count do homage and fealty to him, as the others had done. And while
the Emperor was making these demands, the Count was meditating how he
might take vengeance on the army of the Emperor. But Duke Godfrey and
Robert, Count of Flanders, and the other princes said to him that it would
be unjust to fight against Christians. The wise man, Bohemund, also said that
if the Count should do the Emperor any injustice, and should refuse to do
him fealty, he himself would take the part of the Emperor. Accordingly, the

Count, after receiving the advice of his men, swore that he would not consent to have the life and honor of Alexius sullied either by himself or by anyone else. When he was called upon for homage, he answered that he would not do this at the risk of his head.

Then the host of Lord Bohemund approached Constantinople. Tancred, indeed, and Richard of Principati, and almost the whole of Bohemund's force with him, crossed the Strait by stealth, to avoid the oath to the Emperor. And now the army of the Count of St. Gilles approached Constantinople. The Count remained there with his own band. Therefore the illustrious man, Bohemund, stayed behind with the Emperor, in order to plan with him how they might provide a market for the people who were beyond the city of Nicaea.

10. Raymond of Toulouse: The Version of Anna Comnena

The English translation here is from Krey, 99.

One of them especially, the Count of St. Gilles, he particularly favored because he saw in him superior prudence, tested sincerity, candor of bearing, and finally, such great zeal for truth that he never placed anything before it. He was as far superior to all the other Latins in all virtues as the sun is above the other stars. For this reason, therefore, the Emperor kept him near him for the time being.

When at the wish of the Emperor all had crossed over the Propontis and had arrived at *Damalium*, Alexius, thus relieved from care and trouble, had the Count of St. Gilles summoned and in talks showed him very distinctly what he thought might happen to the Latins on the way. At the same time, he disclosed to him what suspicions he was cherishing about the intentions and plans of the Gauls. He often spoke freely about them with the Count of St. Gilles, opening the doors of his heart to him, as it were, and making everything clearly known to him. He sometimes warned him, also, to keep close watch against the malice of Bohemund, so as to check him immediately if he should try to break his agreement, and to strive in every way to destroy his schemes. The Count of St. Gilles replied: "Since Bohemund has inherited perjury and deceit, as it were, it would be very surprising if he should be faithful to those promises which he has made under oath. However, I will try to carry out what you command, in so far as I can." Then at the wish of the Emperor he departed, joining himself to the forces of the united Gauls. . . .

VI.

The Siege and Capture of Nicaea (May–June, 1097)

On May 6, 1097, the crusading armies reached the city of Nicaea, the capital of the Seljuk ruler of Rum, Kilij Arslan. The city guarded the main land route through Anatolia. The armies besieged the city, and on May 21, 1097, they beat off an attack by Kilij Arslan's army—the first battle victory of the crusade. On June 19, Nicaea surrendered to the forces of Alexius I rather than face a final assault by the Franks. Nicaea was the first of the remarkable victories that sustained the crusaders on the long route to Jerusalem.

1. The *Gesta* Version

The English translation here is from Krey, 101–103.

And thus Duke Godfrey went first to Nicomedia, together with Tancred and all the rest, and they were there for three days. The Duke, indeed, seeing that there was no road open by which he could conduct these hosts to the city of Nicaea, for so great an army could not pass through the road along which the others had passed before, sent ahead three thousand men with axes and swords to cut and clear this road, so that it would lie open even to the city of Nicaea. They cut this road through a very narrow and very great mountain and fixed back along the way iron and wooden crosses on posts, so that the pilgrims would know the way. Meanwhile, we came to Nicaea, which is the capital of all Romania, on the fourth day, the day before the Nones of May, and there encamped. However, before Lord Bohemund had arrived, there was such scarcity of bread among us that one loaf was sold for twenty or thirty *denarii*. After the illustrious man, Bohemund, came, he ordered the greatest market to be brought by sea, and it came both ways at the same time, this by land and that by sea, and there was the greatest abundance in the whole army of Christ.

Moreover, on the day of the Ascension of the Lord we began to attack the city on all sides, and to construct machines of wood, and wooden towers, with which we might be able to destroy towers on the walls. We attacked the city so bravely and so fiercely that we even undermined its wall. The Turks who were in the city, barbarous horde that they were, sent messages to others who had come up to give aid. The message ran in this wise: that they might approach the city boldly and in security and enter through the middle gate, because on that side no one would oppose them or put them to grief. This gate was besieged on that very day—the Sabbath after the Ascension of the Lord—by the Count of St. Gilles and the Bishop of Puy. The Count, approaching from another side, was protected by divine might, and with his most powerful army gloried in terrestrial strength. And so he found the Turks, coming against us here. Armed on all sides with the sign of the cross, he rushed upon them violently and overcame them. They turned in flight, and most of them were killed. They came back again, reinforced by others, joyful and exulting in assured [outcome] of battle, and bearing along with them the ropes with which to lead us bound to Chorosan. Coming gladly, moreover, they began to descend from the crest of the mountain a short distance. As many as descended remained there with their heads cut off at the hands of our men; moreover, our men hurled the heads of the killed far into the city, that they [the Turks] might be the more terrified thereat. Then the Count of St. Gilles and the Bishop of Puy took counsel together as to how they might have undermined a certain tower which was opposite their tents. Men were assigned to do the digging, with *arbalistae* and bowmen to defend them on all sides. So they dug to the foundations of the wall and fixed timbers and wood under it and then set fire to it. However, evening had come; the tower had already fallen in the night, and because it was night they could not fight with the enemy. Indeed, during that night the Turks hastily built up and restored the wall so strongly that when day came no one could harm them on that side.

Now the Count of Normandy came up, Count Stephen and many others, and finally Roger of *Barneville*. At length Bohemund, at the very front, besieged the city. Beside him was Tancred, after him Duke Godfrey, then the Count of St. Gilles, next to whom was the Bishop of Puy. It was so besieged by land that no one dared to go out or in. There all our forces were assembled in one body, and who could have counted so great an army of Christ? No one, as I think, has ever before seen so many distinguished knights or ever will again!

However, there was a large lake on one side of the city, on which the Turks used to send out their ships, and go back and forth and bring fodder, wood, and many other things. Then our leaders counselled together and sent messengers to Constantinople to tell the Emperor to have ships brought to Civitote, where there is a fort, and that he should order oxen to be brought to drag the ships over the mountains and through the woods, until they neared the lake. This was done forthwith, and he sent his Turcopoles with them. They did not want to put the ships on the lake on the very day that they were brought across, but under cover of night they launched them on the lake itself. [The boats were] filled with Turcopoles well decorated with arms. Moreover, at earliest daybreak the ships stood in good order and hastened through the lake against the city. The Turks marvelled upon seeing them, not knowing whether they were manned by their own forces or the Emperor's. However, after they recognized that it was the host of the Emperor, they were frightened even to death, weeping and lamenting; and the Franks were glad and gave glory to God.

The Turks, moreover, seeing that they could have no further aid from their armies, sent a message to the Emperor that they would willingly surrender the city, if he would permit them to go entirely away with their wives and children and all their substance. Then the Emperor, full of vain and evil thinking, ordered them to depart unpunished, without any fear, and to be brought to him at Constantinople with great assurance [of safety]. These he cared for zealously, so that he had them prepared against any damage or hindrance from the Franks. We were engaged in that siege for seven weeks and three days. Many of our men there received martyrdom, and, glad and rejoicing, gave back their happy souls to God. Many of the very poor died of hunger for the name of Christ, and these bore triumphantly to heaven their robes of martyrdom crying with one voice, "Avenge, Lord, our blood which has been shed for Thee, who are blessed and praiseworthy forever and ever. Amen." In the meanwhile, after the city had been surrendered and the Turks had been conducted to Constantinople, the Emperor, more and more rejoiced because the city had been surrendered to his power, ordered the greatest alms to be distributed to our poor.

2. The Version of Raymond d'Aguilers

The English translation here is from Krey, 103–105.

Thereupon, we crossed the sea and went up to Nicaea. For the Duke, Bohemund, and the other princes had preceded the Count and were engaged in the labors of the siege. The city of Nicaea is very strongly fortified by nature, as well as by art. It has on the west a very large lake flowing up to the wall; on the remaining three sides is a moat filled with the overflow of certain little streams; in addition, it is encircled by walls so high that neither the assaults of men nor the attacks of any machine are feared. Indeed, the *ballistae* of the neighboring towers are so turned with reference to one another that no one can approach without danger; however, if anyone wants to approach nearer, he is easily overwhelmed from the top of the towers without being able to retaliate.

Accordingly, this city, such as we have described, was besieged by Bohemund from the north, by the Duke and the Alemanni from the east, by the Count and Bishop of Puy from the middle, for the Count of Normandy was not yet with us. But we believe this one incident should not be passed over: — that when the Count was about to encamp there with his men, the Turks, descending from the mountains in two squadrons, attacked our army. Their plan, indeed, was that while one party of the Turks assailed the Duke and the Alemanni who were on the east, the other party, entering the middle gate of the city and passing out through another, would easily drive our men from the camp at a time when they were not expecting such an attack. But God, who is wont to reverse the plan of the impious, so altered their preparations that, as if it had been arranged, He sent the Count, who was preparing to encamp with his men, upon the squadron of Turks which was now about to enter the city. He put them to flight at the first charge and, after killing several, pursued the rest to the top of the mountain. The other party of Turks which wanted to attack the Alemanni was put to flight in the same way and destroyed. After this, machines were constructed and the wall attacked in vain, for it was very firm against us and was valiantly defended by arrows and machines. So we fought five weeks with no result. At length, through God's will, some men of the household of the Bishop and the Count dangerously enough approached the corner tower which faced the east, and having made a testudo, they began, after a struggle, to undermine one of the towers and by digging threw it to the ground. Thus the city would have been taken, had not the shadows of night prevented. However, the wall was rebuilt during the night, and this rendered our former labor vain. At length the city, terrified with fear, was compelled to surrender. One reason was that the ships of the Emperor which had been dragged over the land were let down into the lake. They therefore gave themselves up to the Emperor, since they now expected no further aid and saw the army of the Franks increasing daily, while they were cut off from their forces. The Count of Normandy had come. Alexius had promised the princes and the people of the Franks that he would give them all the gold, silver, horses, and goods within [the city], and that he would establish there a Latin monastery and hospice for the poor Franks; besides, that he would give to each one of the army so much of his own possessions that they would always want to fight for him. Accordingly, the Franks, placing faith in these promises, approved the surrender. And so, when Alexius had received the city, he afforded the army such an example of gratitude that as long as they live the people will curse him and proclaim him a traitor.

We recognized, then, that the Emperor had betrayed Peter the Hermit, who had long before come to Constantinople with a great multitude. For he compelled him, ignorant of the locality and of all military matters, to cross the Strait with his men and exposed them to the Turks. Moreover, when the Turks from Nicaea saw that unwarlike multitude, they cut them down without effort and delay to the number of sixty thousand. The rest, indeed, fled to a certain fortified place and escaped the swords of the Turks. The Turks, made bold and haughty by this, sent the arms and the captives which they had taken there to the Saracens and the nobles of their own race, and they wrote to the peoples and cities far off that the Franks were of no account in battle.

3. The Version of Anna Comnena

The English translation here is from Krey, 109–110.

But though the Emperor wished to attach himself to the Gauls and advance with them against the barbarians, yet, fearing their countless multitude, he decided to go to *Pelecanum*, in order that by camping near Nicaea he might learn what was happening to the Gauls, and also learn the undertakings of the Turks outside, as well as the conditions in the city. . . .

The august Emperor tarried about *Pelecanum* for some time, since he desired those Gallic counts who were not yet bound to him also to take the oath of loyalty. To this end, he sent a letter to Butumites, asking all the counts in common not to start upon the journey to Antioch until they had said farewell to the Emperor. If they did this, they would all be showered with new gifts by him. Bohemund was the first to prick up his ears at the mention of money and gifts. Quickly won by these words of Butumites, he strove industriously to force all the others to return to the Emperor—so greatly did cupidity move the man. The Emperor received them on their arrival at *Pelecanum* with magnificence and the greatest show of good-will. At length, when they were assembled, he addressed them thus: "You know that you have all bound yourselves to me by oath; if you do not now intend to ignore this, advise and persuade those of your number who have not yet pledged faith to take the oath." They immediately summoned the counts who had not sworn. All of these came together and took the oath.

Tancred, however, nephew of Bohemund and a youth of most independent spirit, professed that he owed faith to Bohemund alone, and would serve him even to death. Rebuked by the loud protest of those of his own fellows who stood near, and of the Emperor's retinue, besides, he turned toward the tent in which the Emperor was then dwelling—the largest and most capacious which anyone has ever seen—and, as if to make sport of them, said, "If you give me this [tent] full of money and, in addition, all the other presents which you gave all the counts, I, too, will take the oath." But Palaeologus, full of zeal for the Emperor, could not endure the mocking speech of Tancred and pushed him away with contempt. Then Tancred, very ready with his arms, sprang upon him. Seeing this, the Emperor arose hastily from his seat and stood between them. Bohemund, too, restrained the youth, saying "It is not fitting shamefully to strike the kinsman of the Emperor." Then Tancred, recognizing the disgrace of his insolence toward Palaeologus, and persuaded by the advice of Bohemund and the others, offered to take the oath himself. . . .

4. The Letter of Emperor Alexius I to the Abbot of Monte Cassino

The English translation here is from Krey, 110–111.

How much you have written to my empire, most venerable servant of God, abbot of the monastery of Monte Cassino! I have read your letter which declares honor and praise to my empire. Toward me and my subjects there is, indeed, very great favor from Almighty and Most Merciful God, for many are His blessings. Through His compassion and by His grace He has honored and exalted my empire. However, not only because I have nothing of good within me, but because I sin above all men, I daily pray that His compassion and patience may be sent to sustain my weakness. But you, filled with goodness and virtue, judge me, sinner that I am, a good man, and truly you have the advantage of me. My empire, though it is praised without having work worthy of praise, holds the praise to its own condemnation.

"I beseech you earnestly to furnish aid to the army of Franks," your most thoughtful letters state. Let your Venerable Holiness be assured on that score, for my empire has been spread over them and will aid and advise them on all matters; indeed, it has already cooperated with them according to its ability, not as a friend, or relative, but like a father. It has expended among them more than anyone can enumerate. And had not my empire so cooperated with them and aided them, who else would have afforded them help? Nor does it grieve my empire to assist a second time. By God's grace, they are prospering up to this day in the service which they have begun, and they will continue to prosper in the future as long as good purpose leads them on. A multitude of knights and foot-soldiers have gone to the Eternal Tabernacle, some of which were killed; others died. Blessed, indeed, are they, since they met their end in good intent! Besides, we ought not at all to regard them as dead, but as living and transported to life everlasting and incorruptible. As evidence of my true faith and my kind regard for your monastery, my empire has sent you an *epiloricum*, adorned on the back with glittering gold.

Sent in the month of June, [1098] sixth Indiction, from the most holy city of Constantinople.

VII.

The Siege and Capture of Antioch, Kerbogha's Attack, and the Discovery of the Holy Lance (October, 1097–July, 1098)

The long siege of Antioch, the exhausted condition of the crusaders, and the dissensions among their leaders constituted the greatest hardships of the whole expedition. The triumphalist crusader perception of the later capture of Jerusalem should be read in the light of the terrible hardships suffered at Antioch. Immediately after their capture of the great city, moreover, the crusaders learned of a massive Muslim counterattack led by Kerbogha, the atabeg *(regent) of Mosul. Kerbogha's name, and transliteration styles generally are treated variously by different sources cited below. The Muslim siege strained the crusaders' resources and determination still further, and the discovery of the Holy Lance (the lance that pierced Christ's side at the Crucifixion) in June, 1098, helped immensely to restore their morale, although not all leaders of the crusade accepted its legitimacy. Kerbogha's army was finally defeated, but the siege had taken a terrible toll. Ademar of Le Puy, the papal legate, died; Stephen, Count of Blois and Chartres and husband of William the Conqueror's daughter Adele, fled home, only to be shamed and pressured to return to the Holy Land (he returned on the Crusade of 1101 and died in 1102). Disease and other physical hardships and further dissension among the leaders kept the armies in Antioch for a year. Not until November, 1098 did the crusaders resume their march to Jerusalem.*

On Stephen's flight, see James A. Brundage, "An Errant Crusader: Stephen of Blois," Traditio *16 (1960), 380–395. On the debate over the Holy Lance, see Colin Morris, "Policy and Visions: The Case of the Holy Lance at Antioch," in* War and Government in the Middle Ages: Essays in Honor of J. O. Prestwich, *ed. John Gillingham and J. C. Holt (Woodbridge, 1984), 33–45. One sign of the enormous effort put forth at Antioch was the beginning of discussions of those killed as*

martyrs. See H. E. J. Cowdrey, "Martyrdom and the First Crusade," in Crusade
and Settlement, *46–56; Jonathan Riley-Smith, "Death on the First Crusade," in*
The End of Strife, *ed. D. M. Loades (Edinburgh, 1984), 14–31; and Colin Morris,*
"Martyrs on the Field of Battle Before and During the First Crusade," Studies
in Church History *30 (1993), 93–104. On the problem of the narrative sources, see*
John France, "The Crisis of the First Crusade: From the Defeat of Kerbogha to the
Departure from Arqa," Byzantion *40 (1970), 131–147.*

    On another body of sources not included here, see J. H. Forse, "Armenians and
the First Crusade," Journal of Medieval History *17 (1991), 13–22. Some sources*
are translated in A. E. Dostourian, ed. and trans., Armenia and the Crusades:
Tenth to Twelfth Centuries *(Lanham, Md., 1993).*

1. Nicaea to Antioch: The Version of Peter Tudebode

The English translation here is from Hill and Hill, 40–42.

The chief body of crusaders, composed of Raymond, Count of Saint-
Gilles, the most learned Bohemond, Duke Godfrey, and other leaders, entered
Armenian land, inflamed and thirsting for Turkish blood. Finally they came
to an impregnable castle which thwarted them. There was a native of the area
named Simeon, who sought the fort so that he could defend it from falling
into Turkish hands. Consequently, they gave him possession, and he dwelled
there with his people. Departing this place we arrived at Caesarea of Cappadocia after a pleasant journey. Leaving Cappadocia we came to a most beautiful
and rich city which the Turks had invested for three weeks but had failed to
capture before our arrival. Upon our advent, the natives happily turned the
place over to us. A petty knight, Peter of Aulps, anxious to secure possession
of the city from all of the lords, promised to defend it in fealty to God, the
Holy Sepulchre, the crusading lords, and Alexius. In a beneficient spirit they
granted it to him freely.

    At sundown Bohemond heard that a large group of Turks who had be-
sieged the city were in our vicinity. Immediately, accompanied by his knights,
he prepared to surround his adversaries but was unable to locate any of them.
Then we arrived at Coxon, a bountiful place stocked with all necessities for
our existence. The Christian inhabitants of Coxon forthwith turned their city
over to the crusaders, who remained there for three days fully recuperating in
the plentiful land.

    At this time Raymond of Saint-Gilles, after receiving reports that the defenders of Antioch had vacated the city, held a council with his Provençals and made plans to send his knights to guard Antioch with great care. Finally he chose those whom he wished to go; namely, Peter, Viscount of Castillon, Peter of Roaix, and Peter Raymond of Hautpoul, along with five hundred knights. On their arrival in a valley near Antioch, they learned at a castle of the Paulicians that the Turks were within the walls of the city prepared to go all-out in its defense. Peter of Roaix left the expeditionary force and, under the cover of darkness, passed near Antioch and without incident entered the valley of Rugia, where he found and battled Turks and Saracens, killing many and ardently chasing the remnants. The Armenian dwellers of the land were so impressed by his formidable victory over the pagans that they promptly put themselves under his protection; whereupon he seized the city of Rusa and many castles.

We, who had remained at Coxon, departed and began to climb a devilish mountain so high and with such narrow defiles that no one dared to pass another on the traillike mountain passes. Horses plunged over cliffs and pack animals tumbled over one another as tearful knights stood everywhere wringing their hands, overcome by grief and shock. Doubtful of the fate of themselves and their arms, they sold their shields, expensive breastplates, and helmets for three or five denarii or more, if possible. Those who could not sell their worthless arms threw them down and marched on. Leaving the devilish mountain we came to Marash. The inhabitants of this town met us joyfully outside the walls and brought ample supplies. Here in the midst of plenty we awaited the arrival of Bohemond.

Our knights then came and neared the valley in which the magnificent city of Antioch is located. Antioch is the capital of all Syria. Lord Jesus Christ handed it over to Saint Peter, foremost of the apostles, that he might return it to the veneration of the true faith, which lives and reigns in the triune God for eternity. Amen.

2. The *Gesta* Version

The English translation here is from Krey, 132–134.

Now grain and all food began to be excessively dear before the birthday of the Lord. We did not dare to go outside; we could find absolutely nothing to eat within the land of the Christians, and no one dared to enter the land of the Saracens without a great army. At last holding a council, our seignors de-

cided how they might care for so many people. They concluded in the council
that one part of our force should go out diligently to collect food and to guard
the army everywhere, while the other part should remain faithfully to watch
the enemy. At length, Bohemund said, "Seignors, and most distinguished
knights, if you wish, and it seems honorable and good to you, I will be the
one to go out with the Count of Flanders on this quest." Accordingly, when
the services of the Nativity had been most gloriously celebrated on Monday,
the second day of the week, they and more than twenty thousand knights and
footmen went forth and entered the land of the Saracens, safe and unharmed.

There were assembled, indeed, many Turks, Arabs, and Saracens from
Jerusalem, Damascus, Aleppo, and other regions, who were on their way to
reinforce Antioch. So, when they heard that a Christian host was being led
into their land, they made themselves ready there for battle against the Christians, and at earliest daybreak they came to the place where our people were
gathered together. The barbarians divided themselves and formed two battle
lines, one in front and one behind, seeking to surround us from every side.
The worthy Count of Flanders, therefore, girt about on all sides with the armor of true faith and the sign of the cross, which he loyally wore daily, went
against them, together with Bohemund, and our men rushed upon them all
together. They immediately took to flight and hastily turned their backs; very
many of them were killed, and our men took their horses and other spoils.
But others, who had remained alive, fled swiftly and went away to the wrath
of perdition. We, however, returning with great rejoicing, praised and magnified God, Three in One, who liveth and reigneth now and forever, Amen.

Finally, the Turks in the city of Antioch, enemies of God and Holy Christianity, hearing that Lord Bohemund and the Count of Flanders were not in
the siege, came out from the city and boldly advanced to do battle with us.
Knowing that those most valiant knights were away, they lay in ambush for
us everywhere, more especially on that side where the siege was lagging. One
Wednesday they found that they could resist and hurt us. The most iniquitous
barbarians came out cautiously and, rushing violently upon us, killed many
of our knights and foot-soldiers who were off their guard. Even the Bishop
of Puy on that bitter day lost his seneschal, who was carrying and managing
his standard. And had it not been for the stream which was between us and
them, they would have attacked us more often and done the greatest hurt to
our people.

At that time the famous man, Bohemund, advancing with his army
from the land of the Saracens, came to the mountain of Tancred, wondering
whether perchance he could find anything to carry away, for they were ran-

sacking the whole region. Some, in truth, found something, but others went away empty-handed. Then the wise man, Bohemund, upbraided them, saying: "Oh, unhappy and most wretched people! O, most vile of all Christians! Why do you want to go away so quickly? Only stop; stop until we shall all be gathered together, and do not wander about like sheep without a shepherd. Moreover, if the enemy find you wandering, they will kill you, for they are watching by night and by day to find you alone, or ranging about in groups without a leader; and they are striving daily to kill you and lead you into captivity." When his words were finished, he returned to his camp with his men, more empty-handed than laden.

3. The Version of Raymond d'Aguilers

The English translation here is from Krey, 136–138.

And since already in the third month of the siege food was bought too dearly, Bohemund and the Count of Flanders were chosen to lead an army into *Hispania* for food, the Count and the Bishop of Puy being left as a guard in the camp. For the Count of Normandy was away at the time, and the Duke was very ill. However, when the enemy learned this, they repeated their customary assaults. The Count, moreover, was compelled to attack them in his usual manner, and, after forming the ranks of the foot-soldiers, he, with some knights, pursued the assailants. He captured and killed two of them on the slope of the little mountain and forced all the enemy to enter by the bridge. As our foot-soldiers saw this, they left their posts and their standards and ran in a mob up to their bridges. And when there, as if already in safety, they cast stones and weapons upon those who were defending the bridge. The Turks, after forming a line, began to rush against our men by the bridge and by a path which was lower down. Meanwhile, our knights chased toward our bridge a certain horse whose master they had overthrown. When our people saw this, thinking our knights in flight, they showed their backs to the attack of the enemy without delay. Then the Turks killed without ceasing those who fled. Even if the knights of the Franks wished to resist and fight for their people, they were caught by the crowd of fleeing footmen, by their arms, and by the manes and tails of the horses, and were either thrown from their horses, or, out of compassion and regard for the safety of their people, were brought to flight. The enemy, indeed, without delay, without pity, slaughtered and pursued the living and despoiled the bodies of the dead. Moreover, it was not enough for our men to leave their arms, take flight, despise shame, but they rushed into the river to be overwhelmed with stones or arrows of the enemy, or to remain under water. If skill and strength in swimming bore anyone across the river, he reached the camp of his companions. However, our flight extended from their bridge to our bridge. They there killed about fifteen of our knights and about twenty foot-soldiers. The standard-bearer of the Bishop was killed there, and his standard was captured. A certain very noble youth, Bernard Raymond of Beziers, died there.

Let the servants of God neither complain nor be angry with us, if our men bequeathed such open shame to the memory of our army; since God, who in this way desired to drive to penance the minds of adulterers and robbers, at the same time gladdened our army in *Hispania*. For a rumor, going forth from our camp, announced to Bohemund and his fellows that all was prosperous, and that the Count had gained a most noble victory. Moreover, this report aroused their spirits no little. After Bohemund had besieged a certain village, he heard some of his peasants suddenly fleeing and shouting, and when he had sent knights to meet them, they saw an army of Turks and Arabs close at hand. Moreover, among those who had set out to determine the cause of the flight and outcry was the Count of Flanders, and with him certain Provençals. For all from Burgundy, Auvergne, Gascony, and all Goths are called Provençals, while the others are called of the Frankish race: that is, in the army; among the enemy, however, all are spoken of as Frankish. This Count of Flanders, as we have said, however, thinking it a disgrace to report about the enemy before attacking them, rushed impetuously against the phalanxes of the Turks. The Turks, indeed, unaccustomed to conduct battles with swords, took to flight for refuge. Nor did the Count sheathe his sword until he had removed a hundred of the enemy from life. When he was now returning to Bohemund as victor, he saw twelve thousand Turks coming behind him, and rising up on the nearest hill toward the left he saw a countless multitude of foot-soldiers. Then, after communicating his plan to the rest of the army, he took a number of men back with him and violently attacked the Turks. Bohemund, indeed, followed at a distance with the rest and guarded the rear lines. For the Turks have this custom in fighting: even though they are fewer in number, they always strive to encircle their enemy. This they attempted to do in this battle also, but by the foresight of Bohemund the wiles of the enemy were prevented. When, however, the Turks, and the Arabs, coming against the Count of Flanders, saw that the affair was not to be conducted at a distance with arrows, but at close quarters with swords, they turned in flight. The Count followed them for two miles, and in this space he saw the bodies of the killed lying like bundles of grain reaped in the field. The ambushes which Bohemund had encountered were scattered and put to flight in the same way. But the countless horde of foot-soldiers, of which we spoke above, slipped away in flight through places impassable to horses. I would dare, I say, were it not arrogant to judge, to place this battle ahead of the fights of the Maccabees, since if Maccabaeus with three thousand felled forty-eight thousand of the enemy, more than sixty thousand of the enemy were here turned in flight by a force of forty knights. I do not, indeed, belittle the valor of the Maccabees, nor exalt the valor of our knights, but I say that God, then marvelous in Maccabaeus, was now more marvelous in our troops.

A [strange] result of this achievement was that after the enemy had been put to flight the courage of our men decreased, so that they did not dare to pursue those whom they saw headlong in flight. Accordingly, when the army returned victorious and empty-handed, there was such famine in the camp that two *solidi* were scarcely enough to keep one man in bread for a day, nor were other things to be obtained less dearly.

4. The Suffering of the Crusaders: The *Gesta* Version

The English translation here is from Krey, 136–139.

When the Armenians and Syrians, however, saw that our men were returning utterly empty-handed, they counselled together and went away through the mountains and places of which they had previous knowledge, making subtle inquiry and buying grain and other bodily sustenance. This they brought to the camp, in which hunger was great beyond measure, and they sold a single ass-load for eight *perpre*, which is worth one hundred and twenty *solidi* of *denarii*. There, indeed, many of our men died because they did not have the means wherewith to buy at such a dear price.

William Carpenter and Peter the Hermit secretly left because of the great sorrow and misery. Tancred pursued and caught them and brought them back in disgrace. They gave him a pledge that they would return willingly to camp and render satisfaction to the seignors. Then William lay all that night, like an evil thing, in the tent of Bohemund. On the next day at early dawn he came shamefacedly and stood in the presence of Bohemund, who, addressing him, said, "O, the misfortune and infamy of all France, the disgrace and villainy of Gaul! O, most evil of all whom the earth endures! Why did you so vilely flee? Was it, perchance, for the reason that you wished to betray these knights and the host of Christ, as you betrayed others in *Hispania*?" He was entirely silent and no speech proceeded from his mouth. Almost all those of Frankish race gathered together and humbly asked Lord Bohemund not to let anything worse befall him. He nodded, with calm countenance, and said, "To this I willingly consent for love of you, if he will swear to me with his whole heart and mind that he will never withdraw from the march to Jerusalem, whether for good or evil; and if Tancred will agree not to let anything untoward befall him, either through him or his men." When William had heard these words, he willingly agreed, and Bohemund forthwith dismissed him. Later, indeed, Carpenter, caught in the greatest villainy, slipped away by stealth without long delay. This poverty and wretchedness God meted out to us because of our sins. Thus in the whole army no one could find a thousand knights who had horses of the best kind.

Meanwhile the hostile *Tetigus*, upon hearing that the army of the Turks had come upon us, said that he was afraid, thinking that we would all perish and fall into the hands of the enemy. Fabricating all the falsehoods which he could industriously scatter, he said: "Seignors and most illustrious men, you see that we are here in the greatest need, and aid is coming to us from no side. So permit me now to return to my country of Romania, and I will, for certain, cause many ships to come hither by sea, laden with grain, wine, barley, meat, butter, and cheese, and all the goods which you need. I shall also cause horses to be brought for sale, and a market to be brought hither in the fealty of the Emperor. So I will swear all this loyally to you and attend to it. Also, my servants and my tent are still in camp, from which you may believe firmly that I will return as quickly as possible." And so he concluded his speech. That foe went and left all his possessions in the camp, and he remains, and will remain, in perjury.

Therefore in this way the greatest need came upon us, because the Turks pressed us on all sides, so that none of us dared now to go out of the tents, for they constrained us on one side, and excruciating hunger on the other; but of succour and help we had none. The lesser folk, and the very poor fled to Cyprus, Romania, and into the mountains. Through fear of the most evil Turks we dared not go to the sea, and the way was never made open to us.

Accordingly, when Lord Bohemund heard that an innumerable host of Turks was coming against us, he went cautiously to the others, saying: "Seignors, most illustrious knights, what are we going to do? For we are not so great that we can fight on two sides. But do you know what we may do? Let us make two lines of ourselves; let a portion of the foot-soldiers remain together to guard the pavilions, and by feinting they will be able to resist those who are in the city. Let the other portion, however, consisting of knights, go with us to meet our enemy, who are lodged here near us in the fortress Aregh beyond the Iron Bridge." Moreover, when evening came the famous man, Bohemund, advanced with the other most illustrious knights and went to lie between the river and the lake. At earliest daybreak he straightway ordered scouts to go out and see how many squadrons of Turks there were, where [they were] and definitely what they were doing. They went out and began to inquire craftily where the lines of the Turks were hidden. Then they saw innumerable Turks, divided into two battle lines, coming from the side of the river, with their greatest valor marching in the rear. The scouts returned very quickly, saying, "Behold! See, they come! Be prepared, therefore, all of you, for they are already near us." And the wise man, Bohemund, spoke to the others, "Seignors, most invincible knights, array yourselves for battle, each one for himself." They answered: "Wise and famous man! Great and magnificent man! Brave and victorious man! Arbiter of battles, and judge of disputes! Make arrangements for us and yourself." Thereupon, Bohemund commanded that each one of the princes should himself form his line in order. They did so, and six lines were formed. Five of them went out together to attack them [the enemy]. Bohemund, accordingly, marched a short distance in the rear with his line.

Thus, when our men were successfully united, one band urged on the other. The clamor resounded to the sky. All fought at the same time. Showers of weapons darkened the air. When their troops of greatest valor, who had been in their rear, came up, they attacked our forces sharply, so that our men fell back a little. As the most learned man, Bohemund, saw this, he groaned. Then he commanded his constable, that is to say Robert, son of Girard, saying: "Go as quickly as you can, like a brave man, and remember our illustrious and courageous forefathers of old. Be keen in the service of God and the Holy Sepulchre, and bear in mind that this battle is not carnal, but spiritual. Be, therefore, the bravest athlete of Christ. Go in peace. The Lord be with you everywhere." And so that man, fortified on all sides with the sign of the cross, went into the lines of the Turks, just as a lion, famished for three or four days, goes forth from his cave raging and thirsting for the blood of beasts and, rushing unexpectedly among the herds of sheep, tears them to pieces as they flee hither and thither. So violently did he press upon them that the tips of his renowned standard flew over the heads of the Turks. Moreover, as the other lines saw that the standard of Bohemund was so gloriously borne before them, they went back to the battle again, and with one accord our men attacked the Turks, who, all amazed, took to flight. Our men, therefore, pursued them even to the Iron Bridge and cut off their heads. The Turks, however, rushed hastily back to their camps and, taking everything they could find there, despoiled the whole camp, set it on fire, and fled. The Armenians and Syrians, knowing that the Turks had utterly lost the battle, went out and watched at the narrow places, where they killed and captured many of them. And so by the favor of God our enemy was overcome on that day. Moreover, our men were sufficiently rewarded with horses and many other things which they greatly needed. And they carried the heads of one hundred dead before the gate of the city, where the envoys of the Emir of Babylon, who had been sent to the princes, were encamped. During the whole day those who had re-mained in the tents had fought before the three gates of the city with those who were inside. This battle was fought on the Wednesday before the begin-ning of Lent, on the fifth day before the Ides of February, with the favor of our Lord Jesus Christ, who, with the Father and the Holy Ghost, liveth and reigneth God forever and ever. Amen. Our men returned triumphant and joy-ful from the victory which, under God's guidance, they had obtained on that day over their defeated enemy. The enemy, entirely beaten, fled, ever roaming and wandering hither and thither. Some [at length] went to Chorosan, but others entered the land of the Saracens.

5. The Suffering of the Crusaders: The Version of Raymond d'Aguilers

The English translation here is from Krey, 139–142.

And so the poor began to leave, and many rich who feared poverty. If any for love of valor remained in camp, they suffered their horses to waste away by daily hunger. Indeed, straw did not abound; and fodder was so dear that seven or eight *solidi* were not sufficient to buy one night's food for a horse. Another calamity also befell the army, for Bohemund, who had become most distinguished in *Hispania* said that he would leave; that he had come for honor, and [now] beheld his men and horses perishing for want; and he [fur-ther] said that he was not a rich man whose private resources would suffice for so long a siege. We found out afterwards that he had said this for the rea-son that he was ambitiously longing to become head of the city of Antioch.

Meanwhile, there was a great earthquake on the third day before the Kalends of January, and we beheld a very marvelous sign in the sky. For in the first watch of the night the sky was so red in the north that it seemed as ·

if dawn had arisen to announce the day. And though in this way God chastised His army, so that we were intent upon the light which was rising in the darkness, yet the minds of some were so blind and abandoned that they were recalled neither from luxury nor robbery. At this time the Bishop prescribed a fast of three days and urged prayers and alms, together with a procession, upon the people; moreover, he commanded the priests to devote themselves to masses and prayers, the clerics to psalms. Thereupon, the merciful Lord, remembering His compassion, put off the punishment of His children, lest the arrogance of their adversaries increase.

There was, besides, in our army a certain member of the Emperor's household whom he had given to us in his place, *Tatius* by name, mangled in nose and all virtue. I had almost forgotten him, since he deserved to be abandoned to oblivion forever. This man, however, was daily whispering in the ears of the princes that they should scatter to the neighboring camp, and then assail the people of Antioch by frequent assaults and ambush. However, as all this was made clear to the Count (for he had been sick since the day when he was forced to flee at the bridge), he called his princes and the Bishop of Puy together. After holding a council, he gave them fifty marks of silver on this condition, truly, that if any of his knights lost a horse, it should be restored to him out of those fifty marks and other [resources] which had been given to the brotherhood. Moreover, this kind of coöperation was of great profit at that time, since the poor of our army, who wanted to cross the river to gather herbs, feared the frequent assaults of the enemy, and since very rarely did any care to go against the enemy, because their horses were starved and weak, and, in addition, so few that scarcely one hundred could be found in the whole army of the Count and Bishop. A similar lot had befallen Bohemund and the other princes. Accordingly, for this reason our knights were not afraid to meet the enemy, especially those who had bad or weak horses, since they knew that if they lost their horses they would obtain better ones. Moreover, something else occurred, namely that all the princes except the Count promised the city to Bohemund, to this agreement, that they would not withdraw from the siege of Antioch for seven years, unless the city was taken.

While these matters were happening in the camp, rumor also announced that the army of the Emperor was coming. It was reported to have been assembled from many peoples; namely, Slavs and Patzinaks and Cumans and Turcopoles. For they are called Turcopoles who either were reared among the Turks, or were born of a Turkish father and a Christian mother. These peoples, moreover, because they had hurt us on the march confessed that they were afraid to meet us. All this, however, that mangled *Tatius* had made up, and he had made such comments in order to be able to get away. This man, after heaping up not only [these] statements, but even the very greatest insults, betrayal of his companions, and perjury, slipped away in flight after having granted to Bohemund two or three cities, *Turso*, Mamistra, Adana. Accordingly, after acquiring everlasting shame for himself and his people in this way, he feigned a journey to the army of the Emperor, and, leaving his tents and his servants, he set out with the curse of God.

It was announced to us at this time that the chief of the Caliph was coming to the help of Antioch with a large army, which he was leading from Chorosan. On this account, after a council had been held in the house of the Bishop, it was decided that the foot-soldiers should guard the camp and the knights should go out of the camp against the enemy; for they said that if the many unwarlike and fearful in our army saw a multitude of Turks, they would afford examples of fright, rather than of boldness. Our men, therefore, set forth at night, lest those in the city should notice [their departure] and report it to those who were coming to aid them, and hid themselves among the little mountains about two leagues distant from our camp.

However, when it became morning, the enemy appeared with the sun. Let them hearken, let them hearken, I beg, who have at one time and another tried to hurt the army, so that, when they recognize that God enlarges His compassion among us, they may hasten to make restitution by lamenations of penance. Accordingly, after the knights had been formed in six squadrons, God multiplied them so much that they who had scarcely seemed to number seventy before the formation, after it were sworn to number more than two thousand in each squadron. What, indeed, shall I say of their boldness, when the knights even sang the military songs so festively that they regarded the coming battle as if it were a game? Moreover, the battle happened to be fought in this place where the swamp and river are a mile apart. This, however, prevented the enemy from spreading out, so that they could not encircle us in their usual manner. For God, who had given us other things, afforded us six successive valleys for advancing to battle. In one hour after going forth the field was taken, and while the sun shone brightly, the battle was committed to arms and shields. Our men, moreover, at first advanced a little, while the Turks, though they scattered to shoot with their bows, yet made a move to retreat. But our men suffered very much until the first ranks of the Turks were pushed into the rear, for as we learned from their deserters, there were said to be not less than twenty-eight thousand horsemen in this battle. And when the first line of the Turks was sufficiently mixed up with the following lines, the Franks called upon the Lord and charged. Nor was there delay; the

Lord, strong and mighty in battle, was present. He protected His children, and hurled down the enemy. So the Franks pursued them even to their very strongly fortified camp, which was about ten miles from the place of battle. But the custodians of the camp, upon seeing this, set fire to it and fled. We were, however, so rejoiced and exultant at this, that we hailed as a second victory the burning of the camp.

And thus on that same day the light in the camp was so great that there was no place toward the city where fighting was not going on. For the enemy had arranged that, while we were most fiercely engaged by the besieged, we should be overwhelmed by their unexpected aid from the rear. But God, who granted victory to our knights, fought among our foot-soldiers [also]. And on that day we obtained no less a triumph over the besieged than our knights reported over the helpers. Accordingly, after the victory and the spoils had been won, the several heads of the dead were brought to the camp. And that we might cause fear among the enemy by the evidence of the [fate of] their scattered allies, the heads that had been brought along were suspended on stakes. This we believed later to have been done by the disposition of God. For when the standard of the Blessed Mary had been captured, they put it point downward in the ground, as if to shame us. And thus it happened that they were restrained from taunting us by the sight of the uplifted heads of their men.

At this time there were in our camp envoys from the King of Babylon, who, upon seeing the wonders which God was working through His servants, glorified Jesus, the son of the Virgin Mary, who through His poor had ground to dust their mightiest tyrants. These envoys, moreover, promised us favor and good will with their king; besides, they told of very many good deeds of their king toward the Egyptian Christians and our pilgrims. Thereupon, our envoys were sent back with them to enter upon a treaty and friendship with the King.

6. The Suffering of the Crusaders: The Version of Peter Tudebode

The English translation here is from Hill and Hill, 72–74, 78–81.

On the third day of the siege Kerbogha made battle preparations, and a large army of Turks accompanied him to the citadel sector. Under the impression that we could match their might, we took up battle positions; but their strength was so awesome that we could not oppose them, and so in disarray we re-entered Antioch. Because of the narrow and cramped gate, many of our fugitives were crushed to death in the jam.

All through this Thursday within and without the walls of Antioch, the Christians fought even until sundown. Likewise, on Friday they battled all day, and the Turks slew many of our men. On this day, Arvedus Tudebodus, a most worthy knight, was wounded. His friends carried him into the city, where he lived until Saturday. On this day between nones and sext he left this world, living now in Christ. His brother, a priest, buried him before the western portal of the church of the blessed Apostle Peter. This brother along with the Christians in Antioch greatly feared death by decapitation. We pray that all readers and listeners give alms and pray for the soul of Arvedus Tudebodus and for all of the departed souls on the journey to Jerusalem.

On this day William Grandmesnil, his brother Alberic, Ivo of Grandmesnil, William of Bernella, Guido Trosellus and William, brother of Richard, and Lambert the Pauper, overwhelmed by fear after yesterday's battle, which had lasted until vespers, secretly lowered themselves from the walls, and in the dark of night fled on foot to the coast. In the course of their flight they stripped the flesh of their hands and feet to the bone. Others, whose names I do not know, secretly fled with them. Upon their arrival at the port of Saint Simeon where ships were docked, they inquired from the sailors: "Why do you wretches stay here? All of our friends are dead, and we almost lost our lives because the Turkish army has besieged Antioch on all sides."

The sailors, upon receipt of this news, stood dumfounded and overwhelmed with fear and therewith rushed to their ships and sailed away. At this time the Turks arrived upon the scene and killed the Christians whom they found, put to torch the ships anchored in the mouth of the river, and seized their goods. We who remained in the city could not equal the power and arms of the Turks, and so we built between the citadel and us a wall which we guarded day and night. In the meantime we were so hungry that we ate horses and asses. Besides we lived in such mortal terror of the Turks that many of our leading men wished to flee by night as had the deserters. . . .

The Turks in the commanding citadel pressed our troops so vigorously that they surrounded three of our knights on a certain day in a tower which stood before their fort. The pagans rushed out of the citadel and struck the Christians so hard that they could not resist their courageous charge. Two of the wounded crusaders abandoned the tower, but the third one defended himself all day so cleverly from the Turkish attacks that on that occasion he knocked down two Turks at the entrance of the walls with broken spears. In the course of the day three spears broke in his hands. The knight was Hugh le Forsenet of the army of Godfrey of Monte Scaglioso.

Bohemond and Tancred could not induce their men to storm the citadel because they were shut up in houses and reluctant to fight, some because of hunger and some because of fear of the Turks. Bohemond, greatly angered by this inaction, at once ordered the quarters of Yaghi Siyan put to the torch. The crusaders, on viewing the mounting flames fanned by a brisk wind, abandoned the houses and fled with booty, some toward the mountain before the citadel, others to the gate of Raymond of Saint-Gilles, and yet others to the gate of Duke Godfrey, and thus each returned to his unit. In the course of the fire Bohemond was greatly distressed because he feared that the churches of Saint Peter and Saint Mary would burn because the conflagration blazed from the third hour until midnight and burned two thousand churches and homes. In the middle of the night the wind calmed and the fire smouldered out.

The Turkish force of the citadel fought day and night with us within Antioch, and nothing separated us but force of arms. At one time four emirs, completely clad in gold armor, came out with the Turks, leading horses likewise encased in gold armor to the knee joints. Our men, who were so hard pressed that they had no time to eat bread or to drink water, were so impressed by this sight that they could endure it no longer. So they erected a wall between them and the mountain and built a fortress-like castle and machines of war so that they could be secure.

Another group of Turks was encamped around Antioch in a valley apart from the others. At nightfall fire from the heavens appeared from the west and fell in among the Turkish troops, astonishing both Turks and Christians. At daybreak the Turks, terrified by the celestial fire, fled hither and thither. However, they surrounded us in Antioch so completely that no one dared enter or leave except stealthily by night. Thus we were besieged and oppressed by the other pagans, enemies of God and Blessed Christianity. They numbered three hundred and sixty-five thousand with the exception of the Emir of Jerusalem, who was there with his soldiers, and the King of Damascus, along with his people, as well as the King of Aleppo with his men.

Consequently, the profane enemies of God held us so closely surrounded in Antioch that many of our people starved to death because of high prices. A small loaf of bread cost a bezant of gold, and of the price of wine I shall not speak; there was not even a jug of it. One hen sold for fifteen *solidi*, an egg cost two *solidi*, a nut brought one *denarius*, three or four beans were worth one *denarius*, and a small goat cost sixty *solidi*. The belly of one goat was worth two *solidi*; the tail of a ram varied in price from three to nine *denari*. The tongue of a camel, which is small, brought four *solidi*. The crusaders likewise ate and sold meat of horses and asses. They cooked leaves of figs, vines, and trees in water and then ate them. Some put the hides of horses, asses, camels, oxen, and wild buffalo, dried for five or six years, into water for two nights and a day; and after mingling them with the water, boiled and ate them. There were many anxieties and hardships suffered in the name of Christ and for the journey of freeing the Holy Sepulchre; in fact, far more than I can recount. As servants of God we suffered such tribulations as well as starvation and fear for twenty-six days.

The shameless Stephen of Blois, head of our army, whom our chieftains had elected their leader before the fall of Antioch, under the pretense of an illness basely retired to another camp called Alexandretta. Deprived of life-saving help while besieged in Antioch, we daily expected him to assist us to the best of his ability. Yet, following news of the Turkish encirclement and blockade of us, Stephen sneaked up a nearby mountain, gazed upon count-less tents of the foe, and as a result retired. Suddenly he was terror stricken and disgracefully fled in wild flight with his army. Upon arrival in his camp, he stripped it of goods and cowardly returned in haste. Afterwards he came to Alexius at Philomelium, approached him in secret and in private related: "You may as well know the truth. Antioch has fallen, but the citadel has not, and all of our men are so grievously beset that I think that at this moment they have been killed by the Turks. Retreat as rapidly as you can lest they find you and your following."

7. The Fall of Antioch: The *Gesta* Version

The English translation here is from Krey, 151–153.

I cannot enumerate all the things which we did before the city was cap-tured, because there is no one in these regions, whether cleric or layman, who can at all write or tell just how things happened. Nevertheless, I will say a little.

There was a certain Emir of the race of the Turks, whose name was *Pirus*, who took up the greatest friendship with Bohemund. By an interchange of messengers Bohemund often pressed this man to receive him within the city in a most friendly fashion, and, after promising Christianity to him most freely, he sent word that he would make him rich with much honor. *Pirus* yielded to these words and promises, saying, "I guard three towers, and I freely promise them to him, and at whatever hour he wishes I will receive him within them."

Accordingly, Bohemund was now secure about entering the city, and, delighted, with serene mind and joyful countenance, he came to all the leaders, bearing joyful words to them in this wise: "Men, most illustrious knights, see how all of us, whether of greater or less degree, are in exceeding poverty and misery, and how utterly ignorant we are from what side we will fare better. Therefore, if it seems good and honorable to you, let one of us put himself ahead of the rest, and if he can acquire or contrive [the capture of] the city by any plan or scheme, by himself, or through the help of others, let us with one voice grant him the city as a gift." They absolutely refused and spurned [the suggestion] saying, "This city shall be given to no one, but we will hold it equally; since we have had equal effort, so let us have equal reward from it."

Bohemund, upon hearing these words, laughed a bit to himself and immediately retired. Not much later we listened to messages concerning [the approach of] an army of our enemy, Turks, *Publicani*, *Agulani*, Azimites, and very many other gentile nations that I know not how to enumerate or name. Immediately all our leaders came together, and held a council, saying: "If Bohemund can acquire the city, either by himself, or with the help of others, let us give it to him freely and with one accord, on condition that if the Emperor comes to our aid and wishes to carry out every agreement, as he swore and promised, we will return it to him by right. But if he does not do this, let Bohemund keep it in his power." Immediately, therefore, Bohemund began meekly to beseech his friend in daily petition, holding out most humbly the greatest and sweetest promises in this manner: "Behold, we have now truly a fit time to accomplish whatever good we wish; therefore, now, my friend *Pirus*, help me." Greatly pleased at the message, he replied that he would aid him in every way, as he ought to do. Accordingly, at the approach of night, he cautiously sent his son to Bohemund as a pledge, that he might be the more secure about his entrance to the city. He also sent word to him in this wise: "Tomorrow sound the trumpets for the Frankish host to move on, pretending that they are going to plunder the land of the Saracens, and then turn back quickly over the mountain on the right. With alert mind, indeed, I will be awaiting those forces, and I will take them into the towers which I have in my power and charge." Then Bohemund ordered a certain servant of his, Malacorona by name, to be called, and bade him, as herald, to admonish most of the Franks faithfully to prepare themselves to go into the land of the Saracens. This was so done. Thereupon Bohemund entrusted his plan to Duke Godfrey, and the Count of Flanders, also to the Count of St. Gilles and the Bishop of Puy, saying, "The grace of God favoring, Antioch will this night be surrendered to us."

All these matters were at length arranged; the knights held the level places and the foot soldiers the mountain. All the night they rode and marched until dawn, and then began to approach the towers which that person [*Pirus*] was watchfully guarding. Bohemund straightway dismounted and gave orders to the rest, saying, "Go with secure mind and happy accord, and climb by ladder into Antioch which, if it please God, we shall have in our power immediately." They went up the ladder, which had already been placed and firmly bound to the projections of the city wall. About sixty of our men climbed up it and were distributed among the towers which that man was watching. *Pirus*, upon seeing that so few of our men had ascended, began to tremble with fear for both himself and our men, lest they fall into the hands of the Turks. And he said, "*Micro Francos echome*—There are few Franks here! Where is most fierce Bohemund, that unconquered knight?" Meanwhile a certain Longobard servant descended again, and ran as quickly [as possible] to Bohemund, saying, "Why do you stand here, illustrious man? Why have you come hither? Behold, we already hold three towers!" Bohemund was moved with the rest, and all went joyfully to the ladder. Accordingly, when those who were in the towers saw this, they began to shout with happy voices, "God wills it!" We began to shout likewise; now the men began to climb up there in wondrous fashion. Then they reached the top and ran in haste to the other towers. Those whom they found there they straightway sentenced to death; they even killed a brother of *Pirus*. Meantime the ladder by which we had ascended broke by chance, whereupon there arose the greatest dismay and gloom among us. However, though the ladder had been broken, there was still a certain gate near us which had been shut on the left side and had remained unknown to some of the people, for it was night. But by feeling about and inquiring we found it, and all ran to it; and, having broken it open, we entered through it.

Thereupon, the noise of a countless multitude resounded through all the city. Bohemund did not give his men any rest, but ordered his standard to be carried up in front of the castle on a certain hill. Indeed, all were shouting in the city together. Moreover, when at earliest dawn those in the tents outside heard the most violent outcry sounding through the city, they rushed out hurriedly and saw the standard of Bohemund up on the mount, and with rapid pace all ran hastily and entered the city. They killed the Turks and Saracens whom they found there, except those who had fled into the citadel. Others of the Turks went out through the gates, and by fleeing escaped alive.

But *Cassianus*, their lord, fearing the race of the Franks greatly, took flight with the many others who were with him and came in flight to the land of Tancred, not far from the city. Their horses, however, were worn out, and, taking refuge in a certain villa, they dashed into a house. The inhabitants of the mountain, Syrians and Armenians, upon recognizing him [*Cassianus*], straightway seized him, cut off his head, and took it into the presence of Bohemund, so that they might gain their liberty. They also sold his sword-belt and scabbard for sixty *besants*. All this occurred on the third day of the incoming month of June, the fifth day of the week, the third day before the Nones of June. All the squares of the city were already everywhere full of the corpses of the dead, so that no one could endure it there for the excessive stench. No one could go along a street of the city except over the bodies of the dead.

8. The Fall of Antioch: The Version of Raymond d'Aguilers

The English translation here is from Krey, 153–155.

Meanwhile, messengers began to come very frequently, saying that aid was coming to the enemy. Moreover, this report came to us not only from the Armenians and the Greeks, but was also announced to us by those who were in the city. When the Turks had obtained Antioch fourteen years before, they had converted Armenians and Greek youths, as if for want of servants, and had given them wives. When such men as these had a chance to escape, they came to us with horses and arms. And when this report became frequent, many of our men and the Armenian merchants began to flee in terror. Meanwhile, good knights who were scattered among the fortresses came and brought arms, fitted, and repaired them. And when the gradually lessening swelling [of pride] had flowed from our army, and courage, ever ready to undergo dangers with brothers and for brothers, had come [in its place], one of the converted who was in the city sent word to our princes through Bohemund that he would surrender the city to us.

Accordingly, when the plan had been communicated, the princes sent Bohemund and the Duke of Lorraine and the Count of Flanders to try it out. And when they had come to the hill of the city at midnight, an intermediary sent back by him who was surrendering the city said, "Wait until the light passes." For three or four men went along the walls of the city with lamps all night, arousing and admonishing the watchers. After this, however, our men approached the wall, raised a ladder, and began to ascend it. A certain Frank, Fulger by name, brother of Budellus of Chartres, was the first boldly to ascend the wall; the Count of Flanders, following, sent word to Bohemund and the Duke to ascend; and since all hurried, each to go ahead of the other, the ladder was broken. But those who had climbed up went down into the city and opened a certain little postern. Thus our men went in, and they did not take captive any of those whom they found. When the dawn of day appeared, they shouted out. The whole city was disturbed at this shout, and the women and small children began to weep. Those who were in the castle of the Count, aroused at this outcry since they were nearer [it], began to say to one another, "Their aid has come!" Others, however, replied, "That does not sound like the voice of joyful people." And when the day whitened, our standards appeared on the southern hill of the city. When the disturbed citizens saw our men on the mountain above them, some fled through the gate, others hurled themselves headlong. No one resisted; in truth, the Lord had confounded them. Then after a long time, a joyful spectacle was made for us, in that those who had so long defended Antioch against us were now unable to flee from Antioch. Even if some of them had dared to take flight, yet they could not escape death. A certain incident occurred there, joyful and delightful enough for us. For when some Turks strove to flee among the cliffs which divide the hill in two from the north, they encountered some of our men, and when the Turks were forced to go back, the repulsed fugitives went with such rapidity that they all fell over the precipice together. Our joy over the fallen enemy was great, but we grieved over the more than thirty horses who had their necks broken there.

How great were the spoils captured in Antioch it is impossible for us to say, except that you may believe as much as you wish and then add to it. Moreover, we cannot say how many Turks and Saracens then perished; it is, furthermore, cruel to explain by what diverse and various deaths they died. When those foes who guarded the castle on the middle hill saw the destruction of their men and that our men were refraining from besieging them, they kept their castle. *Gracianus*, however, who had gone out by a certain postern, was captured and beheaded by some Armenian peasants, and his head was brought to us. This, I believe, was done by the ineffable disposition of God, that he who had caused many men of this same race to be beheaded should be deprived of his head by them. The city of Antioch was captured on the third day before the Nones of June; it had been besieged, however, since about the eleventh day before the Kalends of November.

9. Kerbogha's Attack: The *Gesta* Version

Kerbogha, the atabeg (regent) of Mosul, appeared with a large army before the captured city of Antioch on June 7, 1098. The crusaders, weakened by a long siege and

many desertions, faced yet another battle. They tried to negotiate with Kerbogha, failed, and on June 28 marched out to meet him, and they defeated his army. The capture of Antioch, the defeat of Kerbogha's counterattack, and the discovery of the Holy Lance restored the crusaders' spirits and pointed the way to Jerusalem.
The English translation here is from Krey, 163–168.

Some time before, *Cassianus*, Emir of Antioch, had sent a message to *Curbara*, chief of the Sultan of Persia, while he was still at Chorosan, to come and help him while there was yet time, because a very mighty host of Franks was besieging him shut up in Antioch. If the Emir would aid him, he [*Cassianus*] would give him Antioch, or would enrich him with a very great gift. Since *Curbara* had had a very large army of Turks collected for a long time, and had received permission from the Caliph, their Pope, to kill the Christians, he began a long march to Antioch. The Emir of Jerusalem came to his aid with an army, and the King of Damascus arrived there with a very large host. Indeed, *Curbara* likewise collected countless pagan folk, Turks, Arabs, Saracens, *Publicani*, Azimites, Kurds, Persians, *Agulani*, and countless other peoples. The *Agulani* were three thousand in number and feared neither lances, arrows, nor any kind of arms, because they and all their horses were fitted with iron all around, and they refused to carry any arms except swords into battle. All of these came to the siege of Antioch to disperse the gathering of Franks.

And when they neared the city, *Sensadolus*, son of *Cassianus*, Emir of Antioch, went to meet them, and straightway rushed in tears to *Curbara*, beseeching him with these words: "Most invincible chief, I, a supplicant, pray thee to help me, now that the Franks are besieging me on every side in the city of Antioch; now that they hold the city in their sway and seek to alienate us from the region of Romania, or even yet from Syria and Chorosan. They have done everything that they wished; they have killed my father; now nothing else remains except to kill me, and you, and all the others of our race. For a long time now I have been waiting for your help to succor me in this danger."

To him *Curbara* replied: "If you want me to enter wholeheartedly into your service and to help you loyally in this danger, give that town into my hands, and then see how I will serve you and protect it with my men."

Sensadolus replied, "If you can kill all the Franks and give me their heads, I will give you the town, and I will do homage to you and guard the town in your fealty."

To this *Curbara* answered: "That won't do; hand over the town to me immediately." And then, willy-nilly, he handed the town over to him.

But on the third day after we had entered the town, *Curbara*'s advance guard ran in front of the city; his army, however, encamped at the Iron Gate. They took the fortress by siege and killed all of the defenders, whom we found in iron chains after the greater battle had been fought.

On the next day, the army of the pagans moved on, and, nearing the city, they encamped between the two rivers and stayed there for two days. After they had retaken the fortress, *Curbara* summoned one of his emirs whom he knew to be truthful, gentle, and peaceable and said to him, "I want you to undertake to guard this fortress in fealty to me, because for the longest time I have known you to be most loyal; therefore, I pray you, keep this castle with the greatest care, for, since I know you to be the most prudent in action, I can find no one here more truthful and valiant."

To him the Emir replied: "Never would I refuse to obey you in such service, but before you persuade me by urging, I will consent, on the condition that if the Franks drive your men from the deadly field of battle and conquer, I will straightway surrender this fortress to them."

Curbara said to him: "I recognize you as so honorable and wise that I will fully consent to whatever good you wish to do." And thereupon *Curbara* returned to his army.

Forthwith the Turks, making sport of the gatherings of Franks, brought into the presence of *Curbara* a certain very miserable sword covered with rust, a very worn wooden bow, and an exceedingly useless lance, which they had just recently taken from poor pilgrims, and said, "Behold the arms which the Franks carry to meet us in battle!" Then *Curbara* began to laugh, saying before all who were in that gathering, "These are the warlike and shining arms which the Christians have brought against us into Asia, with which they hope and expect to drive us beyond the confines of Chorosan and to wipe out our names beyond the Amazon rivers, they who have driven our relatives from Romania and the royal city of Antioch, which is the renowned capital of all Syria!" Then he summoned his scribe and said: "Write quickly several documents which are to be read in Chorosan."

"To the Caliph, our Pope, and to our King, the Lord Sultan, most valiant knight, and to all most illustrious knights of Chorosan; greeting and honor beyond measure.

Let them be glad enough and delight with joyful concord and satisfy their appetites; let them command and make known through all that region that the people give themselves entirely to exuberance and luxury, and that they rejoice to bear many children to fight stoutly against the Christians. Let them gladly receive these three weapons which we recently took from a squad of Franks, and let them now learn what arms the Frankish host bears against us; how very fine and perfect they are to fight against our arms which are twice, thrice, or even four times welded, or purified, like the purest silver or gold. In addition, let all know, also, that I have the Franks shut up in Antioch, and that I hold the citadel at my free disposal, while they [the enemy] are below in the city. Likewise, I hold all of them now in my hand. I shall make them either undergo sentence of death, or be led into Chorosan into the harshest captivity, because they are threatening with their arms to drive us forth and to expel us from all our territory, or to cast us out beyond upper India, as they have cast out all our kinsmen from Romania or Syria. Now I swear to you by Mohammed and all the names of the gods that I will not return before your face until I shall have acquired with my strong right hand the regal city of Antioch, all Syria, Romania, and Bulgaria, even to Apulia, to the honor of the gods, and to your glory, and to that of all who are of the race of the Turks." And thus he put an end to his words.

The mother of the same *Curbara*, who dwelt in the city of Aleppo, came immediately to him and, weeping, said: "Son, are these things true which I hear?"

"What things?" he said.

"I have heard that you are going to engage in battle with the host of the Franks," she replied.

And he answered: "You know the truth fully."

She then said, "I warn you, son, in the names of all the gods and by your great kindness, not to enter into battle with the Franks, because you are an unconquered knight, and I have never at all heard of any imprudence from you or your army. No one has ever found you fleeing from the field before any victor. The fame of your army is spread abroad, and all illustrious knights tremble when your name is heard. For we know well enough, son, that you are mighty in battle, and valiant and resourceful, and that no host of Christians or pagans can have any courage before your face, but are wont to flee at the mention of your name, as sheep flee before the wrath of a lion. And so I beseech you, dearest son, to yield to my advice never to let it rest in your mind, or be found in your counsel, to wish to undertake war with the Christian host."

Then *Curbara*, upon hearing his mother's warning, replied with wrathful speech: "What is this, mother, that you tell me? I think that you are insane, or full of furies. For I have with me more emirs than there are Christians, whether of greater or lesser state."

His mother replied to him: "O sweetest son, the Christians cannot fight with your forces, for I know that they are not able to prevail against you;

but their God is fighting for them daily and is watching over them and defending them with His protection by day and night, as a shepherd watches over his flock. He does not permit them to be hurt or disturbed by any folk, and whoever seeks to stand in their way this same God of theirs likewise puts to rout, just as He said through the mouth of the prophet David: 'Scatter the people that delight in wars,' and in another place: 'Pour out Thy wrath upon the nations that know Thee not and against the kingdoms that call not upon Thy name.' Before they are ready to begin battle, their God, all powerful and potent in battle, together with His saints, has all their enemies already conquered. How much more will He now prevail against you, who are His enemies, and who are preparing to resist them with all your valor! This, moreover, dearest, know in very truth: these Christians, called 'sons of Christ' and by the mouth of the prophets 'sons of adoption and promise,' according to the apostle are the heirs of Christ to whom He has already given the promised inheritance, saying through the prophets, 'From the rising to the setting of the sun shall be your border and no one shall stand before you.' Who can contradict or oppose these words? Certainly, if you undertake this battle against them, yours will be the very greatest loss and disgrace, and you will lose many of your faithful knights and all the spoils which you have with you, and you will turn in flight with exceeding fear. However, you shall not die now in this battle, but, nevertheless, in this year, because God does not with quick anger immediately judge him who has offended Him, but when He wills, He punishes with manifest vengeance, and so I fear He will exact of you a bitter penalty. You shall not die, now, I say, but you shall perish after all your present possessions."

Then *Curbara*, deeply grieved in his heart at his mother's words, replied: "Dearest mother, pray, who told you such things about the Christian folk, that God loves only them, and that He restrains the mightiest host from fighting against Him, and that those Christians will conquer us in the battle of Antioch, and that they will capture our spoils, and will pursue us with great victory, and that I shall die in this year by a sudden death?"

Then his mother answered him sadly: "Dearest son, behold the times are more than a hundred years since it was found in our book and in the volumes of the Gentiles that the Christian host would come against us, would conquer us everywhere and rule over the pagans, and that our people would be everywhere subject to them. But I do not know whether these things are to happen now or in the future. Wretched woman that I am, I have followed you from Aleppo, most beautiful city, in which, by gazing and contriving ingenious rhymes, I looked back at the stars of the skies and wisely scrutinized the planets and the twelve signs, or countless lots. In all of these I found that the Christian host would win everywhere, and so I am exceedingly sad and fear greatly lest I remain bereft of you."

Curbara said to her: "Dearest mother, explain to me all the incredible things which are in my heart."

Answering this, she said: "This, dearest, I will do freely, if I know the things which are unknown to you."

He said to her: "Are not Bohemund and Tancred gods of the Franks, and do they not free them from their enemies, and do not these men in one meal eat two thousand heifers and four thousand hogs?"

His mother answered: "Dearest son, Bohemund and Tancred are mortals, like all the rest; but their God loves them greatly above all the others and gives them valor in fighting beyond the rest. For [it is] their God, Omnipotent is His name, who made heaven and earth and established the seas and all things that in them are, whose dwelling-place is in heaven prepared for all eternity, whose might is everywhere to be feared."

Her son said: "[Even] if such is the case, I will not refrain from fighting with them." Thereupon, when his mother heard that he would in no way yield to her advice, she returned, a very sad woman, to Aleppo, carrying with her all the gifts that she could take along.

But on the third day *Curbara* armed himself and most of the Turks with him and went toward the city from the side on which the fortress was located. Thinking that we could resist them, we prepared ourselves for battle against them, but so great was their valor that we could not withstand them, and under compulsion, therefore, we entered the city. The gate was so amazingly close and narrow for them that many died there from the pressure of the rest. Meanwhile, some fought outside the city, others within, on the fifth day of the week throughout the day until the evening.

10. Kerbogha's Attack: The Version of Raymond d'Aguilers

The English translation here is from Krey, 168–169.

In the meantime, while our men, engaged in counting and identifying their spoils, had desisted from the siege of the upper fortress, and, while listening to the pagan dancing girls, had feasted in splendor and magnificence, not at all mindful of God who had granted them so great a blessing, they were besieged by the pagans on the third day, on the Nones of the same June. And so it was brought about that they who by the mercy of God had so long besieged the Turks in Antioch were through His disposition in turn besieged by the Turks. And that we might be the more fearful, the upper fortress which is a kind of citadel, was in the hands of the enemy. Our men, accordingly, under the stress of fear, took up the siege of the fortress.

Corbaga, however, lord of the Turks, expecting the battle to take place there, fixed his tents at a distance of about two miles from the city and, with ranks arrayed, came up to the bridge of the city. Our men, however, had strengthened the fortress of the Count on the first day, fearing that if they proceeded to battle it would be seized by the enemy who were in the citadel, or, if they deserted the fortress which was before the bridge and the enemy occupied it, that the enemy would shut us off from a chance to fight and block our exit.

There was in the army a knight most distinguished and very dear to all, *Roger of Barneville* by name, who, while pursuing the army of the retiring enemy, was captured and deprived of his head. Fear and grief, accordingly, assailed our men, so that many were led to the desperate hope of flight. Thereupon, when the Turks had once and again suffered a repulse in fighting, they besieged the fortress on the third day; and the fighting was carried on there with such violence that the might of God alone was believed to defend the fortress and resist the adversaries. For when the Turks were already prepared to cross the moat and destroy the walls, they were taken with fright, I know not why, and rushed headlong into flight. Then, seeing no reason for their flight, they returned to the siege after they had run a short distance, blaming their own timidity; and, as if to atone for the disgrace of the flight they had made, they attacked more violently and again were more violently terrified by the might of God. Therefore the enemy returned to their camp on that day. On the next day, however, they returned to the fortress with a very great supply of siege machinery, but our men set fire to the fortress and thrust themselves within the walls of the city. And thus, as the fear of the Franks was increased, the boldness of the enemy grew; forsooth, we had nothing outside the city, and the fortress, which was the head of the city, was held by our foes. The Turks, emboldened by this, arranged to enter against us by the fortress. Our men, however, relying on their favorable and lofty location, fought against the enemy and at the first attack overthrew them; but, forgetful of the threatening battle and intent upon plunder, they [in turn] were most vilely put to flight. For more than a hundred men were suffocated in the gate of the city, and even more horses. Then the Turks who had entered the fortress wanted to go down into the city. For the valley between our mountain and their fortress was not large, and in the middle of it was a certain cistern and a little level place. Nor did the enemy have a path down into the city except through our mountain; wherefore they strove with every intent and all their might to drive us out and remove us from their path. The battle was waged with such force from morning to evening that nothing like it was ever heard of. There was a certain frightful and as yet unheard of calamity befell us, for amidst the hail of arrows and rocks, and the constant charge of javelins, and the deaths of so many, our men became unconscious. If you ask for the end of this fight, it was night.

11. The Discovery of the Holy Lance: The *Gesta* Version

The English translation here is from Krey, 174–176.

But one day as our leaders, sad and disconsolate, were standing back before the fortress, a certain priest came to them and said: "Seignors, if it please you, listen to a certain matter which I saw in a vision. When one night I was lying in the church of St. Mary, Mother of God, our Lord Jesus Christ, the Saviour of the world, appeared to me with His mother and St. Peter, prince of the apostles, and stood before me and said, 'Knowest thou me?'

"I answered, 'No.' At these words, lo, a whole cross appeared on His head.

"A second time, therefore, the Lord asked me 'Knowest thou me?'

"To Him I replied: 'I do not know Thee except that I see a cross on thy head like that of Our Saviour.'

"He answered, 'I am He.'

"Immediately I fell at His feet, humbly beseeching that He help us in the oppression which was upon us. The Lord responded: 'I have helped you in goodly manner and I will now help you. I permitted you to have the city of Nicaea, and to win all battles, and I conducted you hither to this point, and I have grieved at the misery which you have suffered in the siege of Antioch. Behold, with timely aid I sent you safe and unharmed into the city, and lo! [you are] working much evil pleasure with Christian and depraved pagan women, whereof a stench beyond measure arises unto heaven.'

"Then the loving Virgin and the blessed Peter fell at His feet, praying and beseeching Him to aid His people in this tribulation, and the blessed Peter said: 'Lord, for so long a time the pagan host has held my house, and in it they have committed many unspeakable wrongs. But now, since the enemy have been driven hence, Lord, the angels rejoice in heaven.'

"The Lord then said to me: 'Go and tell my people to return to Me, and I will return to them, and within five days I will send them great help. Let them daily chant the response *Congregati sunt*, all of it, including the verse.'

"Seignors, if you do not believe that this is true, let me climb up into this tower, and I will throw myself down, and if I am unharmed, believe that this is true. If, however, I shall have suffered any hurt, behead me, or cast me into the fire." Then the Bishop of Puy ordered that the Gospel and the Cross be brought, so that he might take oath that this was true.

All our leaders were counselled at that time to take oath that not one of them would flee, either for life or death, as long as they were alive. Bohemund is said to have been the first to take the oath, then the Count of St. Gilles, Robert of Normandy, Duke Godfrey, and the Count of Flanders. Tancred, indeed, swore and promised in this manner: that as long as he had forty knights with him he would not only not withdraw from that battle, but, likewise, not from the march to Jerusalem. Moreover, the Christian assemblage exulted greatly upon hearing this oath.

There was a certain pilgrim of our army, whose name was Peter, to whom before we entered the city St. Andrew, the apostle, appeared and said: "What art thou doing, good man?"

Peter answered, "Who art thou?"

The apostle said to him: "I am St. Andrew, the apostle. Know, my son, that when thou shalt enter the town, go to the church of St. Peter. There thou wilt find the Lance of our Saviour, Jesus Christ, with which He was wounded as He hung on the arm of the cross." Having said all this, the apostle straightway withdrew.

But Peter, afraid to reveal the advice of the apostle, was unwilling to make it known to the pilgrims. However, he thought that he had seen a vision, and said: "Lord, who would believe this?" But at that hour St. Andrew took him and carried him to the place where the Lance was hidden in the ground. When we were a second time situated in such [straits] as we have stated above, St. Andrew came again, saying to him: "Wherefore hast thou not yet taken the Lance from the earth as I commanded thee? Know, verily, that whoever shall bear this lance in battle shall never be overcome by an enemy." Peter, indeed, straightway made known to our men the mystery of the apostle.

The people, however, did not believe [it], but refused, saying: "How can we believe this?" For they were utterly terrified and thought that they were to die forthwith. Thereupon, this man came forth and swore that it was all most true, since St. Andrew had twice appeared to him in a vision and had said to him: "Rise, go and tell the people of God not to fear, but to trust firmly with whole heart in the one true God and they will be everywhere victorious. Within five days the Lord will send them such a token that they will remain happy and joyful, and if they wish to fight, let them go out immediately to battle, all together, and all their enemies will be conquered, and no one will stand against them." Thereupon, when they heard that their enemies were to be overcome by them, they began straightway to revive and to encourage one another, saying: "Bestir yourselves, and be everywhere brave and alert, since the Lord will come to our aid in the next battle and will be the greatest refuge to His people whom He beholds lingering in sorrow."

Accordingly, upon hearing the statements of that man who reported to us the revelation of Christ through the words of the apostle, we went in haste immediately to the place in the church of St. Peter which he had pointed out. Thirteen men dug there from morning until vespers. And so that man found the Lance, just as he had indicated. They received it with great gladness and fear, and a joy beyond measure arose in the whole city.

12. The Discovery of the Holy Lance: The Version of Raymond d'Aguilers

The English translation here is from Krey, 176–182.

And so, as we said, when our men were in a panic and while they were on the verge of despair, divine mercy was at hand for them; and that mercy which had corrected the children when they were wanton, consoled them when they were very sad, in the following way. Thus, when the city of Antioch had been captured, the Lord, employing His power and kindness, chose a certain poor peasant, Provençal by race, through whom He comforted us; and He sent these words to the Count and Bishop of Puy:

"Andrew, apostle of God and of our Lord Jesus Christ, has recently admonished me a fourth time and has commanded me to come to you and to give back to you, after the city was captured, the Lance which opened the side of the Saviour. To-day, moreover, when I had set out from the city with the rest to battle, and when, caught between two horsemen, I was almost suffocated on the retreat, I sat down sadly upon a certain rock, almost lifeless. When I was reeling like a woe-begone from fear and grief, St. Andrew came to me with a companion, and he threatened me much unless I returned the Lance to you quickly."

And when the Count and Bishop asked him to tell in order the apostolic revelation and command, he replied: "At the first earthquake which occurred at Antioch when the army of the Franks was besieging it, such fear assailed me that I could say nothing except 'God help me.' For it was night, and I was lying down; nor was there anyone else in my hut to sustain me by his presence. When, moreover, the shaking of the earth had lasted a long time, and my fear had ever increased, two men stood before me in the brightest raiment. The one was older, with red and white hair, black eyes, and kindly face, his beard, indeed, white, wide, and thick, and his stature medium; the other was younger and taller, handsome in form beyond the children of men. And the older said to me 'What doest thou?' and I was very greatly frightened because I knew that there was no one present. And I answered, 'Who art thou?'

"He replied, 'Rise, and fear not; and heed what I say to thee. I am Andrew the Apostle. Bring together the Bishop of Puy and the Count of St. Gilles and Peter Raymond of Hautpoul, and say these words to them: "Why has the Bishop neglected to preach and admonish and daily to sign his people with the cross which he bears before them, for it would profit them much?" ' And he added, 'Come and I will show thee the Lance of our father, Jesus Christ, which thou shalt give to the Count. For God has granted it to him ever since he was born.'

"I arose, therefore, and followed him into the city, dressed in nothing except a shirt. And he led me into the church of the apostle of St. Peter through the north gate, before which the Saracens had built a mosque. In the church, indeed, were two lamps, which there gave as much light as if the sun had illuminated it. And he said to me, 'Wait here.' And he commanded me to sit upon a column, which was closest to the stairs by which one ascends to the altar from the south; but his companion stood at a distance before the altar steps. Then St. Andrew, going under ground, brought forth the Lance and gave it into my hands.

"And he said to me 'Behold the Lance which opened His side, whence the salvation of the whole world has come.'

"While I held it in my hands, weeping for joy, I said to him, 'Lord, if it is Thy will, I will take it and give it to the Count!'

"And he said to me 'Not now, for it will happen that the city will be taken. Then come with twelve men and seek it here whence I drew it forth and where I hide it.' And he hid it.

"After these things had been so done, he led me back over the wall to my home; and so they left me. Then I thought to myself of the condition of my poverty and your greatness, and I feared to approach you. After this, when I had set forth for food to a certain fortress which is near Edessa, on the first day of Lent at cock-crow, St. Andrew appeared to me in the same garb and with the same companion with whom he had come before, and a great brightness filled the house. And St. Andrew said 'Art thou awake?'

"Thus aroused, I replied 'No, Lord; my Lord, I am not asleep.'

"And he said to me 'Hast thou told those things which I bade thee tell some time ago?'

"And I answered 'Lord, have I not prayed thee to send some one else to them, for, fearful of my poverty, I hesitated to go before them?'

"And he said 'Dost thou not know why the Lord led you hither, and how much He loves you and why He chose you especially? He made you come hither [to rebuke] contempt of Him and to avenge His people. He loves you so dearly that the saints already at rest, fore-knowing the grace of Divine arrangements, wished that they were in the flesh and struggling along with you. God has chosen you from all peoples, as grains of wheat are gathered from the oats. For you excel in favor and rewards all who may come before or after you, just as gold excels silver in value.'

"After this they withdrew, and such illness oppressed me that I was about to lose the light of my eyes, and I was arranging to dispose of my very meagre belongings. Then I began to meditate that these things had justly befallen me because of my neglect of the apostolic command. Thus, comforted, I returned to the siege. Thinking again of the handicap of my poverty, I began to fear that if I went to you, you would say that I was a serf and was telling this for the sake of food; therefore, I was silent instead. And thus in the course of time, when at the Port of St. Simeon on Palm Sunday I was lying down in the tent with my lord, William Peter, St. Andrew appeared with a companion. Clad in the same habit in which he had come before, he spoke thus to me, 'Why hast thou not told the Count and Bishop and the others what I commanded thee?'

"And I answered 'Lord, have I not prayed thee to send another in my place who would be wiser and to whom they would listen? Besides the Turks are along the way and they kill those who come and go.'

"And St. Andrew said 'Fear not that they will harm thee. Say also to the Count not to dip in the river Jordan when he comes there, but to cross in a boat; moreover when he has crossed, dressed in a linen shirt and breeches, let him be sprinkled from the river. And after his garments are dry, let him lay them away and keep them with the Lance of the Lord.' And this my lord, William Peter, heard, though he did not see, the apostle.

"Thus comforted, I returned to the army. And when I wanted to tell you this, I could not bring you together. And so I set out to the port of Mamistra. There, indeed, when I was about to sail to the island of Cyprus for food, St.

Andrew threatened me much if I did not quickly return to you and tell you what had been commanded me. And when I thought to myself how I would return to camp, for that port was three days distant from the camp, I began to weep most bitterly, since I could find no way of returning. At length, admonished by my lord and my companions, we entered the ship and began to row to Cyprus. And although we were borne along all day by oar and favoring winds up to sunset, a storm then suddenly arose, and in the space of one or two hours we returned to the port which we had left. And thus checked from crossing a second and a third time, we returned to the island at the Port of St. Simeon. There I fell seriously ill. However, when the city was taken, I came to you. And now, if it please you, test what I say."

The Bishop, however, thought it nothing except words; but the Count believed it and handed over the man that had said this to his chaplain, Raymond, to guard.

Our Lord Jesus Christ appeared on the very night which followed to a certain priest named Stephen, who was weeping for the death of himself and his companions, which he expected there. For some who came down from the fortress frightened him, saying that the Turks were already descending from the mountain into the city, and that our men were fleeing and had been defeated. For this reason the priest, wishing to have God witness of his death, went into the church of the Blessed Mary in the garb of confession and, after obtaining pardon, began to sing psalms with some companions. While the rest were sleeping, and while he watched alone, after having said, "Lord, who shall dwell in Thy tabernacle, or who shall rest in Thy holy hill?" a certain man stood before him, beautiful beyond all, and said to him, "Man, who are these people that have entered the city?"

And the priest answered "Christians."

"Christians of what kind?"

"Christians who believe that Christ was born of a Virgin and suffered on the Cross, died, and was buried, and that He arose on the third day and ascended into heaven."

And that man said "And if they are Christians, why do they fear the multitude of pagans?" And he added, "Dost thou not know me?"

The priest replied "I do not know thee, but I see that thou art most beautiful of all."

And the man said, "Look at me closely."

And when the priest intently scrutinized him, he saw a kind of cross much brighter than the sun proceeding from his head. And the priest said to the man who was questioning him, "Lord, we say that they are images of Jesus Christ which present a form like thine."

The Lord said to him, "Thou hast said well, since I am He. Is it not written of me that I am the Lord, strong and mighty in battle? And who is the Lord in the army?"

"Lord," replied the priest, "there never was in the army but one Lord, for rather do they put trust in the Bishop."

And the Lord said, "Say this to the Bishop, that these people have put me afar from them by evil doing, and then let him speak to them as follows: 'The Lord says this: "Return to me, and I will return to you." ' And when they enter battle, let them say this 'Our enemy are assembled and glory in their own bravery; destroy their might, O Lord, and scatter them, so that they may know that there is no other who will fight for us except Thee, O Lord,' And say this also to them 'If ye do whatever I command you, even for five days, I will have mercy upon you!' "

Moreover, while He was saying this, a woman of countenance radiant beyond measure approached and, gazing upon the Lord, said to him, "Lord, what art thou saying to this man?"

And the Lord said to her, "I am asking him about these people who have entered the city, who they are."

Then the Lady replied, "O, my Lord, these are the people for whom I entreat thee so much."

And when the priest shook his companion who was sleeping near him, so that he might have a witness of so great a vision, they had disappeared from his eyes.

However, when morning came the priest climbed the hill opposite the castle of the Turks, where our princes were staying, all except the Duke, who was guarding the castle on the north hill. And thus, after assembling a gathering, he told these words to our princes, and, in order to show that it was true, he swore upon the Cross. Moreover, wishing to satisfy the incredulous, he was willing to pass through fire, or to jump from the top of the tower. Then the princes swore that they would neither flee from Antioch nor go out, except with the common consent of all; for the people at this time thought that the princes wanted to flee to the fort. And thus many were comforted, since in the past night there were few who stood steadfast in the faith and did not wish to flee. And had not the Bishop and Bohemund shut the gates of the city, very few would have remained. Nevertheless, William of Grandmesnil fled, and his brother, and many others, cleric and lay. It befell many, however, that when they had escaped from the city with the greatest danger, they faced the greater danger of death at the hands of the Turks.

At this time very many things were revealed to us through our brethren; and we beheld a marvelous sign in the sky. For during the night there stood over the city a very large star, which, after a short time, divided into three parts and fell in the camp of the Turks.

Our men, somewhat comforted, accordingly, awaited the fifth day which the priest had mentioned. On that day, moreover, after the necessary preparations, and after every one had been sent out of the Church of St. Peter, twelve men, together with that man who had spoken of the Lance, began to dig. There were, moreover, among those twelve men the Bishop of Orange, and Raymond, chaplain of the Count, who has written this, and the Count himself, and Pontius of *Balazun*, and Feraldus of Thouars. And after we had dug from morning to evening, some began to despair of finding the Lance. The Count left, because he had to guard the castle; but in place of him and the rest who were tired out from digging, we induced others, who were fresh to continue the work sturdily. The youth who had spoken of the Lance, however, upon seeing us worn out, disrobed and, taking off his shoes, descended into the pit in his shirt, earnestly entreating us to pray God to give us His Lance for the comfort and victory of His people. At length, the Lord was minded through the grace of His mercy to show us His Lance. And I, who have written this, kissed it when the point alone had as yet appeared above ground. What great joy and exultation then filled the city I cannot describe. Moreover, the Lance was found on the eighteenth day before the Kalends of July.

On the second night, St. Andrew appeared to the youth through whom he had given the Lance to us and said to him "Behold, God has given to the Count that which he never wished to give to anyone and has made him standard-bearer of this army, as long as he shall continue in His love."

When the youth asked mercy from him for the people, St. Andrew replied to him that verily would the Lord show mercy to His people. And, again, when he asked the same saint about his companion, who it was he had so often seen with him, St. Andrew answered, "Draw near and kiss His foot."

And so, when he was about to draw near, he saw a wound on His foot as fresh and bloody as if it had just been made. When, however, he hesitated to draw near because of the wound and blood, St. Andrew said to him:

"Behold, the Father who was wounded on the Cross for us, whence this wound. The Lord likewise commands that you celebrate that day on which He gave you His Lance. And since it was found at vespers, and that day cannot be celebrated, celebrate the solemn festival on the eighth day in the following week, and then each year on the day of the finding of the Lance. Say, also, to them that they conduct themselves as is taught in the Epistle of my brother, Peter, which is read to-day." (And the Epistle was this: "Humble yourselves under the mighty hand of God.") "Let the clerics sing this hymn before the Lance: *Lustra sex qui jam peracta tempus inplens corporis.* And when they shall have said, *Agnus in cruce levatus immolandus stipite,* let them finish the hymn on bended knees."

When, however, the Bishop of Orange and I, after this, asked Peter Bartholomew if he knew letters, he replied, "I do not," thinking that if he were to say "I do," we would not believe him. He did know a little; but at that hour he was so ignorant that he neither knew letters nor had any remembrance of the things he had learned from letters, except the *Paternoster, Credo in Deum, Magnificat, Glory in Excelsis Deo,* and *Benedictus Dominus Deus Israel.* He had lost the others as if he had never heard them, and though he was able afterwards to recover a few, it was with the greatest effort.

13. The Defeat of Kerbogha: The *Gesta* Version

The English translation here is from Krey, 182–185.

From that hour we took counsel of battle among ourselves. Forthwith, all our leaders decided upon the plan of sending a messenger to the Turks, enemies of Christ, to ask them with assured address: "Wherefore have you most haughtily entered the land of the Christians, and why have you encamped, and why do you kill and assail servants of Christ?" When their speech was already ended, they found certain men, Peter the Hermit and Herlwin, and they told them as follows: "Go to the accursed army of the Turks and carefully tell them all this, asking them why they have boldly and haughtily entered the land of the Christians and our own?"

At these words, the messengers left and went to the profane assemblage, saying everything to *Curbara* and the others as follows: "Our leaders and nobles wonder wherefore you have rashly and most haughtily entered their land, the land of the Christians? We think, forsooth, and believe that you have thus come hither because you wish to become Christians fully; or have you come hither for the purpose of harassing the Christians in every way? All our leaders together ask you, therefore, quickly to leave the land of God and the Christians, which the blessed apostle, Peter, by his preaching converted long ago to the worship of Christ. But they grant, in addition, that you may take away all your belongings, horses, mules, asses, camels, sheep, and cattle; all other belongings they permit you to carry with you, wherever you may wish."

Then *Curbara,* chief of the army of the Sultan of Persia, with all the others full of haughtiness, answered in fierce language: "Your God and your

Christianity we neither seek nor desire, and we spurn you and them absolutely. We have now come even hither because we marvelled greatly why the princes and nobles whom you mention call this land theirs, the land we took from an effeminate people. Now, do you want to know what we are saying to you? Go back quickly, therefore, and tell your seignors that if they desire to become Turks in everything, and wish to deny the God whom you worship with bowed heads, and to spurn your laws, we will give them this and enough more of lands, castles, and cities. In addition, moreover, [we will grant] that none of you will longer remain a foot-soldier, but will all be knights, just as we are; and we will ever hold you in the highest friendship. But if not, let them know that they will all undergo capital sentence, or will be led in chains to Chorosan, to serve us and our children in perpetual captivity forever."

Our messengers speedily came back, reporting all this most cruel race had replied. Herlwin is said to have known both tongues, and to have been the interpreter for Peter the Hermit. Meanwhile, our army, frightened on both sides, did not know what to do; for on one side excruciating famine harassed them, on the other fear of the Turks constrained them.

At length, when the three days fast had been fulfilled, and a procession had been held from one church to another, they confessed their sins, were absolved, and faithfully took the communion of the body and blood of Christ; and when alms had been given, they celebrated mass. Then six battle lines were formed from the forces within the city. In the first line, that is at the very head, was Hugh the Great with the Franks and the Count of Flanders; in the second, Duke Godfrey with his army; in the third was Robert the Norman with his knights; in the fourth, carrying with him the Lance of the Saviour, was the Bishop of Puy, together with his people and with the army of Raymond, Count of St. Gilles, who remained behind to watch the citadel for fear lest the Turks descend into the city; in the fifth line was Tancred, son of Marchisus, with his people, and in the sixth line was the wise man, Bohemund, with his army. Our bishops, priests, clerics, and monks, dressed in holy vestments, came out with us with crosses, praying and beseeching the Lord to make us safe, guard us, and deliver us from all evil. Some stood on the wall of the gate, holding the sacred crosses in their hands, making the sign [of the cross] and blessing us. Thus were we arrayed, and, protected with the sign of the cross, we went forth through the gate which is before the mosque.

After *Curbara* saw the lines of the Franks, so beautifully formed, coming out one after the other, he said: "Let them come out, that we may the better have them in our power!" But after they were outside the city and *Curbara* saw the huge host of the Franks, he was greatly frightened. He straightway sent word to his Emir, who had everything in charge, that if he saw a light burn at the head of the army he should have the trumpets sounded for it to retreat, knowing that the Turks had lost the battle. *Curbara* began immediately to retreat little by little toward the mountain, and our men followed them little by little. At length the Turks divided; one party went toward the sea and the rest halted there, expecting to enclose our men between them. As our men saw this, they did likewise. There a seventh line was formed from the lines of Duke Godfrey and the Count of Normandy, and its head was Reinald. They sent this [line] to meet the Turks, who were coming from the sea. The Turks, however, engaged them in battle and by shooting killed many of our men. Other squadrons, moreover, were drawn out from the river to the mountain, which was about two miles distant. The squadrons began to go forth from both sides and to surround our men on all sides, hurling, shooting, and wounding them. There came out from the mountains, also, countless armies with white horses, whose standards were all white. And so, when our leaders saw this army, they were entirely ignorant as to what it was, and who they were, until they recognized the aid of Christ, whose leaders were St. George, Mercurius, and Demetrius. This is to be believed, for many of our men saw it. However, when the Turks who were stationed on the side toward the sea saw that that they could hold out no longer, they set fire to the grass, so that, upon seeing it, those who were in the tents might flee. The latter, recognizing that signal, seized all the precious spoils and fled. But our men fought yet a while where their [the Turks] greatest strength was, that is, in the region of their tents. Duke Godfrey, the Count of Flanders, and Hugh the Great rode near the water, where the enemy's strength lay. These men, fortified by the sign of the cross, together attacked the enemy first. When the other lines saw this, they likewise attacked. The Turks and the Persians in their turn cried out. Thereupon, we invoked the Living and True God and charged against them, and in the name of Jesus Christ and of the Holy Sepulchre we began the battle, and, God helping, we overcame them. But the terrified Turks took to flight, and our men followed them to the tents. Thereupon, the knights of Christ chose rather to pursue them than to seek any spoils, and they pursued them even to the Iron Bridge, and then up to the fortress of Tancred. The enemy, indeed, left their pavilions there, gold, silver, and many ornaments, also sheep, cattle, horses, mules, camels, asses, grain, wine, butter, and many other things which we needed. When the Armenians and Syrians who dwelt in those regions heard that we had overcome the Turks, they ran to the mountain to meet them and killed as many of them as they could catch. We, however, returned to the city with great joy and praised and blessed God, who gave the victory to His people.

Thereupon, when the Emir who was guarding the citadel saw that *Cur-*

bara and all the rest had fled from the field before the army of the Franks, he was greatly frightened. Immediately and with great haste he sought the standards of the Franks. Accordingly, the Count of St. Gilles, who was stationed before the citadel, ordered his standard to be brought to him. The Emir took it and carefully placed it on the tower. The Longobards who were there said immediately: "This is not Bohemund's standard!" Then the Emir asked and said: "Whose is it?" They answered: "It belongs to the Count of St. Gilles." Thereupon, the Emir went and seized the standard and returned it to the Count. But at that hour the venerable man, Bohemund, came and gave him his standard. He received it with great joy and entered into an agreement with Bohemund that the pagans who wished to take up Christianity might remain with him [Bohemund], and that he should permit those who wished to go away to depart safe and without any hurt. He agreed to all that the Emir demanded and straightway sent his servants into the citadel. Not many days after this the Emir was baptized with those of his men who preferred to recognize Christ. But those who wished to adhere to their own laws Lord Bohemund had conducted to the land of the Saracens.

This battle was fought on the fourth day before the Kalends of July, on the vigil of the apostles Peter and Paul, in the reign of our Lord Jesus Christ, who has honor and glory forever and ever. Amen. And after our enemies had now been completely conquered, we gave fitting thanks to God, Three and One, and the Highest. Some of the enemy, exhausted, others, wounded in their flight hither and thither, succumbed to death in valley, forest, fields, and roads. But the people of Christ, that is, the victorious pilgrims, returned to the city, rejoicing in the happy triumph over their defeated foes.

14. The Defeat of Kerbogha: The Version of Raymond d'Aguilers

The English translation here is from Krey, 185–189.

As we have said, when our men were beaten, discouraged, and in narrow straits, divine aid appeared. And the blessed Andrew taught us through the youth who had spoken of the Lance how we ought to conduct ourselves before the battle and in the battle: —

"You have all offended deeply, and you have been deeply humbled; and you have cried out to the Lord, and the Lord has heard you. And now let each one turn himself to the Lord because of his sins, and let him give five alms because of the five wounds of the Lord. If he cannot do this, let him say the *Paternoster* five times. When this has been done, begin battle in the name of the Lord by day or by night, as the judgment of the princes deems best, because the hand of God will be with you. If anyone has doubt of victory, let the gates be opened for him, and let him go forth to the Turks, and he will see how their God will save him. Moreover, if anyone shall refuse to fight, let him be classed with Judas, the betrayer of the Lord, who deserted the apostles and sold his Lord to the Jews. Let them fight in the faith of St. Peter, holding in mind that God promised him that after the third day He would arise and appear to him, and for this reason, also, because this land is justly St. Peter's, and not the pagans'. And let your battle-cry be 'God help us!' and verily God will help you. All your brothers who died since the beginning of the expedition are present with you in this fight; you have only to storm the tenth part of the enemy, because they will assail nine parts in the might and command of God. And do not put off the battle, because [if you do], the Lord will lead as many enemies from the other sides as you have on this side, and He will keep you shut up here until you devour one another. But know certainly that those days are at hand which the Lord promised to the Blessed Mary and to His apostles, saying that He would raise up the kingdom of the Christians, after the kingdom of the pagans had been cast down and ground into dust. But do not turn to their tents in search of gold and silver."

Then the power of God was disclosed, in that He who had commanded the above words to be preached to us through His apostle so comforted the hearts of all that each one in faith and hope seemed to himself already to have triumphed over his enemy. They urged on one another, and in urging regained courage for fighting. The crowd, too, which in the past days seemed to be consumed with want and fright, now reproached the princes and complained of the delay of the battle. However, when the day for battle had been fixed, our princes sent word by Peter the Hermit to *Corbara*, leader of the Turks, to give up the siege of the city, because it was by right the property of St. Peter and the Christians. That proud leader replied that, rightly or wrongly, he was going to rule over the Franks and the city. And he compelled Peter the Hermit, who was unwilling to bow, to kneel to him.

The question was raised at this time as to who should guard the city against those who were in the citadel, while the rest went forth to fight. They built a stone wall and ramparts on our hill against the enemy; these they fortified with many rocks, finally leaving Count Raymond, who was deathly ill, and about two hundred men there.

The day of the fight had come. In the morning all partook of commu-

nion and gave themselves to God, to death, if He willed, or to the glory of
the Roman church and the race of the Franks. Moreover, they decided about
the battle as follows: that two double lines should be made of the Count's
and Bishop's people, so that the foot-soldiers went before the knights and
halted at the command of the princes; and the knights were to follow them
and guard them from the rear. Similar arrangement was made of the people
of Bohemund and Tancred; the like of the people of the Count of Normandy
and the Franks; likewise, of the people of the Duke and the Burgundians.
Moreover, trumpeters went through the city shouting that each man should
stay with the princes of his people. It was likewise ordered that Hugh the
Great, the Count of Flanders, and the Count of Normandy should advance
to the battle first, then the Duke, the Bishop after the Duke, and Bohemund
after the Bishop. They assembled, each man to his own standard and kinfolk,
within the city before the gate of the bridge.

Oh, how blessed is the people whose Lord is God! Oh, how blessed the
people whom God has chosen! Oh, how unaltered His face! How changed
the army from sadness to eagerness! Indeed, during the past days princes
and nobles went along the city streets calling upon the aid of God at the
churches, the common people [walked] with bare feet, weeping and striking
their breasts. They had been so sad that father did not greet son, nor brother
brother, upon meeting, nor did they look back. But now you could see them
going forth like swift horses, rattling their arms, and brandishing their spears,
nor could the bear to refrain from showing their happiness in word and deed.
But why do I grieve about many matters? They were given the power to go
forth, and what had been agreed upon by the princes was fulfilled in order.

Meanwhile *Corbara*, leader of the Turks, was playing at chess within his
tent. When he received the message that the Franks were advancing to battle,
he was disturbed in mind because this seemed beyond expectation, and he
called to him a certain Turk who had fled from Antioch, Mirdalin by name, a
noble known to us for his military prowess. "What is this?" he said. "Didn't
you tell me the Franks were few and would not fight with us?" And Mirdalin
replied to him, "I did not say that they would not fight, but come, and I will
look at them and tell you if you can easily overcome them."

And now the third line of our men was advancing. When he saw how
the lines were arrayed, Mirdalin said to *Corbara*, "These men can be killed;
but they cannot be put to flight."

And then *Corbara* said, "Can none of them be driven back at all?"

And Mirdalin replied, "They will not yield a footstep, even if all the
people of the pagans attack them."

Then, although disturbed in mind, he drew up his many and multiple lines against us. And when at first they could have prevented our exit, they allowed us to go out in peace. Our men, however, now directed their lines toward the mountains, fearing that the Turks might surround them from the rear. However, the mountains were about two long miles from the bridge. We were advancing in open file as the clergy are wont to march in processions. And verily we had a procession! For the priests and many monks, dressed in white robes, went in front of the lines of our knights, chanting and invoking the aid of the Lord and the benediction of the saints. The enemy, on the contrary, rushed against us and shot arrows. *Corbara*, now ready to do what he had just recently refused, likewise sent word to our princes [proposing] that five or ten Turks should do battle with a like number of Franks, and that those whose knights were conquered should peacefully yield to the others. To this our leaders replied, "You were unwilling when we wanted to do this; now that we have advanced to fight, let each fight for his right."

And when we had occupied the whole plain, as we said, a certain portion of the Turks remained behind us and attacked some of our foot-soldiers. But those foot-soldiers, turning about, sustained the attack of the enemy vigorously. When, indeed, the Turks could in no way drive them out, they set fire around them, so that those who did not fear the swords might at all events be terrified by fire. And thus they forced them to give way, for that place had much dry hay.

And when the lines had gone forth, the priests, with bare feet and garbed in their priestly vestments, stood on the walls of the city, calling upon God to defend His people, and through the victory of the Franks in this battle to afford a testimony hallowed by His blood. Moreover, as we were advancing from the bridge up to the mountain, we met with great difficulty because the enemy wanted to surround us. In the midst of this, the lines of the enemy fell upon us who were in the squadron of the Bishop, and though their forces were greater than ours, yet, through the protection of the Holy Lance which was there, they there wounded no one; neither did they hit any of us with arrows. I beheld these things of which I speak and I bore the Lance of the Lord there. If anyone says that Viscount Heraclius, the standard-bearer of the Bishop, was wounded in this battle, let him know that he handed over this standard to another and fell behind our line some distance.

When all our fighting men had left the city, five other lines appeared among us. For, as has already been said, our princes had drawn up only eight, and we were thirteen lines outside the city. In the beginning of the march out to battle the Lord sent down upon all His army a divine shower, little but full of blessing. All those touched by this were filled with all grace and fortitude and, despising the enemy, rode forth as if always nourished on the delicacies of kings. This miracle also affected our horses no less. For whose horse failed until the fight was over, even though it had tasted nothing except the bark or leaves of trees for eight days? God so multiplied our army that we, who before seemed fewer than the enemy, were in the battle more numerous than they. And when our men had thus advanced and formed in line, the enemy turned in flight without giving us a chance to engage in battle. Our men pursued them until sunset. There the Lord worked marvelously as well in the horses as in the men; forsooth, the men were not called away from battle by avarice, and those pack horses which their masters had led into battle, after a scant feeding, now very easily followed the sleekest and swiftest horses of the Turks.

But the Lord did not wish us to have this joy only. For the Turks who were guarding the citadel of the city gave up hope upon seeing the headlong flight of their people; some, on the pledge of their lives alone, surrendered themselves to us, and the rest fled headlong. And though this battle was so terrible and frightful, yet few knights of the enemy fell there; but of their foot-soldiers scarcely any escaped. Moreover, all the tents of the enemy were captured, much gold and silver, and the greatest amount of spoils—grain and cattle and camels without measure or number. And that incident of Samaria about the measures of wheat and barley which were bought for a shekel was renewed for us. Moreover, these events occurred on the vigils of St. Peter and Paul, through which intercessors was granted this victory to the pilgrim church of the Franks by the Lord Jesus Christ, who liveth and reigneth God through all ages. Amen.

15. The Firanj Seize Antioch: The Version of Ibn al-Athir

This is the first selection from the two most important Arabic chronicles of the First Crusade. Ibn al-Athir (555/1160–630/1233) wrote a vast history of the world, drawing on earlier chroniclers for the period considered here. The name Firanj is the Arabic word for Franks, the generic term used by Arab chroniclers for all crusaders.

The English translation here is from Francesco Gabrieli, Arab Historians of the Crusades, *trans. E. J. Costello (Berkeley-Los Angeles, 1969), 3–7.*

The power of the Franks first became apparent when in the year 478/1085–86 they invaded the territories of Islām and took Toledo and other parts of Andalusia, as was mentioned earlier. Then in 484/1091 they attacked and conquered the island of Sicily and turned their attention to the African coast. Certain of their conquests there were won back again but they had other successes, as you will see.

In 490/1097 the Franks attacked Syria. This is how it all began: Baldwin, their King, a kinsman of Roger the Frank who had conquered Sicily, assembled a great army and sent word to Roger saying: "I have assembled a great army and now I am on my way to you, to use your bases for my conquest of the African coast. Thus you and I shall become neighbors."

Roger called together his companions and consulted them about these proposals. "This will be a fine thing both for them and for us!" they declared, "for by this means these lands will be converted to the Faith!" At this Roger raised one leg and farted loudly, and swore that it was of more use than their advice. "Why?" "Because if this army comes here it will need quantities of provisions and fleets of ships to transport it to Africa, as well as reinforcements from my own troops. Then, if the Franks succeed in conquering this territory they will take it over and will need provisioning from Sicily. This will cost me my annual profit from the harvest. If they fail they will return here and be an embarrassment to me here in my own domain. As well as all this Tamīm will say that I have broken faith with him and violated our treaty, and friendly relations and communications between us will be disrupted. As far as we are concerned, Africa is always there. When we are strong enough we will take it."

He summoned Baldwin's messenger and said to him: "If you have decided to make war on the Muslims your best course will be to free Jerusalem from their rule and thereby win great honour. I am bound by certain promises and treaties of allegiance with the rulers of Africa." So the Franks made ready and set out to attack Syria.

Another story is that the Fatimids of Egypt were afraid when they saw the Seljuqids extending their empire through Syria as far as Gaza, until they reached the Egyptian border and Atsiz invaded Egypt itself. They therefore sent to invite the Franks to invade Syria and so protect Egypt from the Muslims. But God knows best.

When the Franks decided to attack Syria they marched east to Constantinople, so that they could cross the straits and advance into Muslim territory by the easier, land route. When they reached Constantinople, the Emperor of the East refused them permission to pass through his domains. He said: "Unless you first promise me Antioch, I shall not allow you to cross into the Muslim empire." His real intention was to incite them to attack the Muslims, for he was convinced that the Turks, whose invincible control over Asia Minor he had observed, would exterminate every one of them. They accepted his conditions and in 490/1097 they crossed the Bosphorus at Constantinople. Iconium and the rest of the area into which they now advanced belonged to Qilij Arslān ibn Sulaimān ibn Qutlumísh, who barred their way with his troops. They broke through in Rajab 490/July 1097, crossed Cilicia, and finally reached Antioch, which they besieged.

When Yaghi Siyān, the ruler of Antioch, heard of their approach, he was not sure how the Christian people of the city would react, so he made the Muslims go outside the city on their own to dig trenches, and the next day sent the Christians out alone to continue the task. When they were ready to return home at the end of the day he refused to allow them. "Antioch is yours," he said, "but you will have to leave it to me until I see what happens between us and the Franks." "Who will protect our children and our wives?" they said. "I shall look after them for you." So they resigned themselves to their fate, and lived in the Frankish camp for nine months, while the city was under siege.

Yaghi Siyān showed unparalleled courage and wisdom, strength and judgment. If all the Franks who died had survived they would have overrun all the lands of Islām. He protected the families of the Christians in Antioch and would not allow a hair of their heads to be touched.

After the siege had been going on for a long time the Franks made a deal with one of the men who were responsible for the towers. He was a cuirass-maker called Ruzbih, whom they bribed with a fortune in money and lands. He worked in the tower that stood over the river-bed, where the river flowed out of the city into the valley. The Franks sealed their pact with the cuirass-maker, God damn him! and made their way to the water-gate. They opened it and entered the city. Another gang of them climbed the tower with ropes. At dawn, when more than 500 of them were in the city and the defenders were worn out after the night watch, they sounded their trumpets. Yaghi Siyān woke up and asked what the noise meant. He was told that trumpets had sounded from the citadel and that it must have been taken. In fact the sound came not from the citadel but from the tower. Panic seized Yaghi Siyān and he opened the city gates and fled in terror, with an escort of thirty pages. His army commander arrived, but when he discovered on enquiry that Yaghi Siyān had fled, he made his escape by another gate. This was of great help to the Franks, for if he had stood firm for an hour, they would have been wiped out. They entered the city by the gates and sacked it, slaughtering all the Muslims they found there. This happened in Jumada I [491/April/May 1098]. As for Yaghi Siyān, when the sun rose he recovered his self control and realized that his flight had taken him several *farsakh* from the city. He asked his companions where he was, and on hearing that he was four *farsakh* from

Antioch he repented of having rushed to safety instead of staying to fight to the death. He began to groan and weep for his desertion of his household and children. Overcome by the violence of his grief he fell fainting from his horse. His companions tried to lift him back into the saddle, but they could not get him to sit up, and so left him for dead while they escaped. He was at his last gasp when an Armenian shepherd came past, killed him, cut off his head, and took it to the Franks at Antioch.

The Franks had written to the rulers of Aleppo and Damascus to say that they had no interest in any cities but those that had once belonged to Byzantium. This was a piece of deceit calculated to dissuade these rulers from going to the help of Antioch.

16. The Firanj Seize Antioch: The Version of Ibn al-Qalanisi

Ibn al-Qalanisi (465/1073–555/1160) wrote earlier than Ibn al-Athir, who used his work, but his focus is more narrow and his narrative more strictly chronological. I have retained the years A.H. (the year from the Hegira, 622, the Muslim system of dating) at the head of Ibn al-Qalanisi's text.

The English translation here is from H. A. R. Gibb, The Damascus Chronicle of the Crusades Extracted and Translated from the Chronicle of Ibn al-Qalanisi *(London, 1932), 41–45.*

A.H. 490 (December 19, 1096, to December 18, 1097)

In this year there began to arrive a succession of reports that the armies of the Franks had appeared from the direction of the sea of Constantinople with forces not to be reckoned for multitude. As these reports followed one upon the other, and spread from mouth to mouth far and wide, the people grew anxious and disturbed in mind. The king, Dā'ud b. Sulaimān b. Qutulmish, whose dominions lay nearest to them, having received confirmation of these statements, set about collecting forces, raising levies, and carrying out the obligation of Holy War. He also summoned as many of the Turkmens as he could to give him assistance and support against them, and a large number of them joined him along with the 'askar of his brother. His confidence having been strengthened thereby, and his offensive power rendered formidable, he marched out to the fords, tracks, and roads by which the Franks must pass, and showed no mercy to all of them who fell into his hands. When he had thus killed a great number, they turned their forces against him, defeated him, and scattered his army, killing many and taking many captive, and plundered and enslaved. The Turkmens, having lost most of their horses, took to flight. The King of the Greeks bought a great many of those whom they had enslaved, and had them transported to Constantinople. When the news was received of this shameful calamity to the cause of Islam, the anxiety of the people became acute and their fear and alarm increased. The date of this battle was the 20th of Rajab (July 4, 1097).

In the middle of Sha'bān [end of July] the amīr Yāghī Siyān, lord of Antioch, accompanied by the amīr Sukmān b. Ortuq and the amīr Karbuqā [lord of Mosul], set out with his 'askar towards Antioch, on receipt of news that the Franks were approaching it and had occupied al-Balāna. Yāghī Siyān therefore hastened to Antioch, and dispatched his son to al-Malik Duqāq at Damascus, to Janāh al-Dawla at Hims, and to all the other cities and districts, appealing for aid and support, and inciting them to hasten to the Holy War, while he set about fortifying Antioch and expelling its Christian population. On the 2nd of Shawwāl [September 12] the Frankish armies descended on Baghrās and developed their attack upon the territories of Antioch, whereupon those who were in the castles and forts adjacent to Antioch revolted and killed their garrisons except for a few who were able to escape from them. The people of Artāh did likewise, and called for reinforcements from the Franks. During Sha'bān a comet appeared in the West; it continued to rise for a space of about twenty days, and then disappeared.

Meanwhile, a large detachment of the Frankish army, numbering about thirty thousand men, had left the main body and set about ravaging the other districts, in the course of which they came to al-Bāra and slaughtered about fifty men there. Now the 'askar of Damascus had reached the neighbourhood of Shaizar, on their way to support Yāghī Siyān, and when this detachment made its descent on al-Bāra, they moved out against it. After a succession of charges by each side, in which a number of their men were killed, the Franks returned to al-Rūj, and thence proceeded towards Antioch. Oil, salt, and other necessaries became dear and unprocurable in Antioch, but so much was smuggled into the city that they became cheap again. The Franks dug a trench between their position and the city, owing to the frequent sallies made against them by the army of Antioch.

Now the Franks, on their first appearance, had made a covenant with the king of the Greeks, and had promised him that they would deliver over to him the first city which they should capture. They then captured Nicaea, and it was the first place they captured, but they did not carry out their word to him on that occasion, and refused to deliver it up to him according to the stipulation. Subsequently they captured on their way several frontier fortresses and passes.

A.H. 491 (December 9, 1097, to November 27, 1098)

At the end of First Jumādā [beginning of June, 1098] the report arrived that certain of the men of Antioch among the armourers in the train of the amīr Yāghī Siyān had entered into a conspiracy against Antioch and had come to an agreement with the Franks to deliver the city up to them, because of some ill-usage and confiscations which they had formerly suffered at his hands. They found an opportunity of seizing one of the city bastions adjoining the Jabal, which they sold to the Franks, and thence admitted them into the city during the night. At daybreak they raised the battle cry, whereupon Yāghī Siyān took to flight and went out with a large body, but not one person amongst them escaped to safety. When he reached the neighbourhood of Armanāz, an estate near Maʿarrat Masrīn, he fell from his horse to the ground. One of his companions raised him up and remounted him, but he could not maintain his balance on the back of the horse, and after falling repeatedly he died. As for Antioch, the number of men, women, and children, killed, taken prisoner, and enslaved from its population is beyond computation. About three thousand men fled to the citadel and fortified themselves in it, and some few escaped for whom God had decreed escape.

In Shaʿbān [July] news was received that al-Afdal, the commander-in-chief [amīr al-juyūsh], had come up from Egypt to Syria at the head of a strong ʿaskar. He encamped before Jerusalem, where at that time were the two amīrs Sukmān and Il-Ghāzī, sons of Ortuq, together with a number of their kinsmen and followers and a large body of Turks, and sent letters to them, demanding that they should surrender Jerusalem to him without warfare or shedding of blood. When they refused his demand, he opened an attack on the town, and having set up mangonels against it, which effected a breach in the wall, he captured it and received the surrender of the Sanctuary of David from Sukmān. On his entry into it, he shewed kindness and generosity to the two amīrs, and set both them and their supporters free. They arrived in Damascus during the first ten days of Shawwāl [September], and al-Afdal returned with his ʿaskar to Egypt.

17. Kerbogha's Attack: The Version of Ibn al-Athir

The English translation here is from Gabrieli, 7–9.

When Qawām ad-Daula Kerbuqā heard that the Franks had taken Antioch he mustered his army and advanced into Syria, where he camped at Marj

Dabiq. All the Turkish and Arab forces in Syria rallied to him except for the army from Aleppo. Among his supporters were Duqāq ibn Tutūsh, the Atabeg Tughtikīn, Janāh ad-Daula of Hims, Arslān Tash of Sanjār, Sulaimān ibn Artūq and other less important amīrs. When the Franks heard of this they were alarmed and afraid, for their troops were weak and short of food. The Muslims advanced and came face to face with the Franks in front of Antioch. Kerbuqā, thinking that the present crisis would force the Muslims to remain loyal to him, alienated them by his pride and ill-treatment of them. They plotted in secret anger to betray him and desert him in the heat of battle.

After taking Antioch the Franks camped there for twelve days without food. The wealthy ate their horses and the poor ate carrion and leaves from the trees. Their leaders, faced with this situation, wrote to Kerbuqā to ask for safe-conduct through his territory but he refused, saying "You will have to fight your way out." Among the Frankish leaders were Baldwin, Saint-Gilles, Godfrey of Bouillon, the future Count of Edessa, and their leader Bohemond of Antioch. There was also a holy man who had great influence over them, a man of low cunning, who proclaimed that the Messiah had a lance buried in the Qusyān, a great building in Antioch: "And if you find it you will be victorious and if you fail you will surely die." Before saying this he had buried a lance in a certain spot and concealed all trace of it. He exhorted them to fast and repent for three days, and on the fourth day he led them all to the spot with their soldiers and workmen, who dug everywhere and found the lance as he had told them. Whereupon he cried "Rejoice! For victory is secure." So on the fifth day they left the city in groups of five or six. The Muslims said to Kerbuqā: "You should go up to the city and kill them one by one as they come out; it is easy to pick them off now that they have split up." He replied: 'No, wait until they have all come out and then we will kill them.' He would not allow them to attack the enemy and when some Muslims killed a group of Franks, he went himself to forbid such behavior and prevent its recurrence. When all the Franks had come out and not one was left in Antioch, they began to attack strongly, and the Muslims turned and fled. This was Kerbuqā's fault, first because he had treated the Muslims with such contempt and scorn, and second because he had prevented their killing the Franks. The Muslims were completely routed without striking a single blow or firing a single arrow. The last to flee were Suqmān ibn Artūq and Janāh ad-Daula, who had been sent to set an ambush. Kerbuqā escaped with them. When the Franks saw this they were afraid that a trap was being set for them, for there had not even been any fighting to flee from, so they dared not follow them. The only Muslims to stand firm were a detachment of warriors from the Holy Land, who fought to acquire merit in God's eyes and to seek martyrdom. The Franks killed them by the thousand and stripped their camp of food and possessions, equipment, horses and arms, with which they re-equipped themselves.

18. Kerbogha's Attack: The Version of Ibn al-Qalanisi

The English translation here is from Gibb, 45–46.

In this year also the Franks set out with all their forces to Ma'arrat al-Nu'mān, and having encamped over against it on 29th Dhu'l-Hijja [November 27], they opened an attack on the town and brought up a tower and scaling-ladders against it.

Now after the Franks had captured the city of Antioch through the devices of the armourer, who was an Armenian named Fīrūz, on the eve of Friday, 1st Rajab [night of Thursday, June 3], and a series of reports were received confirming this news, the armies of Syria assembled in uncountable force and proceeded to the province of Antioch, in order to inflict a crushing blow upon the armies of the Franks. They besieged the Franks until their supplies of food were exhausted and they were reduced to eating carrion; but thereafter the Franks, though they were in the extremity of weakness, advanced in battle order against the armies of Islām, which were at the height of strength and numbers, and they broke the ranks of the Muslims and scattered their multitudes. The lords of the pedigree steeds were put to flight, and the sword was unsheathed upon the foot-soldiers who had volunteered for the cause of God, who had girt themselves for the Holy War, and were vehement in their desire to strike a blow for the Faith and for the protection of the Muslims. This befel on Tuesday, the [twenty] sixth of Rajab, in this year [June 29, 1098].

19. The Firanj Take Ma'arrat an-Nu'mān: The Version of Ibn al-Athir

The English translation here is from Gabrieli 9–10.

After dealing this blow to the Muslims the Franks marched on Ma'arrat an-Nu'mān and besieged it. The inhabitants valiantly defended their city. When the Franks realized the fierce determination and devotion of the defenders they built a wooden tower as high as the city wall and fought from the top of it, but failed to do the Muslims any serious harm. One night a few Muslims were seized with panic and in their demoralized state thought that if they barricaded themselves into one of the town's largest buildings they would be in a better position to defend themselves, so they climbed down from the wall and abandoned the position they were defending. Others saw them and followed their example, leaving another stretch of wall undefended, and gradually, as one group followed another, the whole wall was left unprotected and the Franks scaled it with ladders. Their appearance in the city terrified the Muslims, who shut themselves up in their houses. For three days the slaughter never stopped; the Franks killed more than 100,000 men and took innumerable prisoners. After taking the town the Franks spent six weeks shut up there, then sent an expedition to 'Arqa, which they besieged for four months. Although they breached the wall in many places they failed to storm it. Munqidh, the ruler of Shaizar, made a treaty with them about 'Arqa and they left it to pass on to Hims. Here too the ruler Janāh ad-Daula made a treaty with them, and they advanced to Acre by way of an-Nawaqir. However they did not succeed in taking Acre.

20. The Firanj Take Ma'arrat an-Nu'mān: The Version of Ibn al-Qalanisi

The English translation here is from Gibb, 46–47.

A.H. 492
(November 28, 1098, to November 16, 1099)

In Muharram of this year [December, 1098], the Franks made an assault on the wall of Ma'arrat al-Nu'mān from the east and north. They pushed up the tower until it rested against the wall, and as it was higher, they deprived the Muslims of the shelter of the wall. The fighting raged round this point until sunset on 14th Muharram [December 11], when the Franks scaled the wall, and the townsfolk were driven off it and took to flight. Prior to this, messengers had repeatedly come to them from the Franks with proposals for a settlement by negotiation and the surrender of the city, promising in return security for their lives and property, and the establishment of a [Frankish] governor amongst them, but dissension among the citizens and the fore-ordained decree of God prevented acceptance of these terms. So they captured the city after the hour of the sunset prayer, and a great number from both sides were killed in it. The townsfolk fled to the houses of al-Ma'arra, to defend themselves in them, and the Franks, after promising them safety, dealt treacherously with them. They erected crosses over the town, exacted indemnities from the townsfolk, and did not carry out any of the terms upon which they had agreed, but plundered everything that they found, and demanded of the people sums which they could not pay. On Thursday 17th Safar [January 13, 1099] they set out for Kafr Tāb.

VIII.

The Siege and Capture of
Jerusalem (June–July 1099)

Divided as to how to proceed from Antioch, greatly reduced in size, exhausted, but also by now convinced that they had been saved by the hand of God, the crusading army turned southward toward Jerusalem, taking Jabala, Maraclea, and Tortosa in February and March, 1099. Rejecting the inland route via Damascus, they proceeded along the coastal road from Akkar, taking Tripoli, Beirut, Sidon, Tyre, and Acre in May, and turning inland toward Jerusalem, seizing Ramla on June 3. The siege of Jerusalem itself lasted from June 7 to July 15. The best account is that of France, Victory in the East: A Military History of the First Crusade *(Cambridge, 1994), 297–366.*

1. The March to Jerusalem: The *Gesta* Version

The English translation here is from Krey, 242–243.

Accordingly, we left the fortified town and came to Tripoli on the sixth day of the week on the thirteenth day of incoming May, and we stayed there for three days. At length, the King of Tripoli made an agreement with the leaders, and he straightway loosed to them more than three hundred pilgrims who had been captured there and gave fifteen thousand *besants* and fifteen horses of great value; he likewise gave us a great market of horses, asses, and all goods, whence the whole army of Christ was greatly enriched. But he made an agreement with them that if they could win the war which the Emir of Babylon was getting ready against them and could take Jerusalem, he would become a Christian and would recognize his land as [a gift] from them. In such manner it was settled.

We left the city on the second day of the week in the month of May and, passing along a narrow and difficult road all day and night, we came to a fortress, the name of which was Botroun. Then we came to a city called Gibilet near the sea, in which we suffered very great thirst, and, thus worn out, we reached a river named Ibrahim. Then on the eve of the day of the Ascension of the Lord we crossed a mountain in which the way was exceedingly narrow, and there we expected to find the enemy lying in ambush for us. But God favoring us, none of them dared to appear in our way. Then our knights went ahead of us and cleared the way before us, and we arrived at a city by the sea which is called Beirut, and thence we went to another city called Sidon, thence to another called Tyre, and from Tyre to the city of Acre. But from Acre we came to a fortified place the name of which was Cayphas, and then we came near Caesarea. There was celebrated Pentecost on the third day of outgoing May. Then we came to Ramlah, which through fear of the Franks the Saracens had left empty. Near it was the famous church in which rested the most precious body of St. George, since for the name of Christ he there happily received martyrdom from the treacherous pagans. There our leaders held a council to choose a bishop who should have charge of this place and erect a church. They gave tithes to him and enriched him with gold and silver, and with horses and other animals, that he might live the more devoutly and honorably with those who were with him. He remained there with joy.

2. The March to Jerusalem: The Version of Raymond d'Aguilers

The English translation here is from Krey, 243–248.

Meanwhile the Count and the other princes inquired of the inhabitants of that region how the march to Jerusalem might be better and more easily made. For there are the mountains of Lebanon, in which almost sixty thousand Christian men dwell. The Christians who are near the city of Tyre (now commonly called Sur, whence they are called Surians) have possessed that land and mountains for a long time. But when the Saracens and Turks arose through the judgment of God, those Surians were in such great oppression for four hundred and more years that many of them were forced to abandon their fatherland and the Christian law. If, however, any of them through the grace of God refused, they were compelled to give up their beautiful children to be circumcised, or converted to Mohammedanism; or they were snatched from the lap of their mothers, after the father had been killed and the mother mocked. Forsooth, that race of men were inflamed to such malice that they overturned the churches of God and His saints, or destroyed the images; and they tore out the eyes of those images which, for lack of time, they could not destroy, and shot them with arrows; all the altars, too, they undermined. Moreover, they made mosques of the great churches. But if any of those distressed Christians wished to have an image of God or any saint at his home, he either redeemed it month by month, or year by year, or it was thrown down into the dirt and broken before his eyes. In addition, too harsh to relate, they placed youths in brothels, and, to do yet more vilely, exchanged their sisters for wine. And their mothers dared not weep openly at these or other sorrows. Why do we say much about them? Surely that people had conspired against the Holy of Holies and His inheritance! Except by the command and direction of God, the people of the Franks would have encountered these ills, had not God straightway armed brute animals against their enemies, as He did once in our presence. And so much for this.

When those Surians who, as we said above, came to the Count, were asked about the better route, they replied: "The way through Damascus is level and full of vituals; but you will not find water for two days. The other way through the mountains of Lebanon is safe enough and well watered, but it is very hard for the pack animals and camels. There is another way along the sea, where there are so many and such narrow passes that if fifty or a hundred Saracens want to hold them, they can do so against all mankind. And yet it is contained in the Gospel of St. Peter, which we have, that if you are the people who are to take Jerusalem, you will pass along the sea-coast, though because of the difficulty it seems impossible to us. Moreover, there is written in that Gospel among us not only what you have done, but also what you ought to do about this march and many other things."

While some were urging in this and other ways, and others were contradicting, William Hugo of Monteil returned with the Cross of which we spoke above. Moreover, when the friends of the Count likewise beheld this Cross, they became so eager for the march that, except for the counsel of the Count and the other princes, the servants of the Count would have burned their huts and been the first to leave the siege of Archas. Thereupon, the Count was disturbed to tears and even to hatred of himself and his people. But the Duke of Lorraine especially wished this journey and admonished the people to it. Accordingly, having set forth from that detestable and hateful siege of Archas, we came before Tripoli. Even then Count Raymond with prayers and gifts urged all the nobles to besiege the city of Tripoli, but all opposed him.

At this time, St. Andrew appeared to Peter Desiderius, of whom we have made mention above, and said to him, "Go and speak to the Count, saying:

'Do not molest thyself or others, for unless Jerusalem shall first have been taken, thou shalt have no help. Do not trouble thyself about the unfinished siege of Archas; let it not weigh upon thee that this city, or others which are on the journey, are not taken at present, because a fight will soon come upon thee in which these and many other cities shall be captured. Furthermore, do not trouble thyself or thy men, but distribute freely in His name whatever God shall grant to thee, and be a companion and loyal friend to thy vassals. If thou shalt do this, God will grant thee Jerusalem and Alexandria and Babylon. But if thou dost not do this, thou shalt neither acquire the things promised by God nor have a message, until thou art placed in such straits that thou knowest not how to escape!'" So the Count accepted the words of the priest; he accepted them, truly, in words, but he refused them in deeds. For when he had received great wealth from the King of Tripoli, he was never willing to give anyone any of it, but he even daily afflicted his people with blows and insults. Not only this, however, did that priest tell us, but also many other things, some of which we have added to this work.

For once, when we wanted to set out from Antioch, that priest came to me, Raymond, and said to me that a certain person had appeared to him in a vision who said to him, "Go into the church of St. Leontius, and thou wilt find there the relics of four saints; take them with thee and carry them to Jerusalem." And he showed him in that vision the relics and locations of the relics, and he taught him the names of the saints. When that priest had awakened, not fully believing in his vision, he began to urge God with prayers and entreaties to make known to him a second time if this vision was from Him. Several days later the same saint stood before him in a vision and threatened him much because he had neglected the command of God, and [said that] unless he had taken those relics away by the fifth day of the week, it would be a great hurt to him and his lord, Count Ysoard. Ysoard, Count of Die, was a man loyal to God as far as he knew, and helpful to all of us for his wisdom and uprightness.

When the priest had narrated this to me, Raymond, I told it to the Bishop of Orange and to the Count of St. Gilles and to some others. We took candles and went to the church of St. Leontius. We offered the candles and vows to God and to the saints of the same church, [praying] that Almighty God, who had sanctified them, might give them to us as companions and helpers; and that those saints might not spurn the company of pilgrims and exiles for God, but, rather, out of charity might join us and link us with God. When it became morning, we went with the priest to the places where the relics were kept, and we found everything just as it had been foretold. Moreover, these are the names of the saints: Cyprian, *Omechios*, Leontius, John Chrysostom. And, furthermore, at the place where the relics were kept we found a little chest filled with relics. When he asked a priest about these, of which saint they were the relics, he replied that he did not know. But when we inquired of the inhabitants if they knew of which saint these were the relics, some said of St. Mercurius, others, however, of other saints. But the priest wished to take them up and put them with the collection of other relics. To him, I, Raymond, said angrily in the presence of all who were there, "If this saint wishes to come with us to Jerusalem, let him make known his name and wish; otherwise let him remain here. Why should we weight ourselves with unknown bones and carry them along?" Therefore on that day those relics were left behind. But when the priest had collected the other relics and had rolled them up in cloths and a covering, on the night which followed, as he lay awake, there appeared to him a youth of about fifteen years, exceedingly beautiful, who said to him, "Why didst thou this day not take any relics with the rest?"

The priest replied to this, "Who art thou?"

"Dost thou not know who is the standard bearer of this army?" he replied.

The priest answered, "I do not, Sire."

When the priest had made the same reply to the same question a second time, the youth threatened the priest terribly, saying, "Tell me the truth."

And then the priest said, "Sire, it is said of St. George that he is the standard-bearer of this army."

He replied, "Thou hast said well. I am he. Take, therefore, my relics and put them with the others."

When, however, the priest had deferred doing this for several days, the same George came to him and commanded the priest sternly, saying, "Do not delay longer than the morning to take up my relics; and near by in a little ampule thou wilt find some of the blood of the virgin and martyr St. Tecla, which likewise take; and after this chant mass." And the priest found all this, and did it.

But before we go on to the remainder, we ought not to pass over these men who did not hesitate, for love of the most holy expedition, to sail through the unknown and very long water of the Mediterranean and the Ocean. For when the Angles heard the name of the Lord's vengeance against those who unworthily occupied the birthplace of Jesus Christ and His apostles, they embarked upon the Anglican Sea. Rounding Spain, crossing the ocean and thus ploughing through the Mediterranean Sea, with great labor they gained the port of Antioch and the city of Laodicaea, before our army came thither by land. Their ships, as well as those of the Genoese were of advantage to us at this time, for during the siege we had trade with the island of Cyprus and the remaining islands because of these ships and the security which they offered. Forsooth, these ships passed daily over the sea, and for this reason the ships of the Greeks were safe, since the Saracens feared to encounter them. But when the Angles saw the army setting forth for Jerusalem, and that the strength of their own ships was impaired by the long wait (for though they had thirty ships in the beginning, they now had scarcely nine or ten), some abandoned their ships and exposed them; others, however, burned theirs and hastened with us on the journey.

When our princes were entangled in delay before Tripoli, the Lord sent such great desire of going to Jerusalem that no one could there restrain himself, or another, but, setting out at evening against the decrees of the princes and the custom of our army, we walked along all that night and came on the following day to Beirut. After this, when the narrow passages which are called The Twisted Mouth had been suddenly seized in advance, we came in a few days and without baggage to Acre. The King of Acre, however, afraid that we would besiege his city, and hoping that we would withdraw, took oath to the Count that if we captured Jerusalem, or were in the region of Judaea for twenty days, and the King of Babylon did not meet us in battle, or if we were able to overcome that king, he would surrender himself and his city to us; but that in the meanwhile he would be our friend.

Setting forth from Acre one day at vespers, we pitched camp by the swamps which are near Caesarea. And while, according to custom, some ran here and there below the camp, as need demanded, and while others were inquiring from acquaintances where their companions were lodged, a dove, mortally wounded by a hawk, fell down in the midst of those running about. When the Bishop of Agde took it up, he found a letter which it was carrying. And the sense of the letter was as follows:

"The King of Acre to the Duke of Caesarea: A canine breed, a foolish and troublesome host without order, passed me. As you love your law, try by yourselves and through others to hurt them; this you can easily do, if you wish. Send this likewise to other cities and fortresses."

In the morning, when we were commanding the army to rest, the letter was shown to the princes and to all the people, and [it was manifest] how God had been kind to us, so that not even the birds could cross through the air to harm us, and that He likewise disclosed to us the secrets of our foes. Wherefore, we rendered praise and thanks to Almighty God. And thence setting forth securely and willingly, we went forward, frequently in the front rank of the army, and also at the end.

But when the Saracens who lived in Ramlah heard that we had crossed the river near by, they left their fortifications and arms, and much grain in the fields, and crops, which we gathered. And when we came to it on the next day, we found out that God was truly fighting for us. So we offered vows to St. George because he had confessed himself our guide. The leaders and all the people agreed that we should there choose a bishop, since that was the first church which we found in the land of Israel, and, also, in order that St. George might entreat God in our behalf, and might lead us faithfully through the land in which He was not worshipped. Moreover, Ramlah is about fifteen miles from Jerusalem. Therefore, we there held a conference.

Some said, "Let us not go to Jerusalem at present, but towards Egypt; we will obtain not only Jerusalem, but likewise Alexandria and Babylon and very many kingdoms. If we go to Jerusalem and, failing of sufficient water, give up the siege, we will accomplish neither this nor the other afterwards."

But others said in opposition, "There are scarcely fifteen hundred knights in the army, and the number of armed men is not great; and yet it is now suggested that we go to very distant and unknown regions, where we will be able neither to get help from our people nor to place a garrison in a city, if we capture one; nor, even if it should be necessary, would we be able to return thence. But none of this; let us hold to our way, and let God provide for His servants for the siege, for thirst, for hunger, and for other things!"

Accordingly, after leaving a garrison in the fortress of Ramlah with the new Bishop, we loaded our camels and oxen, and then all our baggage animals and horses, and turned our march to Jerusalem. However, the word which Peter Bartholomew had commanded us—that we should not approach Jerusalem except with bared feet—we forgot and held in low regard, each one, from ambition to occupy castles and villas, wishing to go ahead of the next. For it was a custom among us that if any one came to a castle or villa first and placed his standard there with a guard, it was touched by no one else afterward. Therefore, because of this ambition they arose at midnight and, without waiting for companions, gained all those mountains and villas which are in the meadows of the Jordan. A few, however, to whom the command of God was more precious, walked with naked feet and sighed heavily for the contempt of the Divine word; and yet no one recalled a companion or friend from that ambitious chase. Moreover, when by such arrogant procedure we had come near Jerusalem, the people of Jerusalem came forth to meet the first of our men and wounded the horses severely. Of those men three or four fell on that day, and many were wounded.

3. The Fall of Jerusalem: The Version of Peter Tudebode

The English translation here is from Hill and Hill, 112–120.

Raymond of Saint-Gilles and Godfrey, along with other happy pilgrims, arrived before Jerusalem, rejoicing and boasting on Tuesday of the seventh day of entering June and set up a formidable siege. Robert the Norman occupied the zone to the north next to the church of the Blessed Protomartyr, Stephen, where the saint happily for the name of Christ was stoned. Adjoining his sector was that of the Count of Flanders; Duke Godfrey and Tancred encamped to the west, while Raymond of Saint-Gilles took position on Mount Zion next to the church of the Blessed Mary, Mother of the Lord. It was in this place that Mary departed the world, that the Lord broke bread with the disciples, and that the Holy Spirit entered the hearts of the disciples.

On the third day of the siege knights of our army of the Holy Sepulchre, namely Raymond Pilet, Raymond of Turenne, and others moved out intent on plundering. The knights of Christ came upon two hundred Arabs, gave battle to the pagans, and with God's aid and that of the Holy Sepulchre overwhelmed them, slaughtering many and seizing thirty horses. On the second day of the following week [Monday] the crusaders launched such a staunch attack that Jerusalem would have fallen if scaling ladders had been available. However, they tumbled a lesser wall, pushed a ladder against a major wall, and our knights mounted it, and engaged the pagans in close combat with swords and lances. Raginaldus, seneschal of Hugh of *Liziniacensis*, and many other Christians met death there, but the enemy casualties were heavier.

For ten days the Christians were without bread, when news came that our ships were anchored in a nearby port of Jaffa. So at daylight one hundred knights from the army of Raymond of Saint-Gilles, including Raymond Pilet, Geldemar Carpinel, Achard of Montmerle, William of Sabran, and others whose names I do not know, left the siege. When they marched to the port thirty of our knights, among whom were Geldemar and Achard, made a diversionary move and encountered six hundred Arabs, Turks, and Saracens. The Christian knights charged valiantly, but the superiority of the pagans over our men was such that they hemmed the crusaders in on all sides, and killed Achard of Montmerle and poor footmen.

While the Christians were so trapped that they only awaited death, a messenger rushed to Raymond Pilet and questioned: "Why do you dally here with your knights? Lo! All your comrades are in the clutches of Arabs, Turks, and Saracens, perhaps even dead at this very minute. Hurry, hurry to their aid!" The messenger's report brought the crusaders to life, and they rushed hurriedly to the scene of the battle. The infidels formed two lines when they sighted the Jerusalem knights. The Christians countered by calling upon the name of Christ and the Holy Sepulchre and hurled themselves so spiritedly against the foe that every individual knight overcame his adversary. Realizing that they were no match for the derring-do of the crusaders, the enemy became paralyzed with fear, called retreat, and fled. Our troops chased them almost four miles, killing numerous infidels, and holding one alive as an informer. In addition they seized one hundred and three horses.

In the course of the siege scarcity of water plagued the crusaders so much that they stitched skins of oxen, buffalo, and goats into leather bottles and lugged water in them for six miles. Such foul and stinking water was drunk from these canteens that daily we were in great misery and torment because of the fetid water and barley bread. The Fountain of Siloam, situated at the foot of Mount Zion, sustained us for the moment. But even the water was sold among Christians of God and the Holy Sepulchre so that one man could scarcely quench his thirst for a penny. The Saracens, lying in ambush around all fountains and wells, slew those whom they could find, and led away animals into caverns, caves, or mountains. In other places the infidels slaughtered those who foraged in the vineyards.

When our lords saw these atrocities, they were greatly angered and held a council in which the bishops and priests recommended that the crusaders hold a procession around the city. So the bishops and priests, barefooted, clad in sacred vestments, and bearing crosses in their hands, came from the church of the Blessed Mary, which is on Mount Zion, to the church of Saint Stephen, the Protomartyr, singing and praying that the Lord Jesus Christ deliver his holy city and the Holy Sepulchre from the pagan people and place it in Christian hands for His holy service. The clerks, so clad, along with the armed knights and their retainers, marched side by side.

The sight of this caused the Saracens to parade likewise on the walls of Jerusalem, bearing insignia of Mohammed on a standard and pennon. The Christians came to the church of Saint Stephen and there took their stations as is customary in our processions. In the meantime the Saracens stood on the walls, screamed, blared out with horns, and performed all kinds of acts of mockery. To add insult to injury they made from wood a cross similar to the one on which, pouring forth His blood, the most merciful Christ redeemed the world. Afterward they inflicted great sorrow upon the Christians when, in the sight of all, they beat upon the cross with sticks and shattered it against the walls, shouting loudly, *"Frango agip salip,"* which means "Franks, is this a good cross?"

The Christians were greatly distressed by this sight, but continued with their prayers as they wound their way up in the procession to the church of the Mount of Olives, from which place Christ ascended to heaven. There a most respected clerk, Arnulf, preached a sermon elaborating on the mercy which God would bestow upon Christians who followed Him even to His grave, from which He mounted to heaven. So the Saracens, seeing the Christians standing there in a most advantageous view, began to threaten them by running to and fro between the Temple of the Lord and the Temple of Solomon. But the Christians continued the procession and came to the monastery of the Blessed Mary in the Valley of Jehosaphat, from which her most holy body was snatched up to heaven. Thence they returned to the Mount of Olives in which place a clerk, wishing to enter the church when the procession came to the entrance of the monastery, was struck in the middle of his forehead and died on the spot. I believe his soul will dwell with Christ through eternity, world without end. Amen. This is believed by him who first wrote this, since he was in the procession and saw it with his worldly eyes—namely, Peter Tudebode.

Immediately thereafter our lords studied means by which they could take Jerusalem and enter the Sepulchre for the purpose of adoring their Lord and Savior. They constructed two wooden towers and many other machines of war. Both Godfrey and Raymond of Saint-Gilles equipped their towers with war devices. Wooden beams for the construction of these towers had to be dragged from distant places. Fifty or sixty captive Saracens bore the timbers on their shoulders, and thus the Christians disconcerted the enemy with their own men. Sight of the building of these machines caused the Saracens to take extraordinary measures to fortify the city and to strengthen the towers by night and day.

On a certain day the enemy sent a Saracen for the purpose of spying on the building of war machines of the Christians. But Syrians and Greeks, seeing the Saracen, pointed him out to the crusaders, saying: "*Ma te Christo caco Sarrazin*," which in our language means: "By Christ, this a dastardly Saracen." After grabbing him the Christians interrogated the Saracen through an interpreter asking him why he had come. In reply the captive said: "The Saracens sent me here to discover what were your inventions." In response the Christians pronounced judgment. They took the spy with bound hands and feet and placed him on the bottom of a machine called a petrary. They thought that with all of their might they could propel him within Jerusalem. They found it impossible, for he was ejected with such force that his bonds broke before he came to the walls and he was dismembered.

After spotting the most vulnerable part of Jerusalem's defenses, the leaders, on a Saturday night, moved our war machines and wooden towers to the eastern sector of the siege. At sunrise they erected them and for the next three days of the week put the towers in order and made them battle worthy. On the fourth and fifth days of the week they blitzed Jerusalem on all sides. On the sixth day very early in the morning they again assaulted the city, but became dumfounded and terrified when their efforts availed them naught. Despite this setback, at the approach of the hour in which our Lord Jesus Christ decided to be crucified on the Cross for us, our knights, Duke Godfrey, and his brother Count Eustace, battled valiantly on a siege tower. Then a knight named Lethold scaled a wall of the city, closely followed by our knights of Christ along with Count Eustace and Duke Godfrey. The defenders scurried from the wall and scattered throughout Jerusalem, while our men pursued them, killing, and lopping off heads.

In the meantime, Raymond of Saint-Gilles was stymied by a deep ditch near the wall as he rolled his siege tower toward it. After counseling on measures to be taken to fill the ditch, Raymond announced that anyone dumping three stones into the ditch would be paid one denarius. Upon completion of the fill after three days and two nights, the Christians moved the siege tower next to one of the city towers.

The defenders struck back spiritedly against our forces with fire and rocks so that they shattered the upper part of Raymond's tower. So when the count and his knights were angered and confused because the defenders had broken most of the upper part of the tower and it appeared to be burning, he suddenly saw three knights from the army of Duke Godfrey approaching from the Mount of Olives and yelling that Duke Godfrey and his men were in Jerusalem. At news of the Frankish break into Jerusalem, Raymond shouted to his men: "Why do you hang back? Listen, all of the Franks are in the city." At this command they picked up their ladders, pushed them against the wall, and thus battling entered Jerusalem.

The emir, who commanded the Tower of David, relinquished it to Raymond of Saint-Gilles and opened the gate through which the pilgrims were accustomed to pay tribute. By this treaty Raymond agreed to conduct the emir and his retainers in the Tower of David safe and unharmed as far as Ascalon. This he did. Upon entering Jerusalem the pilgrims pursued and killed Saracens and other infidels even to the Temple of Solomon and the Temple of the Lord. Gathered there the enemy waged a hot battle until sundown, but our men killed so many that blood flowed through all of the Temple. Finally, after having overwhelmed the pagans, our men grabbed a large number of males and females in the Temple, killing some, and sparing others as the notion struck them. Tancred and Gaston of Béarn gave their banners to a great number of the infidels of both sexes crowded on the roof of the Temple.

Soon the crusaders ran through all the city taking gold, silver, horses, mules, and houses packed with all kinds of riches. Afterwards, all came rejoicing and weeping with joy to the Holy Sepulchre of our Savior. On the next morning Tancred sent forth the command that the Christians go to the Temple to kill Saracens. Upon their arrival some began to draw their bows and to kill many. Another group of crusaders climbed to the roof of the Temple and rushed the Saracens huddled there, decapitating males and females with naked sword blades. They caused some to plunge from the Temple roof and others found their death above.

On another day the Christians held a meeting before the Temple and agreed that each one should say prayers, give alms, and fast so that God would elect someone pleasing to Him to reign over the others, to govern Jerusalem, and to despoil the pagans. But the bishops and priests commanded that the crusaders first drag the bodies of Saracen dead from Jerusalem lest the unbearable stench harm them. Actually all of Jerusalem was clogged with cadavers. The Saracen survivors pulled out the corpses of their fellows to the gate exits, corded them up in mounds like houses, and put them to the torch. Has anyone ever seen or heard of such a holocaust of infidels? God alone knows the number for no one else does.

Throughout the city Christians celebrated the Feast of the Octave of the capture of Jerusalem, and on the same day they held a council in which they elected Duke Godfrey prince of Jerusalem, so that he would battle the pagans and protect the Christians. In a similar manner they selected a most wise and noted patriarch named Arnulf on the Feast of Saint Peter in Chains. The city was captured on the fifteenth day of July, the sixth day of the week, with the aid of our Lord Jesus Christ to Whom is the honor and glory forever and forever. Amen.

4. The Fall of Jerusalem: The Version of Raymond d'Aguilers

The English translation here is from Krey, 250–256.

Duke Godfrey and the Count of Flanders and the Count of Normandy besieged the city from the north side, that is from the church of St. Stephen, located in the center of the city, southward to the angular tower next to the tower of David. Count Raymond and his army, however, settled down on the West and besieged Jerusalem from the camp of the Duke to the foot of Mount Zion. But since his men could not come close to besiege the wall because of a gully which intervened, the Count wished to move his camp and change his position. One day, while he was reconnoitering, he came to Mount Zion and saw the church which is located on the Mount. When he heard of the miracles that God had performed there, he said to his leaders and companions, "If we neglect to take this sacred offering, which the Lord has so graciously offered us, and the Saracens there occupy this place, what will become of us? What if through hatred of us they should destroy and pollute these sacred things? Who knows that God may not be giving us this opportunity to test our regard for Him? I know this one thing for certain: unless we carefully protect this sacred spot, the Lord will not give us the others within the city." And so Count Raymond, against the wishes of the leaders of his army, ordered his tents to be moved to that spot. As a result, he incurred such great hatred from his men that they were neither willing to encamp with him nor to do guard duty during the night; each stayed where he had first pitched his tent, with the exception of a few who accompanied the Count. However, by great rewards the Count daily induced knights and footmen to guard his camp. There are in that church these sacred treasures—the tombs of the kings, David and Solomon, as well as that of the first martyr, St. Stephen. There the Blessed Mary departed from this world; the Lord supped there and, after rising from the dead, appeared there to His disciples and to Thomas. On this spot, also, the disciples were filled with the Holy Spirit.

Thereupon, when the siege had been set, it happened one day that some of the leaders of the army met a hermit on the Mount of Olives, who said to them, "If you will attack the city tomorrow till the ninth hour, the Lord will deliver it into your hands." They replied, "But we do not have the necessary machinery for storming the walls." The hermit replied: "God is all powerful. If He wills, He will storm the walls even with one ladder. The Lord aids those who labor for the Truth." So, with such machinery as could be constructed during the night, an attack was made on the city in the early morning, and it lasted till the third hour. The Saracens were compelled to retreat behind the inner walls, for the outer wall was broken down by our men, some of whom even climbed to the top of the inner walls. Now when the city was about to be captured, in the confusion of desire and fear the attack was interrupted, and we then lost many men. On the next day no attack was attempted.

After this, the whole army scattered throughout the surrounding country to collect provisions, and nothing was even said of the necessity of preparing the machines that were needed to capture the city. Each man was serving his mouth and stomach; what was worse, they did not even ask the Lord to free them from such great and manifold evils, and they were afflicted even unto death. Just before our arrival, the Saracens had filled up the springs, destroyed the cisterns, and dammed up the brooks from the springs. And the Lord Himself had turned rivers into wilderness and water-springs into thirsty ground for the wickedness of them that dwell therein. Therefore water was obtained with great difficulty. There is a fountain at the foot of Mount Zion, which is called the Pool of Siloam. Indeed, it is a large spring, but the water flows forth only once in three days, and the natives say that formerly it emptied itself only on Saturdays; the rest of the week it remained stagnant. We do not know how to explain this, except that the Lord willed it to be so. But when, as we have said, the water did flow forth on the third day, it was consumed with such great crowding and haste that the men pushed one another into it, and many baggage animals and cattle perished in it. And so when the pool was filled with the crowd and with the bodies of dead animals, the stronger, even at the price of death, forced their way to the very opening in the rocks through which the water flowed, while the weak got only the water which had already been contaminated. Many sick people fell down by the fountain, with tongues so parched that they were unable to utter a word; with open mouths they stretched forth their hands toward those who had water. In the field were many horses, mules, cattle, and sheep, most of the animals without strength enough to move. And when they had become parched and died because of extreme thirst, they rotted where they had long stood, and there was a most sickening stench throughout the camp. Because of such affliction it was necessary to fetch water a distance of two or three leagues, also to drive the cattle to distant watering places. When the Saracens noticed that our people were going unarmed to the watering places through the dangerous passes in the hills, they lay in wait for them in ambush. They killed many of them and drove away the flocks and herds. The situation was so bad that when any one brought foul water to camp in vessels, he was able to get any price that he cared to ask, and if any one wished to get clear water, for five or six *nummi* he could not obtain enough to satisfy his thirst for a single day. Wine, moreover, was never, or very rarely, even mentioned. In addition, the heat, the dust, and the wind increased their thirst, as though this was not bad enough in itself. But why say so much about these troubles? None, or few, were mindful of the Lord, or of such work as was needed to capture the city; nor did they take heed to beseech the Lord's favor. And thus we did not recognize God in the midst of our affliction, nor did He show favor to the ungrateful.

Meanwhile, messengers came to camp, announcing that our ships had arrived at Joppa and that the sailors demanded that a guard be sent to hold the tower of Joppa and to give them protection at the port; for the town of Joppa had been destroyed except the castle, and that was nearly in ruins, with the exception of one tower. However, there is a harbor there, and it is the one nearest to Jerusalem, being about one day's journey distant. All of our people rejoiced when they heard the news of the ships, and they sent out Count Galdemar, surnamed *Carpinellus*, accompanied by twenty knights and about fifty footmen. Later, they sent Raymond Piletus with fifty knights and William of Sabran with his followers.

As Galdemar and his contingent approached the plains that are on this side of Ramlah, they encountered a force of four hundred chosen Arabs and about two hundred Turks. Galdemar, because of the small number of his men, arranged his knights and bowmen in the front ranks and, trusting in the Lord, advanced upon the enemy without hesitation. The enemy, however, thought that they would be able to crush this band, and, rushing upon them and shooting arrows, they encircled them. Three or four of Galdemar's knights were killed, including Achard of Montemerle, a noble youth and renowned knight; others were wounded, and all our bowmen fell. However, many of the enemy were also killed. Nevertheless, the attack of the enemy did not slacken on account of all this, nor did the courage of our knights, nay God's knights, falter; though oppressed by wounds and death itself, they stood up to their enemies all the more fiercely, the more they suffered from them. But when our leaders, rather from weariness than from fear, were about to withdraw, a cloud of dust was seen approaching. Raymond Piletus was rushing headlong into the fight with his men. Moreover, his men raised so much dust that the enemy thought there were very many knights with him. Thus, by the grace of God, our men were delivered. The enemy scattered and fled, about two hundred of them were killed, and much plunder was taken. It is the custom of this people, when they flee and are hard pressed by the enemy, first to throw away their arms, then their clothes, and lastly their saddle bags. Thus it happened in this fight that our few knights continued killing the enemy until they were worn out, and they kept the spoils obtained from the rest, even of those whom they did not kill.

After the pursuit was over our men assembled, divided the spoils, and then marched to Joppa. The sailors received them with great joy and felt so secure after their arrival that they forgot their ships and neglected to place watches on the sea, but entertained the crusaders with a feast of bread, wine, and fish from their ships. The sailors, careless of their security, failed to post lookouts for the night, and in the darkness they were suddenly surrounded by enemies from the sea. When dawn came, they realized that the enemy was too strong to be resisted, and they abandoned their ships, carrying only the spoils. Thus our knights returned to Jerusalem after winning one battle and losing another. However, one of our ships which had gone on a plundering expedition was not captured. It was returning to port with the greatest plunder when it saw the rest of our ships surrounded by so great a fleet of the enemy. By the use of oars and sail it made its escape to Laodicaea and told our friends and companions at that port what had been happening at Jerusalem. We knew that we had deserved this misfortune, for we had refused to place faith in the words sent to us by the Lord. Despairing of God's mercy, the men went to the plain of the river Jordan, collected palms, and were baptized in its waters. They did so chiefly with the intention of abandoning the siege, having seen Jerusalem, and of going to Joppa, thence to return home by whatever means they could. But the Lord looked after the ships for His unfaithful.

About this time a public assembly was held, for the leaders of the army were quarreling with each other. There was dissatisfaction because Tancred had occupied Bethlehem and had placed his standard over the church of the Nativity, as though it was an ordinary house. An effort was also made to elect one of the princes king to have custody of the city, lest what had been achieved in common should be destroyed in common for want of anyone to take care of the city, if God should give it to us. The bishops and clergy replied [to this suggestion], "You ought not to choose a king where the Lord suffered and was crowned. For if a David, degenerate in faith and virtue, should say in his heart, 'I sit upon the throne of David and hold his kingdom,' the Lord would probably destroy him and be angry with place and people. Besides, the prophet proclaims, saying, 'When the Holy of Holies shall come, unction shall cease, because it will be manifest to all peoples that He has come.' But there should be an advocate to guard the city and divide the tributes and rents of the region among the guardians of the city." For this and many other reasons the election was stopped and put off until the eighth day after the capture of Jerusalem. Not in this matter alone, but in other ways, our affairs did not prosper, and the troubles of the people increased every day. Nevertheless, the merciful and propitious Lord, both for His name's sake and lest our enemies should insult His law and say, "Where is their God?" sent word to us through the Bishop of Puy, Lord Ademar, how we could placate His anger and obtain His mercy. We, however, preached that this be done without mentioning the command of God, lest if the people transgressed this command of the Lord, they should be especially afflicted, as they would then be the more culpable. For the Lord was so kind to us that He had sent His messengers to us often, but because they were our brothers we had not heeded them.

The Bishop [Ademar] appeared before Peter Desiderius, saying: "Speak to the princes and all the people, and say to them: 'You who have come from distant lands to worship God and the Lord of hosts, purge yourselves of your uncleanliness, and let each one turn from his evil ways. Then with bare feet march around Jerusalem invoking God, and you must also fast. If you do this and then make a great attack on the city on the ninth day, it will be captured. If you do not, all the evils that you have suffered will be multiplied by the Lord.'"

When the priest had said this to William Hugo, the brother of the Bishop, to his lord, Count Ysoard, and to certain of the clergy, they assembled the princes and the people and addressed them. "Brothers, you know why we undertook this expedition, and what we have suffered, and that we are acting negligently in that we are not constructing the machines that are needed to capture the city. Likewise, we are not careful to reconcile the Lord to us, for we offend Him in many ways and through our evil deeds have driven Him from us. Now, if it seems right to you, let each one become reconciled to his brother whom he has offended, and let brother graciously forgive brother. After this, let us humble ourselves before God; let us march around Jerusalem in bare feet and, through the patronage of the saints, invoke the mercy of the Lord, so that Almighty God, who for us, His servants, laid aside the form of His Godhead, assumed the flesh, and humbly rode into the city on an ass to suffer death on the Cross for our sins, may come to our aid. If we make this procession around the walls, for the honor and glory of His name, He will open the city to us and give us judgment upon His enemies and ours, who now with unjust possession contaminate the place of His suffering and burial, the enemy who seek to deny us the great blessing of the place of God's humiliation and our redemption."

These words were pleasing to both princes and people, and it was publicly commanded that on the next Friday the clergy should lead the procession with crosses and relics of the saints, while the knights and all able-bodied men, with trumpets, standards, and arms, should follow them, barefooted. All this we did according to the commands of God and the princes. When we reached the spot on the Mount of Olives whence the Lord had ascended into heaven after the resurrection, the following exhortation was made to the people: "Now that we are on the very spot from which the Lord made His ascension and we can do nothing more to purify ourselves, let each one of us forgive his brother whom he has injured, that the Lord may forgive us." What more? All were reconciled to each other, and with generous offerings we besought the mercy of God, that He should not now desert His people, whom He had led so gloriously and miraculously to this goal. Thus the mercy of God was obtained, since every thing that had been against us was now favorable.

Although we have passed over many matters, this one we ought to record. While we marched around the city in procession, the Saracens and Turks made the circuit on the walls, ridiculing us in many ways. They placed many crosses on the walls in yokes and mocked them with blows and insulting deeds. We, in turn, hoping to obtain the aid of God in storming the city by means of these signs, pressed the work of the siege day and night.

5. The Fall of Jerusalem: The *Gesta* Version

The English translation here is from Krey, 256–257.

At length, our leaders decided to beleaguer the city with siege machines, so that we might enter and worship the Saviour at the Holy Sepulchre. They constructed wooden towers and many other siege machines. Duke Godfrey made a wooden tower and other siege devices, and Count Raymond did the same, although it was necessary to bring wood from a considerable distance. However, when the Saracens saw our men engaged in this work, they greatly strengthened the fortifications of the city and increased the height of the turrets at night. On a certain Sabbath night, the leaders, after having decided which parts of the wall were weakest, dragged the tower and the machines to the eastern side of the city. Moreover, we set up the tower at earliest dawn and equipped and covered it on the first, second, and third days of the week. The Count of St. Gilles erected his tower on the plain to the south of the city.

While all this was going on, our water supply was so limited that no one could buy enough water for one *denarius* to satisfy or quench his thirst. Both day and night, on the fourth and fifth days of the week, we made a determined attack on the city from all sides. However, before we made this assault on the city, the bishops and priests persuaded all, by exhorting and preaching, to honor the Lord by marching around Jerusalem in a great procession, and to prepare for battle by prayer, fasting, and almsgiving. Early on the sixth day of the week we again attacked the city on all sides, but as the assault was unsuccessful, we were all astounded and fearful. However, when the hour approached on which our Lord Jesus Christ deigned to suffer on the Cross for us, our knights began to fight bravely in one of the towers— namely, the party with Duke Godfrey and his brother, Count Eustace. One of our knights, named Lethold, clambered up the wall of the city, and no sooner had he ascended than the defenders fled from the walls and through the city. Our men followed, killing and slaying even to the Temple of Solomon, where the slaughter was so great that our men waded in blood up to their ankles. . . .

Count Raymond brought his army and his tower up near the wall from the south, but between the tower and the wall there was a very deep ditch. Then our men took counsel how they might fill it, and had it proclaimed by heralds that anyone who carried three stones to the ditch would receive one *denarius*. The work of filling it required three days and three nights, and when at length the ditch was filled, they moved the tower up to the wall, but the men defending this portion of the wall fought desperately with stones and fire. When the Count heard that the Franks were already in the city, he said to his men, "Why do you loiter? Lo, the Franks are even now within the city." The Emir who commanded the Tower of St. David surrendered to the Count and opened that gate at which the pilgrims had always been accustomed to pay tribute. But this time the pilgrims entered the city, pursuing and killing the Saracens up to the Temple of Solomon, where the enemy gathered in force. The battle raged throughout the day, so that the Temple was covered with their blood. When the pagans had been overcome, our men seized great numbers, both men and women, either killing them or keeping them captive, as they wished. On the roof of the Temple a great number of pagans of both sexes had assembled, and these were taken under the protection of Tancred and Gaston of *Beert*. Afterward, the army scattered throughout the city and took possession of the gold and silver, the horses and mules, and the houses filled with goods of all kinds.

6. The Frankish Triumph:
The Version of Raymond d'Aguilers

The English translation here is from Krey, 257–262.

Later, all of our people went to the Sepulchre of our Lord, rejoicing and weeping for joy, and they rendered up the offering that they owed. In the morning, some of our men cautiously ascended to the roof of the Temple and attacked the Saracens, both men and women, beheading them with naked swords; the remainder sought death by jumping down into the temple. When Tancred heard of this, he was filled with anger.

The Duke and the Counts of Normandy and Flanders placed Gaston of *Beert* in charge of the workmen who constructed machines. They built mantlets and towers with which to attack the wall. The direction of this work was assigned to Gaston by the princes because he was a most noble lord, respected by all for his skill and reputation. He very cleverly hastened matters by dividing the work. The princes busied themselves with obtaining and bringing the material, while Gaston supervised the work of construction. Likewise, Count Raymond made William *Ricau* superintendent of the work on Mount Zion and placed the Bishop of Albara in charge of the Saracens and others who brought in the timber. The Count's men had taken many Saracen castles and villages and forced the Saracens to work, as though they were their serfs. Thus for the construction of machines at Jerusalem fifty or sixty men carried on their shoulders a great beam that could not have been dragged by four pair of oxen. What more shall I say? All worked with a singleness of purpose, no one was slothful, and no hands were idle. All worked without wages, except the artisans, who were paid from a collection taken from the people. However, Count Raymond paid his workmen from his own treasury. Surely the hand of the Lord was with us and aided those who were working!

When our efforts were ended and the machines completed, the princes held a council and announced: "Let all prepare themselves for a battle on Thursday; in the meantime, let us pray, fast, and give alms. Hand over your animals and your boys to the artisans and carpenters, that they may bring in beams, poles, stakes, and branches to make mantlets. Two knights should make one mantlet and one scaling ladder. Do not hesitate to work for the Lord, for your labors will soon be ended." This was willingly done by all. Then it was decided what part of the city each leader should attack and where his machines should be located,

Meanwhile, the Saracens in the city, noting the great number of machines that we had constructed, strengthened the weaker parts of the wall, so that it seemed that they could be taken only by the most desperate efforts. Because the Saracens had made so many and such strong fortifications to oppose our machines, the Duke, the Count of Flanders, and the Count of Normandy spent the night before the day set for the attack moving their machines, mantlets, and platforms to that side of the city which is between the church of St. Stephen and the valley of Josaphat. You who read this must not think that this was a light undertaking, for the machines were carried in parts almost a mile to the place where they were to be set up. When morning came and the Saracens saw that all the machinery and tents had been moved during the night, they were amazed. Not only the Saracens were astonished, but our people as well, for they recognized that the hand of the Lord was with us. The change was made because the new point chosen for attack was more level, and thus suitable for moving the machines up to the walls, which cannot be done unless the ground is level; and also because that part of the city seemed to be weaker, having remained unfortified, as it was some distance from our camp. This part of the city is on the north.

Count Raymond and his men worked equally hard on Mount Zion, but they had much assistance from William Embriaco and the Genoese sailors, who, although they had lost their ships at Joppa, as we have already related, had been able, nevertheless, to save ropes, mallets, spikes, axes, and hatchets, which were very necessary to us. But why delay the story? The appointed day arrived and the attack began. However, I want to say this first, that, according to our estimate and that of many others, there were sixty thousand fighting men within the city, not counting the women and those unable to bear arms, and there were not many of these. At the most we did not have more than twelve thousand able to bear arms, for there were many poor people and many sick. There were twelve or thirteen hundred knights in our army, as I reckon it, not more. I say this that you may realize that nothing, whether great or small, which is undertaken in the name of the Lord can fail, as the following pages show.

Our men began to undermine the towers and walls. From every side stones were hurled from the *tormenti* and the *petrariae*, and so many arrows that they fell like hail. The servants of God bore this patiently, sustained by the premises of their faith, whether they should be killed or should presently prevail over their enemies. The battle showed no indication of victory, but when the machines were drawn nearer to the walls, they hurled not only stones and arrows, but also burning wood and straw. The wood was dipped in pitch, wax, and sulphur; then straw and tow were fastened on by an iron band, and, when lighted, these firebrands were shot from the machines. [They were] all bound together by an iron band, I say, so that wherever they fell, the whole mass held together and continued to burn. Such missiles, burning as they shot upward, could not be resisted by swords or by high walls; it was not even possible for the defenders to find safety down behind the walls. Thus the fight continued from the rising to the setting sun in such splendid fashion that it is difficult to believe anything more glorious was ever done. Then we called on Almighty God, our Leader and Guide, confident in His mercy. Night brought fear to both sides. The Saracens feared that we would take the city during the night or on the next day, for the outer works were broken through and the ditch was filled, so that it was possible to make an entrance through the wall very quickly. On our part, we feared only that the Saracens would set fire to the machines that were moved close to the walls, and thus improve their situation. So on both sides it was a night of watchfulness, labor, and sleepless caution: on one side, most certain hope, on the other doubtful fear. We gladly labored to capture the city for the glory of God, they less willingly strove to resist our efforts for the sake of the laws of Mohammed. It is hard to believe how great were the efforts made on both sides during the night.

When the morning came, our men eagerly rushed to the walls and dragged the machines forward, but the Saracens had constructed so many machines that for each one of ours they now had nine or ten. Thus they greatly interfered with our efforts. This was the ninth day, on which the priest had said that we would capture the city. But why do I delay so long? Our machines were now shaken apart by the blows of many stones, and our men lagged because they were very weary. However, there remained the mercy of the Lord which is never overcome nor conquered, but is always a source of support in times of adversity. One incident must not be omitted. Two women tried to bewitch one of the hurling machines, but a stone struck and crushed them, as well as three slaves, so that their lives were extinguished and the evil incantations averted.

By noon our men were greatly discouraged. They were weary and at the end of their resources. There were still many of the enemy opposing each one of our men; the walls were very high and strong, and the great resources and skill that the enemy exhibited in repairing their defenses seemed too great for us to overcome. But, while we hesitated, irresolute, and the enemy exulted in our discomfiture, the healing mercy of God inspired us and turned our sorrow into joy, for the Lord did not forsake us. While a council was being held to decide whether or not our machines should be withdrawn, for some were burned and the rest badly shaken to pieces, a knight on the Mount of Olives began to wave his shield to those who were with the Count and others, signalling them to advance. Who this knight was we have been unable to find out. At this signal our men began to take heart, and some began to batter down the wall, while others began to ascend by means of scaling ladders and ropes. Our archers shot burning firebrands, and in this way checked the attack that the Saracens were making upon the wooden towers of the Duke and the two Counts. These firebrands, moreover, were wrapped in cotton. This shower of fire drove the defenders from the walls. Then the Count quickly released the long drawbridge which had protected the side of the wooden tower next to the wall, and it swung down from the top, being fastened to the middle of the tower, making a bridge over which the men began to enter Jerusalem bravely and fearlessly. Among those who entered first were Tancred and the Duke of Lorraine, and the amount of blood that they shed on that day is incredible. All ascended after them, and the Saracens now began to suffer.

Strange to relate, however, at this very time when the city was practically captured by the Franks, the Saracens were still fighting on the other side, where the Count was attacking the wall as though the city should never be captured. But now that our men had possession of the walls and towers, wonderful sights were to be seen. Some of our men (and this was more merciful) cut off the heads of their enemies; others shot them with arrows, so that they fell from the towers; others tortured them longer by casting them into the flames. Piles of heads, hands, and feet were to be seen in the streets of the city. It was necessary to pick one's way over the bodies of men and horses. But these were small matters compared to what happened at the Temple of Solomon, a place where religious services are ordinarily chanted. What happened there? If I tell the truth, it will exceed your powers of belief. So let it suffice to say this much, at least, that in the Temple and porch of Solomon, men rode in blood up to their knees and bridle reins. Indeed, it was a just and splendid judgment of God that this place should be filled with the blood of the unbelievers, since it had suffered so long from their blasphemies. The city was filled with corpses and blood. Some of the enemy took refuge in the Tower of David, and, petitioning Count Raymond for protection, surrendered the Tower into his hands.

Now that the city was taken, it was well worth all our previous labors and hardships to see the devotion of the pilgrims at the Holy Sepulchre. How they rejoiced and exulted and sang a new song to the Lord! For their hearts offered prayers of praise to God, victorious and triumphant, which cannot be told in words. A new day, new joy, new and perpetual gladness, the consummation of our labor and devotion, drew forth from all new words and new songs. This day, I say, will be famous in all future ages, for it turned our labors and sorrows into joy and exultation; this day, I say, marks the justification of all Christianity, the humiliation of paganism, and the renewal of our faith. "This is the day which the Lord hath made, let us rejoice and be glad in it," for on this day the Lord revealed Himself to His people and blessed them.

On this day, the Ides of July, Lord Ademar, Bishop of Puy, was seen in the city by many people. Many also testified that he was the first to scale the wall, and that he summoned the knights and people to follow him. On this day, moreover, the apostles were cast forth from Jerusalem and scattered over the whole world. On this same day, the children of the apostles regained the city and fatherland for God and the fathers. This day, the Ides of July, shall be celebrated to the praise and glory of the name of God, who, answering the prayers of His Church, gave in trust and benediction to His children the city and fatherland which He had promised to the fathers. On this day we chanted the Office of the Resurrection, since on that day He, who by His virtue arose from the dead, revived us through His grace. So much is to be said of this.

7. "The Vision of Peace": The *Gesta* Version

English translation here is from Krey, 262.

Then our leaders in council decided that each one should offer alms with prayers, that the Lord might choose for Himself whom He wanted to reign over the others and rule the city. They also ordered all the Saracen dead to be cast outside because of the great stench, since the whole city was filled with their corpses; and so the living Saracens dragged the dead before the exits of the gates and arranged them in heaps, as if they were houses. No one ever saw or heard of such slaughter of pagan people, for funeral pyres were formed from them like pyramids, and no one knows their number except God alone. But Raymond caused the Emir and the others who were with him to be conducted to Ascalon, whole and unhurt. However, on the eighth day after the city was captured, they chose Godfrey as head of the city to fight the pagans and guard the Christians. On the day of St. Peter ad Vincula they likewise chose as Patriarch a certain very wise and honorable man, Arnulf by name. This city was captured by God's Christians on the fifteenth day of July, the sixth day of the week.

8. "The Vision of Peace": The Version of Raymond d'Aguilers

The English translation here is from Krey, 262–264.

Accordingly, after six or seven days the princes solemnly began to consider the matter of choosing a ruler, who, assuming charge of all matters, should collect the tributes of the region, to whom the peasants of the land could turn, and who would see to it that the land was not further devastated. While this was taking place, some of the clergy assembled and said to the princes, "We approve your election, but if you proceed rightly and properly, you will first choose a spiritual vicar, as eternal matters come before temporal; after this, a ruler to preside over secular matters. Otherwise, we shall hold invalid whatever you do." The princes were exceedingly angered when they heard this and proceeded the more quickly with the election. The clergy had been weakened by the departure of Lord Ademar, Pontiff of Puy, who, in his life had held our army together with holy deeds and words, like a second Moses. After him, however, William, Bishop of Orange, a man of good repute, wished to minister to our strength, but he rested in peace at Marra within a short time. Accordingly, therefore, the good men having been taken off, the clergy conducted themselves humbly, all except the Bishop of Albara and some others. However, the Bishop of Martirano, advancing by other than the right road, since he had obtained the church of Bethlehem by fraud, was captured by the Saracens on the third or fourth day and never again appeared among us. The princes, disregarding admonition and opposition, urged the Count of St. Gilles to accept the kingdom. But he said that he abhorred the name of king in that city, though he would consent to have others accept it. For this reason they together chose the Duke and placed him in charge of the Sepulchre of the Lord.

After this, however, the Duke required the Tower of David from the Count. But the latter refused, saying that he wished to stay in that region until Easter, and meanwhile he wanted to keep himself and his men in honorable state. But the Duke said that he would give up other places rather than the Tower. And so the disputes were multiplied. The Counts of Flanders and Normandy favored the Duke. Almost all from the land of Count Raymond did likewise in the belief that if the Tower were surrendered he would thereupon return home. Not alone did the Provençals oppose their lord, the Count, in this matter, but they also made up many vile statements about him so that he would not be chosen King. And so the Count, without the help of companions or friends, handed over the Tower to the Bishop of Albara for the sake of avoiding judgment. But the latter, without waiting for judgment, handed it over to the Duke, and when he was called traitor for having done this, he said that he had been compelled [to do so] and had suffered violence. I found this out, in truth, that very many arms were brought into the house of the Patriarch where the Bishop was staying near the Holy Sepulchre. But he spoke, also, of violence done himself and often secretly charged the friends of the Count with this affair.

So when the Tower had been surrendered, the Count blazed forth into great anger against his people, saying that he could not remain disgraced in that country. Accordingly, we set out from Jerusalem to Jericho, took palms and went to the Jordan. There, as Peter Bartholomew had commanded, a raft was constructed from twigs, and with the Count on it we pulled it across the river; since, forsooth, we had no ship, this plan seemed better to us. When after this the multitude had been called together, we commanded that they pray God for the life of the Count and the other princes. Therefore we proceeded to dress only in a shirt and new breeches, as we had been commanded about baptism; but why the man of God so commanded, we still do not know. When these matters had been accomplished, we returned to Jerusalem.

At this time, Arnulf, chaplain of the Count of Normandy, was chosen Patriarch by some, the good [clergy] opposing it not only because he was not a subdeacon, but especially because he was of priestly birth and was accused of incontinence on our expedition, so much so that they shamelessly composed vulgar songs about him. But, led on by such ambition, and disregarding the decrees of the canons and the infamy of his birth and conscience, he stirred up the people against the good [clergy] and had himself raised upon the patriarchal seat with hymns and chants and the great applause of the people. The divine vengeance exacted from the Bishop of Martirano, who had been the instigator and executor of this affair, not only did not terrify Arnulf, but, furthermore, did not prevent him from depriving of their benefices the clergy who had altars in the church of the Holy Sepulchre, or those in whose custody indulgence funds had been established.

And thus Arnulf, increasing his power, began to inquire from the inhabitants of the city where the Cross was which pilgrims had been accustomed to adore before Jerusalem was taken. Although they denied [this knowledge], and by oath and other signs were willing to show that they did not know, they were at length compelled [to yield] and said this: "It is manifest that God has chosen you, has delivered you from all tribulation, and has given you this and many other cities, not by the strength of your valor, but by blinding the impious in His wrath. Your Lord and Guide has opened to you the most strongly fortified cities and has won fearful battles for you. Therefore, why should we stubbornly conceal from you His good gifts, since we see that God is with you?" After this, they led them to a certain hall in the church, and, unearthing the Cross, they gave it up. Thereupon, all our men rejoiced, and we returned praise and thanks to Almighty God, who not only gave us the city in which He had suffered, but likewise the symbols of His Passion and victory, that we might the more closely embrace Him with the arms of faith, the more certain the signs of our salvation that we beheld.

9. "May God Restore It Forever": The Geniza Letters

For many years no Jewish sources for the capture of Jerusalem and the fate of its Jews were known; that is, there were no Hebrew narrative accounts as there had been in western Europe. In 1952, however, S. D. Goitein, in his extensive research in the scattered remains of the Cairo Geniza, published two letters written in Arabic in Hebrew characters that were authentic statements from Jews who had escaped the Christian conquest. Goitein published similar materials over the next several decades, and he summed up his great work in A Mediterranean Society: The Jewish Communities in the Arab World, as Portrayed in the Documents of the Cairo Geniza, *6 vols. (Berkeley-Los Angeles, 1967–1993). Goitein has suggested that the essential differences between the Hebrew sources in western Europe and those of Palestine and Egypt are attributable to the fact that in the East the problems Jews faced were those of refugees and exiles; their work therefore was focused on charitable concerns rather than on recording heroic suffering. The following four letters are in approximate chronological order.*

A

Letter from the three leaders of the community of Ascalon to the Jewish community in Alexandria or Cairo, summer, 1100. The letter is one of several attempts to raise money for the enormous expenses incurred by Jews because of the crusader's capture of Jerusalem. The text is from S. D. Goitein, "Contemporary Letters on the Capture of Jerusalem by the Crusaders," Journal of Jewish Studies 3 (1952), 162–177.

We thank the Most High who gave us the opportunity of fulfilling this pious deed, and granted to you to take a share in it with us. We spent the money for the ransom of some of the captives, after due consideration of the instructions contained in your letter, that is, we send what was available to those who [had already been ransomed(?)].

We did not fail to reply to what you had written us, and indeed we answered, but we were seeking a man who would bring our reply to you. Afterwards it happened that these illnesses came upon us; plague, pestilence, and leprosy, which filled our minds with anxiety, that we ourselves or some of our relatives might be stricken with disease. A man whom we trust went from here and must have explained to you the position with respect to the sums you had sent: that they reached us safely and that they were spent in the manner indicated [in your letter].

News still reaches us that among those who were redeemed from the *Franks* and remained in *Ascalon* some are in danger of dying of want. Others remained in captivity, and yet others were killed before the eyes of the rest, who themselves were killed afterwards with all manner of tortures; [for the enemy murdered them] in order to give vent to his anger on them.

We did not hear of a single man of Israel who was in such plight without exerting ourselves to do all that was in our power to save him.

The Most High has granted opportunities of relief and deliverance to individual fugitives, of which the first and most perfect instance—after the compassion of Heaven—has been the presence in *Ascalon* of the honourable shaykh *'Abu' l-Fadl Sahl son of Yusha' son of Shay'a* (may God preserve him), an agent of the Sultan (may God bestow glory upon his victories), whose influence is great in *Alexandria* where his word is very much heeded. He arranged matters wisely and took great pain in securing the ransom; but it would require a lengthy discourse to explain how he did it. But he could only ransom some of the people and had to leave the others. In the end, all those who could be ransomed from them [the Franks] were liberated, and only a few whom they kept remained in their hands, including a boy of about eight years of age, and a man, known as [?] *the son of the Tustari's wife*. It is reported that the Franks urged the latter to embrace the Christian faith of his own free will and promised to treat him well, but he told them, how could he become a Christian priest and be left in peace by them [the Jews], who had disbursed on his behalf a great sum. Until this day these captives remain in their [Franks] hands; as well as those who were taken to *Antioch*, but these are few; and not counting those who abjured their faith because they lost patience as it was not possible to ransom them, and because they despaired of being permitted to go free.

We were not informed, praise be to the Most High, that the accursed ones who are called '*Ashkenazim* (Germans) violated or raped women, as did the others.

Now, among those who have reached safety are some who escaped on the second and third days following the battle and left with the governor who was granted safe conduct; and others who, after having being caught by the *Franks*, remained in their hands for some time and escaped in the end; these are but few. The majority consists of those who were ransomed. To our sorrow, some of them ended their lives under all kind of suffering and affliction. The privations which they had to endure caused some of them to leave for this country without food or protection against the cold, and they died on the way.

Others in a similar way perished at sea; and yet others, after having arrived here safely, became exposed to a "change of air"; they came at the height of the plague, and a number of them died. We had, at the time, reported the arrival of each group.

And when the aforementioned honoured shaykh arrived, he brought a group of them, *i.e.*, the bulk of those who had reached *Ascalon*; he spent the Sabbath and celebrated Passover with them on the way in the manner as is required by such circumstances. He contracted a private loan for the sum that he had to pay the camel drivers and for their maintenance on the way, as well as the caravan guards and for other expenses, after having already spent other sums of money, which he did not charge to the community. All this is in addition to the money that was borrowed and spent in order to buy back two hundred and thirty volumes, a hundred codices and eight Torah Scrolls. All these are communal property and are now in *Ascalon.*

The community, after having disbursed about five hundred dinars for the actual ransom of the individuals (40 interlinear), for maintenance of some of them and for the ransom, as mentioned above, of the sacred books remained indebted for the sum of two hundred dinars. This is in addition to what has been spent on behalf of those who have been arriving from the beginning until now, on water and other drinks, medical treatment, maintenance and, in so far as possible, clothing. If it could be calculated how much this has cost over such a long period, the sum would indeed be great.

Had the accepted practice been followed, that is, of selling three Jewish captives (in the margin) for a hundred [dinars], the whole available sum would have been spent for the ransom of only a few. However, the grace of the Lord, may His name be exalted, and His ever-ready mercy, has been bestowed upon these wretched people, the oppressed, the captives, the poor and indigent, who may, indeed, groan, lament, and cry out as it is written [Ps. 44:12–13]: "Thou hast given us like sheep appointed for meat, and hast scattered us among the heathen. Thou sellest Thy people for nought and dost not increase Thy wealth by their price." And we ourselves may say [Is. 1:9]: "Except the Lord of Hosts had left unto us a very small remnant, we should have been as Sodom, and we should have been like unto Gomorrah." We declare that all the silver which we have weighed [*i.e.,* the money we have spent] in this catastrophe, from the beginning until now is but light and insignificant in relation to its magnitude and the greatness of the sorrow it has entailed.

Some adduce as an excuse the impoverishment of this class of financial magnates and property holders . . . and [?] the harshness of the winter season . . . and . . . enfeebled it.

We could not refrain ourselves from reporting what we know and the outcome of what we have done in this juncture, for we are convinced that you, just like ourselves, regret and mourn for those who have died and strive for the preservation of those who are alive; especially since your determination to distinguish yourselves was clearly shown and the loftiness of your aspiration and generosity became apparent. You were the first and the most consistent in the fulfilment of this "good deed" which you were granted to perform, and which gained for you great superiority over the other communities as well as much honour. Thus, you may be, indeed, compared with that class of people to whom it was assigned to perform generous deeds and to strive to do praiseworthy acts, as it is written [Deut. 33:21]: "And he came with the heads of the people, he executed the justice of the Lord, and his judgments with Israel."

We have already indicated that we remained in debt of over two hundred dinars, apart from the moneys that are required for the maintenance of the captives who remained in *Ascalon*—they number more than twenty persons—for their transfer and other needs until they arrive here. Among those who are in *Ascalon* is the honoured elder *'Abi al-Khair Mubarak* the son of the teacher *Hiba b. Nisan* (may God protect him for a long time). It is well known how much he is revered, wise, God-fearing, and endowed with high virtues; he is bound by an old vow not to benefit in anything from charity together with the whole of the community, but only from what is explicitly destined for him by name. [He should be enabled] to come here, after [you] our Lords, elders and masters—may God preserve your happiness—have graciously offered us the sum needed for cancelling the debt incurred for the ransom of our and your brethren. Gird now your loins together with us in this matter, and it will be accounted for you as a mark of merit in the future, as it has been in the past . . . the generous deed which you began, by helping us to lighten our burden and by assisting us with your generosity in order to put us back on our feet, for we have no one in this country to whom we could write as we are writing to you. It is proper that we should turn to you and cause you some disturbance. The main tenor of this letter ought to be read out to your [entire] community, after you have announced that everyone must attend [the meeting]. For the benefit will [thus] be complete and general, both to those who pay and to those who receive payment. For it is unlikely that there should lack among the public those who had made a vow, or those who had undertaken an obligation to perform "holy deeds" which have not yet been determined; such should, then, be invited to contribute as much as may be seen fitting. Or there may be those who had previously intended to make contribution to charity, or others may wish to make a specific contribution to one cause rather than to another. In this manner you will achieve your purpose, and deal with us in your accustomed generosity and excellent manner . . . and you will deserve, through this charitable act, to acquire "both worlds." Only rarely does such a juncture present itself, in which "commerce" is beneficial and "business" entirely profitable. We do not call your attention to such a matter in order to remind you of the duty of doing it, but . . . your own lofty [virtues] are the strongest urger and reminder.

We dispatched a messenger to you and what he will tell you about the details of this misfortune exempts us from discoursing on it at a greater length. We beg of you, may God preserve you in long life, to deal with him kindly until he returns; and concerning that which God may cause him [to collect] amongst you—may God preserve you—if you could write out for him a bill of exchange, it would make things easier for him, since he is but a messenger, and speed up his return. If this cannot be done, arrange that an exact statement of how much has been collected be made, and have your letter sent through him [the messenger] and mention the sum in it. The God of Israel, etc. . . . .

(There follow nine lines with complimentary phrases in Hebrew.)

(In the margin)

The writer of the above, the pained, sorrowful, and grieving *Yesha'ya ha-Kohen b. Maṣliaḥ the Enlightened* sends respectful greetings to all the gentlemen, and begs them to accept his apology. They are not unaware of what he has gone through from the time he took leave of them until this day.

(To the left of preceding lines)

David b. R. Shelomo b. R. . . . . sends his greeting to your excellencies and begs you to note . . . *al-Fadl Abu.* . . .

(To the right of the first signature, in Arabic characters)

Hanina b. Mansur b. 'Ubayd (peace be on him) reserves for the venerable lords and masters, may God preserve their excellencies, the best greeting and most excellent salutation and attention; expresses his longing for them and begs them to take note of the contents of this letter. Peace.

B

Letter from Egypt to North Africa or Spain in 1100 by a pilgrim who could not reach Palestine because of the wars. The text appears in S. D. Goitein, "Contemporary Letters on the Capture of Jerusalem by the Crusaders," 162–177.

In Your name, You Merciful.

If I attempted to describe my longing for you, my Lord, my brother *and cousin*,—may God prolong your days and make permanent your honour, success, happiness, health, and welfare; and [. . .] subdue your enemies—all the paper in the world would not suffice. My longing will but increase and double, just as the days will grow and double. May *the Creator of the World* presently make us meet together in joy when I return under His guidance to my homeland *and to the inheritance of my Fathers* in complete happiness, *so that we rejoice and be happy through His great mercy and His vast bounty; and thus may be His will!*

You may remember, my Lord, that many years ago I left our country to seek God's mercy and help in my poverty, to behold Jerusalem and return thereupon. However, when I was in Alexandria God brought about circumstances which caused a slight delay. Afterwards, however, "the sea grew stormy," and many armed bands made their appearance in Palestine; *"and he who went forth and he who came had no peace,"* so that hardly one survivor out of a whole group came back to us from Palestine and told us that scarcely anyone could save himself from those armed bands, since they were so numerous and were gathered round . . . every town. There was further the journey through the desert, among [the bedouins] and whoever escaped from the one, fell into the hands of the other. Moreover, mutinies [spread throughout the country and reached] even Alexandria, so that we ourselves were besieged several times and the city was ruined; . . . the end however *was good*, for the Sultan— may God bestow glory upon his victories—conquered the city and caused justice to abound in it in a manner unprecedented in the history of any king in the world; not even a dirham was looted from anyone. Thus I had come to hope that because of his justice and strength God would give the land into his hands, and I should thereupon go to Jerusalem in safety and tranquillity. For this reason I proceeded from Alexandria to Cairo, in order to start [my journey] from there.

When, however, God had given Jerusalem, the blessed, into his hands this state of affairs continued for too short a time to allow for making a journey there. The Franks arrived and killed everybody in the city, whether of *Ishmael or of Israel*; and the few who survived the slaughter were made prisoners. Some of these have been ransomed since, while others are still in captivity in all parts of the world.

Now, all of us had anticipated that our Sultan—may God bestow glory upon his victories—would set out against them [the Franks] with his troops and chase them away. But time after time our hope failed. Yet, to this very present moment we do hope that God will give his [the Sultan's] enemies into his hands. For it is inevitable that the armies will join in battle this year; and, if God grants us victory through him [the Sultan] and he conquers Jerusalem—and so it may be, with God's will—I for one shall not be amongst those who will linger, but shall go there to behold the city; and shall afterwards return straight to you—if God wills it. My salvation is in God, for this (35) [is unlike] the other previous occasions [of making a pilgrimage to Jerusalem]. God, indeed, will exonerate me, since at my age I cannot afford to delay and wait any longer; I want to return home under any circumstances, if I still remain alive—whether I shall have seen Jerusalem or have given up the hope of doing it—both of which are possible.

You know, of course, my Lord, what has happened to us in the course of the last five years: the plague, the illnesses, and ailments have continued unabated for four successive years. As a result of this the wealthy became impoverished and a great number of people died *of the plague*, so that entire families perished in it. I, too, was affected with a grave illness, from which I recovered only about a year ago; then I was taken ill the following year so that (on the margin) for four years I have remained [. . .]. He who has said: *The evil diseases of Egypt* [Deut. vii, 15] . . . he who hiccups does not live . . . ailments and will die . . . otherwise . . . will remain alive.

C

The following letter is from around 1100, from a noble woman in Tripoli, Lebanon, who was a refugee from Jerusalem. She writes to her relatives, imploring them for aid, since she and her children are now destitute. The text appears in S. D. Goitein, "Tyre-Tripoli-ʿArqa: Geniza Documents from the Beginning of the Crusader Period," Jewish Quarterly Review *66 (1975), 69–88.*

[My lord and] illustrious master, may God make your welfare and happiness permanent. [I have to convey] to you, my dear boy, something which I shall immediately describe, . . . Abu 'l-Khayr [was] with al-Muntaṣir. Al-Muntaṣir died [and Abu 'l-Khayr disappeared]. Consequently we are lacking clothing and food to a degree I am unable to describe. But [our relative] Joseph was not remiss in providing us with cash, wheat, and other things. Moreover, he returned to me the collaterals, which I had given him, so that I could place them with someone else. God the exalted, deserves thanks and has imposed on us to thank Him. You must write him a letter of thanks. . . .

About the books of Abu 'l-Khayr I learned only in Tripoli. For the crate was locked and I learned about its contents only in Tripoli . . . I witnessed much bloodshed and experienced everything terrible. I was told that, as soon as al-Muntaṣir died, Abu 'l-Khayr disappeared. He had books and I [pawned] his books and yours for 5 dinars. Your letters concerning them have arrived. If the Nagid—may God keep him in his honored position—manages to send 5 dinars, he will do so in the way of charity and thus ransom all the books, whereupon I shall send them to you. If he (Abu 'l-Khayr) is all right, he will ransom them and send them [to you].

I learned that Abu 'l-Wafāʾ was taken by the Bedouins at the time when his brother disappeared. I am a luckless young woman, suffering both by the hunger of the family, and especially the baby girl, who are with me, and by the bad news I heard about my boy. If my lord, the Nagid, has sworn that he would not go to my aid and visits on me the iniquities committed by Abu 'l-Khayr, have mercy upon me you, your sister, and your mother, as far as you are able to do so.

As far as I am concerned, by our religion, it is better to be captured by the Rūm (the Crusaders), for the prisoners find someone who gives them food and drink, but I, by our religion, am completely without clothing, and I and my children are starving.

Now, do not neglect me. Be mindful of the family bonds and the blood. Show your affection for me by writing to me.

The brother of this man was not remiss towards him, when he first arrived here, until he sued them for an inheritance. This led to a complete rupture between them, and no one of them talks to me . . . Miserable days have come upon me. Must it be so? At the time when I was in Jerusalem, your letters and contributions came to me plentifully, as is proper between two sisters, but now you cut me.

I am writing these lines while the people are on the point of sailing. I have not described in this letter even a fraction of my real state.

Accept for yourself my greeting of peace. And may God extend his peace to my lord the Nagid and my lord the Ḥāvēr. Greetings also to your mother and sister, and to his excellency, your paternal uncle. And regards to everyone under your care.

Address (written upside down as usual):

Right side: To my lord and illustrious master [. . .] Abu 'l-A 'lā, may God keep him.

Left side: [From] his grate[ful] A[bu 'l] Riḍā. Convey and be rewarded! Between the two lines in small script: son of Abu 'l-Khayr, son of . . .

D

This letter is probably the oldest document illustrating the reaction of indigenous Jewish residents to the fall of Jerusalem. Written from the Jewish community of Cairo to that of Ascalon, it illustrates the difficulty of transmitting much-needed funds due to the insecure conditions caused by the crusader conquests. The text appears in S. D. Goitein, "Geniza Sources for the Crusader Period: A Survey," in Outremer, *306–322.*

Boundless [blessings . . .] from the Lord of Peace, who makes peace, [and the angels of peace, and from the Torah,] [the per]fect, all the paths of which are peace, [may come upon] the excellent [congrega]tions, the communal assembly of Ascalon [with greetings from us,] the community at Cairo, known as the residential city, your loving brothers, who inquire about your welfare and wish you all the best. May it please our God to accept from us all prayers and supplications on your behalf.

We beg to inform you—may God grant you permanent welfare and bestow upon you his mercy and grace—that we received tidings of the great disaster and all-comprising visitation, which befell *our brothers, the Jews living in the Holy City, may God restore it forever, the holy Torah scrolls, and the captives*, suffering multiple vexations inflicted upon them *by the enemies of God and haters of his people. We assembled* at *his Excellency, our lord, his Hon(or), Great(ness), and Hol(iness), our master and teacher Mevōrākh, "Leader of the Deliberations," "Sage of the Yeshiva," "the Great Council,"* etc., and found him, his garments rent, sitting on the floor, and shedding tears about what had happened. He addressed us, admonishing and urging us to donate sums for redeeming *the Torah scrolls and the people of God held in captivity by the wicked kingdom, may God destroy and exterminate it.*

We were moved by his warm and *heart-winning* words—*may God preserve his high rank*—and, responding to him, collected one hundred twenty-three dinars for retrieving the Torah scrolls and ransoming *the remnants of Israel who had escaped from the sword.*

This sum we handed over to Mr. Manṣūr, son of Mr. ———, known as "the Son of the Schoolmistress," to bring it to Ascalon. He will let you know what he is carrying and how he acted. We explained to him how he should proceed in this matter. We are sending you these lines in a great hurry because we are afraid *lest our sins might cause failure and, God forbid, our iniquities will be visited upon us. For indeed we are unable to control and console ourselves. Our kidneys are in flames, because of the burning of the house of our God, our glorious sanctuary, may God forgive—, our sun has darkened and our stature is bent . . ."*

10. The Firanj Conquer Jerusalem: The Version of Ibn al-Athir

The English translation here is from Gabrieli, 10–12.

Taj ad-Daula Tutūsh was the Lord of Jerusalem but had given it as a feoff to the amīr Suqmān ibn Artūq the Turcoman. When the Franks defeated the Turks at Antioch the massacre demoralized them, and the Egyptians, who saw that the Turkish armies were being weakened by desertion, besieged Jerusalem under the command of al-Afdal ibn Badr al-Jamali. Inside the city were Artūq's sons, Suqmān and Ilghazi, their cousin Sunij and their nephew

Yaquti. The Egyptians brought more than forty siege engines to attack Jerusalem and broke down the walls at several points. The inhabitants put up a defence, and the siege and fighting went on for more than six weeks. In the end the Egyptians forced the city to capitulate, in Sha'bān 489/August 1096. Suqmān, Ilghazi, and their friends were well treated by al-Afdal, who gave them large gifts of money and let them go free. They made for Damascus and then crossed the Euphrates. Suqmān settled in Edessa and Ilghazi went on into Iraq. The Egyptian governor of Jerusalem was a certain Iftikhār ad-Daula, who was still there at the time of which we are speaking.

After their vain attempt to take Acre by siege, the Franks moved on to Jerusalem and besieged it for more than six weeks. They built two towers, one of which, near Sion, the Muslims burnt down, killing everyone inside it. It had scarcely ceased to burn before a messenger arrived to ask for help and to bring the news that the other side of the city had fallen. In fact Jerusalem was taken from the north on the morning of Friday 22 Sha'bān 492/July 15, 1099. The population was put to the sword by the Franks, who pillaged the area for a week. A band of Muslims barricaded themselves into the Oratory of David and fought on for several days. They were granted their lives in return for surrendering. The Franks honoured their word, and the group left by night for Ascalon. In the Masjid al-Aqsa the Franks slaughtered more than 70,000 people, among them a large number of Imams and Muslim scholars, devout and ascetic men who had left their homelands to live lives of pious seclusion in the Holy Place. The Franks stripped the Dome of the Rock of more than forty silver candelabra, each of them weighing 3,600 drams, and a great silver lamp weighing forty-four Syrian pounds, as well as a hundred and fifty smaller silver candelabra and more than twenty gold ones, and a great deal more booty. Refugees from Syria reached Baghdād in Ramadan, among them the qadi Abu Sa'd al-Hárawi. They told the Caliph's ministers a story that wrung their hearts and brought tears to their eyes. On Friday they went to the Cathedral Mosque and begged for help, weeping so that their hearers wept with them as they described the sufferings of the Muslims in that Holy City: the men killed, the women and children taken prisoner, the homes pillaged. Because of the terrible hardships they had suffered, they were allowed to break the fast. . . .

It was the discord between the Muslim princes, as we shall describe, that enabled the Franks to overrun the country. Abu l-Muzaffar al-Abiwardi composed several poems on this subject, in one of which he says:

We have mingled blood with flowing tears, and there is no room left in us for pity[?]

To shed tears is a man's worst weapon when the swords stir up the
     embers of war.

Sons of Islām, behind you are battles in which heads rolled at your feet.

Dare you slumber in the blessed shade of safety, where life is as soft as
     an orchard flower?

How can the eye sleep between the lids at a time of disasters that would
     waken any sleeper?

While your Syrian brothers can only sleep on the backs of their
     chargers, or in vultures' bellies!

Must the foreigners feed on our ignominy, while you trail behind you
     the train of a pleasant life, like men whose world is at peace?

When blood has been spilt, when sweet girls must for shame hide their
     lovely faces in their hands!

When the white swords' points are red with blood, and the iron of the
     brown lances is stained with gore!

At the sound of sword hammering on lance young children's hair turns
     white.

This is war, and the man who shuns the whirlpool to save his life shall
     grind his teeth in penitence.

This is war, and the infidel's sword is naked in his hand, ready to be
     sheathed again in men's necks and skulls.

This is war, and he who lies in the tomb at Medina seems to raise his
     voice and cry: "O sons of Hashim!

I see my people slow to raise the lance against the enemy: I see the
     Faith resting on feeble pillars.

For fear of death the Muslims are evading the fire of battle, refusing to
     believe that death will surely strike them."

Must the Arab champions then suffer with resignation, while the
     gallant Persians shut their eyes to their dishonour?

11. The Firanj Conquer Jerusalem:
The Version of Ibn al-Qalanisi

*The problems of defining the settlement at Jerusalem in the summer of 1099 were
considerable. Many crusaders planned to return to western Europe, their vows fulfilled and their sins forgiven. Others needed to organize a community and prepare
against a Muslim counterattack. On July 22 Godfrey of Bouillon was elected Guardian of the Holy Sepulcher, the first title given to a Christian ruler in the Holy Land.*

Upon Godfrey's death in 1100 his brother Baldwin assumed the title of King of the Latin Kingdom of Jerusalem. On August 12 the armies of the Caliphate of Cairo met the crusaders in battle at Ascalon. The crusaders won the battle, but political disagreements prevented them from occupying the city. The battle signaled a wave of Islamic resistance, which was made stunningly evident in the destruction of the Crusade of 1101. On the Crusade of 1101, see Jonathan Riley-Smith, The First Crusade and the Idea of Crusading, *(Philadelphia, 1986) 120–134.*

The English translation here is from Gibb, 47–48.

Thereafter they proceeded towards Jerusalem, at the end of Rajab [middle of June] of this year, and the people fled in panic from their abodes before them. They descended first upon al-Ramla, and captured it after the ripening of the crops. Thence they marched to Jerusalem, the inhabitants of which they engaged and blockaded, and having set up the tower against the city they brought it forward to the wall. At length news reached them that al-Afdal was on his way from Egypt with a mighty army to engage in the Holy War against them, and to destroy them, and to succour and protect the city against them. They therefore attacked the city with increased vigour, and prolonged the battle that day until the daylight faded, then withdrew from it, after promising the inhabitants to renew the attack upon them on the morrow. The townsfolk descended from the wall at sunset, whereupon the Franks renewed their assault upon it, climbed up the tower, and gained a footing on the city wall. The defenders were driven down, and the Franks stormed the town and gained possession of it. A number of the townsfolk fled to the sanctuary [of David], and a great host were killed. The Jews assembled in the synagogue, and the Franks burned it over their heads. The sanctuary was surrendered to them on guarantee of safety on the 22nd of Sha'bān [14th July] of this year, and they destroyed the shrines and the tomb of Abraham.

12. Ascalon and Its Aftermath: The Version of Ibn al-Qalanisi

The English translation here is from Gibb, 48–51, 53–54.

Al-Afdal arrived with the Egyptian armies, but found himself forestalled, and having been reinforced by the troops from the Sāhil, encamped outside Ascalon on 14th Ramadān [4th August], to await the arrival of the fleet by sea and of the Arab levies. The army of the Franks advanced against him and attacked him in great force. The Egyptian army was thrown back towards Ascalon, al-Afdal himself taking refuge in the city. The swords of the Franks were given mastery over the Muslims, and death was meted out to the foot-men, volunteers, and townsfolk, about ten thousand souls, and the camp was plundered. Al-Afdal set out for Egypt with his officers, and the Franks be-sieged Ascalon, until at length the townsmen agreed to pay them twenty thousand dinars as protection money, and to deliver this sum to them forth-with. They therefore set about collecting this amount from the inhabitants of the town, but it befel that a quarrel broke out between the [Frankish] leaders, and they retired without having received any of the money. It is said that the number of the people of Ascalon who were killed in this campaign—that is to say of the witnesses, men of substance, merchants, and youths, exclusive of the regular levies—amounted to two thousand seven hundred souls.

A.H. 493
(November 17, 1099, to November 5, 1100)

Al-Malik Shams al-Mulūk Duqāq, son of Tāj al-Dawla, set out from Da-mascus for Diyār Bakr with his 'askar in order to recover possession of it from a governor who had forcibly seized it. He reached al-Rahba by the desert route and thence entered Diyār Bakr, where he occupied Mayyā-fāriqīn, and established a garrison in it for its protection and defence.

In Rajab of this year [May–June, 1100], Bohemond, King of the Franks and lord of Antioch, marched out to the fortress of Afāmiya [Apamea], and besieged it. He remained there for some days and laid waste its crops, when he received news of the arrival at Malatiya of al-Dānishmand with the 'askar of Qilij Arslān b. Sulaimān b. Qutulmish. On learning of this, Bohemond returned to Antioch, and having collected his forces, marched against the Muslim army. But God Most High succoured the Muslims against him, and they killed a great host of his party and he himself was taken captive together with a few of his companions. Messengers were dispatched to his lieutenants at Antioch, demanding the surrender of the city, in the second decade of the month of Safar in the year 494.

In this year also, reports arrived that the water in the wells had sunk at a number of places in the northern districts, and likewise the springs in most of the forts, and the water was low and prices were high in those parts.

A.H. 494
(November 6, 1100, to October 25, 1101)

In this year, the amīr Sukmān b. Ortuq collected a great host of Turkmens, and marched with them against the Franks of al-Ruhā [Edessa] and Sarūj, in the month of First Rabī' [January, 1101]. He captured Sarūj, and was joined by a large body [of volunteers], while the Franks also collected their forces. When the two armies met, the Muslims were on the point of victory over them, but it happened that a party of the Turkmens fled and Sukmān lost heart and retired. The Franks then advanced to Sarūj, recaptured it, and killed and enslaved its inhabitants, except those of them who escaped by flight.

In this year also, Godfrey, lord of Jerusalem, appeared before the fortified port of 'Akkā and made an assault upon it, but he was struck by an arrow and killed. Prior to this he had rebuilt Yāfā [Jaffa] and given it in charge to Tancred. When Godfrey was killed, his brother Baldwin the count, lord of al-Ruhā, set out for Jerusalem with a body of five hundred knights and footmen. On hearing the report of his passage, Shams al-Mulūk Duqāq gathered his forces and moved out against him, together with the amīr Janāh al-Dawla, lord of Hims, and they met him near the port of Bairūt. Janāh al-Dawla pressed forward towards him with his 'askar, and he defeated him and killed some of his companions.

In this year the Franks captured Haifā, on the sea coast, by assault, and Arsūf by capitulation, and they drove its inhabitants out of it. At the end of Rajab also [end of May] they captured Qaisarīya by assault, with the assistance of the Genoese, killed its population, and plundered everything in it.

13. Ascalon and Its Aftermath: The Version of Peter Tudebode

The English translation here is from Hill and Hill, 121–127.

In the meantime a courier came to Tancred and Count Eustace with instructions for them to make preparations to move out to take Nablus. They did so, and accompanied by many knights and footmen arrived at Nablus, where its inhabitants immediately turned over the city to them. Then Duke Godfrey through a messenger commanded Tancred and Godfrey's brother Eustace to rush to him because he had heard that the emir of Babylon was in the city of Ascalon, where he was making plans to capture Jerusalem. He was even bringing chains and other iron shackles with which he could fetter young Christians, whom he would enslave for years. But he had ordered all of the old Christians killed.

When Count Eustace and Tancred received this message, they came with great joy through the mountains, eager for a fight with the Saracens, and so arrived at Caesarea. Finally they turned down the seacoast and came to Ramla, where they spotted many Arabs who were in the vanguard of the approaching conflict. The Christians pursued and seized many captives who reluctantly related complete news on battle plans, location of the enemy, size of their forces, and where they planned to fight. When Count Eustace and Tancred received this information, they immediately dispatched to Jerusalem a courier with these words to Duke Godfrey, the Patriarch Arnulf, and all of the princes: "Know you, battle preparations are being made against us in the city of Ascalon. For this reason hasten there with all possible strength you can muster."

Duke Godfrey commanded all of the people to take energetic steps to move to Ascalon against the enemies of God. Then Godfrey, in company of the Patriarch, the Count of Flanders, and the Bishop of Marturana, went out of Jerusalem on the third day of the week. However, Raymond of Saint-Gilles and Robert the Norman said: "We shall not budge unless we are sure that there will be a battle." Consequently, they commanded their men to move out and verify the report of an approaching encounter. If they found this true the counts ordered: "You return posthaste, and we shall be on the alert."

Their men reconnoitered, saw evidence of battle preparations, rushed back, and reported: "Certainly it is true because we have seen it with our own eyes." Afterwards Duke Godfrey sent the Bishop of Marturana to Jerusalem with commands to Raymond of Saint-Gilles, Robert the Norman, and other lords that they hurry to his side if they wished to engage the enemy. The Bishop of Marturana, returning with messages from the Patriarch and the duke, met Saracens who seized him and led him to a place unknown to us.

Raymond and the other leaders left Jerusalem on the fourth day of the week; and prepared for battle, they marched to serve Godfrey. Peter the Hermit remained in Jerusalem making arrangements and advising the Greeks and Latins for God's sake to form processions, offer prayers, and give alms so that God would bestow victory upon His people. So the clergy, barefooted, clad in sacred garments, and carrying crosses in their hands, made a procession from the Holy Sepulchre to the Temple of the Lord with the litany and other prayers. So the clerics made a procession.

Duke Godfrey, Raymond of Saint-Gilles, the Patriarch, other bishops, and all the remaining leaders gathered at a river which flows on this side of Ascalon. There they found countless numbers of animals, oxen, camels, sheep, donkeys, and other cattle which the Saracens had sent out to hide. But the Christian knights and their retainers seized all of the animals.

At sundown the Patriarch, carrying with him the Cross of our Lord Jesus Christ, which the pilgrims had found in Jerusalem, and also the chaplain of Raymond of Saint-Gilles, carrying with him the Lance of our Lord Jesus Christ, began to order in the name of God, the Holy Sepulchre, the most precious Lance, and the most sacred Cross that no man should turn to any booty until the battle's end and the defeat of God's enemies. But afterwards they could return happily because of their good luck and great victory and seize whatever God had alloted to them.

Because of these instructions the pilgrims of the Holy Sepulchre and the Christian knights at dawn on the sixth day of the week went into a beautiful valley nearby the seacoast and there arrayed their battle lines. Duke Godfrey, who had now been elected king of Jerusalem, drew up his lines; and likewise Raymond of Saint-Gilles, Robert the Norman, Robert of Flanders, Count Eustace, Tancred, and Gaston of Béarn formed their ranks. So six lines began to do battle while the archers were moving out front. Joining them on the right and left flanks, all the animals, camels and other beasts moved out without a leader. The assistance of the animals was indeed a miracle of God. Immediately the Christians began to fight in the name of Jesus Christ and of the Holy Sepulchre as they carried the Lance of our Saviour, and the Patriarch bore a part of the Cross of our Lord.

On the left flank was Duke Godfrey with his troops, and on the right side near the seacoast rode Raymond of Saint-Gilles. In the middle the Count of Normandy, the Count of Flanders, Count Eustace, Tancred, and Gaston of Béarn rode. Then our troops began to move back and forth while the pagans stood at attention prepared for battle.

Each one of the enemy had a water bag strung to his neck to use while fighting the Christians. Count Robert of Flanders charged the enemy hotly, followed by Tancred and all of the others. This sight caused the enemy to turn in flight at once. The battle was on a very large scale because the multitude of pagans was innumerable, and only God knew their number. But divine strength followed us and was so great and powerful that numbers counted little against our soldiers. The enemies of God stood blinded and stunned with open eyes staring at the Jerusalem knights of Christ, but seeing nothing and, trembling because of God's might, they dared not challenge the Christians.

In their great fright they climbed and hid in trees, only to plunge from boughs like falling birds when our men pierced them with arrows and killed them with lances. Later the Christians uselessly decapitated them with swords. Other infidels threw themselves to the ground groveling in terror at the Christians' feet. Then our men cut them to pieces as one slaughters cattle for the meat market. By the seacoast Raymond of Saint-Gilles put to the sword countless numbers, and those who could not flee plunged into the sea. Yet others fled to Ascalon.

The emir approached Ascalon in a dispirited and mournful state and bewailed his fate: "Oh! Mohammed and our God, who ever heard of such a catastrophe? Such might, such spirit, such fortitude, such a hitherto invincible army in the face of Christian or pagan, now overwhelmed by such a puny people who could be squeezed to death in the fist of anyone and overwhelmed. Alas! What sorrow and grief. What else can I say? Why am I conquered by a mendicant people, unarmed and most miserably poor, who have neither scrip nor bag. They now chase our Egyptian people, who often gave them charity when they begged throughout our fatherland in ancient times. To this place I led a great force of knights and footmen including Turks, Saracens, Arabs, Agulani, Kurds, Asurpates, Azymites, and other pagans, whom I now see basely scurrying away on unbridled steeds on the road back to Cairo and who dare not return to face this frail race. So I swear by Mohammed and the names of all of our gods that I shall no longer retain knights by compact because I have been overthrown by this most indolent people. I brought all kinds of arms and apparatus such as machines, and many iron chains with which I thought I could lead the Christians back to Cairo in manacles. All of these preparations I made that I might besiege them in Jerusalem. Instead they came against me two days' journey from Jerusalem. What would have happened to me if I had led my men to the Holy City? Certainly I believe that neither I nor any of my men could have fled from the place. What more can be said? I shall always be disgraced in the land of Cairo."

One of our men seized the standard of the emir. Above the standard was a golden apple on a spear, all encased in silver. Incidentally a standard is called a banner by us. Count Robert of Normandy bought the standard for twenty marks of silver and, in turn, gave it to the Patriarch in honor of God and the Holy Sepulchre. A pilgrim also bought the sword of the emir for sixty bezants. Thus by God's approval all of our enemies were uniformly overwhelmed because they had no more fight left in them. The fleet from all the lands of the infidels lay in harbor there, when the sight of the rout of the emir and his army caused them to hoist sails at once, to take the emir aboard, and put out to the high seas.

Our soldiers returned to the enemy tents and seized huge amounts of gold, silver, garments, and a pile of many goods, in addition to horses, mules, camels, sheep, cattle, asses, and many other animals. Actually all the mountains, hills, and plains were covered with great numbers of their animals. The Christians also found a great cache of arms and proceeded to carry away those things they desired and to pile together those which they did not want and put them to the torch. Then our soldiers returned joyously and gladly, having conquered all of the pagans, and brought back many spoils with them such as camels, asses loaded with biscuits, flour, grain, cheese, bread, oil, and all essential goods.

Because of this booty there was such an abundance among the Christians that an ox could be bought for eight or ten *nummi*, a peck of grain for twelve *nummi*, and a peck of barley for eight *nummi*. For fear that this is not known to all Christians, let them be informed that this battle was fought the day before the Ides of August by the grace of our Lord Jesus Christ, to Whom is the honor and glory now and forever throughout eternity. Amen.

14. The Latins in the Levant: From the Chronicle of Fulcher of Chartres, Book III

The English translation here is from Krey, 280–281.

Consider, I pray, and reflect how in our time God has transferred the West into the East. For we who were Occidentals now have been made Orientals. He who was a Roman or a Frank is now a Galilaean, or an inhabitant of Palestine. One who was a citizen of Rheims or of Chartres now has been made a citizen of Tyre or of Antioch. We have already forgotten the places of our birth; already they have become unknown to many of us, or, at least, are unmentioned. Some already possess here homes and servants which they have received through inheritance. Some have taken wives not merely of their own people, but Syrians, or Armenians, or even Saracens who have received the grace of baptism. Some have with them father-in-law, or daughter-in-law, or son-in-law, or step-son, or step-father. There are here, too, grand-children and great-grandchildren. One cultivates vines, another the fields. The one and the other use mutually the speech and the idioms of the different languages. Different languages, now made common, become known to both races, and faith unites those whose forefathers were strangers. As it is written, "The lion and the ox shall eat straw together." Those who were strangers are now natives; and he who was a sojourner now has become a resident. Our parents and relatives from day to day come to join us, abandoning, even though reluctantly, all that they possess. For those who were poor there, here God makes rich. Those who had few coins, here possess countless besants; and those who had not had a villa, here, by the gift of God, already possess a city. Therefore, why should one who has found the East so favorable return to the West? God does not wish those to suffer want who, carrying their crosses, have vowed to follow Him, nay even unto the end. You see, therefore, that this is a great miracle, and one which must greatly astonish the whole world. Who has ever heard anything like it? Therefore, God wishes to enrich us all and to draw us to Himself as His most dear friends. And because He wishes it, we also freely desire the same; and what is pleasing to Him we do with a loving and submissive heart, that with Him we may reign happily throughout eternity.

IX.

Letters of the Crusaders

The First Crusade, more than any earlier event, produced a vast number of both private and public documents. The letters translated here, with the exception of the last three, were written around the time of the siege of Antioch, the darkest moment of the three-year campaign.

1. The Patriarch of Jerusalem to the Church in the West (Antioch, January 1098)

The English translation here is from Krey, 142–144.

The Patriarch of Jerusalem and the bishops, Greek as well as Latin, and the whole army of God and the Church to the Church of the West; fellowship in celestial Jerusalem, and a portion of the reward of their labor.

Since we are not unaware that you delight in the increase of the Church, and we believe that you are concerned to hear matters adverse as well as prosperous, we hereby notify you of the success of our undertaking. Therefore, be it known to your delight that God has triumphed in forty important cities and in two hundred fortresses of His Church in Romania, as well as in Syria, and that we still have one hundred thousand men in armor, besides the common throng, though many were lost in the first battles. But what is this? What is one man in a thousand? Where we have a count, the enemy have forty kings; where we have a company, the enemy have a legion; where we have a knight, they have a duke; where we have a foot-soldier, they have a count; where we have a camp, they have a kingdom. However, confiding not in numbers, nor in bravery, nor in any presumption, but protected by justice and the shield of Christ, and with St. George, Theodore, Demetrius, and Basil, soldiers of Christ, truly supporting us, we have pierced, and in security are piercing, the ranks of the enemy. On five general battle-fields, God conquering, we have conquered.

But what more? In behalf of God and ourselves, I, apostolic Patriarch, the bishops and the whole order of the Lord, urgently pray, and our spiritual Mother Church calls out: "Come, my most beloved sons, come to me, retake the crown from the hands of the sons of idolatory, who rise against me—the crown from the beginning of the world predestined for you." Come, therefore, we pray, to fight in the army of the Lord at the same place in which the Lord fought, in which Christ suffered for us, leaving to you an example that you should follow his foot-steps. Did not God, innocent, die for us? Let us therefore also die, if it be our lot, not for Him, but for ourselves, that by dying on earth we may live for God. Yet it is [now] not necessary that we should die, nor fight much, for we have [already] sustained the more serious trials, but the task of holding the fortresses and cities has been heavily reducing our army. Come, therefore, hasten to be repaid with the twofold reward—namely, the land of the living and the land flowing with milk and honey and abounding in all good things. Behold, men, by the shedding of our blood the way is open everywhere. Bring nothing with you except only what may be of use to us. Let only the men come; let the women, as yet, be left. From the home in which there are two, let one, the one more ready for battle, come. But those, especially, who have made the vow, [let them come]. Unless they come and discharge their vow, I, apostolic Patriarch, the bishops, and the whole order of the orthodox, do excommunicate them and remove them utterly from the communion of the Church. And do you likewise, that they may not have burial among Christians, unless they are staying for suitable reasons. Come, and receive the twofold glory! This, therefore, also write.

2. Anselm of Ribemont to Manasses II, Archbishop of Rheims (Antioch, February 10, 1098)

Anselm of Ribemont was one of those remarkable fighting men whose generosity to churches and religious communities was conspicuous. He founded the monastery of Ribemont and was a friend of Manasses II of Rheims. The first letter echoes crusaders' concerns for the safety of their property back home, recounts the course of the crusade from Nicaea to Antioch, and lists the dead, for whom the archbishop's prayers are requested. English translation here is from Munro, Letters, 2–5.

To his reverend lord M., by God's grace archbishop of Reims, A. of Ribemont, his vassal and humble servant—greeting.

Inasmuch as you are our lord and as the kingdom of France is especially dependent upon your care, we tell to you, our father, the events which have happened to us and the condition of the army of the Lord. Yet, in the first place, although we are not ignorant that the disciple is not above his master, nor the servant above his lord, we advise and beseech you in the name of our Lord Jesus to consider what you are and what the duty of a priest and bishop is. Provide therefore for our land, so that the lords may keep peace among themselves, the vassals may in safety work on their property, and the ministers of Christ may serve the Lord, leading quiet and tranquil lives. I also pray you and the canons of the holy mother church of Reims, my fathers and lords, to be mindful of us, not only of me and of those who are now sweating in the service of God, but also of the members of the army of the Lord who have fallen in arms or died in peace.

But passing over these things, let us return to what we promised. Accordingly after the army had reached Nicomedia, which is situated at the entrance to the land of the Turks, we all, lords and vassals, cleansed by confession, fortified ourselves by partaking of the body and blood of our Lord, and proceeding thence beset Nicaea on the second day before the Nones of May. After we had for some days besieged the city with many machines and various engines of war, the craft of the Turks, as often before, deceived us greatly. For on the very day on which they had promised that they would surrender, Soliman and all the Turks, collected from neighboring and distant regions, suddenly fell upon us and attempted to capture our camp. However the count of St. Gilles, with the remaining Franks, made an attack upon them and killed an innumerable multitude. All the others fled in confusion. Our men, moreover, returning in victory and bearing many heads fixed upon pikes and spears, furnished a joyful spectacle for the people of God. This was on the seventeenth day before the Kalends of June.

Beset moreover and routed in attacks by night and day, they surrendered unwillingly on the thirteenth day before the Kalends of July. Then the Christians entering the walls with their crosses and imperial standards, reconciled the city to God, and both within the city and outside the gates cried out in Greek and Latin, "Glory to Thee, O God." Having accomplished this, the princes of the army met the emperor who had come to offer them his thanks, and having received from him gifts of inestimable value, some withdrew, with kindly feelings, others with different emotions.

We moved our camp from Nicaea on the fourth day before the Kalends of July and proceeded on our journey for three days. On the fourth day the Turks, having collected their forces from all sides, again attacked the smaller portion of our army, killed many of our men and drove all the remainder back to their camps. Bohemond, count of the [Normans] count Stephen, and the count of Flanders commanded this section. When these were thus terrified by fear, the standards of the larger army suddenly appeared. Hugh the Great and the duke of Lorraine were riding at the head, the count of St. Gilles and the venerable bishop of Puy followed. For they had heard of the battle and were hastening to our aid. The number of the Turks was estimated at 260,000. All of our army attacked them, killed many and routed the rest. On that day I returned from the emperor, to whom the princes had sent me on public business.

After that day our princes remained together and were not separated from one another. Therefore, in traversing the countries of Romania and Armenia we found no obstacle, except that after passing Iconium, we, who formed the advance guard, saw a few Turks. After routing these, on the twelfth day before the Kalends of November, we laid siege to Antioch, and now we captured the neighboring places, the cities of Tarsus and Laodicea and many others, by force. On a certain day, moreover, before we besieged the city, at the "Iron Bridge" we routed the Turks, who had set out to devastate the surrounding country, and we rescued many Christians. Moreover, we led back the horses and camels with very great booty.

While we were besieging the city, the Turks from the nearest redoubt daily killed those entering and leaving the army. The princes of our army seeing this, killed 400 of the Turks who were lying in wait, drove others into a certain river and led back some as captives. You may be assured that we are now besieging Antioch with all diligence, and hope soon to capture it. The city is supplied to an incredible extent with grain, wine, oil and all kinds of food.

I ask, moreover, that you and all whom this letter reaches pray for us and for our departed brethren. Those who have fallen in battle are: at Nicaea, Baldwin of Ghent, Baldwin *Chalderuns*, who was the first to make an attack upon the Turks and who fell in battle on the Kalends of July, Robert of Paris, Lisiard of Flanders, Hilduin of *Mansgarbio* [Mazingarbe], *Ansellus* of *Caium* [Anseau of Caien], Manasses of *Claromonte* [Clermont], *Laudunensis*.

Those who died from sickness: at Nicaea, Guy of *Vitreio*, Odo, of *Vernolio* [Verneuil (?)], Hugh of Reims; at the fortress of Sparnum, the venerable abbot Roger, my chaplain; at Antioch, Alard of *Spiniaeco*, Hugh of *Calniaco*.

Again and again I beseech you, readers of this letter, to pray for us, and you, my lord archbishop, to order this to be done by your bishops. And know for certain that we have captured for the Lord 200 cities and fortresses. May our mother, the western church, rejoice that she has begotten such men, who are acquiring for her so glorious a name and who are so wonderfully aiding the eastern church. And in order that you may believe this, know that you have sent to me a tapestry by Raymond *"de Castello."* Farewell.

3. Stephen, Count of Blois and Chartres, to His Wife, Adele (Antioch, March 29, 1098)

The English translation here is from Munro, Letters, *5–8.*

Count Stephen to Adele, his sweetest and most amiable wife, to his dear children, and to all his vassals of all ranks—his greeting and blessing.

You may be very sure, dearest, that the messenger whom I sent to give you pleasure, left me before Antioch safe and unharmed, and through God's grace in the greatest prosperity. And already at that time, together with all the chosen army of Christ, endowed with great valor by Him, we had been continuously advancing for twenty-three weeks toward the home of our Lord Jesus. You may know for certain, my beloved, that of gold, silver and many other kind of riches I now have twice as much as your love had assigned to me when I left you. For all our princes, with the common consent of the whole army, against my own wishes, have made me up to the present time the leader, chief and director of their whole expedition.

You have certainly heard that after the capture of the city of Nicaea we fought a great battle with the perfidious Turks and by God's aid conquered them. Next we conquered for the Lord all Romania and afterwards Cappadocia. And we learned that there was a certain Turkish prince Assam, dwelling in Cappadocia; thither we directed our course. All his castles we conquered by force and compelled him to flee to a certain very strong castle situated on a high rock. We also gave the land of that Assam to one of our chiefs and in order that he might conquer the above-mentioned Assam, we left there with him many soldiers of Christ. Thence, continually following the wicked Turks, we drove them through the midst of Armenia, as far as the great river Euphrates. Having left all their baggage and beasts of burden on the bank, they fled across the river into Arabia.

The bolder of the Turkish soldiers, indeed, entering Syria, hastened by forced marches night and day, in order to be able to enter the royal city of Antioch before our approach. The whole army of God learning this gave due praise and thanks to the omnipotent Lord. Hastening with great joy to the aforesaid chief city of Antioch, we besieged it and very often had many conflicts there with the Turks; and seven times with the citizens of Antioch and with the innumerable troops coming to its aid, whom we rushed to meet, we fought with the fiercest courage, under the leadership of Christ. And in all these seven battles, by the aid of the Lord God, we conquered and most assuredly killed an innumerable host of them. In those battles, indeed, and in very many attacks made upon the city, many of our brethren and followers were killed and their souls were borne to the joys of paradise.

We found the city of Antioch very extensive, fortified with incredible strength and almost impregnable. In addition, more than 5,000 bold Turkish soldiers had entered the city, not counting the Saracens, Publicans, Arabs, Turcopolitans, Syrians, Armenians, and other different races of whom an infinite multitude had gathered together there. In fighting against these enemies of God and of our own we have, by God's grace, endured many sufferings and innumerable evils up to the present time. Many also have already exhausted all their resources in this very holy passion. Very many of our Franks, indeed, would have met a temporal death from starvation, if the clemency of God and our money had not succoured them. Before the above-mentioned city of Antioch indeed, throughout the whole winter we suffered for our Lord Christ from excessive cold and enormous torrents of rain. What some say about the impossibility of bearing the heat of the sun throughout Syria is untrue, for the winter there is very similar to our winter in the west.

When truly Caspian [Bagi Seian], the emir of Antioch—that is, prince and lord—perceived that he was hard pressed by us, he sent his son Sensodolo [Chems Eddaulah] by name, to the prince who holds Jerusalem, and to the prince of Calep, Rodoam [Rodoanus], and to Docap [Deccacus Ibn Toutousch], prince of Damascus. He also sent into Arabia to Bolianuth and to Carathania to Hamelnuth. These five emirs with 12,000 picked Turkish horsemen suddenly came to aid the inhabitants of Antioch. We, indeed, ignorant of all this, had sent many of our soldiers away to the cities and fortresses. For there are one hundred and sixty-five cities and fortresses throughout Syria which are in our power. But a little before they reached the city, we attacked them at three leagues' distance with 700 soldiers, on a certain plain near the "Iron Bridge." God, however, fought for us, His faithful, against them. For on that day, fighting in the strength that God gives, we conquered them and killed an innumerable multitude—God continually fighting for us—and we also carried back to the army more than two hundred of their heads, in order that the people might rejoice on that account. The emperor of Babylon also sent Saracen messengers to our army with letters, and through these he established peace and concord with us.

I love to tell you, dearest, what happened to us during Lent. Our princes had caused a fortress to be built before a certain gate which was between our camp and the sea. For the Turks daily issuing from this gate, killed some of our men on their way to the sea. The city of Antioch is about five leagues' distance from the sea. For this reason they sent the excellent Bohemond and Raymond, count of St. Gilles, to the sea with only sixty horsemen, in order that they might bring mariners to aid in this work. When, however, they were returning to us with those mariners, the Turks collected an army, fell suddenly upon our two leaders and forced them to a perilous flight. In that unexpected flight we lost more than 500 of our foot-soldiers—to the glory of God. Of our horsemen, however, we lost only two, for certain.

4. Anselm of Ribemont to Manasses II, Archbishop of Rheims (Antioch, July 1098)

The English translation here is from Munro, Letters, 229–232.

In the name of the Lord!

To his lord and father, Manasses, by grace of God venerable Archbishop of Reims, Anselm of Ribemont, his loyal vassal and humble servant; greeting.

Let your Eminence, reverend father and lord, know that, even though absent and not present, we are daily asking aid in our hearts from you—not only from you, but, also, from all the sons of the Holy Mother Church of Reims, in whom we have the greatest faith. Likewise, inasmuch as you are our lord, and the counsel of the whole kingdom of France is especially dependent upon you, we are keeping you, father, informed of whatever happy and adverse events have happened to us. Let the others, moreover, be informed through you, that you may share equally in our sufferings, and rejoice with us in our success.

We have informed you how we fared in the siege and capture of Nicaea, in our departure thence and our journey through all Romania and Armenia. It now remains for us to tell you a little about the siege of Antioch, the many kinds of danger we there tasted, and the innumerable battles which we fought against the King of Aleppo, the King of Damascus, and against the adulterous King of Jerusalem.

Antioch has been besieged by the army of the Lord since the thirteenth day before the Kalends of November with exceeding valor and courage beyond words. What unheard of battles you might have perceived there at a certain gateway to the west! How marvelous it would seem to you, were you

present, to see them daily rushing forth through six gates—both they and ourselves fighting for safety and life! At that time our princes, seeking to enclose
the city more and more closely, first besieged the eastern gate, and Bohemund,
having built a fort there, stationed a part of his army in it. However, since
our princes then felt somewhat elated, God, who chasteneth every son whom
he loveth, so chastened us that hardly seven hundred horses could be found
in our army; and thus, not because we lacked proven and valiant men, but
from lack of horses, or food, or through excessive cold, almost all were dying.
The Turks, moreover, supplied with horses and all necessities in abundance,
were wont daily to ride around our camp, a certain stream which lay between
serving as a wall. There was likewise a castle of the Turks almost eight miles
away; and these Turks were daily killing many of our men, who were going
back and forth from our army. Our princes went out against them and with
God's help put them to flight and killed many of them. Therefore the ruler of
Antioch, seeing himself afflicted, called the King of Damascus to his aid. By
God's providence, this King met Bohemund and the Count of Flanders, who
had gone to find food with a part of our army, and, God's help prevailing, he
was defeated and routed by them. The ruler of Antioch, still concerned about
his safety, sent to the King of Aleppo and aroused him with promises of very
great wealth, to the end that he should come with all his forces. Upon his arrival, our princes went forth from camp, and that day, God being their helper,
with seven hundred knights and a few foot-soldiers they defeated twelve thousand Turks with their King, put them to flight, and killed many of them. Our
men regained not a few horses from that battle, and returned rejoicing with
victory. Growing stronger and stronger, therefore, from that day our men
took counsel with renewed courage as to how they might besiege the western
gate which cut off access to the sea, wood, and fodder. By common agreement, therefore, Bohemund and the Count of St. Gilles went to the coast to
fetch those who were staying there. Meanwhile, those who had remained to
look after the possessions, seeking to acquire a name for themselves, went
out incautiously one day after breakfast, near that western gate from which
they were ingloriously repulsed and put to flight. On the third day after this,
Bohemund and the Count of St. Gilles, on their way back, sent word to the
princes of the army to meet them, [intending] together to besiege the gate.
However, since the latter delayed for a short time, Bohemund and the Count
of St. Gilles were beaten and put to flight. Therefore all our men, grieving
and bewailing their disgrace, as well, for a thousand of our men fell that day,
formed their lines and defeated and put to flight the Turks, who offered great
resistance. On this day, moreover, almost fourteen hundred of the enemy perished both by weapons and in the river, which was swollen with winter rains.

And so, when this had been accomplished, our men began to build the fortress, which they strengthened, also, with a double moat and a very strong wall, as well as with two towers. In it they placed the Count of St. Gilles with machine men and bowmen. Oh, with what great labor we established the fortress! One part of our army served the eastern front, another looked after the camp, while all the rest worked on this fortress. Of the latter, the machine men and bowmen kept watch on the gate; the rest, including the princes themselves, did not stop in the work of carrying stones, and building the wall. Why recount the trials of many kinds, which, even if passed over in silence, are sufficiently evident in themselves—hunger, intemperate weather, and the desertion of faint-hearted soldiers? The more bitter they were, the more ready our men were in enduring them. Yet, indeed, we think that we should by no means pass in silence the fact that on a certain day the Turks pretended that they would surrender the city and carried the deception so far as to receive some of our men among them, and several of their men came out to us. While this was going on in this manner, they, like the faithless people that they were, set a trap for us in which Walo, the Constable, and others of them as well as of us were destroyed. A few days after this, moreover, it was announced to us that *Corbara*, chief of the army of the king of the Persians, had sworn to our death. God, however, who does not desert those who place their trust in Him, did not abandon His people, but on the Nones of June compassionately gave to us the city of Antioch, which three of its citizens betrayed. We, however, devastated the city, and on that same day killed all the pagans in it, except some who were holding out in the castle of the city.

5. The People of Lucca on Crusade to All Faithful Christians (Antioch, October 1098)

The English translation here is from Krey, 161–162; the Latin text is in Hagenmeyer, 165–167.

To the primates, archbishops, bishops, and other rectors, and to all the faithful of the lands of Christ anywhere; the clergy and people of Lucca [send] greeting full of peace and gladness in the Lord.

To the praise and glory of the Redeemer, our Lord Jesus Christ, we are truly and faithfully making known to all [the news] which we received truly and faithfully from participants in the affairs themselves—at what time, with what great triumph, the most mighty right hand of Christ gave complete victory over the pagans to our brethren, His champions, after trial and perils.

A certain citizen of ours, Bruno by name, known and very dear to all of us, in the year preceding this, went with the ships of the Angles even to Antioch itself. There, as a partner in work and danger, sharer of triumph and joy, he fought along with the fighters, starved with the starving and conquered, also, with the conquering; and when the complete victory had already been achieved, and he had rejoiced three weeks there with all, he returned to us, after a happy voyage. Placing him in our midst, we received from him the pure and simple truth of the matter—lo! in his own account, as follows:

"When we who were voyaging by sea had come to Antioch, the army, which had gathered together from everywhere by land, had already surrounded the city in siege, though not very well. On the following day, our princes proceeded to the sea, for the sake of visiting us. They urged us to get together an abundant supply of wood for the construction of war engines, which we did at great expense. On the third day, moreover, before the Nones of March, that is the first Friday, our princes decided to erect a fortress at the western gate of the city. This fortress, a very short ballista-shot away [from the city], is now called by the name of the Blessed Mary. There, on that same day, in an attack of the Turks, in which they killed 2,055 of our men, we killed 800 of the enemy. From the third day, moreover, when the fortress had been erected, until the third day before the Nones of June, our men endured many hardships, and, weakened by hunger and the sword, they toiled there at great cost. However, on this day the city was captured in the following manner: Four brothers, noble men of Antioch, on the second day of June promise to surrender the city to Bohemund, Robert Curtose, and Robert, Count of Flanders. These, however, with the common assent of all our princes, at nightfall conduct the whole army to the wall of the city, without the knowledge of the Turks. And in the morning, when the citizens of Antioch open the gates to receive the three named princes alone, according to promise, all of our men suddenly rush in together. There is the greatest clamor: our men obtain all the fortified places, except the very high citadel; the Turks—these they kill, those they hurl to destruction over the precipice."

6. Godfrey of Bouillon, Raymond of St. Gilles, and Daimbert to Pope Paschal II (Laodicea, September 1099)

Urban II had died on July 29, 1099. His successor, Paschal II (1099–1118), continued his policies and reminded bishops and archbishops that those who had assumed the cross and had not yet gone on crusade must now do so unless poverty alone held them back. If they did not go, they were to be considered infamous, a legal condi-

tion that entailed substantial disabilities. Paschal also insisted that the deserters at Antioch were to remain excommunicated unless they promise to return to the East. (See below, "Pope Paschal II to the Clergy in Gaul," in this section.) Paschal's statement was especially important because, as this letter states, the crusaders' capture of Jerusalem came at a great cost in men and resources. The English translation here is from Munro, Letters, 8–11.

To lord Paschal, pope of the Roman church, to all the bishops, and to the whole Christian people, from the archbishop of Pisa, duke Godfrey, now, by the grace of God, defender of the church of the Holy Sepulchre, Raymond, count of St. Gilles, and the whole army of God, which is in the land of Israel, greeting.

Multiply your supplications and prayers in the sight of God with joy and thanksgiving, since God has manifested His mercy in fulfilling by our hands what He had promised in ancient times. For after the capture of Nicaea, the whole army, made up of more than three hundred thousand soldiers, departed thence. And, although this army was so great that it could have in a single day covered all Romania and drunk up all the rivers and eaten up all the growing things, yet the Lord conducted them amid so great abundance that a ram was sold for a penny and an ox for twelve pennies or less. Moreover, although the princes and kings of the Saracens rose up against us, yet, by God's will, they were easily conquered and overcome. Because, indeed, some were puffed up by these successes, God opposed to us Antioch, impregnable to human strength. And there He detained us for nine months and so humbled us in the siege that there were scarcely a hundred good horses in our whole army. God opened to us the abundance of His blessing and mercy and led us into the city, and delivered the Turks and all of their possessions into our power.

Inasmuch as we thought that these had been acquired by our own strength and did not worthily magnify God who had done this, we were beset by so great a multitude of Turks that no one dared to venture forth at any point from the city. Moreover, hunger so weakened us that some could scarcely refrain from eating human flesh. It would be tedious to narrate all the miseries which we suffered in that city. But God looked down upon His people whom He had so long chastised and mercifully consoled them. Therefore, He at first revealed to us, as a recompense for our tribulation and as a pledge of victory, His lance which had laid hidden since the days of the apostles. Next, He so fortified the hearts of the men, that they who from sickness or hunger had been unable to walk, now were enbued with strength to seize their weapons and manfully to fight against the enemy.

After we had triumphed over the enemy, as our army was wasting away at Antioch from sickness and weariness and was especially hindered by the dissensions among the leaders, we proceeded into Syria, stormed Barra and Marra, cities of the Saracens, and captured the fortresses in that country. And while we were delaying there, there was so great a famine in the army that the Christian people now ate the putrid bodies of the Saracens. Finally, by the divine admonition, we entered into the interior of Hispania, and the most bountiful, merciful and victorious hand of the omnipotent Father was with us. For the cities and fortresses of the country through which we were proceeding sent ambassadors to us with many gifts and offered to aid us and to surrender their walled places. But because our army was not large and it was the unanimous wish to hasten to Jerusalem, we accepted their pledges and made them tributaries. One of the cities forsooth, which was on the sea-coast, had more men than there were in our whole army. And when those at Antioch and Laodicea and Archas heard how the hand of the Lord was with us, many from the army who had remained in those cities followed us to Tyre. Therefore, with the Lord's companionship and aid, we proceeded thus as far as Jerusalem.

And after the army had suffered greatly in the siege, especially on account of the lack of water, a council was held and the bishops and princes ordered that all with bare feet should march around the walls of the city, in order that He who entered it humbly in our behalf might be moved by our humility to open it to us and to exercise judgment upon His enemies. God was appeased by this humility and on the eighth day after the humiliation He delivered the city and His enemies to us. It was the day indeed on which the primitive church was driven thence, and on which the festival of the dispersion of the apostles is celebrated. And if you desire to know what was done with the enemy who were found there, know that in Solomon's Porch and in his temple our men rode in the blood of the Saracens up to the knees of their horses.

Then, when we were considering who ought to hold the city, and some moved by love for their country and kinsmen wished to return home, it was announced to us that the king of Babylon had come to Ascalon with an innumerable multitude of soldiers. His purpose was, as he said, to lead the Franks, who were in Jerusalem, into captivity, and to take Antioch by storm. But God had determined otherwise in regard to us.

Therefore, when we learned that the army of the Babylonians was at Ascalon, we went down to meet them, leaving our baggage and the sick in Jerusalem with a garrison. When our army was in sight of the enemy, upon our knees we invoked the aid of the Lord, that He who in our other adversities had strengthened the Christian faith, might in the present battle break the strength of the Saracens and of the devil and extend the kingdom of the church of Christ from sea to sea, over the whole world. There was no delay; God was present when we cried for His aid, and furnished us with so great boldness, that one who saw us rush upon the enemy would have taken us for a herd of deer hastening to quench their thirst in running water. It was wonderful, indeed, since there were in our army not more than 5,000 horsemen and 15,000 foot-soldiers, and there were probably in the enemy's army 100,000 horsemen and 400,000 foot-soldiers. Then God appeared wonderful to His servants. For before we engaged in fighting, by our very onset alone, He turned this multitude in flight and scattered all their weapons, so that if they wished afterwards to attack us, they did not have the weapons in which they trusted. There can be no question how great the spoils were, since the treasures of the king of Babylon were captured. More than 100,000 Moors perished there by the sword. Moreover, their panic was so great that about 2,000 were suffocated at the gate of the city. Those who perished in the sea were innumerable. Many were entangled in the thickets. The whole world was certainly fighting for us, and if many of ours had not been detained in plundering the camp, few of the great multitude of the enemy would have been able to escape from the battle.

And although it may be tedious, the following must not be omitted: On the day preceding the battle the army captured many thousands of camels, oxen and sheep. By the command of the princes these were divided among the people. When we advanced to battle, wonderful to relate, the camels formed in many squadrons and the sheep and oxen did the same. Moreover, these animals accompanied us, halting when we halted, advancing when we advanced, and charging when we charged. The clouds protected us from the heat of the sun and cooled us.

Accordingly, after celebrating the victory, the army returned to Jerusalem. Duke Godfrey remained there; the count of St. Gilles, Robert, count of Normandy, and Robert, count of Flanders, returned to Laodicea. There they found the fleet belonging to the Pisans and to Bohemond. After the archbishop of Pisa had established peace between Bohemond and our leaders, Raymond prepared to return to Jerusalem for the sake of God and his brethren.

Therefore, we call upon you of the catholic church of Christ and of the whole Latin church to exult in the so admirable bravery and devotion of your brethren, in the so glorious and very desirable retribution of the omnipotent God, and in the so devoutly hoped-for remission of all our sins through the grace of God. And we pray that He may make you—namely, all bishops, clerks and monks who are leading devout lives, and all the laity—to sit down at the right hand of God, who liveth and reigneth God for ever and ever. And we ask and beseech you in the name of our Lord Jesus, who has ever been with us and aided us and freed us from all our tribulations, to be mindful of your brethren who return to you, by doing them kindnesses and by paying their debts, in order that God may recompense you and absolve you from all your sins and grant you a share in all the blessings which either we or they have deserved in the sight of the Lord. Amen.

7. Manasses II, Archbishop of Rheims, to Lambert, Bishop of Arras (1099)

The English translation here is from Krey, 264–265.

Manasses, by grace of God Archbishop of Reims, to Lambert, his brother, Bishop of Arras; greeting in Jesus Christ.

Be it known to you, dearest brother, that a true and joyful rumor has recently come to our ears, which we believe to have come down not from human knowledge, but from the Divine Majesty—to wit: Jerusalem stands on high with joy and gladness which it has so gloriously received from God in our times. Jerusalem, the city of our redemption and glory, delights with inconceivable joy, because through the effort and incomparable might of the sons of God it has been liberated from most cruel pagan servitude. And let us also be joyful, whose Christian faith in such times as these has been placed in a mirror of eternal clarity.

We, therefore, admonished, summoned, and compelled, not only through the letters of Lord Pope Paschal, but, also, through the most humble prayers of Duke Godfrey, whom the army of Christ by divine direction elevated as King, as well as through the mellifluous entreaties of Lord Arnulf, whom they have unanimously chosen as Patriarch of the see of Jerusalem— we command with equal affection that you have every one of your parish churches, without fail, pray with fasts and almsgiving that the King of Kings and the Lord of Lords crown the King of the Christians with victory against the enemy, and the Patriarch with religion and wisdom against the sects and deceptions of heretics. We command, likewise, and admonish, through your obedience, that you constrain by threat all who vowed to go on the expedition and took the sign of the cross upon themselves to set out for Jerusalem, if they are vigorous of body and have the means to accomplish the journey. As for the others, however, do not cease skilfully and most devoutly to admonish them not to neglect aiding the people of God, so that not only the first, but likewise the last, may receive the shilling which is promised to those laboring in the vineyard. Farewell.

Pray for the Bishop of Puy, for the Bishop of Orange, for Anselm of Ribemont, and for all the others who lie at rest, crowned with so glorious a martyrdom.

8. Pope Paschal II to the Clergy in Gaul (1099)

The English translation here is from Krey, 279.

Paschal, bishop, servant of the servants of God, to all archbishops, bishops, and abbots throughout Gaul; greeting and apostolic blessing.

We owe boundless gratitude to the compassion of Almighty God, since in our time He has deigned to wrest the Church in Asia from the hands of the Turks and to open to Christian soldiers the very city of the Lord's suffering and burial. However, we ought to follow Divine grace with what means He has given us, and effectively aid our brethren who have remained in those districts which were once the lands of the people of Palestine or Canaan. Urge, therefore, all the soldiers of your region to strive for remission and forgiveness of their sins by hastening to our Mother Church of the East; especially compel those who have assumed the sign of the cross in pledge of this journey to hasten thither, unless they are prevented by the hindrance of poverty. Moreover, we decree that those be held in disgrace who left the siege of Antioch through weak or questionable faith; let them remain in excommunication, unless they affirm with certain pledges that they will return. We furthermore command that all their possessions be restored to those brethren who are returning after the victory of the Lord, just as you recall was ordained in a synodal decree by Urban, our predecessor of blessed memory. Do thus in all matters, being so zealous in your duty that by common zeal our Mother Church of the East may be restored to her due state, the Lord granting it.

X.

Three Problematic Texts

The three texts that conclude this volume illustrate a few of the problems still posed by the full range of source materials. The first is a letter attributed to Pope Sergius IV (1009–1012) that has been interpreted as prefiguring Urban II's crusade call by nearly a century. The second is the opening of the earliest written part of the "Epic Cycle of the Crusades," one of the means by which the idea of crusading was conveyed to a vernacular-speaking audience in the twelfth, thirteenth, and fourteenth centuries. The third is a triumphal song whose focus is the glory of the city of Jerusalem and its conquest in 1099, found in the same manuscript that contains the better known poems known as the Carmina Burana. *All three texts offer dimensions of crusade history that need to be considered along with the narrative and epistolary sources printed above.*

1. The "Encyclical" of "Sergius IV"

*In 1857 the French historian Jules Lair edited and published the text of a letter attributed to Pope Sergius IV (1009–1012), which an earlier collector of manuscripts, Nicholas-Joseph Foucault (1643–1722), had discovered in the monastery of Moissac in Languedoc and passed on to Colbert, the minister of Louis XIV, whose collection later went to the Bibliothèque National in Paris, where Lair found and printed it. The letter purports to be an invitation to European Christians to take the Holy Land (in the wake of the destruction of the Church of the Holy Sepulcher by the Caliph al-Hakim in 1009). Shortly after the publication of the document, a number of scholars challenged its authenticity, and the debate has continued until the present. Until very recently, the dominant view has been that of Alexander Gieysztor, presented in "The Genesis of the Crusades: The Encyclical of Sergius IV (1009–1012)" (*Medievalia et Humanistica, *fasc. 5 [1948], 3–23, and fasc. 6 [1950], 3–34), with a new Latin edition of the letter, which holds that the letter is a late eleventh-century forgery, probably created at Moissac in 1096 and intended to serve as part of the* excitatoria, *or propaganda, for the First Crusade. More recently, Hans Martin*

Schaller, in "Zur Kreuzzugsenzyklika Papst Sergius' IV" (in Papsttum, Kirche und Recht im Mittalalter: Festschrift für Horst Fuhrmann zum 65. Geburtstag, ed. Hubert Mordek [Tübingen, 1991], 135–153), has re-edited the letter and argued for a date far closer to—and very likely contemporary with—Sergius's pontificate, exploiting sources not used by earlier scholars but also distinguishing sharply between the letter of Sergius and later statements of Urban II.

The text remains a puzzle, and it is included here to suggest both the problem of the chronology of "the crusade idea" and the ambiguity of some of the source material for it. It is worth pointing out that John France, in "The Destruction of Jerusalem and the First Crusade" (Journal of Ecclesiastical History 47 [1996], 1–17), accepts the Gieysztor thesis and also argues that the destruction of the church was largely forgotten in western Europe by the end of the eleventh century: "It was an event that has passed out of human memory."

The text has been translated for this volume by Thomas G. Waldman from the Latin edition of Hans Martin Schaller cited above.

Sergius, bishop, servant of the servants of God, to all catholic kings, archbishops, bishops, abbots, priests, deacons, subdeacons, and all other members of the clergy, dukes, marquises, counts, and greater and lesser persons having perpetual hope in almighty God, dearest greeting and apostolic blessing.

Since we, my sons, recognize that we have been redeemed by the precious blood of our Lord Jesus Christ, all the more we ought to bless and praise him and with constant and great humility offer him pleasing gifts. For God, dearest sons, humbly bore many things on our behalf so that he might free us unharmed from the jaws of demons: blows, abuse, the crown of thorns, the cross, and even death he underwent for us, and, on the third day, as the sacred history testifies, he rose from the dead and in the sight of the disciples he returned to the heaven eternal in the glory of the Father. Therefore, some brethren, led by the love of Jesus, have sought out that place, which he touched with his own feet, even searching for the Mount of Calvary, where he healed us by his own wounds, and venerating the Mount of Olives, and especially the tomb in which he lay. Honoring Jesus by their devotion, these brethren have left their own homelands, and in the words of Paul, "in toil and hardship, through many a sleepless night, in hunger and thirst, often without food, in cold and exposure [2 Cor. 11:27]," have not ceased throughout Jerusalem, a place foreign to them, to follow the route of Jesus Christ. They put aside temporal possessions and bore their own crosses as if they might become disciples and, as it is ordered, trod the way of Jesus with only the cross. Christ committed his tomb to us where some penitents sought the celestial kingdom.

We are making this known to all Christian people since a messenger coming to the Apostolic See from eastern parts announced that the holy tomb of the redeemer our Lord Jesus Christ has been destroyed to its very foundations by the unclean hands of pagans. On account of its destruction the universal church and the city of Rome are deeply troubled and put in a state of great lamentation. Even the whole world stands in lamentation and the people tremble with great sighs. I will remove the dream from my eyes and I will make my heart a companion to grief, since never did we read—not in the writings of the prophets or the psalms or any doctor of the church—that the tomb of the redeemer would be destroyed, but rather that it would stand till the end of time. For the prophet said: "His tomb shall be glorious forever [Is. 11:10; Geb. 13:15]."

Therefore, may the Christian intention be known. I myself, if it will be pleasing to the Lord, desire to set sail with all the Romans, Italians, and Tuscans, and any other Christian who wishes to go with us to the Saracens, God willing, since with anger in my heart I desire to kill them all and restore the holy tomb of the redeemer.

My sons, let not the rising sea frighten you or the fury of war scare you, for the divinity has promised: He who in the present will lose his life for Christ, let him not lose courage, for he will regain it in the future. For this fight is not concerning some poor kingdom, but the eternal dominion. It is our task to make a beginning; however, it is the Lord's to punish. For we who are about to pass through this world, let us fight against the enemies of God so that we are worthy to rejoice with him in heaven. It seems right concerning what can be done that we receive your counsel and aid. Inspired by the divine clemency, with all the Romans and all of Italy and equally Venice and the citizens of Genoa, with your reward and aid from all the people, we wish to construct a thousand ships in this year, with which we may go into parts of Syria so we might avenge the redeemer and his tomb. Any time now, vigorous defenders, cross the high seas; before your eyes recognize the day of judgment when with Christ, if you act well, you will possess all joys. Come, sons, defend God and gain the eternal kingdom. I hope, I believe, and most certainly I hold true that through the virtue of our Lord Jesus Christ victory will be ours as it was in the days of Titus and Vespasian, who avenged the death of the son of God even though at that time they had not received baptism, but when after, through victory, they attained the imperial honor of the Romans, they received a pardon for their sins. And we, if we will do likewise, without a doubt may remain in eternal life.

We make known to you that we have found out that many people who are from the city placed by the seashore are most faithful to us. They have sent their own letter, because on their own they have sold their things; for this purpose they sent away their sons and parents, work on the ships, make arms, and for all the expeditions they prepare the means so they may seek to show themselves on those shores across the sea. They are making haste to avenge the holy tomb, and they desire to fulfill these words of the evangelist: "And everyone who has left houses or brothers or sister or father or mother or children or lands, for my name's sake, will receive a hundred-fold and inherit eternal life [Matt. 19:29]." Through all these words we command you and caution you concerning the safety of your souls so you may persevere in good works.

The blessed apostle Peter desired to warn the sheep entrusted to him by the Lord saying, "Humble yourselves therefore under the mighty hand of God that in due time he may exalt you [1 Peter 5:6]." And elsewhere, "Be sober, be watchful. Your adversary the devil prowls around like a roaring lion seeking someone to devour. Resist him, firm in your faith [1 Peter 5:8–9]. For faith without works is dead [James 2:20, 26]. For faith separates good from evil and does good."

We ought to know and understand that before the coming of our Lord Savior the devil was ruling in the world. He held sway over the empire of death and all people (sinners and the just), leaving the body descended into hell for the reason that Adam the first man in paradise had disobeyed the commandment of God. But because God saw that the whole world would perish he had mercy on the human race. "He sent forth his Son, born of woman, born under the law to redeem those who were under the law [Gal. 4:4–5]."

The Son of God deigned to descend from the seat of the Father, that is the word in the womb of the blessed virgin Mary, and thus he humbly came so he might conquer the devil, the author of death, and free the human race through the cross. If God, who is without sin, bore so much for us, how much more we ought to bear for our sins.

We wish and we order that for the safety of your soul by the authority of almighty God and all the saints and our own counsel that all churches, provinces, places, and persons—great and small—may have peace among themselves, since without peace no one can serve God, as he himself said to the apostles: "Peace I leave with you; my peace I give to you [John 14:27]. In peace I sent you away, in peace I will find you." And in another place: "Blessed are the peacemakers, for they shall be called sons of God [Matt. 5:9]." And so he will be called son of God who now begins to make peace; for he does not wish to be called son of God who is unwilling to embrace peace. He denies for himself to have God the Father who scorns to make peace. The peace of Christ leads to eternal salvation; the peace that is in the devil leads to perpetual damnation, as Judas showed, who through peace betrayed the Lord our redeemer. A bitter kiss is the damnation of the soul. And you, dearest sons, may you have perfect peace, so you may acquire eternal life. And he who will not have done this or will not have fulfilled this, as is written above, may he know that he is not catholic or to be received by the Lord, since through the peace and prayer of all Christians concerning the tomb of the redeemer we wish to have victory and without end reign with him in heaven. Therefore, whoever wishes to come to this battle of the Lord, as we said above, let him come with us. However, he who cannot do this, may he help now in working on the ships and preparing arms and by the hand of bishop John may he contribute aid to this so the pontifical order can be carried out and so that he may be a councillor of peace and be numbered among the defenders of God. May our *nuntio* be commended to you all and be received with our letter so that when he will have returned to us through the divine aid we may be worthy to give manifold thanks to God and to you.

Farewell, farewell everywhere and always in the Lord.

2. *La Chanson d'Antioche*

La Chanson d'Antioche *(The Song of Antioch) as it has come down to us is the work of the late twelfth-century poet Graindor de Douai, who wrote between 1175 and 1200. The oldest materials in the poem, however, appear to have dated from the earlier twelfth century, and Graindor and his successors through the mid-fourteenth century added more and more episodes to the original account of the siege of Antioch in 1097. Just how early the original materials are is hard to ascertain, although the passages translated here echo some of the material in sources more or less contemporary with the First Crusade. Graindor himself seems to indicate that he is narrating a much older poem, and there is plenty of evidence of songs and stories contemporary with the events of 1097–1099.*

There is a fascinating account in Colin Morris, "Propaganda for War: The Dissemination of the Crusading Ideal in the Twelfth Century," Studies in Church History *15 (1978), 79–101. See also Richard Crocker, "Early Crusade Songs," in* The Holy War, *78–98, and Michael Routledge, "Songs," in* The Oxford Illustrated History, *91–111. The extensive study by Norman Daniel, "Crusade Propaganda," in* A History of the Crusades, *vol. 6, 39–97, is invaluable. The* Chanson d'Antioche *has been edited by Suzanne Duparc-Quioc,* La Chanson d'Antioche *(Paris, 1976); the translation here may be found on 19–21, 25–28. The entire cycle is being edited under the direction of Jan Nelson at the University of Alabama*

Press. See The Old French Crusade Cycle, *vol. 1,* La Naissance du chevalier au cygne, *ed. Jan A. Nelson and Emmanuel J. Mickel, Jr. (University, Ala., 1977). See also Albert Foulet, "The Epic Cycle of the Crusades," in* A History of the Crusades, *vol. 6, 98–115; Karl-Heinz Bender, "La Geste d'Outremer ou les epopées françaises des croisades," in* La Croisade: Realités et Fictions, *ed. Danielle Buschinger (Göppingen, 1989), 19–30; Lewis M. Sumberg,* La Chanson d'Antioche: Étude historique et littéraire *(Paris, 1968); and Robert Francis Cook, "Chanson d'Antioche,"* Chanson de Geste: Le Cycle de la croisade est-il epique? *(Amsterdam, 1980).*

The section translated here gives some sense of the themes of crusade song and poetry (and some of its manner, as well as approximate blank verse can convey it), in this case particularly the theme of the crusade as an expression of the "Revenge of Jesus Christ," here predicted at the crucifixion and blamed on the Jews. The chanson thus places the crusade in the context of sacred time. The opening verses of the chanson reflect the prominence of Peter the Hermit, who is here alleged to have led an army to the Holy Land before the First Crusade, seen its defeat, and returned to assemble a larger army.

I

Be still, my lords, leave off your chatter now,
If you want to hear a glorious song be sung.
No jongleur ever sang a better song;
Hold this song in your heart and love it deep,
It tells a story great, and of brave men.
You ought to love this song and hold it dear;
In it you'll find examples of brave men
And other things you need to keep in mind.
No better song is sung, as we all know,
About that holy city that we praise,
Where God let weak men pierce and harm His body
Strike it with lance and hang it on a cross,
Jerusalem, by right the city's named.
Those new-style poets who try to make this song
Always leave out the best of all beginnings,
But Graindor of Douai will leave out nothing,
And he has made all its old verses new.
Now you will hear the city's song entire,
And the song of those who traveled to the tomb,
How all the hosts assembled everywhere,

From France, Berry, and neighboring Auvergne,
From Calabria, Apulia, sea-town Barletta,
From distant Wales, they gathered all their forces
And from lands, too, whose names I do not know.
Of such a pilgrimage there's never been the like,
For God alone they went, and suffered much,
Thirst, hunger, heat and cold, no food nor sleep,
How could God not reward them for all this,
And lead their souls to Heaven and to His glory.

II

Barons, now hear me—stop all your jabbering,
A song I'll sing, one that will bring me praise,
You'll start to hear about Jerusalem,
Where God let weak men pierce and harm His body,
And strike Him with a lance and torture Him,
But warriors whom God loves and holds most dear
Went out across the sea for vengeance there.
Peter then led them, whom God made messenger.
But they began with great noise and confusion,
They were captured, died, and nothing could recover.
Only Peter escaped, returning now,
Then he assembled counts, and noble princes;
Hugh of Maine, and many other knights,
Tancred and Bohemund, the faithful vassal,
And the duke Godfrey, whom all men do praise,
The duke of Normandy, Normans and Poihier,
And the count of Flanders, and Flemish warriors bold.
When they assembled, close to Montpellier
The story says they were one hundred thousand.
They took Nicaea by force and stormed the palace,
Then Rohais, Antioch, and other towns,
Then took Jerusalem, they broke the walls,
But there they suffered, too, and thirsted, starved,
And saw great storms and rains, and snow and hail,
And God saw them through this and gave reward
Because their arms had brought them glory, too.
The song begins—the song that tells of this.

III

God, who raised Lazarus in Bethany,
And who for us gave up His life in passion,
He holds out to all men a true confession
To those who love Him and serve with good intention!
But He also sends wicked confusion
To those who love Apollo and Mahomet!
Oh Lord, there is no fable in our song,
Only pure truth and holy, moral message.

. . . .

VIII

Lords, for the love of God, make peace and listen,
So that, leaving this world, you'll be the better.
When God was first tortured by the Jews,
Wounded and pierced by nail, lance, and thorn,
To His right there hung a robber crucified,
Dismas his name, with that he was baptized;
He believed in God well, and he was rewarded!
When he saw Jesus being so tormented
He spoke to Him, a man condemned to death:
"Oh King, oh Virgin's Son, so great Your pity,
Please save me and Yourself when You're in Heaven.
It would be good to see Yourself avenged
On these treacherous Jews who torment You."

IX

Our Lord, hearing him speak, turned toward him, saying:
"My friend," He said, "The people are not yet born
Who will avenge my death with their steel lances,
Who for me will come kill the faithless pagans
Who spurn my just commandments every day,
By later people will Christendom be honored,
They will regain my land and free my country;
A thousand years from now they will be raised
And baptized, regain the Sepulcher and then adore it.
And they will serve me as if I had begat them,
They all will be my children, that I promise,
Their heritage will be in Paradise,
With me today you, too, will soon be crowned."

X

To Jesus' left there hung another robber,
He had been baptized with the name of Getas,
A companion of the thief with faith in Jesus,
Whom he saw tormented by the bitter passion
From nails and lance and from the bitter drink
That treacherous felons gave Him.
The disbelieving thief then contradicted:
"My friend, you're wrong," he said, "It can't be hidden,
You think this man can help you in your need,
He can't save his own life—can He save yours?
He says that help a thousand years from now
Will come, but on that day that He has mentioned
You and all others who await this gift,
Will be confounded and will have no ransom,
It's foolishness to hope in such a promise."

XI

The true-believing thief then turned to him,
"Alas, that you defame Almighty God!
We both deserve to hang and die in torment,
Always have we been thieves and criminals,
But this man is Lord of worlds, sees all, allows
To happen all that happens. The believing man
Knows this and never doubts and never will
That sinners go to Hell and there they stay."
"Friend," said Our Lord, "Know this for certainty,
From over the sea a great new race will come,
That will take vengeance for its own Lord's death.
The only pagans left will move far east;
The Franks will take this land, deliver it,
Those captured or else killed on their great journey
Their souls will rise from bodies to salvation.
By my command your soul is saved today,
Together with souls of all those who believe."

3. *Nomen a solemnibus*

The text of this lyric is illustrative of an often neglected dimension of both pilgrimage and warfare—the role of collective prayer and song. Not only The Song of Roland *but many other shorter pieces of verse, whether as prayer or pastime, have come down from the late eleventh and early twelfth centuries. Around 1100, for example, Anselm, archbishop of Milan, urged the young men in his army to sing "the song* Ultreia, Ultreia" *as they marched into battle. There are a number of songs and hymns associated with the capture of Jerusalem in 1099, discussed in Goswin Spreckelmeyer,* Das Kreuzzugslied des Lateinischen Mittelalters *(Munich, 1974), and by Joseph Szövérffy,* Secular Latin Lyrics and Minor Poetic Forms of the Middle Ages: A Historical Survey and Literary Repertory from the Tenth to the Late Fifteenth Century, *vol. 1 (Concord, N.H., 1992), 369–373. The text and music of* Nomen a solemnibus *are printed in Goswin Spreckelmeyer,* Mittellateinische Kreuzslieder: Texte und Melodien, *Göppinger Arbeiten zur Germanistik, nr. 216 (Göppingen, 1987), 9, 67–68. The poem is particularly striking because it employs three very different rhythmic patterns (only approximately achieved in this translation) and has a peculiar opening verse that no one has ever explained satisfactorily. The name* Solemnicum *may refer to the monastery of Solignac, and the first line may not refer to "feast," but rather "place," if the identification with Solignac is correct. The references to Dagon, Amalec, and the sons of Hagar are to 1 Samuel 5:1–5, Exodus 17:8–16, and Genesis 21:9–21. The city of the song is Jerusalem.*

> This feast is named from solemn rites   it takes the name
>   Solemnicum
> Therefore we all will solemnize   all except a certain monk,
> Serracus, who has maimed himself   by cutting off his private parts;
> Because he has we will accept him   just as if he were a demon;
> Let him mourn, and mourn alone   and stand accused before Eacus!

>   Let us exalt, and let us sing a canticle of victory,
>   And let us sing, as sing we must, the praises due to Glory's King,
>   Who today has saved the city   David's city from the pagans!

>   *Refrain:*
>   The festival begins,
>   we cherish now the day
>   when Dagon lies in pieces smashed
>   and Amalec defeated, quashed

the sons of Hagar driven back
Jerusalem is snatched away
Restored again to Christian ways,
And so we celebrate the day!

This city the most beautiful   noblest of all, had first a King
In this city vast and great   that King was pleasing to the Lord
Here on account of humankind   that King wished to be crucified
Here to this city came the Spirit   who resounded to Apostles.

City wond'rous, fire descending, fire descending once a year,
This it shows us, generations, how God loves it through the ages,
Be it honored, be it filled up, be it filled with kings and peoples!

Refrain

This city is from Heaven blessed   set in the Heavens, how it loves
Of Law the tabernacle true   temple of ark of covenant
Shelter of wretched of the earth   of all the poor the sanctuary,
Never will you have to fear   as long as you reside in it.

With the brightness of its light, the city outshines sun and moon
With its holiness this city conquers and absorbs all cities
Gebuseus Areuna does not choose His place in vain.

Refrain

Bibliographical Essay

The Historiography of the First Crusade and the Crusade Movement

The historiography of the First Crusade began with the accounts written and rewritten during and shortly after the crusade itself, and it continued as a component of the works of later historians of the Latin Kingdom of Jerusalem between the twelfth and seventeenth centuries, especially that of William of Tyre.[1] The crusade also inspired a long line of literary works in both Latin and the vernacular languages of Europe, and it included Latin hymns as well as vernacular lyrics and epic poetic accounts beginning with the *Chanson d'Antioche* in the twelfth century and the additions to it made later. During the sixteenth century it continued to be a subject of literary interest, culminating in Tasso's epic poem, the *Gerusalemme Liberata* ("Jerusalem Delivered"), in 1581.

Its early modern historiography began with the great compilation of Jacques Bongars, *Gesta Dei per Francos*, a vast printed collection of narrative sources of all the crusades which appeared in 1611. The English historian Thomas Fuller used Bongars's collection in his own *History of the Holy Warre* of 1639, which, although it was a virulently anti-papal work, was a substantial contribution to early crusade historiography. But Fuller himself was writing toward the close of the great series of religious wars that had torn Europe since the mid-sixteenth century and had produced in competing Protestant and Catholic histories both great scholarship and violent polemic.

In the eighteenth century many thinkers reacted with equal violence against religious passions in civil affairs and against religious wars of any kind, and the denunciations of the crusades and crusaders appeared thick and fast. "Among the Franks," said De Guignes in his *History of the Huns* of 1756, "a large number of people without devotion and with many vices

---

1. Peter W. Edbury and John Gordon Rowe, *William of Tyre, Historian of the Latin East* (Cambridge, 1988). On the mythological dimensions of the earliest historiography, see James M. Powell, "Myth, Legend, Propaganda, History: The First Crusade, 1140–ca. 1300," *Autour de la Première Croisade*, 127–141.

left Europe and passed over into Asia only so that they might enrich themselves, to indulge their vices more than ever with impunity. Their crimes,
and the fanaticism of others, as well as the bizarre combination of religion
and chivalry, has made a more enlightened century disdain their wars."[2] For
Diderot the crusades produced for Europe only "an infinity of vexations"; for
David Hume they were "the most durable monument of human folly that
has yet appeared in any age or nation"; for Edward Gibbon they were "the
world's debate," a vast and useless waste of men and material that should
have been used to enrich Europe and cultivate peaceable relations with the
Middle East.

But Enlightenment scorn gave way in its turn to political expansion and
Romantic sensibilities with Napoleon's occupation of Malta in 1798. At the
time Malta was still occupied by the last of the original cursading military
orders. Napoleon's expedition to Egypt in 1798–99 opened a new age of
European interest in the Middle East, its present and past. One of its earliest
manifestations was the seven-volume *Histoire des Croisades* and *Bibliothèque
des croisades*, which Joseph Michaud (1767–1839) published between 1811 and
1840, as well as U. Wilken's seven-volume history of the crusades in German
between 1807 and 1832. Unlike his predecessors, Wilken had used Arabic and
Syriac sources for the first time and strongly influenced Michaud's later revisions of his own work.[3] The work of Michaud and the new interest in
"Orientalism" colored much nineteenth-century interest in the crusades and
the Middle East. An edition of Michaud's history was illustrated in 1877 by
the artist Gustave Doré in a series of pictures that captured much of the sen-
sibility of the nineteenth-century taste for the heroic and sentimental, as did
the novels of Sir Walter Scott, particularly *Ivanhoe* and *The Talisman*.[4]

In 1839 King Louis-Philippe of France added a new wing to the palace
at Versailles that was dedicated to the crusades (conceived exclusively as a
component of French history). The wing was decorated with a number of
historical paintings by H. A. S. Serrur and others, introducing the crusades

---

2. There is an excellent brief account in J. J. Saunders, *Aspects of the Crusades* (Christchurch,
New Zealand, 1962), 9–16. See also Jonathan Riley-Smith, "The Crusading Movement and Historians," in *The Oxford Illustrated History*, 1–12.

3. Michaud's history appeared in English translation, *Michaud's History of the Crusades*,
3 vols., trans. W. Robson (London, 1852).

4. The Doré illustrations recently have been reproduced in *Storia delle Crociate illustrata
da Gustave Doré*, 3 vols., ed. Roberto Gervaso (Milan, 1978). See also Elizabeth Siberry, "Vic-
torian Perceptions of the Military Orders," in *Fighting for the Faith and Caring for the Sick*, ed.
Malcolm Barber (London, 1995), 365–372, and Siberry, "Images of the Crusades in the Nineteenth and Twentieth Centuries," in *The Oxford Illustrated History*, 364–385; in the same volume,
see Jonathan Riley-Smith, "Revival and Survival," 386–391.

as an attractive topic for large historical paintings as well as book illustrations and, later, for long narrative poems and operas.[5] Louis-Philippe also permitted members of families whose ancestors had fought in the crusades to place their coats of arms in the new room. As Riley-Smith has pointed out, this privilege generated a market in forged documents that could be used by ambitious parvenus to prove crusade ancestry, and any reader of Stendhal's novel *The Red and the Black* knows the value of crusading ancestry, actual or professed, in nineteenth-century France.[6] But scholarly method could also be used to verify professedly historical documents, and during the next few years in France scholarly interest in the crusades flowered. The work of Michaud inspired the French Academy of Inscriptions to begin its immense enterprise of printing the narrative sources of the crusades, both Occidental and Oriental (Arabic, Syriac, and Armenian), in the *Recueil des historiens des croisades*, which began in 1841 and was completed in 1906. French scholarship continued its substantial work on crusade history through the nineteenth and early twentieth centuries. One of the most important later landmarks was the influence of Paul Riant (1836–1888), whose first major work was an edition of the forged letters allegedly sent from the Byzantine emperor Alexius I to Robert I, Count of Flanders. Riant's influence started the important journal *Revue de l'Orient latin* in 1883.

In 1841 the young German historian Heinrich von Sybel, a pupil of Leopold von Ranke, published his *History of the First Crusade*, a penetrating study that effectively swept away much crusade mythology and became the model for later critical historical studies.[7] Von Sybel's work inspired a number of later German scholars, including R. Röhricht's *History of the Kingdom of Jerusalem* in 1898, and the publication in 1901 of Heinrich Hagenmayer's great edition of the letters associated with the First Crusade.[8] By the turn of the twentieth century crusade historiography had been captured largely by learned academies and professional academic historians.[9]

---

5. Some of the paintings are reproduced in *The Oxford Illustrated History of the Crusades* and in Paul Lesourd and Jean Marie Ramiz, *On the Path of the Crusaders*, trans. Jerry O'Dell (Ramat-Gan, 1969). There are numerous illustrated histories of the crusades, not all of them reliable. There is a particularly interesting example of the genre from a Marxist scholarly perspective in Martin Erbstösser, *The Crusades*, trans. C. S. V. Salt (Leipzig, 1978).

6. Riley-Smith, "The Crusading Movement and Historians." On the forgery "industry," see also Giles Constable, "Medieval Charters as Sources for the History of the Crusades," in *Crusade and Settlement*, 73–89, and for diplomatic in general, Marcus Bull, "The Diplomatic of the First Crusade," *The First Crusade*, 35–54.

7. Von Sybel's work appeared in an English translation: *The History and Literature of the First Crusade*, trans. Lady Duff Gordon (London, 1861).

8. Heinrich Hagenmayer, *Die Kreuzzugsbriefe aus den Jahren 1088–1100* (Innsbruck, 1901).

9. And there is where its history can be most reliably traced, since the subject remains

And not only in Europe. In the 1890s the American scholar Dana C. Munro began a series of publications on crusade history that included his pioneering pamphlets of crusade sources in translation for the benefit of students at the University of Pennsylvania and elsewhere whose Latin was not yet up to scholarly exactness.[10] Munro also produced graduate students. The most distinguished of these in crusade history was John LaMonte, whose study *Feudal Monarchy in the Latin Kingdom of Jerusalem* appeared in 1932. LaMonte also inspired the collective enterprise of research that appeared as the first two volumes of *A History of the Crusades*, whose general editor was LaMonte's successor at the University of Pennsylvania, Kenneth M. Setton.[11] The enterprise moved with Setton to the University of Wisconsin in 1965, and the first two volumes were reprinted in 1969–70. The final work in six volumes was completed in 1989.[12]

During the twentieth century historical research in Germany, France, Great Britain, Italy, and the United States has continued to illuminate both the genesis and the complexity of the crusade movement in western Europe and the perspectives of non-Western cultures.[13] The French historian Paul Chalandon published his history of the First Crusade, *Histoire de la première croisade*, in 1925, focusing on the military history of the expedition, and René

---

popular and generates a large literature and filmography that is often quite innocent of any scholarship at all. See the reflections of Theodore L. Steinberg, "The Use and Abuse of Medieval History: Four Contemporary Novelists and the First Crusade," *Studies in Medievalism* 2 (1982), 77–92; James M. Powell, "Rereading the Crusades," *Journal of International History* 17 (1995), 663–669; and Lorraine Atreed and James F. Powers, "Lessons in the Dark: Teaching the Middle Ages with Film," *Perspectives: American Historical Association Newsletter* 35 (1997), 11–16. *Indiana Jones and the Last Crusade* (1989) is a wonderful movie, but it has nothing to do with the crusades—or with archaeology.

10. Dana C. Munro, *Urban and the Crusaders*, University of Pennsylvania, Translations and Reprints from the Original Sources of European History, vol. 1, no. 2 (Philadelphia, 1895); idem, *Letters of the Crusaders*, University of Pennsylvania, Translations and Reprints from the Original Sources of European History, vol. 1, no. 4 (Philadelphia, 1896); idem, *The Kingdom of the Crusaders* (1936); and L. J. Paetow, ed., *The Crusades and Other Historical Essays Presented to Dana C. Munro* (New York, 1928).

11. Philadelphia, 1955, 2 vols.; Madison, Wis., 1969–1989, 6 vols. On the place of this series in crusade historiography and the later development of the field, see Jonathan Riley-Smith, "History, the Crusades and the Latin East, 1095–1204: A Personal View," in *Crusaders and Muslims*, 1–17.

12. In one sense, the present volume, edited by Setton's successor at the University of Pennsylvania, is the most recent example of the local influence of Dana C. Munro.

13. Two excellent examples of contemporary Italian crusade historiography are those of Raoul Manselli, *Italia e Italiani alla Prima Crociata* (Rome, 1983), and Franco Cardini, *Studi sulla Storia e sull'Idea di Crociata* (Rome, 1993). Cardini's work is extremely wide-ranging and includes an important historiographical study, "Le Crociate tra Illuminismo ed Età Napoleonica," 23, 465–501, treating the history of the idea of the crusades between the Enlightenment and the Romantic movement of the early nineteenth century.

Grousset's *Histoire des Croisades*, published in three volumes between 1934 and 1936, offered a new and important perspective from the point of view of the Muslim Middle East.

In 1935 the great German historian Carl Erdmann published his masterpiece, *Die Entstehung des Kreuzzugsgedankens* ("The Origins of the Idea of Crusade"), opening a new line of research into the origins of the First Crusade as an extension of changes in Christian society which had taken place in the ninth and tenth centuries. Erdmann's work centered on the increasing practice and forms of expression of the role of war and warriors as integral and virtuous components of God's plan for the Christian world—that is, on treating "crusade ideology" as a product of the history of ideas that found expression in the widespread understanding of ritual, political symbolism, sacred objects (holy banners), wars against heathens, and the great movement of ecclesiastical and lay reform of the earlier eleventh century.[14] Erdmann's work resonated in the subsequent research of several French scholars. Between 1941 and 1954 the historian of devotion Etienne Delaruelle published a series of articles that extended Erdmann's approach and focused on the opportunity for salvation that the crusade movement offered to lay people as a component of the reform movement of the eleventh century.[15] On the side of social and collective psychology the research begun in the 1920s by the French scholar Paul Alphandéry and continued, after his untimely death in 1932, by his colleague and literary executor Louis Dupront finally appeared in two volumes in 1954 and 1959.[16]

In French scholarship the work of Delaruelle and Alphandéry-Dupront had been joined in 1940 by Claude Cahen's *La Syrie du Nord à l'époque des croisades et la principauté franque d'Antioche* (Paris, 1940), in 1942 by Maurice Villey's study of the legal status and privileges of crusaders, and in 1947

14. Carl Erdmann, *The Origin of the Idea of Crusade*, trans. Marshall W. Baldwin and Walter Goffart, foreword and additional notes by Marshall W. Baldwin (Princeton, N.J., 1977). Baldwin's foreword is an excellent survey of international historiographical opinion as of the late 1970s, and a thorough bibliography of works on the subject from 1935 to 1975 appears on pp. 410–477. For a similar and still extremely valuable discussion a decade earlier than the Baldwin-Goffart translation of Erdmann, see James A. Brundage, "Recent Crusade Historiography: Some Observations and Suggestions," *Catholic Historical Review* 49 (1964), 493–507, and more recently, Brundage, "The Crusades: Past Achievements and Future Agenda," in *The Meeting of Two Worlds: Cultural Exchange Between East and West During the Period of the Crusades*, ed. Vladimir P. Goss (Kalamazoo, Mich., 1986), 447–453.

15. Delaruelle's articles have been collected in his *L'Idée de croisade au Moyen Age* (Turin, 1980). For an assessment, see Erdmann/Baldwin, *The Origin of the Idea of Crusade*, xxii–xxiii.

16. *La Chrétienté et l'idée de croisade* (Paris, 1954, 1959; rept. Paris, 1990). For the fascinating history of this collaboration, see the *Postface* to the 1990 reprint edition by Michel Balard, vol. 2, 565–593. See Erdmann/Baldwin, *The Origin of the Idea of Crusade*, xxv–xxvi.

by Philippe Rousset's study of the crusade in twelfth-century thought and imagination.[17] Clearly, by the 1950s crusade history in general had broadened considerably from its political, diplomatic, and military origins into the entire eleventh- and twelfth-century medieval world of ecclesiology, culture, and mentalities.

Although British historiography did not initially contribute as substantially as did German, French, and U.S. research, it did produce substantial contributions through the work of Arabists and Byzantinists. The major work of the Byzantine historian Steven Runciman, *History of the Crusades*, a three-volume narrative history that appeared between 1951 and 1954, instantly became the most widely known and respected single-author survey of the subject in English. Since Runciman's work, British scholarship has assumed a dominant role in crusade research and historiography, particularly under the influence of R. C. Smail and Jonathan Riley-Smith and their students and associates.[18]

As early as the first volumes of Setton's *A History of the Crusades*, it was clear that crusade history encompassed virtually the entire spectrum of the historical discipline, from legal, military, and economic history to the history of ideas and devotion, and that any historian who worked in the field had to be aware of the work of all the others, often in quite different areas of research, because all of these areas shed light on each other. This concern is reflected in the establishment in 1980 of the Society for the Study of the Crusades and the Latin East, whose bulletins and conferences are usually the focus of much of the international scholarship on crusade history. In the case of the First Crusade this range is evident in the four most recent single-author histories of the First Crusade and the crusades in general, those of Hans Eberhard Mayer, Jean Flori, Alfons Becker, and Jonathan Riley-Smith.[19]

17. Maurice Villey, *La croisade: Essai sur la formation d'une théorie juridique* (Paris, 1942); Philippe Rousset, *Les origines et charactères de la première croisade* (Neuchâtel, 1947); see Erdmann/Baldwin, *The Origin of the Idea of Crusade*, xxiii–xxiv.

18. Stephen Runciman, *History of the Crusades*, 3 vols. (Cambridge, 1951–54). Most recently in the second edition of R. C. Smail, *Crusading Warfare, 1097–1193* (Cambridge, 1956; 2d ed., 1995) and in Jonathan Riley-Smith, ed. *The Oxford Illustrated History*. See also Riley-Smith, "History, the Crusades, and the Latin East."

19. Hans Eberhard Mayer, *The Crusades*, trans. John Gillingham (German original version, 1965; Oxford and New York, 1972, 2d ed. 1988); Jean Flori, *La première croisade: L'Occident chrétien contre l'Islam (Aux origines des idéologies occidentales)* (Brussels, 1992); Alfons Becker, *Papst Urban II (1088–1099)*, Schriften der Monumenta Germaniae Historia, Band 19, II (Stuttgart, 1988), "*Deus vult*—Urbans II. Kreuzzug," 272–457; Jonathan Riley-Smith, *The First Crusade and the Idea of Crusading* (Philadelphia, 1986), and *The Crusades: A Short History* (New Haven, Conn., 1987). See also the memorial volume for Donald Queller, *Prayer, War, and Crusade: Essays Commemorating the Nine-Hundredth Anniversary of the Proclamation of the First Crusade*, International History Review 17 (1995), and the most recent publications of conference proceedings cited below.

For the late twentieth-century (or early twenty-first century) student of crusade history there now exist vast collections of edited, printed, and often translated source materials as well as much that is still in manuscript. Not only are there excellent general and particular histories of the crusades, but there are extensive bibliographies, studies of methodology, and guides to cross-disciplinary research as well. Crusade scholarship, if it sometimes appears to have become something of a scholarly industry, also offers the reader of history the opportunity to investigate not only a series of related episodes along a time axis, but also a number of problems perennially important in the history of Western society and other societies: the social force of changing ideologies; the social and economic consequences of large-scale enterprises on underdeveloped, or agro-literate, societies, and the cultural response to the shock of contact with members of other cultures. In the changing concepts of peace and war which the sources reveal, in the changing character and forms of expression of Christian beliefs in the eleventh and early twelfth centuries, and in the slowly developing consciousness on the part of people from many different backgrounds that "Christendom" could be a compelling and organizing idea, that it preceded the idea of "Europe," and that it played a powerful role in defining the identity of both the West and western Europeans long after the city of Jerusalem had been lost again, crusade studies continue to play an important role.

And the idea echoes down to the late twentieth century. Not only did Dwight Eisenhower entitle his memoirs of World War II *Crusade in Europe*, but two recent studies of U.S. foreign policy have also adapted the term. In their study of foreign policy in the "post-superpower age" J. Clarke and J. Clad call their subject *After the Crusade* (Lanham, Md., 1995), and Walter MacDougall's recent survey of the history of U.S. foreign policy is entitled *Promised Land/Crusader State* (New York, 1997). Nine hundred years after they were created, neither the history nor the image is exhausted.

Recent Research on the First Crusade

The best recent analysis of the First Crusade in English is that of Jonathan Riley-Smith, *The First Crusade and the Idea of Crusading* (Philadelphia, 1986), particularly valuable in its discussion of the progressive development of the idea of crusade in the wake of the events of 1095–1099 and for its important discussion of the Crusade of 1101. The best military history is that of John France, *Victory in the East: A Military History of the First Crusade* (Cambridge,

1994), which should be supplemented by Randall Rogers, *Latin Siege Warfare in the Twelfth Century* (Oxford, 1997); Kelly DeVries, *Medieval Military Technology* (Peterborough, Ont., 1992); Bernard S. Bachrach, "On Roman Ramparts, 300–1300," in *The Cambridge Illustrated History of Warfare: The Triumph of the West*, ed. Geoffrey Parker (Cambridge, 1996), 64–91; and *The Cambridge Illustrated Atlas of Warfare: The Middle Ages, 768–1487*, ed. Nicholas Hooper and Matthew Bennett (Cambridge, 1996). Most of these works have extensive and up-to-date bibliographies.

The best study of the motivations of crusaders is that of Marcus Bull, *Knightly Piety and the Lay Response to the First Crusade: The Limousin and Gascony, c. 970–c. 1130* (Oxford, 1993), and Bull, "The Roots of Lay Enthusiasm for the First Crusade," *History* 78 (1993), 353–372.

The best general bibliography in English through 1982 is that of Hans Eberhard Mayer and Joyce McLellan, "Select Bibliography of the Crusades," in *A History of the Crusades*, gen. ed. Kenneth M. Setton, vol. 6, *The Impact of the Crusades on Europe*, ed. Harry W. Hazard and Norman P. Zacour (Madison, Wis., 1989), 511–664. This essay is partly a recapitulation and partly an expansion of Mayer's earlier bibliographies, *Bibliographie zur Geschichte der Kreuzzüge* (Hannover, 1960), and "Literaturbericht über die Geschichte der Kreuzzüge," *Historische Zeitschrift, Sonderheft* 3 (1969), 641–731. Bibliographies of work produced after 1982 may be found in *The Oxford Illustrated History of the Crusades* and in works by individual authors cited in the introduction, particularly those of Jonathan Riley-Smith and John France.

A good historical survey of medieval Europe is that of Edward Peters, *Europe and the Middle Ages*, 3d ed. (Englewood Cliffs, N.J., 1996).

On topography and crusade routes, see Jonathan Riley-Smith, *The Atlas of the Crusades* (London-New York, 1991).

Two recent collections of scholarly essays on the First Crusade have appeared: Michel Balard, ed., *Autour de la première croisade*, Papers from the Fourth Conference of the Society for the Study of the Crusades and the Latin East (Paris, 1996), with essays in English, French, and German; and Jonathan Phillips, ed., *The First Crusade: Origins and Impact* (Manchester, 1997). On the occasion of the nine-hundredth anniversary of the First Crusade, other collections of papers will also appear.

Internet Sites for Crusade History

The home page for the Society for the Study of the Crusades and the Latin East is

http://www.wcslc.edu/pers_pages/m.markow/ssclehome.html

Links to other Crusade sites are available through

http://gator.naples.net/~nfn05074/jason4.html

and

http://www.mcgnw.com/~mcmcconn/edieval.html

There is also an ORB site that provides bibliography and some translated texts:

http://orb.rhodes.edu

For medieval subjects generally see LABYRINTH:

http://www.georgetown.edu/labyrinth

Discussion Lists

To subscribe to the listserv MEDIEVAL-L, send a message to:

listserv@ukanvm.cc.ukans.edu

Leave the subject line blank; your text should consist of the following message (and nothing more):

subscribe mediev-l [your name]

To subscribe to MEDIEVAL RELIGION, use the same protocol, except that the message "subscribe medieval-religion" should be sent to mailbase@mail base.ac.uk